THE RUSSIAN
RELIGIOUS MIND (I)
KIEVAN CHRISTIANITY
The 10th to the 13th Centuries

VOLUME THREE
IN THE COLLECTED WORKS OF
GEORGE P. FEDOTOV

About the Author

George P. Fedotov was born in 1886 in Saratov, Russia. He began his academic life as a student of engineering but, while studying in Germany and Italy, he changed his scope of study to history. When he returned to Russia in 1914, he became Assistant Professor of European Medieval History at the University of St. Petersburg (1914-1918) and, later, Professor at the University of Saratov (1920-1922). Unable to pursue creative scholarship in Soviet Russia, Professor Fedotov left his homeland in 1925. From 1926 to 1940 he was Professor of Church History at the Russian Theological School in Paris. During this time in Paris he also worked on the journals *Sovremennyi zapiski* [*Contemporary Notes*], *Put'* [*The Way*] and *Chisla* [*Dates*]. In 1931 he co-founded the important journal *Novyi Grad* [*The New City*] which he edited until 1939. In 1941 he came to the United States where, until his death in 1951, he was Professor of Church History at St. Vladimir's Theological School.

ABOUT *THE COLLECTED WORKS* OF
GEORGE P. FEDOTOV

George P. Fedotov wrote prolifically and his interests ranged over several fields of inquiry—Russian history, literature, theology, spirituality and Russian culture in general as well as political thought and the Latin West. *The Collected Works* of George P. Fedotov will be published in English and will include his numerous articles as well as his books—including reprints of those books which were already published in English.

The Russian Religious Mind (I)

Kievan Christianity
The 10th to the 13th Centuries

BY

GEORGE P. FEDOTOV

VOLUME THREE

IN THE COLLECTED WORKS OF

GEORGE P. FEDOTOV

NORDLAND PUBLISHING COMPANY
BELMONT, MASSACHUSETTS 02178
1975

BY THE SAME AUTHOR

THE COLLECTED WORKS OF GEORGE P. FEDOTOV
[Nordland Publishing Company]

Volume I — *St. Filipp: Metropolitan of Moscow*
Volume II — *A Treasury of Russian Spirituality*
Volume III — *The Russian Religious Mind (I): Kievan Christianity— The 10th to the 13th Centuries*
Volume IV — *The Russian Religious Mind (II): The Middle Ages*
Volume V — *Peter Abelard*

[Other volumes forthcoming]

Library of Congress Catolog Card Number 75-27465
ISBN 0-913124-18-4

PRINTED IN THE UNITED STATES OF AMERICA

PREFACE

Although the present work is an independent whole in itself, it represents the beginning of a series which, it is hoped, will cover the history of the Russian religious mind from the early Kievan period to the present day. This volume is concerned with Kievan Russia, the period extending from the tenth to the thirteenth century.

Despite the fact that I have been cut off from the Russian libraries and archives, wih their rich funds of manuscript materials, this book has not been seriously handicaped, since most of the sources, and all the essential ones, are printed. Most of the literature could be located in the libraries of Europe and America. During the last five years in the United States I have become much indebted to the staffs of the many excellent libraries for their courtesy and assistance; in particular to those of the New York Public Library, the Library of Congress, the libraries of Yale, Harvard, and Columbia universities, and others. The Divinity School of Yale University gave shelter to the exile and excellent conditions for work, accepting me as a visiting fellow in the first and most difficult year of my American life. The Humanities Fund and also the Protestant Episcopal Church supported my material existence for years and contributed generously toward publishing the present book.

This does not diminish the kindness of the Harvard University Press which bravely took the risk of publishing an author unknown in this country. I also feel obliged to express my hearty gratitude to my friends Professors Michael Karpovich, George Vernadsky, and Roman Jacobson, who read my manuscript and assisted me with very valuable suggestions. Miss M. N. Shelly and Ruth A. Whitman are responsible for giving a more literary form to my imperfect English. Indeed, I received much more encouragement and help in America than I had the right to hope for.

May 17, 1946   G. P. F.

Contents

THE ORDINARY CHRISTIAN

CONCLUSION

INTRODUCTION

It is not without some hesitation that I have chosen as my title *The Russian Religious Mind*. Although in English the word *mind* has mainly an intellectual connotation, it can also be used in the sense of the whole content of consciousness. Since I am writing the history not of Russian religious thought, but of Russian religious consciousness, it is in this larger sense that I employ the term throughout the book. Were I writing in Russian, I would choose a word corresponding to the German *Religiosität* (*religioznost'*). The French prefer *sentiment religieux*, which has a richer meaning than merely religious feeling. For the English reader, "religious mind" appears to be the nearest approximation to the idea.

But it needs a further qualification. My intention is to describe the subjective side of religion as opposed to its objective side; that is, opposed to the complex of organized dogmas, sacraments, rites, liturgy, Canon Law, and so on. I am interested in man, religious man, and his attitude towards God, the world, and his fellow men; his attitude is not only emotional, but also rational and volitional, the attitude of the whole man. This wholeness of religious personality is the invisible center out of which the main phenomena not only of religious but of cultural life in general have their origin and receive their meaning. The history of theology, of liturgy, of Canon Law ceases to be an assembly of antiquities only when light is thrown on it from the source of religious man or religious mind. At the core of these investigations stands, of course, the study of "spiritual life" in the sense of ascetic-mystical life and of religious ethics—religious experience and religious action—of which theology, liturgy, and canons can be considered the expression and form.

ix

In all religious societies—churches and sects—the objective structure of religion can but to a very small degree express or reflect the religious mind of contemporary man. It is the heritage of a remote past, sacred and untouchable. It changes little, but it is the infinitesimal changes which bear witness to the deep religious processes going on. Spiritual life and ethics, despite their being rooted in tradition, move more freely than the objective elements and are in this respect similar to religious art. The degree of subjectivity of the different spheres of religious life determines their value as historical sources. The disparity between objective and subjective elements becomes tremendous in a Christian nation which confesses dogmas and practices, sacraments and rites inherited from an alien and long extinct civilization. In a society like ancient Russia, which had no theology of its own and which preserved unchanged liturgical rites and prayers inherited from Byzantium, theology and liturgy are practically eliminated as historical sources for the student of the Russian religious mind. Spiritual life, ethics, arts, and religiously tinged social norms will therefore be our chief subjects of investigation.

I am fully aware that this approach to religion from its subjective human side may appear not sufficiently up-to-date. In fact, some modern currents in the theology of various Christian confessions (Barthianism is typical of the Protestant representatives) break sharply with the humanism of the nineteenth century. Modern theology, in this restricted sense, begins with God rather than man and discards not only the term *Religiosität* but often "religion" itself as far too human. Faith is regarded as a call of God to man rather than man's response to God. This attitude emphasizes the objective, unchangeable elements in religion. The human side of religion is easily thrown into a refuse heap with all kinds of psychologisms. I do not deny the supernatural, divine character of Christianity as a religion of revelation. But I believe that its realization begins with the human response to Grace. The history of Christianity is the history of this response; its culture is the culture of this experience. History and culture are, in essence, human.

The history of spiritual life is still a youthful branch of historical science. It was born in the beginning of this century, in the spiritual atmosphere of Roman Catholic modernism which was extremely favorable to it. Abbé Brémond was a major pioneer in this new field of research with his monumental *Histoire Littéraire du Sentiment Religieux en France.* The Catholic modernism died or was strangled; but Catholic theology took over its historical legacy, and the new historical research of spirituality, the religious mind, and religious ethics is now being fruitfully cultivated by Catholic as well as Protestant students.

The Eastern Orthodox and Russian fields have been singularly neglected until the present day. This was chiefly because of the lack of religious understanding among secular historians in Russia, and the lack of historical outlook among authors and writers on spiritual life and Christian ethics. During the nineteenth century two kinds of scholars approached the problems of the Russian religious mind: the secular historians of literature who studied the ancient sources of Russian religious tradition, and the Church historians who dealt in part with the same material. The first had no key to religious problems; for them these matters had no intrinsic value. Literature was studied for its linguistic form or cultural content. As to the religious kernel—and we must realize that practically all ancient Russian literature was concerned primarily with religion—this was considered something extremely simple and stable. One is now appalled by the simplicity of characterization used by authors in comparatively recent times. Qualifications such as "Christian," "ec-

clesiastical," "monastic," "ascetic" seemed to meet all requirements. The reader asked for nothing more. Exactly the
same monotony is found in the ecclesiastical writers of the
nineteenth century. Some of them had themselves lost their
sympathetic feeling for the problems of religious life in the
generally discouraging atmosphere of the age. Others accepted without criticism the common premise of Orthodox
traditionalism: that everything which is essential in Orthodox
life, feeling, and thinking is eternal and changeless. The
continually changing face of Western Christendom was held
to be a sign of its depraved character. We know that the
Christian East is much more conservative and traditional
than the Christian West. All movements and changes in the
East go slowly, but still they progress in every sphere of
religious life. Nevertheless, the old prejudice in favor of
stability prevented scholars from making a really searching
inquiry into the history of spiritual life. External forms and
the data of religion were studied, sometimes with great success, but the depths remained unstirred and even unsuspected.

There were, of course, some happy exceptions. In Russia's past we observe, from time to time, great movements
in which religious issues were tied up with social and political
problems. Such was the great schism in the Russian Church
in the middle of the seventeenth century which led to the
secession of the "Old Believers" and to the formation of
various dissenting sects. Such was, on a lesser scale, the clash
between two religious parties about 1500, the Josephites and
the Trans-Volgans, which involved many spiritual and social
issues. These periods of turmoil represent the two focal
points around which historical studies have been concentrated.
On the one hand, the religious mind of the Old Believers
and sectarians has been studied and is possibly better known
than that of the Orthodox. On the other hand, the study of
the conflict between the Josephites and the Trans-Volgans

led at least one of our scholars to deeper inquiry into the spiritual tendencies of Russian monasticism in previous times. The book by Kadlubovsky, *Essays on the History of Ancient Russian Lives of Saints,* is perhaps the only serious research in this field. I am much indebted to this rather forgotten scholar for both inspiration and method. My two small studies in Russian on the *Saints of Ancient Russia,* and on the religious content of the Russian "Spiritual Songs" were preliminaries to the present work. The scholarly and rich book by G. Florovsky on the *Ways of Russian Theology* covers much of the same ground but comprises only the two or three centuries since Russian theology came into being, so late as the seventeenth century. In fact, Florovsky's book is less the history of theological ideas than of the religious mind of theologians and the Russian educated society in general. The simple folk are left out of the picture.

Fifteen years ago I came to this work with empty hands, having devoted myself to the study of western medieval culture. I let the Russian sources speak for themselves, with unexpected and overwhelming results. At every step the living image of the past contradicted the accepted opinions of historians. This result is to be accounted for not by any special perspicacity but simply by the introduction of western methods and viewpoints into the Russian field. Some western writers of former days, such as Leroy-Beaulieu in France, had been able to see features of Russian mind and life which had escaped Russian observers who were dulled by nearness and habit.

In recent years, however, there have been many efforts to describe the Russian mind and, in particular, the Russian religious mind. These efforts bear witness to a vivid interest in Russia, aroused, of course, by the Russian Revolution. Most of these studies—including those written by Russians— have failed. Works by Russians are perhaps less reliable than those written by foreigners, for, instead of suffering from the insufficiency of a too remote observation, they suffer from partiality and preconceptions. A foreigner judges the Russian people by a few striking features, a Russian by his own religious and political standards. Everybody sees what he wishes to see. The contemporary moment, extracted from the thousand years of Russian history, is taken by practically all writers as the expression of Russia's eternal soul. Her past either is little known or is deformed by a false approach.

Does this mean that the problem of discovering the Russian religious mind is to be rejected as unreal or mythical? On the contrary, for religious as well as cultural reasons, I believe that the phenomena of both the Russian mind and the Russian religious mind do exist. But it is extremely arduous to subject them to scientific investigation, that is, to comprehend them in exact concepts. All collective life is unity in multiformity; it exists only in individuals, each of whom reflects only a few features of the common being. We cannot take a single individual as representative of the whole, nor can we add together particular properties which are contradictory and inconsistent. The only way to meet this difficulty is to select types which are representative of different spiritual groups, and which in their totality, if properly chosen, can represent the collective being. Intellectual desire for unity tempts the student to reduce the number of typical groups to a single generality, thereby damaging the concreteness and exactness of the picture. In this process of reduction one may arrive at duality, but there one must stop. Only in duality can the real be grasped with all its contradictions. There is something eternally true in the Hegelian way of contemplating all historical reality in contradictory pairs. To reduce the duality of life to monism is to kill it.

If we approach the present problem with these principles

in mind, we shall not lose sight of the multiform constituents
of the material, particularly of those cultural, geographical,
and historical divisions which, coinciding in part with the
various classes of society, bring an enormous influence to bear
on the moral character of a people. In Russia, social divisions during the last two centuries and geographical divisions
of a much longer period have been of great cultural and
religious importance. Furthermore, certain historical cata-
clysms, such as the Mongolian conquest and the "reform"
of Peter the First, have been pregnant with spiritual and
religious consequences and suggest, in sharp contrast to the
traditional view of the immobility of eastern life, a real break
in the continuity of national thought.

In view of the poverty of preparatory works, the question
arises whether the time has come for presenting a book on
this subject to American readers. Where preliminary research is almost lacking, the synthesis, from a strictly scientific point of view, cannot have a solid foundation. Yet I am
moved to this enterprise by the conviction that, in historical
science, the point of departure is not analysis but synthesis,
a kind of preliminary synthesis, even though intuitional or
subjective. Analysis comes secondly to test and modify the
primary form of synthesis. The science of Russian religion
has not yet reached the analytical stage. For more than a century the best scholars in literary and ecclesiastical history have
been studying sources, accumulating materials, and writing
excellent monographs, with the result that not even the problems of the history of spiritual life have been set. When
there are no problems there will be no answers. But historical problems are revealed only by a preliminary, clearcut,
provocative synthesis.

The historical problems of spiritual life are the challenge
of our time, especially in regard to Russian history. Despite
changes and revolutions, Russian historical development

shows a continuity which makes the unity of the Russian religious mind not a myth, but a reality. Yet this unity cannot be expressed by one ideological formula, for a national mind does not cease to manifest new forms of its being until the end of national life. While a nation is living, its definition remains incomplete and uncertain. On the other hand, not one of the essential features of the past has completely disappeared. Some traits may have lost their predominance; some may have gone underground to the lower social strata or less conscious strata of the national soul, but they still exist and can still illuminate the past as well as determine the present and the future of the Russian religious mind.

The Religious Background

I

PRE-CHRISTIAN PAGANISM

*A*LL Christian nations must be "twice-born," but since Grace transforms nature rather than destroys it, they carry deep within them traces of their heathen past. The process of transformation is never complete. In the most civilized of modern peoples there are survivals of the prehistoric ages, now degraded to the rank of superstitions or "folklore." Perhaps this tincture of native heathendom accounts primarily for the characteristic national features of Christianity. Oriental in its origins, universal in its message, Christianity was incorporated into each nation by undergoing a kind of adaptation to, or investment of the pre-Christian legacies which hide in the subconscious of the national soul. The devotional life of a modern German and that of a medieval Frenchman are each respectively influenced by the character of pre-Christian Teutonic and Celtic gods.

The Russians are no exception. With them the tie between Christian and pre-Christian elements is perhaps still stronger than in most of the nations of the west. Not that Slavic heathendom proved to be exceptionally powerful; rather the contrary is the truth. But Russia did not know either the Reformation or the Counter-Reformation with their cleansing, spiritualizing, and sweeping out of medieval superstitions. The Russian peasant had been living in the Middle Ages through the nineteenth century. Many an author has said, after personal contact, that the Russians are the

3

most religious people of Europe. But it is rather the difference of age than of the quality of mind or culture. The same historical reasons which had preserved religious freshness in the Russian folk in the midst of an age of rationalism also kept many elements of heathen customs, heathen cults, and even heathen world-view in a state of good preservation both in and out of the Christian Church. Therefore an acquaintance with Russian paganism is an important preliminary for understanding Russian Christianity.

HISTORICAL BACKGROUND

History finds eastern Slavic tribes in the ninth century settled on the western side of the great east European plain, which is the European Russia of today. They came there from the south, the coast of the Black Sea, and from the west, and were drawn into a continual process of expanding towards the east and the north. The common name "Russians" which came later is of an uncertain origin. Historians argue about whether the name derives from the Norsemen conquerors or from the pre-Slavic population of southern Russia. Before the coming of the Slavs to the Russian plain, its northern forests, virgin and wild, were occupied by half-savage Finnish tribes; and the open spaces of the southern steppes by various nomadic peoples of Iranian (the Scythians and Sarmatians) and of Turkish extraction.

No fixed boundaries ever existed between Slavic and neighboring peoples. In the process of continuous colonization of new territories, Slavic tribes fused easily with the aborigines. The influence which had been mutual since prehistoric times appeared in language, customs, and anthropological types. The northern Great Russian, that is, the Russian in a narrow sense as distinct from the Ukrainian and White Russian, in his physical outlook is a product of both the Slavic and Finnish races. The infiltration and blending

of the newcomers with the Finnish aborigines was mostly
a peaceful process; history and legend do not preserve any
memory of battles. But with the inhabitants of the southern
steppes, that is, the nomads, the struggle never ceased. The
annals of ancient Kievan Russia are full of wars or rather
of one continual war against Turkish nomads: Pechenegs,
Polovtsi, and finally, Tartars. The Russian folk epics, even
in the last centuries, lived on the legendary glory of these
campaigns. The southern Russians, however, were also
touched by oriental influences, especially since, in spite of the
Nomadic character of the population, the northern coasts of
the Black Sea were saturated with ancient culture. The girdle
of Greek colonies surrounded it from the Danube to the
Caucasus, and the Byzantine emperors still possessed many
towns in the Crimea, of which Chersonesus or Korsun was
the chief.

Beneath the Graeco-Roman civilization, another cultural
current, and a more ancient one, connected the Russian
steppes with Asia, through the Iranian nomads. Assyro-
Babylonian and particularly Persian influences can still be
clearly read on archaeological relics. Iranianism was the first
traceable cultural element in these areas which was preparing
the soil for the future Russian state on the Dnieper River.
Between the seventh and ninth centuries, the southern steppes
belonged to the vast Turkish Empire of Khazars whose
capital was on the lower Volga. The Slavs of Kiev, the
biggest town on the Dnieper, paid them tribute. The half-
civilized Khazar state opened the Dnieper and the Volga
for the oriental commerce practised by the Moslem merchants. Strangely enough, the Khazars themselves were
not Moslems but were converted to Judaism, at least in the
person of their rulers (Kahans) and their upper classes: this
is one of the rare cases of Jewish proselytism on a national
scale.

At the same time, the northern Slavs, whose main center was Novgorod on the Volkhov River near the Baltic Sea, were harrassed by the inroads of Norsemen, who inundated the whole of Europe in the ninth century as robber-soldiers, merchants, and founders of kingdoms. The Norsemen founded some principalities among the Russian Slavs, too, in Novgorod and neighboring countries, moving steadily to the south towards the legendary Byzantium, which attracted them by its wealth and political glory. Probably about the middle of the eighth century, the Norsemen, or "Varangians" as they were called by Russians and Greeks, appeared on the Black Sea and began their inroads upon Constantinople. In eastern Europe, Norsemen figured more commonly as merchants than as conquerors and managed to organize the regular commerce between Slavic-Finnish forest hunters and the Byzantine Empire. They tied the Baltic basin (Novgorod) and the Dnieper-Black Sea basin into the famous "Great Road from the Varangians to the Greeks." This commercial road, a system of water-ways, was the beginning of the first Russian state.

The Varangians were not very numerous, and their expeditions in Russia were not of a violent character. They acted rather as a police force for the native population whose Slavic language, now called Russian, they soon adopted. The Kiev-Varangian dynasty of the Rurikovichi was the first dynasty of Russian princes. From Kiev, in the course of the tenth and the eleventh centuries, they succeeded in uniting all the other Norse principalities and Slavic tribes on the eastern European plain. A powerful though loosely knit state was created which entered into military and diplomatic relations with Byzantium as well as with the neighbors in the West: Bulgars, Hungarians, Czechs, Poles, and Lithuanians. No natural frontiers delineated the new state, which was geographically shapeless, always moving eastward, and open to the most various cultural influences: oriental, occidental, and southern. The western neighbors of the Russians were heathens until the tenth century; those on the east were Jews and Moslems. Christianity was coming from the south, from Byzantium. Under these circumstances, the Russian Slavs had no opportunity to develop their primitive paganism into an independent culture.

SOURCES

Our knowledge of Slavic paganism in general, and Russian paganism in particular, is extremely small. The primitive religion, without any priestly organization, even without temples (the Baltic Slavs are an exception), could hardly elaborate a complex mythology. Nothing in it would attract the attention of foreign observers. Native Christian preachers of later times, attacking pagan survivals in rites, sacrifices, and divinations, rarely mention the names of heathen gods. Since many of these preachers use Greek homiletic originals, it is perilous to deduce from their statements any conclusions about the real conditions in Russia. And yet these ancient Russian sermons are our chief source of information. Further evidence is given by a few lines in the *Chronicles* and by a heroic epic of the twelfth century, *The Tale of Igor's Campaign*. The *Chronicles* give the names of idols standing before the palace of Prince Vladimir about A.D. 980; they are strange names, most of them non-Slavic, a real puzzle for mythologists. *The Tale of Igor*, on the contrary, besides offering some fresh mythological reminiscences, reflects such a strong feeling of a cosmic life, of a primary accord between man's passions and external nature, as to bring us immediately into contact with the pre-Christian religious mind.

But our chief source for understanding this mind is Russian popular religion observed in modern times. Russian paganism, lacking the protection of any social organization or dogmatic mythological system, yielded almost without struggle to the official Christianity imposed upon the people by the will of the Kievan princes. Yet its passive resistance was tough and tenacious. Indeed, Church historians are right in describing the Russian medieval religion as a "dual faith." The great gods whose pantheon was, probably, the recent creation of Prince Vladimir, disappeared. But lesser spirits, the whole substructure of the people's attitude toward nature and life, remained. Some historians date the true conversion of the lower classes of the Russian people as late as the fifteenth century. But exact dating has no meaning because even in the nineteenth century pagan survivals were still deeply rooted. Long ago these pagan elements blended with Christian Orthodox ritualism and became hardly distinguishable from it. The Russian Church, which formerly waged a merciless war against the dual faith and had redoubled its efforts in the eighteenth century, the age of enlightenment, gave up the struggle in the nineteenth century. Thus in modern days Russia still possessed in its rich folklore an immense hoard of heathen rites, sayings, and songs.

Ethnographical science, in the course of a hundred years, has gathered a huge amount of raw material for the reconstruction of the primitive religion. Unfortunately, this material is little worked over. The first great study of Slavic mythology by A. N. Afanas'ev was a failure, in spite of the author's erudition and wealth of ideas. Afanas'ev started from a German-Aryan mythological background and was under the spell of the solar theory, which, as we shall see, does not explain much in Russian mythology. The grand ruin of his work still stands like a scarecrow in the field of Russian folklore. Modern students became too skeptical, and nobody except a few popularizers has dared until now to approach the hard task under which Afanas'ev was crushed. Some two or three special investigations in Russian religious folklore must be considered only as stepping stones to the synthesis. Happily, we are concerned neither with mythology nor with rites and forms of worship, but with the religious mind, which speaks clearly in every fragment of Russian folklore.

THE ROLE OF NATURE

Nature, of course, is the necessary source of every primitive world view. It is even commonly, if not correctly, accepted that paganism is identical with nature worship. The Russian peculiarity is one of quantity rather than quality. But the quantitative difference is very large, especially from the Western folk mind. One can hardly imagine any Russian lyrical song without a background of nature, used not merely as a framework or scenery for human drama. A human being—a young lad or a maiden—is identified with, rather than compared to some animal or vegetative being—a bird: falcon, swan, duck, dove; a tree: birch; a flower; or, particularly Russian, a fruit or berry such as the raspberry. The destiny of human and animal or vegetative beings are blended in one: they blossom and die together.

In prosaic folk tales, beasts are familiar actors and partakers in human life. Besides the purely animal epic belonging to the common store of mankind there are many Russian stories of animals carrying on business with men in a friendly or cunning but rarely mischievous way. In case of conflicts the guilt lies more often on the side of the man than the beast, who represents the less sophisticated and more straightforward moral standard. The bear particularly appears as an honest, even venerable and mighty being. Some features in the bear tales suggest the idea of a religious bear cult in prehistoric times.

Among the actors in Russian tales one encounters the elementary forces of nature: wind, frost, sun, and moon. They are treated in an intimate, cordial, sometimes ironical way which does not presuppose a real awe or fear before overwhelming powers. Certainly, the laws of the artistic form of the folk tale partly account for the lighthearted treatment of the beings who obviously were objects of worship for the heathen ancestors. Yet some conclusions can be drawn from the tone in which the dethroned gods are treated. The most wanton being is, of course, Wind. The most serious, godlike, or demonlike figure is, curiously enough, Frost. Grandfather Frost is surely the most thoroughly mythological image in Russian tales. It is striking how much more human, familiar, and less divine are Sun and Moon in whom, according to old solar theories, we ought to see the core of the Russian religion.

The cult of solar deities has left noticeable traces in Russian folklore, particularly in the yearly feast calendar. The days of the summer and winter solstice (Saint John and Christmas) are marked by pagan rites which are similar to those of other Indo-European nations. And yet, in spite of the tenets of the traditional school of Russian ethnographers, we venture to say that Russian paganism was perhaps less "solar" than any other in the Aryan religious world. Our Slavic ancestors at the time of Vladimir, about A.D. 1000, must have had some solar deity: the names of Khors (probably Iranian) and Dazhbog (Slavic) are given in different sources. Yet even the attribution of these names is not quite certain. We do not share the mythological skepticism of most modern scholars (Iagitch, Anichkov, Mansikka), yet the uncertainty and dearth of evidence points toward the relative vagueness of the primitive myths. The names of Perun, God of Thunder, and Veles (or Volos), God of Cattle (or Wealth) are more stable in the literary tradition, although not without some difficulties of interpretation.

These difficulties, however, are beyond our field of interest. What is essential in order to understand specifically Russian features against the western background is to mark the secondary character of celestial deities in Russian paganism. Perhaps this is the reason for the general underdevelopment of Russian mythology. Throughout the world the most plastic and picturesque mythological ideas are connected with the celestial world. The eastern Slav did not look passionately at the night sky, like the Semite in the desert, nor was he particularly struck by the might of the sun, though he used to celebrate the stages of its annual life by the winter, spring, and summer festivals. His attention was more attracted by the mysteries beneath, by what happened on earth where his personal and tribal life took place.

THE CULT OF MOTHER EARTH

The sky or the heavens is rarely mentioned by a Russian Slav with particular warmth, awe, or romantic longing. It is on the earth that he has concentrated all his religious devotion to natural powers. We must understand the earth in a narrow sense as soil, as a grain-bearing field, as the earth of the ploughman.

In Russia many relics of the cult of stones, trees, and wells are still partly preserved. Most of them, especially the sacred wells, have long been Christianized. Some sacred trees and stones, however, received no Christian sanctification at all, or like many sacred birches, are associated with the cult of *Paraskeva* (Friday), a mythological rather than hagiological figure. Ancient preachers accused the Russian folk of sacrificing to trees and wells. But even if there were beyond doubt a cult of individual trees and wells surviving as the remainder of a universal fetishism or animism, it would be premature to deduce that there was a particular orientation toward waters or forests in Russian worship of nature elements as images of Mother Earth. Russian folklore preserves quite vividly the belief in both water and forest spirits as half-human male lords or kings of their respective elements. Both species are ugly and malicious; wanton, although not fundamentally evil. They are not devils, and their favor can be bought by some small sacrifices. Besides the male water and forest kings, the Russian people believe in female spirits dwelling in rivers and forests, called *Rusalki*. They are very dangerous and wanton; their pleasure is to lure young men and to tickle them to death. We can guess that Christianity has contributed much to the degradation of these nature spirits, yet it is hardly credible that they once enjoyed a kind of filial affection from their worshippers. Forest and water were always objects of apprehension and distrust for the Russian. The immense forests of the North are indeed a very inhospitable and sometimes dangerous element for the agricultural settler. The beginning of history, however, finds the northern Russians as hunters and honey-seekers in their virgin forests. Perhaps they were at that time more familiar and more intimate with the forest lords. Yet we must not forget that the Slavs were chiefly agricultural people, since the times of the Indo-European unity, and this period of Russian hunting was not an experience which left an indelible mark on the national soul. In this respect, the difference between Slavs and Finns must have been immense.

In Mother Earth, who remains the core of Russian religion, converge the most secret and deep religious feelings of the folk. Beneath the beautiful veil of grass and flowers, the people venerate with awe the black moist depths, the source of all fertilizing powers, the nourishing breast of nature, and their own last resting place. The very epithet of the earth in the folk songs, "Mother Earth, the Humid," known also in the Iranian mythology, alludes to the womb rather than to the face of the Earth. It means that not beauty but fertility is the supreme virtue of the earth, although the Russian is by no means insensible to the loveliness of its surface. Earth is the Russian "Eternal Womanhood," not the celestial image of it: mother, not virgin; fertile, not pure; and black, for the best Russian soil is black.

As a mother who nourishes man during his life and after death gives him rest, the Earth is the embodiment of kindness and mercy. There is, however, something impersonal and generic in her. Unlike the spirits of water and forest, Earth had no indwelling spirits nor was she embodied in human form. She was shapeless as her body under the surface is shapeless. Many myths connected with her are now forgotten, for Christianity succeeded in destroying all traces of sexual associations in the cult of Earth. Yet, Mother Earth must have had a mate, a celestial god of the Sun or of Thunder. Of this marriage between Earth and Heaven in Russian folklore we know nothing. Some remnants of fertilizing rites still point in the direction of the former phallic cult. It is remarkable, however, that Motherhood alone survived through the ages, thereby proving itself stronger than the eroticism of the primitive myth. Speaking in classical terms, this means that in the Russian Earth-goddess, Demeter was more strongly expressed than Aphrodite.

But was Mother Earth once a goddess? We have no positive evidence for this assertion, yet it seems most likely. As we shall see later, the worship of divine Motherhood is an outstanding feature of Russian religion in Christian times. As remnants of the prehistoric periods, there are found on the Russian soil many archeological relics of the worship of an unnamed Great Goddess. Probably, the Slavs had then not yet descended into the southern steppes. This great anonymous goddess was a Scythian, or rather, pre-Scythian, deity. The Greeks of the Black Sea colonies worshipped her as Artemis; the *Iphigenia in Tauris* of Greek tragedy gives the best literary evidence of the Great Goddess worshipped on Rusian soil. The eastern Slavs received this Goddess together with other legacies of Iranian culture. Khors, mentioned among the Gods of Vladimir, was most probably the Iranian Sun-god. Among other mysterious divine names in Vladimir's pantheon is found Mokosh, the supposedly female deity whose name, according to some scholars, survived in Russian topography. Was not Mokosh then the name of the great Earth-goddess of the Russian Slavs? Or did the Mother remain nameless, the more venerable in her anonymity, like the Greek Gaia, or Demeter, the Magna Mater of the Romans or the Mother Earth the Humid of the Iranians?

The erotic element, obliterated in the cult of Mother Earth, survived up to recent times in the form of a male godhead, called Iarilo. Forgotten by the ancient chroniclers —obviously not belonging to the supreme gods of the Slavs— Iarilo enjoyed greater longevity. The popular feasts in his honor were still celebrated in Russian towns in the eighteenth century; and in the countryside even in the nineteenth century, to the accompaniment of wild gaity and obscenities. Iarilo (a Slavic name) was undoubtedly the god of male power and passion—by no means a celestial deity. The nearest parallel to him is the barbarian Dionysus. Dionysus is of Thracian origin, akin to the Iranian, and in his mother country was called Sabazius. In view of the proximity of the Iranians to the Slavs on the Danube and in the south of Russia it would not be too daring to discover in the Russian Iarilo the analogon to Sabasios the Thracian. Even if there were no direct influence of the Iranian deity upon this Slavic fellow-god, their functions must have been essentially identical.

We do not know and shall never know whether Iarilo was once the bridegroom of Mother Earth. Nor can it be discovered of Perun, god of thunder. The ancient chroniclers assign to him the place of supreme deity over the Russian Slavs. The conversion to Christianity in Kiev and Novgorod meant, first of all, the breaking of Perun's wooden idols. It is quite possible that the Scandinavian warriors had shaped the Slavic godhead into the image of the Teutonic Thor. Yet once upon a time he was a Slavic god whose former power is attested to, among other remains, by his long survival in the Russian cult of the prophet Elijah, his successor as thunderlord.

THE GENS RELIGION

The mythology of the Russian Slavs is very obscure. But, should it ever be known in every detail, it would probably not lead us to the heart of Russian paganism. Russian folk religion seems to have been essentially impersonal and even the cult of the Mother Earth gives only one side of it. The other and not the less sacred aspect must be sought in the cult of the dead as the parents, as the ancestors of the eternal kinship-community. The Russian word for it is *rod*. The nearest analogon to it is the classical *gens*. The Latin *gens*, the Celtic *clan*, are now the dead colorless shadows of once-vital social realities. In Russian language and life, the *rod* is full of vitality and vigor; the *rod* is more vigorous than the *sem'ia* (family), which did not succeed in inheriting all the religious meaning of the former.

Among the European peoples only the Russians, together with the Balkan Slavs, preserved personal patronymic names. Every Russian has two personal names, the second being a derivative from his father's. The simple folk sometimes use only the patronymic, like the Homeric Greeks: Atrides, Pelides resemble the Russian Ivanovich, Petrovich. The denominations of the kinship relation are very complicated in detail: the educated people could not keep in their memory all the kinship names which are continually on the lips of the peasants. Still more typical of the Russian's *gens* mentality is the use of kinship names in addressing strangers, as a title of civility. The appellations "father," "grandfather," "uncle," "brother," as well as the corresponding feminine titles, spring to the lips of the Russian peasant addressing either known or unknown persons. Out of the rich store of kinship designations, the most appropriate is chosen in accordance with the age or the degree of moral and social importance of the person addressed. In this procedure all social life is shaped as the extension of family life and all moral relations among men are raised to the level of blood kinship. This is of tremendous importance in understanding Russian social ethics. The Russian village community, the *mir*, has long been based not upon kinship, but upon neighborhood and property. Yet the *mir* inherited from the *gens* the warmth and the patriarchal character of life. The whole Russian nation from an idealistic viewpoint could once be thought of as an immense *gens* or *rod*, of whom the Tsar was the father. This was, indeed, the conception of Russian Slavophiles, based upon the moral and political idea of the people.

This gens-ethic acquires its religious aspect in relation to the deceased parents, the ancestors. In modern Christian Russia the commemoration of the dead occupies a prominent place in the liturgical worship of the Church. No less than ten Saturdays in the year—so-called "Parents' Saturdays"— are consecrated to prayer for the dead. Even the liturgical service preserved the traces of the pagan funeral banquet, at which the dead were believed to participate in the meal with the living. A sacred food now composed of wheat or rice and raisins is brought into the Church and put on the table with the Crucifix. This funeral meal takes much freer forms in the churchyard, on the graves, where wine plays a great part, and which ends sometimes in real orgies. It is a spring feast of the dead (*Radunitsa*), coinciding with the Easter week which has preserved most faithfully the character of the pagan Slavic *Trizna*, or funeral banquet. The old Slavic mead was until recently served at the social banquet following the funeral, and the sacred rice, *kut'ia*, replaced the ancient Slavic millet.

In western or White Russia, there still existed in the nineteenth century the profane or substantially pagan feast in honor of the dead, the so-called *Dziady* (Grandfathers). It consisted of an abundant and prolonged meal in a house where all the living relatives were asembled under the presidency of the oldest member of the *rod*, and where the dead received their part of each dish and drink. Strange prayers or incantations were recited by the old man, after which the dead were solemnly expelled from the house.

In pagan times all the dead became minor gods whose cult represented the very core of the Slavic religion. The dead were mighty enough to help or to endanger the living, according to the formers' character or to the latters' ritual zeal. The chief of the ancestors, or the founder of the *rod* became a particular patron of the house, who was, and still is called by the general name of "house spirit" (*Domovoi*). The belief in *Domovoi* was very common among the peasants in the nineteenth century. Every house had its particular house spirit who was thought of as an old dwarf living under the threshold, in the stove, or in the horse stall. Although he can be seen by the living, he dislikes to be seen and punishes people for their curiosity or neglect of him. For he, like all the dead, must be fed and treated with respect. The Russian Domovoy has his correspondent in the Roman *Penates*, and the Russian "parents" or grandfathers in the *Manes*.

The strength and extension of the parents' cult to modern times indicated the central place dead relatives held in the Slavic cult. On the other hand, they were closely connected with minor deities of nature. Indeed, the modern ethnographists see in *Rusalki*, the female spirits of waters and woods, the souls of the dead maidens or children who had committed suicide or had met a violent death. In the Spring festivities in honor of the *Rusalki*—in the *Rusalii* (from the Roman *Rosalia*) feast—these unhappy female spirits are treated with kindness and pity. Some modest gifts are brought to them, especially wreaths of flowers. The period from Easter to Pentecost is the time of relief and release for all the spirits in the underworld. They dare to appear on earth to share the communion and gifts of the living. The Pentecost, which coincides, approximately, with the Roman Rosalia or the Greek Anthesteria, brings this privilege to an end. When the spirits have been expelled from earth, the *Rusalki* return to their water element. We do not know in what measure Christianity influenced the moral character of these spirits; their mischievous mood may or may not be comparatively recent. But the idea of violent death or lack of orderly burial as the ground for damnation is, obviously, non-Christian. It must have originated in the cult of the dead where strict ritualistic forms were considered a necessary condition for the post-mortem welfare of the soul.

The minor spirits of nature are not the only extension of the cult of the dead. Mother Earth becomes clearer to us against the background of the *gens* religion. The sacred motherhood of the earth is intimately akin to the worship of the parents. The double mystery of birth and death is experienced as well in the life of a *rod* as in the yearly cycle of the earth. From the sperm of the parents man is brought forth into the everlasting *rod* for his short existence, just as the seed, buried in the earth's womb, gives a new life to the ear of corn which is procreated through the death of the seed itself. Was not this symbolical association of the life of man and corn the fundamental mystery of Eleusis? But while the Greek mysteries promised immortality to the human soul, Russian paganism (as well as the primitive Greek) considered the individual only as a transient moment in the eternal life of the *rod*. From the parents man comes and to the parents he returns, into the womb of the Mother Earth. During his earthly life, his whole existence is determined by the parents, by the will of the living and by the traditions of the departed. For the freedom and will of the individual there is left very little place. The consciousness of personality, of its own ways, vocations, and rights developed tardily and slowly on the Russian soil both in pagan and in Christian times. This is the deepest religious root of Russian collectivism.

A well-known Orphic verse found in many tombs of southern Italy puts into the mouth of the departed:

> I am the son of the Earth
> And of the starred Heaven.

The Russian Slav could hardly make a claim upon the second, celestial origin. He was the fatherless son of the Great Mother. This mother taught him kindness and fidelity, but not freedom and valor—the male virtues. Of course, we must not exaggerate this characteristic and imagine Russian paganism completely lacking in the male features which are so manifest in the other Indo-European religions. We speak only of determinants, of the main emphasis.

Some Byzantine writers, in describing the customs of the Slavs, stress their peaceful character. Is it an accidental fact that we do not know the Russian god of War? Perun could play the part of such a one under the Norsemen's influence, sharing thus the career of the Teutonic Thor. But we cannot prove that he was a warlike god from the beginning.

There is no Russian parallel to Athena, or any other Virgin Goddess, and it seems that neither purity nor beauty was essential to the Russian worship of Sacred Womanhood. Even the Rusalki are conceived by the Great Russians in the north as ugly beings; their alluring loveliness in south Russia can be explained by the southern Slavic influence. Mother Earth is shapeless and faceless. The beauty to which the Russian is so sensitive is not embodied primarily in the woman. Beauty dwells in nature. And the beauty of nature for the Russian is the embracing, the enveloping, rather than the contemplated. Man is lost in nature, unwilling to master her.

Hence it follows that the greatest religious temptation for a Russian will be pantheism of a sensual (hylozoistic) kind. Sacred matter rather than spirit is the object of veneration. Personality is underdeveloped, social ties extremely strong, on the basis of blood relationship. Romanticism in any form is basically un-Russian. Sensual mysticism, however, is a necessary complement to the social discipline of the *rod*. The spirit of Dionysus is perpetually attempting to infringe upon the laws of Mother Earth.

II

RELIGIOUS BYZANTINISM

HISTORICAL BACKGROUND

*A*BOUT 1000 A.D. (tradition says 988) Russia was officially converted to Christianity by the baptism of the Kievan Prince Vladimir and his subjects. Of course, it was only the beginning of the Christian mission, supported by the state, among Slavic and Finnic tribes of the eastern European plain. Yet from the very outset Vladimir had to make a choice of tremendous historical significance: between the Eastern and Western forms of Christianity, between Byzantium and Rome. The Christian Church was still united at the time of the conversion. But the relations between its Greek and Latin halves were hopelessly spoiled and were moving towards the final break of 1054. Vladimir chose the Greek Church—not perhaps without hesitation—and thus determined the destiny of Russia. She became a province of Byzantine culture and the bearer of the Eastern Orthodoxy, the usual name for the Greek form of Catholicism. The whole Russian mind and heart were shaped by this Eastern Christian mould. After 1054 official ecclesiastical relations with Western Catholic Europe became practically impossible: after the Mongolian conquest of 1240, the political and cultural ties with the West were almost severed. These two facts are the source of both the originality and the limitations of Russian culture; of both its greatness and its flaws.

After 1037—the previous years are shrouded in mist

21

—the Russian Church was headed by the Metropolitan appointed by the Patriarch of Constantinople. It was, indeed, an ecclesiastical province of Constantinople standing under the supreme jurisdiction of the oecumenical Patriarch. The decisions of the Greek councils, the Greek Canon Law, and the Greek ritual were obligatory on Russian territory. With two exceptions, the Metropolitans of Kiev of the pre-Mongolian time were Greek by nationality and subjects of the Byzantine Emperor. In Russia they found no political counterbalance to the Greek influence. The loose monarchy of Kiev, after reaching its climax under Vladimir who died in 1015, and his son Iaroslav, who died in 1054, began to split into a multiplicity of local principalities, not dissimilar, at first glance, to the feudal Europe of the same time. Their ties were very weak, and of moral rather than legal character; the primacy of the prince of Kiev was merely honorary. In every local state the prince had to face many social forces: his retainers (*druzhina*), the landed and commercial aristocracy (*boyars*) and popular assembly (*veche*). The Church was the most powerful of these social elements and the princes could not even dream of dominating it. If they had an influence upon the election of the diocesan bishops, the appointment of the Metropolitan was still outside their sphere. Canonically, the Greek element was predominant. Modern Russian scholars have discovered some traces of western institutions in the ancient Russian Church (the ecclesiastical tithes, for instance); they were due to continuous political and cultural relations with the West during the pre-Mongolian period. But they are not strong enough to change the predominance of the Greek institutions, as well as the Greek doctrines and forms of worship, in the Russian Church. The Church was born in the body of Byzantinism and to determine these Byzantine elements in ancient Russian Christianity will be our next task.

THE FORMULA OF BYZANTINISM

It is an extremely arduous undertaking to attempt, in a few pages, a summary sketch of Byzantine culture and religion, especially since the contents of Byzantine religious culture has by no means been thoroughly investigated. We are faced in this field with many "clichés" and prejudices which must at least partly disappear upon closer study.

It is certainly untrue to say that medieval Greece, or the "Roman Empire," as she called herself, was a barbarian state. On the contrary, until the twelfth century, Byzantine civilization surpassed, beyond question, that of the European West. Until the year 1000—the time of the Russian conversion—western Europe can be considered as a dark and backward province of the one Christian civilization, the center of which was definitely not in Rome, but in Constantinople. The latter was the treasure store of classical literature which preserved for us the ancient pagan and Christian traditions of Greece. The preservation of these traditions constituted the main historic role played by Byzantium. It was conservative rather than creative, the role of a schoolmaster and custodian. Byzantium was a museum and a library of Christian Greece. When the West began to spread its wings for original thought and art it soon overtook Byzantium in creative richness and power, although the privilege of refinement remained with Byzantium until 1453.

The relative immobility of Byzantium must not be conceived in too literal a sense. There were changes, but they were slow; there were conflicts, but they were less acute than in the West. Byzantium never had a sufficient cleavage with antiquity to allow it to start a new culture. The term "Middle Ages," therefore, has no application, in its full sense, to the Christian East. The tradition of Hellenistic culture was never broken. Yet there were periods of decadence followed by revivals which did not exactly repeat previous patterns, but brought some new elements or some stylistic innovations. The first great decline covered the seventh and eighth centuries, the time of the Persian and Arabian conquests; the second, the time of the Latin invasion and the temporary conquest by the Crusaders (1204-1260). These periods of depression distinctly divide Byzantine history into three epochs: the age of Justinian, the age of the Macedonian and Comnene dynasties (ninth to twelfth centuries), and the age of the Paleologues (thirteenth to fifteenth centuries).

The pictorial arts definitely changed from age to age. But the content of religious interests and literary forms did not change in the same way. Yet there was always some tension between heterogeneous elements in the culture which led, from time to time, to open conflicts. Such were the tensions between secular and theological knowledge, between rationalism and mysticism, between Platonism and Aristotelianism, which counterbalanced one another up to the end of the Empire. These spiritual conflicts had their social parallel in the tension between Church and State, notwithstanding the organic coöperation claimed in this field, or the tension between the centralizing and the feudal forces of political life. All this gives a dramatic movement to Byzantine history, but ,in all scenes of the drama one always sees the same actors and the same forces in struggle.

Can there be found then something like a general formula for Byzantine culture? Remaining on the ground of merely formal definitions one has the choice between "Orientalized Hellenism" or "Hellenized Orientalism." Despite Strzigovsky and so many other modern partisans of orientalism it seems a truer view to regard Byzantium as the survival of the Hellenistic world. Hellenism, from its very beginning with Alexander the Great, continued to

undergo the steady process of orientalization. Diocletian's
reforms and Constantine's conversion to an oriental religion could only reinforce this influence. Yet somewhere
in Justinian's or the following age this process was stopped
and Byzantium found its balance between the West and the
East. It cannot be denied that in some spheres of life the
Orient prevailed: in the state, in the conception of sovereignty, in the hierarchical structure of society. In art,
orientalism was very strong; whether it was predominant
is a question. The truth is that in art Byzantium achieved
a real synthesis of both cultural traditions. It may be that
this was her only original creation—sacred painting, the
icon—apart from hymnic poetry and the new mystical methods of contemplation which developed later. But in the
humanities—theology, philosophy, literature—and in science
Byzantium remained faithful to the Greek heritage. It
succeeded in preserving—throughout a thousand years—
the Greek literary language and style in a relatively pure
state. Byzantium continued the literary forms bequeathed by
antiquity—the Hellenistic novel, mythological poetry, and
so on. This purity is the cause of barrenness, for which it is
merely a polite name. Except for religious poetry, Byzantine literature absorbed nothing from the East, nothing
from the barbarians of the North—mostly Slavs who had
inundated the Balkan peninsula leaving there but little of
the ancient pure Greek blood. Barbarians succeeded one
another on the sacred throne of *basileus*—Isaurians, Armen-
ians, Slavs—yet nothing changed in the written language,
in school education, or in scholarship. In the eleventh and
twelfth centuries, Lucian, Thucydides, and Homer were still
imitated and were always at the base of the "grammatical"
education. Philosophy had the choice only between Plato
and Aristotle. Inasmuch as culture in Byzantium never
died out as in the West, so also it never experienced a resur-

rection. Every new inflorescence meant a restoration, a return: there was no *vita nuova,* no new life.

This lack of creative vitality prevented Byzantium from
achieving the final synthesis between the pagan and Christian
elements of its heritage. It was, in principle, a totalitarian
culture claiming a Christian (orthodox) sanctification of the
whole life: state, war, economics, family, school, art, and
learning. And yet big undefined elements of paganism
remained, without any serious attempt at transformation.
The school was the guardian of pagan traditions, blended
only superficially with Christianity. The monastery, on
the contrary, never was in Byzantium the place of learning
it often was in the West. From time to time a strange figure
arises out of the twilight of the Byzantine schoolrooms: a
semi-pagan philosopher, a neoplatonist or occultist. On the
other hand, the fulminations against culture by monastic
representatives of saintly simplicity never ceased. Palace
and hermitage were the two foci of the Byzantine world.
The tension between them was the only serious drama in
this static culture.

THE RELIGIOUS MIND OF BYZANTIUM

Until we possess extensive monographs on Byzantine
theology, liturgy, and spiritual life, all general characteri-
zations of the Byzantine religious mind will remain un-
proven and hypothetical. They are grounded in general
impressions rather than in critical studies. Yet a summary
picture of religious Byzantium is indispensable as a natural
background for the Russian religion with which the Byzantine is constantly, but wrongly, confused. In trying to
discriminate between these two forms of Eastern Orthodoxy
we come to a rather unconventional conception of Byzantine
Christianity.

Byzantium was a direct heir of Greek classical theology

of the fourth and fifth centuries. This means that Byzantium inherited the organic fusion of the two streams of
ancient Christian spirituality: that of Asia Minor and that of
Alexandria. The Johannine tradition of Saint Ignatius,
of Irenaeus, was merged with the Platonism of Clement and
Origen, into an organic whole by Athanasius and the Cap-
padocian fathers. This fusion remained forever the discriminating character of the Eastern Christianity as distinct
from the Christian West which united Platonism with the
Latin or Roman patristic tradition in the person of Saint
Augustine. Alexandrian Platonism is common to the whole
Catholic Church; Romanism versus Asianism is the principle of individuation. Platonism initiates into the mystics
of spirit; Johannine Christianity is the religion of Incarnation in the sense of the fourth Gospel: the revelation of the
spirit incarnate. The latter develops into the Eastern
mysticism of sacramental life, whereas Platonism lays the
ground for the mystical contemplation in the Eastern, as
well as in Western, monasticism. Thus, Byzantium had
inherited and kept alive—even enriched—the two sources
of spiritual life: the sacramental and the ascetic-mystical.
The whole original theological thought of Byzantium is
concentrated upon these two points; the doctrine of sacraments and the doctrine of spiritual life. The first word of
Byzantinism was Pseudo-Dionysius of about the year 500;
the last, Gregorius Palamas and Nicholas Kabasilas of the
fourteenth century. Through Dionysius the whole tradition of late neoplatonic theurgical mystics of Iamblichus and
Proclus merged into the mysteries religion of the ancient
Christian Church; it was the reinforcement of the previous,
already mighty, sacramental stream. The mysticism of
personal ascetic life finds its climax and its adequate literary
expression much later, in the tenth century with Simeon
the New Theologian. Both currents are parallel and closely

akin. This is the double process of "deification" which
Athanasius and all Greek fathers taught. Byzantium never
knew a real tension between ascetic and sacramental forms
of spirituality.

The doctrinal theology underlying this spirituality was
that of the ancient Church and the seven oecumenical councils—in principle, identical with the Western Church. There
is, however, an essential, although never formulated and
very delicate distinction in Christology, at the very core of
Christian dogma. There are two types of Catholic orthodoxy in the dogma of Incarnation: Leo the Great and Cyril
of Alexandria. Cyril stood for the unity of the person in
Christ, and Leo for the distinction between the divine and
human natures. Western Christology was and remains
faithfully Leonine; and eastern Byzantine, Cyrillian.
Cyril was the father of the third Ephesian Oecumenical
Council of 431, and Leo of the Chalcedonian 451. They
both were proclaimed guardians of orthodoxy at a time when
it was very difficult to retain this title, and yet they stood
for the opposite tendencies of the two theological schools,
Cyril representing Alexandria and Leo representing Antioch. They came from opposite directions to the verge of
orthodoxy. Yet Cyril was the acknowledged father of the
Monophysites to whom he bequeathed his incorrect formula:
"One nature of the God-Logos incarnate." To the Monophysites Leo was simply a Nestorian, the head of the other
heretical dissident Church. The balance between the Greek
East and the Latin West was found only with difficulty and
at the price of the Oriental provinces of the Empire lost to
Islam. But the whole religious development of the
Christian West and East in their divergent ways was, per-
haps, determined by this primordial opposition: Leo and
Cyril. Leonine Christology, emphasizing strongly the human nature in Christ, was the necessary condition of the

Jesus-mystics of the Middle Ages, as well as of the modern humanism. Both remained strange to Byzantium.

Monophysitism was a perpetual temptation to the Christian East. Rejected overtly, although not wholeheartedly, it returned again and again in official conciliatory creeds and in the ecclesiastical policy of Justinian who managed to condemn some of the ancient fathers of Chalcedon, if not the Chalcedonian council itself. Cyril, who never was condemned despite his obviously anti-Chalcedonian terminology, (one nature in Christ), became the last great father and the authority of the Byzantine Church. His Christology was adopted, in corrected form, by John of Damascus who lived in the eighth century, the classical exponent of Eastern orthodoxy. And, what is more important, it became the main source of inspiration for Byzantine hymnographers, and thus assured for itself the predominant place in Eastern worship.

Let us now consider what were the questionable features in the Cyrillic legacy. While affirming the perfect humanity as well as the perfect divinity of Christ, Saint Cyril limited the weakness of human nature in Christ to the bodily side. Jesus knew hunger, weariness, pains, tortures, and death on the cross. Yet Cyril denied in Him human ignorance, human development, human nonsinful emotions, sorrow and fear. According to Cyril, Jesus lived with men, from childhood, as omniscient, omnipotent God, who voluntarily took upon Himself the cross of human sufferings, but not human nature itself. Hardly could He be considered and worshipped as man or God-man. What remained real in His humanity was the human body. As to the human soul, it might be accepted in theological treatises, but in practice, in devotional life, it shrank into nothingness. God in human flesh—this was the Christ of the Byzantine worshipper, as He was revealed in the icons and addressed in the prayers of the Church.

The typical Byzantine icon of Christ is that of the
Pantocrator, the Lord Omnipotent. It is the image of
the glorified Christ regnant on His heavenly throne. We
are not even sure that it is not an image of the Eternal God
rather than that of Christ. In fact, He bears the designation
O Ω N around His head as God who spoke to Moses. The
Greek tradition did not know any image of God the Father
as distinct from the Son because in the theology of icons
only the Incarnation makes legitimate and humanly possible
the representation of the Godhead. But, as the Son is the
image of the Father, so through the face of the Son we see
the Father as well. Thus, the Pantocrator is really the
icon of both Father and Son: the Godhead in all His glory
and majesty. It was said that the iconographic type itself
originated in the Zeus of Phidias. This was, indeed, the
evolution of Christ's image in the pictorial arts: after the
Good Shepherd (Hermes Cryophoros), came Christ as
Asclepius, the mild healer of the fourth and fifth centuries;
then Christ as Zeus. Yet the expression of Phidias'
Olympian god had changed. Sorrow and severity are written upon this divine face as if it were forced, unwillingly, to
contemplate men's crimes and sins. Christ-Pantocrator is,
indeed, the Christ of the Last Judgment or of the "Terrible
Judgment" as it is called by the Greeks, not the Redeemer,
but the Judge—as He is expected by the faithful.

Byzantium knew no other more evangelical icons of
Christ, except in the compositions of the Lord's feasts
(scenes from the Gospel) where His figure is but one among
many. The Pantocrator icon leads us to the very heart of
Byzantine piety. It is the worship of the transcendent almighty God whom the sinful man can approach only in awe
and terror. The old Biblical "numinous"—to use the term
of R. Otto—concept of Jahve was rediscovered in Byzantium
in the process of the retrogressive evolution. A thousand

years later, at the other pole of Christianity, the same Old
Testament concept of God was revived by Calvin. It is
curious to observe how many common features the radical
form of Protestantism has with oriental monophysitism or
with some radical trends of Oriental monasticism. In both
a miserable man stands before the terrible God, finding no
words strong enough for self-humiliation.

The hope for salvation is small. Hell is the lot of the
average, not only of the worst people. But there is a hope
and a way of salvation. Byzantium knew and cultivated,
in doctrine and life, two ways of salvation already referred
to: monastic asceticism and sacrament. In the Eastern
Church monasticism became not one form of Christian life
among others, but Christian life in its perfection, the norm
for everyone who did not trifle with his salvation. In the
course of time the monks succeeded in imposing upon the
laity not only their penitential discipline (private confession),
the monastic "black" espiscopacy (not in Canon Law but in
practice), and their fast regulations, but even the order and
the contents of the liturgical prayers. The liturgical rules
(*typica*) of the great monasteries, *Studion* (or better *Studios*)
in Constantinople and Saint Sabbas in Palestine gradually
superseded the liturgy of the Patriarchal Church of Saint
Sophia and other episcopal cities. This is the explanation
for the extreme length of the Eastern services: designed,
in the first place, for monks, they had practically no time
limitations. In Mount Athos, where they are celebrated in
unabridged form, they occupy the whole night.

In being thus universalized, the monastic life needed
to be mitigated and humanized. Byzantium had to restrict
those heroic and superhuman exploits of bodily asceticism
admired in the Egyptian and, particularly, in the Syrian
fathers. This humanization of the Eastern asceticism was
already completed in Palestine—in the circles of Saint

Euthymius and Saint Sabbas in the fifth and sixth centuries
—and in this mitigated form monasticism was spread throughout the Byzantine empire; the old classical countries of
monasticism became the prey of monophysitism and, later,
of Islam. The Palestinian and Studite monastic life was an
harmonious combination of prayer, work, and social charity.
The work consisted mostly of physical labors, and Byzantine
monasteries never grew to be cultural centers as in the West.
Since social work was limited, prayer was the main purpose
of the monastic life. Prayer absorbed asceticism, becoming
itself a kind of ascetic labor and thus approached the lay
ideal of salvation through prayer and sacrament. The high
mystical contemplation was rather exceptional. Ascetic
treatises of the early Byzantine era contain mostly rules for
self-examination, for the inner discipline and the struggle
against passions. This struggle embraces, among the inner
foes, all "cogitations," not only sinful, but also neutral, that
is, the whole contents of the "psychic" as opposed to the
"pneumatic" life of thought and heart: Spirit against Soul.
The pity is that the spiritual life often stops at this stage
of the *via purgativa*. Mystical contemplation was for the
few. Prayer for the average ascetic, particularly liturgical
prayer, fills his whole consciousness, emptied of all other
contents, and works out, or is believed to work out, the
process of "deification."

Two developments connect the monastic way of salvation with the sacramental one: very early the initiation
to monastic life, a rite called in the East "tonsuring," was
considered by many as a real sacrament bestowing pardon
for the sins of the foregoing life. On the other hand, this
sacrament was open to the moribund. Every layman who
had time—which was, of course, a great uncertainty—could
die a monk, thereby increasing enormously his chances of
salvation.

The other way of "deification"—through sacraments—
was open to everybody. It was embedded and enshrouded
in prayer to prevent its becoming degraded into a simple
magic. The gorgeous rituals enhanced the symbolism of
sacred words and gestures inherited from early Christian
mysteries. The mysteries themselves were extended in
number and meaning; in fact, they became innumerable.
The number of the seven sacraments was fixed first by the
Western Church in the twelfth century. The Greek Church
took over this doctine only in the seventeenth century and
not without some hesitations which have lasted up to the
present. In the Middle Ages Byzantine liturgical writers
emphasized some major sacraments which had greater theological bearing: Baptism, Chrismation (Confirmation), the
Holy Eucharist. The other sacraments tended to merge
with the undetermined mass of *Sacramentalia* such as the
anointing of the Emperor, the monastic "tonsuring," the
"Great Consecration" of water (on the Epiphany), the
minor sanctifications of water, wine, bread and oil, fruits,
homes, fields, and of elements and matter in general. Every
icon was a mystery in itself, not only as an image of the
divine world but as its real presence on earth. The saints
were really present in their relics as well as in their icons.
From all these sacraments, sacral actions and sacred objects,
streams of grace flood upon this sinful world purifying and
deifying it.

In this sacramental religion the Deity ceases to be trans-
cendant. It takes its abode in the temple. The Church
becomes "heaven on earth," according to a classical Orthodox
saying. The Divinity is accessible through matter, that of
sacraments and sacred objects; it can be not only seen, but
even smelled, tasted, kissed. This is not merely coarse
materialism as most Protestants think; there is a world of
higher emotions tied up with this bodily adoration: awe,

contrition, tenderness, gratitude, joy, the consciousness of
one's unworthiness, and the unmerited grace of God. Sacramentalism also is an instrument of the mystical life as
asceticism is, though in a more rudimentary form: not mystical life itself, but sparks which can, though not necessarily,
be kindled into a flame of personal spirituality.

We are, apparently, very far from the severe religion of
a transcendent God which is so unpromising for man's salvation. Sacramentalism and transcendentalism were the two
poles of the Byzantine religion, as can be found in every
religion. They were not divided as sharply in reality as
they are in logical analysis. In fact, they were merged into
one organic religious complex in which one could not
exist without the other. The pure religion of universal
damnation is unthinkable, as is the religion of easy salvation through material elements. The Church, despite the
high appreciation of its sacramental treasures, never could
promise salvation through them alone. It insisted, in
principle, on personal holiness, for which sacraments were
only the means. On the other hand, this holiness was un-
attainable, except by the ascetic way. There is no security
in the religious life. Before the God of justice and the
God of mercy man lived, oscillating between fear and hope.
This religious situation or "crisis" (to use Barth's expression) is, of course, a general Christian situation; Byzantinism was distinguished from Western Christianity only
by the radical emphasis put upon the two terms of its religious complex and by the particular fashion of their presentation.

From the historical point of view, one cannot help
seeing in this religious dualism of Byzantium the heritage
of the two religious worlds: Judaism and Hellenism. If
it is true that the whole of Byzantine culture was a blending
of Orientalism and Hellenism, the Orientalism was repre-

sented in the religious sphere by Judaic transcendentalism, and the Hellenism by the mystical and sacramental elements of Christianity. What is amazing in this synthesis is the small place left to the New Testament and to the historical God-man Christ. Practically the whole of Byzantine religion could have been built without the historical Christ of the Gospels, upon a simple myth of the heavenly saviour similar to Hellenistic saviour myths. The divine, glorified Christ is, certainly, the main object of the Byzantine cult— together with His Mother, the Queen of Heaven. Yet, strangely, His earthly life, and His good news of the Kingdom of God, and particularly His teaching, attracted little attention. The Gospels became a book of mysteries of Christ; a source of theological speculations. Since Christ Himself was the Word of God, His own spoken word was little heeded—or rather, was almost inaccessible beneath all the allegorical exegesis. Of the ethical teaching of Jesus what remained most forceful was His uncompromising commandments, obviously beyond human achievement, reinforced by the promise of Terrible Judgment.

A corollary of this attitude toward Christ was in the character of Byzantine preaching. The Greek sermon was mostly theological. Its paramount aim was to disclose the meaning of a particular feast in the Church calendar and its mystical significance. The sermon itself was a continuation of the liturgy, sharing in its solemn, theurgical style, but the moral implications were often neglected. This gives us the key to a tremendous gap in the Byzantine religion: the weakness of ethical life.

The Greek fathers of the fourth century, with all their Platonic and mystical interests, had been prophetic teachers to their nation. They considered the struggle against evil in personal and social life the main task of a Christian. But after some real efforts at transforming and Christianizing the national life in the first century after Constantine, the Church seems to have exhausted herself and given up the fruitless struggle. The sanctification of the whole life became a symbolic consecration, not a real change. The Orientalism of the state, rebuilt by Diocletian, was paralleled by the orientalization of social life which had fallen to the level of oriental, pagan societies. Slavery was not only one of the basic social institutions but the model type of all social relationships. Everyone was the slave of his superiors and master to his inferiors. The ethics of slavery, in the disguise of Christian humility, were accepted and idealized by the Byzantine Church. In reading the Byzantine historians one is appalled by the amount of cruelty and perfidy occurring at every step: regicides; tortures and mutilations of vanquished foes; blinding and castration not only of individuals but of whole captive armies. Perhaps half of the Byzantine emperors came to the throne through revolt, and often by shedding the blood of their predecessors, despite the sacred character of the monarchy. Certainly there was cruelty in the western Middle Ages too, but in Byzantium one is confronted by a cold, passionless cruelty which finds no moral opposition from either the narrating authors or—with rare exceptions—from the contemporary Church. The mixture of cruelty and perfidy is often considered as typically oriental. Yet stepping out of the Byzantine into the Moslem world one is breathing a purer air. The combination of these "oriental" features with deep and sincere piety makes the Byzantine complex quite unique in the Christian world.

It is true that one draws this impression from the descriptions of life in high society and the imperial palace. The middle classes and the simple folk may have led a more decent life. Unfortunately, we know very little about the life of the lower classes in Byzantium. Byzantium had its religious focus not at the base but at the top of the social pyramid. The *basileus* was the model of devotion, and the palace the center of theological and ecclesiastical interests. The patriarch who headed the Church was always connected with the palace and often shared in its political activities and crimes. Spiritual independence and sometimes real holiness could be achieved in seclusion from the world, in a monk's cell. But this cell was more remote from the folk life than the cell of a western or a Russian monk. The monks in Byzantium did not preach to the people and rarely taught them. They did little to change the fundamentally pagan character of society, which continued the life of the ancient Hellenistic empires in a considerably deteriorated form. A certain amount of hypocrisy was naturally created by the half-conscious feeling of incompatibility between the pagan structure of society and Christian standards. The refusal to adjust society to these standards, together with great personal, rather superstitious, piety imprints upon this refined society the mark of a fundamental mendacity. This was the general impression of the Russian Slavs when they came into contact with their Byzantine teachers: "The Greeks have been deceivers up to this day," was the verdict of an ancient Russian annalist.

SLAVIC BYZANTINISM

Nobody can understand the destiny of Russian culture and religion without being aware of a primordial difference between Russia and the Christian West. Both had inherited their culture and their religion from the ancient Hellenistic world: the one from the Latin source, the other from the Greek. The Greek tradition was undoubtedly richer and more original: the Romans were disciples and imitators of Greece. Besides, Rome had long lost its political existence and even had ceased to be a cultural center,

whereas Byzantium was a powerful and flourishing state.
It would seem that all conditions were turned in favor of
the southern and eastern Slavs against the Latinised Germans
and Celts, and we could expect the blossoming of medieval
culture in Russia instead of in France, Germany, or England.
Yet the contrary was the case. The poverty of intellectual
culture in ancient Russia is amazing. For seven centuries—
that is, until the seventeenth—we know of no scientific work
in Russian literature, not even a dogmatic treatise. The
whole of literary production had a practical, moral, or religious character, with the exception of the Chronicles, whose
great artistic value vividly emphasizes, by contrast, the
complete lack of scientific culture. Modern Russian historians, of a new nationalistic brand in the USSR, are
unanimous in overestimating the level of ancient Kievan
culture, which, according to them, was not inferior to and
even surpassed the contemporary western civilization. Their
complete failure to substantiate their claim constitutes by
itself a new proof of the poverty, at least the intellectual
poverty, of that culture.

What is the reason for this anomaly which has had such
tragic consequences for Russian life? Was it a natural organic incapacity of the Russians—or Slavs in general—for
rational thinking? Yet in the last century Russia developed
a rich production in all branches of science second only to
the few most civilized nations of the West. Was it the
perennial struggle against the nomad tribes of the steppes
which exhausted all the national energies? But a never-
ceasing feudal war was the background of the medieval
monastic schools and universities of the West. Was it the
geographical remoteness from the areas of ancient classical
culture? Yet Scandinavia and northern Europe in general
were still more distant from Rome than Russia from Byzantium. However, the last consideration brings us nearer

the truth. Russia, in fact, did not receive, together with Greek Christianity, the classical culture of Greece. Byzantium itself still possessed the ancient treasures; it did not transmit them to Russia, or rather, Russia did not care to receive them. What was the reason? Here again comparison with the West gives an illuminating answer.

The western barbarians, before they were able to think their own thoughts and to speak their own words—about 1100 A.D.—had been sitting for five or six centuries on the school bench, struggling with the foreign Latin language, learning by heart the Latin Bible and the Latin grammar with Vergil as the introduction to the Bible. Men of the dark ages had no independent interest in culture. They were interested only in the salvation of their souls. But Latin gave them the key to salvation. As the language of the Church, Latin was a sacred tongue and everything written in it became invested with a sacred halo. Hence the popularity of Ovid in medieval monasteries, and the Latin versifying of Irish saints, such as Columban, who in their severe asceticism and primitive rudeness of life did not yield to the anchorites of Egypt and Syria. For the Irish the Trivium and Quadrivium were the way to the Latin Bible.

The Slavs converted by the Greeks did not need a similar vehicle to Christianity: they received the Bible and divine service in Slavonic translations. In the second half of the ninth century, two Greek brother missionaries, Saint Cyril and Saint Methodius, performed with their disciples a great work of translating Greek sacred books into Old Slavonic, which at that time could be considered more or less as a common Slavic literary idiom. In the next century the cultivated circle around the Bulgarian Tsar Simeon completed the work of the Cyrillic generation by translating some works of theological and scientific content. A Slavonic library was thus created from which medieval Russia was spiritually fed. Russia received her ecclesiastical organization from Greece but the books and perhaps the first priests came from Bulgaria. The bulk of this literature was more than sufficient for the needs of a newly converted people. Some of these books even exceeded the level of their understanding. Upon this store of learning, obtained from abroad, Russia lived for centuries; most of the additions, new translations from the Greek, came from the same South Slavic source, the Serbs and Bulgarians. There was no religious motive to look in Greek libraries for a new supply. The available Slavonic literature had an overwhelmingly practical and didactic character. Theoretical interests had not been awakened. And the Russian intellect was dwarfed in its development for a long time, not because of the predominance of mystical tendencies, as has often been claimed, but because of the absence of external occasions for exercise. So the Slavonic Bible and the Slavonic liturgy proved to be an ambiguous gift to Russian culture. At the same time, it cannot be denied that these were a priceless endowment for Russia's spiritual life. The people could listen to the word of God and pray to Him in an idiom very near their own. The Gospel was accessible in some measure even to the illiterate. It is obvious then that the fruits of the Christian mission in Russia were, from the very beginning, richer than those yielded by the western Latin soil. It would be no exaggeration to suppose that the imprint of the Gospel was deeper there than in Teutonic and even Romance nations. And this *a priori* conclusion is, indeed, confirmed by the general impression one receives from the documents of ancient Russian literature.

The same must be said of other Slavic nations who inherited the Cyrillo-Methodian tradition. The Bulgarians of the tenth century, the medieval Serbs, and in a lesser degree the Czecho-Moravians through the eleventh century conveyed to the Russians not only a selection of Greek literature, but also some original works of Bulgarian and perhaps even Czech authorship. To single these works out of the bulk of original Russian literature, with the exception of a few names, is very difficult. Future investigation has to determine accurately the extent and character of the Bulgarian and Czech contributions to Russian religious and cultural life. We can here venture only two remarks, based upon the authentic documents. First, the writings of the Bulgarian authors, such as Clement and Constantine the Junior, are marked by evangelical moralism, inspired by Chrysostom. Second, they preserve and develop the great Cyrillo-Methodian concept of the national calling and the particular gifts of every nation within the oecumenical Church. Both features, so essential to Russian Christianity, were thus originated in the Slavic West and found in Russia an extremely fertile soil.

SLAVONIC TRANSLATIONS

The original Russian and Slavic literature represented only a small part of the whole written tradition under the influence of which the Russian religious mind was growing. All the rest was translation. In the sixteenth century, Metropolitan Macarius made an attempt to unite in one collection "all the books" (of religious content) "which are to be found in the Russian land." The number of texts translated from the Greek was overwhelming. Among about a thousand lives of saints, only about forty were of Russian saints, written by Russians. It would not be far from the truth to suppose the same proportion to exist in other branches of literature. One has to search for the sources of Russian religious thought in this translated literature. Since the literature originated outside Russia, the existence of an ancient work in a Russian library does not prove its influence or popularity in Russia. One must look for other evidence. This can be found in the quantity of Russian manuscripts, in the quotations by Russian authors, and in the direct influence upon their thought or style. All these preliminary investigations have as yet borne far from definite results.

Let us begin with the Holy Scripture. It is not certain whether ancient Russia possessed the whole Bible; there is no copy of the Russian Bible in one manuscript before 1500. All sacred books circulated separately for both liturgical and private use. As the Church made only a limited liturgical use of the Old Testament the prescribed lections were excerpted and collected into a special liturgical book which made the complete edition less necessary. When, at the end of the fifteenth century, a zealous Russian bishop, Gennadius of Novgorod, wanted a complete copy of the Bible for the polemics against the heretics, he could find nowhere twelve books of the Old Testament and was obliged to have a new translation made from Latin. At any rate, the New Testament was complete, divided into two books, the Gospel and the Apostle (Epistles). The most widely read book was, however, not the Gospel, but the Psalter, thanks to its extensive liturgical use. It was the first reader for the child, a common devotional book for the layman and a book used even for divinations. After the Psalter, the prophets were read and commented upon, often with the aim of anti-Jewish polemics. Among the didactic, or "Wisdom" literature of the Old Testament, it was the deutero-canonical or apocryphal book of Jesus, son of Sirach, which was the most popular in Russia because of its plain and practical character. The historical books of the Bible were early supplanted by a compendium of sacred history, called *Palaea* (The Old Testament). The *Palaea* merged the shortened content of the canonical books with popular

apocrypha. Speaking of apocrypha, we do not mean the
deutero-canonical books accepted into the canon by the Roman
and partly by the Greek Church, but the Jewish and Christian
legends rejected by the Church, such as the Book of Enoch,
Testaments of the Twelve Patriarchs, and so on.

Some of these apocrypha were undoubtedly read in
Russia among canonical books. The attitude of the Church
towards these apocrypha vacillated. On the one hand,
there existed in Greece, and were translated into Slavonic,
the indexes of the "false" books which were prohibited.
But these indexes contradicted one another. On the
other hand, the Church made a large use of those other
prohibited writings, like the Gospel of Saint James or that
of Nicodemus, in liturgical hymns, in sermons, even those
of the ancient fathers, and in the narrations about Biblical
and ecclesiastical history. In Russia, the notion of the
Biblical canon, distinguishing strongly between the inspired
Holy Scripture and the works of the fathers, never existed.
All religious writings were called sacred and divine insofar
as they were not heretical. The Russian people had a particular predilection for the apocrypha because of its fab-
ulous content which appealed to their imagination. It was
often claimed that through the apocrypha heretical influences penetrated into Russia, especially from the Bogomils,
a Bulgarian dualistic sect. Some insignificant details can,
indeed, betray a Bogomil's hand, but their general world-
outlook has nothing of dualistic or other heresies; besides,
most of these writings date from the times of the early
Church.

The Holy Scripture, together with the apocrypha were
equalled or perhaps surpassed by the lives of saints in popular
favor. The latter afforded religious elevation, moral lessons, even the thrill of romance. Very few Greek legends
of saints were not translated or known in Russia. Among

the passions of the martyrs the most popular were, naturally, those of the "megalomartyrs," enjoying the solemn veneration of the Church, such as Saint George, Saint Theodore (or rather, the two Saint Theodores), and Saint Demetrius of Salonika. These legends gave birth, later on, to popular songs in honor of these saints. We shall mention later the names of the most popular Greek ascetic saints. One apocryphal monastic legend can be cited here which particularly struck the imagination of the Russian people. It was the legend of Buddha, the history of the conversion of the young Indian prince which passed through many national and religious transformations before receiving its Christian and Greek form, as the life of Saint Barlaam and Joasaph. According to tradition, the author was no less a person than Saint John of Damascus. Its oriental color, its wise parables and the dramatization of ascetic renunciation profoundly moved the Russian soul.

Among the third category of the Greek saints, that of canonized bishops, no one had such fame or enjoyed such veneration as Saint Nicholas. He became at once Russia's national saint. His legends were supplemented in Russia by new miracles. Two things in the figure of the saint most impressed them: the superhuman power of miracles, an almost Godlike domination of the elements, and the charitable trend of his heroic activity. Saint Nicholas lives in the imagination of Christendom not as a hero of asceticism, but as a pattern of compassionate love.

After the lives of saints the next most important subject matter in Russian manuscripts is the vast and vague literature of sermons, admonitions, and moral treatises. But this leads us into the field of the patristics and raises the question of how much of the immense theological library of the Greek fathers was accessible to the Russians.

This question sometimes was answered in an optimistic

way. The catalogue of the names of the fathers whose works were known in Russia is really very long. But if one passes from names to writings, the impression is changed. Very few of the classical works of Greek theology were known in Russia. Most of the translations pursued merely practical and edifying aims.

From Athanasius of Alexandria the only dogmatic work was available: his sermons *Contra Arianos*, a rather casual choice by a Bulgarian translator. Since Arianism was unknown in Russia there are no traces of the popularity of its refutation. Nothing, except fragments and sermons, was read of Saint Cyril of Alexandria; nothing in this early period from the mystical school of theology, Gregory of Nyssa, Maxim the Confessor, Dionysius the Areopagite. Of the works of Basil the Great were studied his ascetic treatises and the *Hexaemeron*, the cosmological commentary on Genesis. A selection of sermons from Gregory of Nazianzus represented for the Russians the summit of Greek theological thought. The sermons were saturated with high dogmatic ideas construed upon Platonic metaphysical background. Unfortunately, they were translated in Bulgaria in such an involved style, word for word, that they were hardly understandable without the Greek original. Even in Greece they demanded the work of commentators to explain their elevated and highly rhetorical language to the medieval reader. In Russia they were studied and admired by the most learned men, and difficulties occurring in them provoked disputes among the readers. One of the Byzantine exegetes, Nicetas, was translated as well.

For general summaries of Christian doctrine the Russians could use two expositions, one of the earliest and one of the latest summaries of Greek theology: *The Catechetic Sermons* of Saint Cyril of Jerusalem in the fourth century and the *Exposition of the Orthodox Faith* by Saint John of

Damascus in the eighth century. The latter work was translated only in an abridged form, with the exclusion of many
philosophical and dogmatic developments. These two
works were, by themselves, sufficient for an introduction into
Orthodox dogma. Unhappily, they did not belong to the
popular writings in Russia. Practically none of the Latin
fathers were known in Russia or in Greece either.

The dogmatic interests of the Greek fathers could not
evoke a response from the Slavs, which explains the scarcity
of their translations. There were, however, among the
ancient fathers, two men whose spirit deeply influenced
Russian Christianity. It can be said that these two men
represented for the Russian people the whole patrisitic tradition. They were John Chrysostom and Ephrem the
Syrian. More than two hundred sermons of Chrysostom
were spread in pre-Mongolian Russia, in manifold editions,
partly united in collections under different titles: *Chrysostom*
(Golden Mouth), *Golden Stream,* and *Margarite* (the
Pearl). The selected sermons of Saint Ephrem bore the
Greek name of *Paraenesis* which was interpreted in the
Slavonic text as "parable, comfort, prayer, instruction." What
is common to both authors is their practical, moral purpose
combined with high impressive eloquence. Ephrem the
Syrian was a poet in the true sense of the word. Even the
double translation into Greek and Slavonic could not efface
his artistic spirit.

In content and inspiration the two authors were very
different. Chrysostom, through his brilliant Hellenistic
rhetoric led directly to the Gospel and dwelled not upon
its symbolic-mystical but upon its ethico-religious meaning.
He was the teacher of *agape,* of caritative love, especially
of the social aspect of it, defender of the poor, and an in-
veigher against the rich. A courageous prophetic spirit
emanated from his writing as well as his whole personality.

In spite of his moral severity he represented the bright side
of Christianity, the joy and hope of redemption.

The Syrian poet, whose language was imbued with Biblical lyricism, struck another chord: he was a prophet of repentance. His predominant attitude was the contemplation of the
sin and death reigning in this world. With prophetic power
and artistic vision he pointed to the final coming of the Lord
and His Terrible Judgment. His tone was dark compared
to the brighter Chrysostom. But this darkness was saturated
with emotionalism and warmed by tears. The Russian people have never abandoned these two first teachers of their
Christianity, their spiritual leaders through a thousand
years. Russian legends tell about two celestial birds singing in Paradise; Sirin and Alconost, the bird of Joy and that
of Sorrow. They could well be an emblem of the two poet-
preachers: Saint John and Saint Ephrem.

A separate and much-appreciated branch of Greek
patristic literature was the ascetic treatises on monastic
"spiritual" life, in the narrow sense. From the classics of
Greek spirituality ancient Russia knew and held in high
esteem the works of Saint Nilus of Sinai, about 450, and
the *Climax* (*Scale*) of Saint John Climacus (d. 563). No one
of the great mystic writers of the Greek Church, Macarius,
Isaac the Syrian, or Simeon the New Theologian, was translated before the Mongolian conquest.

With these great names the Russian patristic library
was by no means exhausted. Its main content was not that
of books, in the modern sense of separate literary works.
There was a large mass of anonymous writings often circulating under false authorship, of fragments and even simple
sentences whose attributions are a puzzle for literary criticism. Among this heterogeneous material one finds exegetic
commentaries (particularly to Psalms), and sermons on feast
and fast days of the Calendar. Under the names of ancient

fathers, Saint John, Gregory, or Cyril, some later Byzantine homilists found, in this disguise, their way into the Russian Church. The remainder was a formless mass of so-called articles or chapters of various contents, which fills the Slavonic *Collections*. Most of the Russian books were, indeed, nothing but collections of fragments, sometimes unified as to subject; sometimes entirely heterogeneous. A book was a library of fragments. The origin of this sort of literature was Byzantine. Since the end of the ancient Church, the patristic tradition in Greece became current in excerpts, joined together in *Catenae* (*Chains*). Some compilers left their names and titles to their collections. The title of the *Pandects* was fixed to the collections of the monks Antioch (seventh century) and Nicon (eleventh century), both translated into Slavonic. Very popular in Russia was the *Bee* (*Melissa*); various versions of short sentences, partly of religious and partly of secular-moral content,—some even taken from Greek pagan authors. Perhaps even more popular was the form of *Questions and Answers* (Anastasius Sinaitas, in the seventh century and Pseudo-Athanasius). To such sources rather than to great works the Russian student looked for his theological and scientific knowledge.

As a result of this brief survey, we can draw some conclusions. At first the main bulk of the translated literature belonged to the Christian antiquity of the fourth and fifth centuries. The purely Byzantine theological and mystical tradition was rather weak, but the overwhelming mass of this literature pursued practical, moral, and ascetical aims. Beyond the practical sphere, religious needs were satisfied more by apocrypha than by works of dogmatic theology. The Slavic soul craved more for mythology than for dogma, and it received mythology in Christian disguise. It can be added that the translators showed a great predilection for problems of eschatology, partly in apocryphal form. Most of the genuine treatises and sermons of the ancient fathers concerning the end of the world, the coming of the Antichrist and Christ, were translated with the addition of many pseudepigraphs. This explains the strange popularity in Russia of some pre-Nicean fathers of the third century who left or were supposed to have left writings on the Antichrist: Hippolytus and Methodius of Olympus or Patara.

Concerning the principles by which the Slavic translators were guided in their choice, one naturally sees them motivated primarily by the needs of the primitive Bulgarian people, recently converted to Christianity. But, on the other hand, in studying the few preserved medieval catalogues of Byzantine monastic libraries, one finds their items mostly coinciding with the lists of ancient Slavic literature. The monastery in Byzantium, as we know, was neither a school nor a theological school. For higher learning the Byzantine scholar had to turn to the libraries of the Imperial and Patriarchal universities of Constantinople or to the schools of big cities, like Salonika. Learned Bulgarian clerics had no such ambition; they simply transplanted into their country and their idiom the library of an average Greek monastery, with some few additions of apocrypha after their taste.

Russia had nothing to do with this choice, but she had to bear its consequences for centuries. She was able to manifest her original tastes only by the choice within the choice already made; and these tastes can be traced by the relative frequency of manuscripts or by their influence upon the original works of Russian literature. In this connection, we have to add one interesting fact.

So far we have not yet mentioned one secular work among the literature of translations. Such works practically did not exist. One monastic chronicle of John Malalas, a half-legendary world history, very unlike the excellent chronicler-memoirists of Byzantine history; some other short chronicle, perhaps that of Nicephorus or Georgius Syncellus; and some fragments of logical and grammatical content almost comprised the body of secular translations. Modern philologists, particularly Sobolevsky, basing their conclusions upon linguistic marks—sometimes a very questionable procedure—succeeded in separating from the large mass of Slavonic literature some works translated in Russia during the pre-Mongolian period. There can be counted two or three dozen works in this group, attributed mainly to the translators of Prince Iaroslav, of whose activity we are informed by the chronicler. And curiously enough, among these few Russian translations most are the works of secular or half-secular literature: the *Cosmography* of Cosmas Indicopleustes; the *World Chronicle* of Georgius Hamartolos; the *Judaic War* of Flavius Josephus, the only monument of non-Christian antiquity; and some Greek writings of fictional or half fictional character. Among them was the unique medieval epic of Byzantium—the poem on Diogenes Acritas—which, together with Flavius Josephus, contributed much to the elaboration of literary historical style in Russia. This choice bears witness to the cosmological and historical interests of the Russian readers, confirmed, besides, by original Russian literature. Religious cosmology and history, based upon an eschatological background, were the two theoretical poles of the Russian mind, devoid as it was of metaphysical or rational thought.

THE GREEK LITURGY

Greek literature, even in Slavonic translation, was designed only for the Russian elite. In addition, the volume and the frequency of circulation of this literature in Russia was a changing element. The Russian copyist and reader had a choice. Compared with literature, Greek liturgy constituted a more powerful, universal, and stable factor of religious education. It was universal and permanent. Nothing forms and transforms personality like prayer. Through liturgical prayer in the Slavonic idiom, the Greek religious mind and feeling made a tremendous impact on the Russian soul. And today it maintains its effectiveness in the same way as it did in the time of Vladimir.

The Eastern liturgy is one of the most beautiful and original creations of Byzantine culture. So it became the main vehicle of Byzantinism in Russia. In what measure, however, Eastern liturgy and Byzantinism can be regarded as identical, we shall see later. But first let us consider the general impression of this liturgy upon the mind of the newly-converted Russian Slav. The impression was overwhelming and quite the same as that produced today on western observers: the impression of supreme beauty. We are even told by the Russian chronicler that the beauty of the Byzantine cult was the chief reason which determined Prince Vladimir's choice of faith. His special envoys, according to legend, were sent to observe the services of different religions. They found the Moslem cult ugly, the Catholic not particularly attractive, but attending the service in the Saint Sophia, they were spellbound: "We did not know whether we were on earth or in heaven." One remembers that "heaven upon earth" is one of the favored Greek definitions of the Church.

The beauty of the Byzantine cult is expressed in words and gestures, in liturgical vestments, in dramatic actions, in choral song and icon paintings, as well as in sacred architecture. The particular style of Byzantine beauty can be defined as baroque, used in its largest sense. It is solemn, magnificent, overladen with ornaments, resplendent with gold and precious stones. It is properly a palace style with, however, mystical depth beneath it. In fact, the Byzantine temple is, at the same time, the palace of God and the *adytum* of mysteries.

The ancient Church was the heir of the cult of both the Synagogue and the Hellenistic mysteries. From the Synagogue came, and remained forever, the Psalm type of prayer and Scripture reading; from Hellenism, the framework of mysteries in words and symbolical actions. The mysteries were destined for the few, for the initiates only. Yet since the whole Empire belonged to the initiates, the mysteries were brought forth to the masses. The danger of this vulgarization was met by a retroactive process. The Church now tried to protect and to hide the mysteries again, particularly the Eucharist, which is the core of the Church life and its cult. Hence the tendency, and afterward the rule of pronouncing secretly the prayers of consecration as well as many others; the development of the altar railing into the high Iconostasis, completely hiding the sanctuary from the lay people. Hence also, under the use of late neoplatonic theurgical language, the new verbal vestment of mysteries, which made them sublime and inaccessible, even dangerous for the unworthy, in its full sense, *mysteria tremenda*.

At the same time, between the sixth and eighth centuries, another mighty influence helped to shape the Eastern cult: the imperial palace. Many of the court ceremonies and adoration formulas, the silk and gold vestments, were adopted by the Church. Even now, after more than a thousand years and on foreign Slavic soil, the Constantinopolitan palace still lives in every Orthodox Church, particularly in the Cathedral. The beginning of the episcopal Mass, for instance, closely follows the ceremony of the Emperor's dressing.

The Byzantine liturgists undertook the task of enrichment of the ancient liturgical heritage. This heritage itself was truly preserved within a new shrine. Thus in the

Orthodox liturgy we distinguish, living side by side, prayer
strata of various epochs. Let us try to make a summarized
inventory of the secular treasures and of their relative values
in the Greek liturgy. The most ancient layer is, of course,
that of the Old Testament and it remains still the most powerful. The Psalter ever has been the matrix of Christian
prayer. From the outset of monasticism the Psalter became, however strange it may seem, the daily bread of
ascetic worship. Day and night services in a monastery, so-
called "canonical hours," consisted mainly in reading psalms.
As the Greek Church incorporated the monastic services into
its universal cult, the Psalter became predominant as a
liturgical factor.

The New Testament bequeathed, besides the lections of
the Gospel and the Epistles the Dominical Prayer recurring
perpetually in all services, the *Nunc Dimittis*, the *Ave Maria*
(with Byzantine additions), and the *Magnificat*, all common
both to the Western and Eastern Churches. From early
pre-Nicean times are preserved two of the most beautiful
hymns of the Greek Church—*Phos hilaron*—(*O gladsome
light*) and *Gloria in excelsis*, of which the latter is western
as well. Also preserved are the general structure of the
Mass and some sacramental formulas leading us into the
world of Hellenistic mysteries. To the classical Church of
the fourth and fifth centuries the East owes its Mass, relatively little changed in the later Byzantine epoch, the monastic hours, and the main frame of the Vesper and Matins
which received the richest development in later times.
Litanies or ectenes, perpetually recurrent in every service,
also belong, in their general inspiration and wording, to the
classical Church. They are full of evangelical spirit. Pro-
nounced very loudly by the deacon to the laymen outside the
sanctuary, they had great educational value. Repeating
the words after the deacon, the simple man, uninitiated into

the high theological mysteries, found himself in the midst of the evangelical atmosphere.

What remains from Byzantium itself? Mainly hymnology extremely rich in the East, which serves, particularly, for the calendar development of the Matins. The center of the Greek Matins, so-called Canon (not to be confused with the Canon of the Mass), consists of many scores of hymns, both sung and read. They abound throughout other places of the Matins and Vespers too; but only three Byzantine hymns belong to the body of the Mass. As to the other sections of liturgy, the Byzantines are responsible mainly for their stylistic ornamentation, especially for invocations and doxologies in the beginning and at the end of prayers. With their highly developed hierarchical sense they did not dare address the beings of the celestial world without a convenient and rich titulation. They never said: "Jesus," or "Christ," or "Mary," but, for the simplest, "Our Lord Jesus Christ," or "Most Holy Mother of God." Sometimes the whole prayer consists of an extended titulation like the one concluding every litany, recurring many times in every service and dedicated to the glory of the Virgin Mary. To introduce the name of Mary and hymns to Mary into all possible pieces of ancient liturgical treasure was one of the predominant concerns of the Byzantine liturgists.

The poetic structure of Byzantine hymnology is an organic blending of Jewish and Greek artistic forms. The Psalms and Homer (with other classic poets) contributed to a common store of images and rhetorical means. The dominant feature, however, was Greek thought, clearly felt in the logical construction and in the theological formulas introduced even into lyrical parts. It was a highly intellectual poetry grown from the soil of classical rhetorics. It is impossible to draw a strict line between poetry and rhetorics in this school, since the age saw no difference between them at all. Poetry here is never a free outburst of heart, but always an art severely controlled by literary rules, as personal piety is controlled by scholarly theology. By far the larger part of this semipoetical literature one would justly classify under rhetoric—sometimes very dry and monotonous rhetoric. Yet the Byzantine Church has produced two or three real poets whose works touch, stir, and extort tears, even up to the present: such was Saint John of Damascus, the author of the funeral service and of the Easter Matins.

What is the general impression of the Byzantine liturgy in its ensemble of the ancient and later elements, of words, symbols, and acts? The opinions of Orthodox people themselves would diverge in answering this question. Everybody finds what he needs in this rich store. Nowadays, it has become fashionable to speak of Paschal joy as the main tune of the Eastern liturgy and even Eastern Christianity as a whole. This feeling corresponds to some modern mystic tendencies of the Russian Orthodox intelligentsia and is supported by the sad fact that most of the Russian intelligentsia attend the Church services but once a year: namely on Easter night, when they cannot resist the charm of the hymns of the Damascene. This nocturnal service in its almost Dionysian joy has, indeed, nothing parallel in the liturgies of the West. Yet it is only one day (or one week) in the year. Passion week, preceding it, is saturated with terror and tragedy which, in the eyes of many, surpasses in power of emotion the Paschal Joy, and this week is but the climax of the fifty-day fast.

On the other hand, it is true that, compared with the Orthodox service, the Roman liturgy makes the impression of greater distance between two worlds, one of ascetic longing, of thirst without quenching. The Eastern pathos is: heaven on earth, God's presence here in His temple in

His mysteries, icons, relics, in sacred matter. The dome of the Byzantine temple is large and round, a living symbol of heaven descending upon earth. Therefore, longing is not the most essential emotion of the faithful, nor joy, but fear and exaltation. Man, sinful and unworthy man, is called to contemplate the Divine glory. He stands in the palace of the Heavenly King who is imagined seated upon the throne behind the Iconostasis, seeing everything in man's heart and mind. The contrition, self-humiliation, fear, and beseeching of man on the one side, and the radiant glory of God on the other: between these two religious poles runs the whole gamut of liturgical emotions. The most frequently recurring invocations are: "Kyrie eleison" (Lord, have mercy) and "Doxa tō patri" (Glory to the Father). Only in the Mass the part of the "numinous" is more limited; the Glory of the Divine Presence dominates. The tragedy of the Golgotha sacrifice is hidden in secret prayers behind the "Royal" doors, and the whole drama takes the aspect of the Eucharistic banquet: solemn and grandiose.

The last question concerning the Byzantine liturgy is in what measure was it accessible, in Slavonic translation, to the newly-converted Russian? This is not easy to answer. Nowadays, since the Russian spoken language has departed far from the Old Slavonic, the people have lost the understanding of the language of the Church; they need a special education. In Kiev of the eleventh century, the distance between the Old Church Slavonic and Russian was very small, and the congregation could understand everything at the level of their intelligence. Then, of course, this average level was still lower than that of the present Russian peasant. The translations by Cyril and Methodius were excellent, although they were forced to omit much of the poetic forms of the Greek hymnology. But the language of the primitive Bulgarian people was mostly inadequate for the expression of Greek mysteries. Many religious ideas required new words which were coined without becoming any more intelligible than their Greek equivalents. Thus the general impression of the service was more of actions, tunes, and pictures, than of words and ideas that shaped the Russian soul. The impression was overwhelming but vague. And yet, becoming more accustomed to ever-recurring words, the layman began to distinguish something. Fragments of ideas dimly perceived were completed from imagination, according to old heathen traditions. The seed was sown into the soil.

One fact is of paramount importance. Within the whole liturgical content the Gospel as part of the New Testament was, certainly, the most accessible to the simple mind, and the Byzantine elements least of all. As to the Epistles of Saint Paul, their involved language, their high theology, and obscure translation always rendered and still render them quite beyond the understanding of the average Russian. To the Gospel, on the contrary, the people were attentive; they began to understand. During the first half of the Middle Ages, until the twelfth century, only the Slavic nations of Europe listened to the Gospel and could understand something of it. Russia was one of the few so privileged.

THE GREEK LANGUAGE IN RUSSIA

We have seen that the Slavonic liturgy and the Slavonic Bible cut off the Russian people from immediate contact with Greek culture in its Byzantine as well as its classical forms. This barrier, however, was not unsurpassable; at least, Byzantine culture was living and flourishing close at hand and Russia had constant intercourse with the Byzantine empire in political, commercial, and ecclesiastical matters. The last was most fertile for spiritual culture. Greek pre-

lates came to Russia as Metropolitans of Kiev, sometimes as
bishops of provincial cities. They came, naturally, with a
more or less numerous suite of Greek clerics, possessing at
first probably only a limited knowledge of Russian, if any
at all. A few Russians in their immediate surroundings
had to acquire some rudiments of Greek from the prelates and
their clerics. It is possible also, though not certain, that
the foreign bishops celebrated in Greek before they had
mastered the Slavonic idiom. On the other hand, Russians travelled to Greece as pilgrims, living as monks in the
monasteries of Constantinople and on Mount Athos. On
Athos there had even been a Russian monastery from early
times. As for the laymen, we are told of some princes who
mastered many foreign languages: Greek was certainly one
of them. This must be particularly true of Prince Vsevolod,
son of Iaroslav, learned in six languages, who married a
Byzantine princess. His son Vladimir was even surnamed
with the Greek derivative Monomach after his imperial
grandfather.

And yet the knowledge of Greek seems to have been
not much extended among Russians. In the *Chronicles* or
in the *Lives* of Saints we never find them speaking Greek,
nor is there any mention of the Greek language being taught
in schools. What is still more significant, there have been
preserved no Greek manuscripts written in Russia, no Greek
quotations or even single words in Greek letters in Russian
manuscripts. It appears that Greek was for the Russians
a language of practical intercourse with foreigners and not
an instrument of culture. Studying the theological and
scientific fund of the most learned Russian authors, one cannot discover, among their sources, direct Greek originals.
Attempts were made to credit Cyril of Turov or Clement of
Smolensk with the knowledge of direct Greek sources. These
are not convincing. Everything in their writings can be ex-

plained on the ground of the existent literature of translations.

But the direct use of Greek books by some highly educated persons cannot be dismissed. We know at least one
instance which occurred in the fourteenth century. A holy
monk, Saint Stephen, is said to have chosen for his seclusion
a monastery in the city of Rostov, because of the Greek
library there. Stephen was one of the most remarkable
men of his time. The circle of translators in Kiev under
Iaroslav has been previously mentioned. The few Russian
translations could have been made in the Athos monasteries.
In some cases, the idiom of these translations indicating
both Bulgarian and Russian elements confirms this hypothesis. The philological study of the Slavonic Bible has led
to the conclusion that at different times the old Slavonic
text was revised in Russia or by Russians, with two opposite
intentions, sometimes to bring the sacred text nearer to
the spoken idiom and sometimes to achieve a more literal
approximation of the Greek original. One of these translations, still existing in the original manuscript of the
fourteenth century, is attributed traditionally to Metropolitan Alexius, a Russian by birth. Alexius and Stephen
were contemporaries and are the only Russians of medieval
times whom the positive evidence of sources credits with the
knowledge of Greek. They were, certainly, not unique.
But, however many Russians might have known Greek, the
fact remains: no one of the Russian authors, even if he had
possessed knowledge of Greek, ever betrayed it. No one was
tempted to transgress the circle or to surmount the level of
that second-rate Greek theological tradition accessible in
Slavonic translations.

As for spirituality, the direct Greek influence was transmitted by the monasteries on Greek soil which were, for
the Russians of all times, seminaries of ascetic life. Studion

in Constantinople and Xylurgu and Saint Panteleimon on Athos were monastic beacons. How Russian monasticism followed in the steps of its Greek precursors we shall see later.

Scholars and Saints

III

THE RUSSIAN BYZANTINISTS

*T*HREE figures stand out against the background of Russian culture in the pre-Mongolian age: Clement Smoliatich, Hilarion of Kiev, and Cyril of Turov. All of them were bishops and two were metropolitans of Kiev, the only two Russians of the Kievan see; they merited the chroniclers' description of the most learned men of their time. Here, if anywhere, one might seek the expression of Russian Byzantinism at its best.

CLEMENT SMOLIATICH

In 1147, when a Russian abbot, Clement, born in Smolensk was elected by the Kievan prince to the metropolitan see of Russia, the chronicler remarked: "Such a philosopher there has not yet been in the Russian land." Everyone acquainted with ancient Russian literature knows that the title of "philosopher" was given to every scholarly or highly educated person, with no particular relation to philosophy as a science. Unfortunately, we possess only one fragmentary work of Clement, a missive to a priest Thomas. The manuscript, which contains later additions, is in bad condition and completely confused in the order of the pages. Yet this fragmentary piece remains the highest known level of Russian-Byzantine scholarship. Some students of Russian literature have imagined to have found in it proof that Clement had read Homer, Plato, and Aristotle—of course in

Greek, for no Slavonic translations of these authors ever existed. Upon closer examination, however, one sees that this supposed acquaintance with Greek classics is only attributed to Clement by his adversaries, obviously as indication of his profane secularism. The priest Thomas accused Clement of interpreting the Holy Scripture with the aid of Homer, Plato, and so on. The subject of discussion between the two Russian churchmen was the question of the legitimacy of allegory in Biblical exegesis, which the Smolensk circle of Thomas and his friends denied and Clement defended. Instead of the doctrinal justification of allegorism, Clement in his missive shows by concrete examples the necessity of this method. He selects many passages from the Old Testament which, in their literal meaning, seem to have no religious bearing: "What is to me the lameness of Jacob? What sorrow is it to me if Jacob limps?" asks Clement. He gives his own interpretations in order to convince his adversary of the effectiveness of allegory. He quotes no secular writer nor does he take a logical or purely rational approach to Scripture. All his examples are taken from the patristic literature already existent in Slavonic. He uses no original ideas to enrich or deform the Greek tradition. There are many parallels to the text of Clement in the favorite Russian literature of short *Questions and Answers*, anthologies of theological and exegetical propositions. The fact of the existence of two exegetical schools and the discussion between them gives, of course, evidence of the awakening of thought. Yet this thought is still childish in both camps: in Smolensk with its rather obscurantist suspicion of Hellenism; in Kiev with its "higher" exegesis, a slavish transcription of artificial Greek allegories.

His cultural apex is exhibited in some comments upon obscure passages in the sermons of Saint Gregory of Nazianzus. From Clement, or better, from his Greek sources, also known in translation, the Russian reader could learn about the "Alcyon's days," the griffins of Alexander, the salamander or some other geographical, historical, or mythological details which, however, were quite useless to him because of the complete lack of knowledge about the extinct culture of classic Greece. These curiosities could only tickle the vanity of a few snobbish litterateurs.

More serious and religiously significant is Clement's Biblical exegesis. Following Theodoret and Nicetas of Heracleia, he revels in allegory. Every detail in the narration of the Old Testament evokes for him a New Testament parallel or some moral implication. Seldom is this parallelism based upon the inward affinity of things. Otherwise the exegetical attitude would deserve the name of symbolism. In a symbolic interpretation the connection between two things, or one thing and its image, is so close and inherent that it cannot be arbitrarily broken, once having been perceived. The exodus from Egypt, with its climax in the passage through the Red Sea, will remain forever the symbol of rescue and of redemption and therefore, of Christian atonement and the Easter feast. Adam and Christ, Noah's ark and the Church, circumcision and baptism, the tree of life and the cross of Jesus are connected for a Christian thinker by the bonds of essential nature. But Melchizedek and Christ, the brass serpent and the cross, are connected only by the way of allegory, by an artificial way. Certainly this distance between allegory and symbol is not unbridgeable. An allegory may grow into a symbol through doctrinal ingraining. And Christian symbols may seem merely allegorical for an outsider foreign to Christian tradition. The medieval exegesis which knew no measure in the use of allegory, obviously was not aware of the distinction between it and a true symbol. The prevailing idea was that nothing in the Revelation could belong to the realm of contingencies

and every detail in the Bible must have its essential, ontological connotations. This circumstance deprives their exegetical literature of religious value for us.   One feels in
sympathy with the priest Thomas and his friends who refused to be edified by childish playing with the Sacred Book.

To justify the legitimacy of his scholarly method Clement marshals a review of scores of Biblical texts, without any
apparent connection between them.   The comments of
Clement are now sublime, now ridiculous, depending on who
happened to be his Greek informant.

"Wisdom hath builded her house; she hath hewn her
seven pillars." (Proverbs 9:1) "Wisdom is the Divinity of
our Lord," says Clement, "and the house is his humanity.
God dwelled in the flesh as in the house. The seven columns
mean seven councils of the holy god-bearing fathers." The
ruminating animals, chewing their food, remind us of the
necessity of meditating upon the law of God day and night.
"The sons of Jacob are the virtues, his cattle—the evil
cogitations." "What is the woman of Samaria to me?" insists Clement, in his egotism of personal salvation, "whether
she is holy or has five or six husbands?   But the bishop of
Heracleia (Nicetas) tells me: The woman of Samaria is the
soul, her five husbands are the five senses, and her sixth is
the mind. . ."

Here Clement gives us a key to one of his sources. He,
certainly, has no claim to originality in his interpretations, for
such would appear rather a heresy to him. Thus, all his
exegetical examples are familiar to those well-read in patristic
literature. Sometimes, when his scholarship fails, he leaves the
heights of allegory and simply tells at length whole chapters
of the Bible in paraphrase. Such is his treatment of the fall of
Adam and, strangely enough, of Genesis 38, where he literally quotes the story of Tamar's widowhood and incest.
In the latter instance, however, the exegesis immediately

follows and a very prolix one it is. This Biblical episode has a particular significance for Clement. For out of the incest between Tamar and Judah, her father-in-law, the line of David took its origin and, consequently, the genealogy of Jesus Christ. Thus, the whole economy of redemption is tied up with this incest, and Clement is seriously at pains to erase the suspicion of sin from the memory of Jesus' ancestors. Not from sensual lust, but for the sake of motherhood did Tamar assume the disguise and conduct of a harlot.

The historical connection between Judah and Christ appears to have such an importance for Clement that he transcribes the entire pedigree, with some comments upon the Mosaic rule of Levirate. Here we are far remote from the allegory of the Alexandrine school. The historicity of Antioch inspires him through the mediation of Theodoret, Clement's authority in this case. It is then impossible to see in Clement, as has often been done, an adept of the Alexandrine school: he is eclectic, and entirely dependent upon his sources.

The aftermath of Tamar's adventure leads us to the predominant theological interest of Clement. A particular theme recurring over and over again in his exegesis is the opposition between the Old and the New Testament. Allusions to it occur whenever he finds some kind of duality in the Bible. Now it is Jacob's two wives, of whom Leah symbolizes the Jews, living under the Law, and Rachel the Gentiles or Christians, living under Grace; this is indicated by Leah's tender eyes and Rachel's beauty.

Clement interprets the birth of Zarah and Pharez, Tamar's twins, in the following way. Zarah first showed his hand out of his mother's womb, and the midwife tied this hand with a scarlet thread. But subsequently he retreated into the womb and his brother Pharez was born before him. Zarah is the symbol of all the people saved before and after

the Law. The Mosaic law occupies the middle place between them: thus, Zarah precedes his brother and at the
same time follows him. The scarlet thread is the blood
of sacrifices offered before the Law. This explanation is
taken from Theodoret, but the idea seems to be particularly
dear to Clement. When he speaks on the abolition of the
Law by Grace, Clement arrives at the height of sacred eloquence, although without becoming any more original. This
time he probably takes his pattern from another much greater
Russian Byzantinist, Hilarion of Kiev. "The Law abolished
the primordial Covenant, and Grace abolished both the
Covenant and the Law." Here is a tripartite instead of the
dual scheme.

When the sun shines it is impossible for the world to dwell
in darkness but it becomes it to be enlightened with the brightest
rays. Thus Christ, our God, the Sun of Justice, illuminated us with
divine dawns and enlightened us with the holy baptism. Fallen is
all that is old, all is become new (II Corinthians 5:17). And mankind is not anymore confined by the Law but walks in freedom.
And all the shadow of the Law is fallen being the image of the future
and not the truth itself.

The short extent of Clement's work does not allow us
to draw any further implications as to his religious tendencies. We have a better idea of his theological method than
of his underlying religious interests. If, in one passage, he
speaks about the grave which he digged for his continual
meditation of death, we have no right to draw conclusions
about his radical asceticism. Put as a polemic weapon of self-
justification and invective, this passage has the savor of af-
fectation, particularly in the mouth of such an ambitious
Church leader as Clement undoubtedly was. His exaggerated
expressions of humility have purely literary value since they
are inserted into invective of the most biting and sarcastic
kind. We can take them, at the best, as the expressions of

Byzantine ecclesiastical fashions of intercourse. On the other hand, if one of his exegetic examples is a true hymn in honor of man and his godlike rational nature, it is only the reflection of a patristic humanism of the best epoch, represented by Gregory of Nazianzus. At the present state of our knowledge we are bound to give up the insoluble task of reconstructing the spirituality of Clement Smoliatich and instead look upon him as merely a formal pupil and imitator of Byzantine literary style. For a representative of the Byzantine religious mind we have to approach another man, Clement's junior contemporary.

CYRIL OF TUROV

Cyril, who lived in the middle of the twelfth century, was bishop of Turov, a small town not far from Kiev. His personality is shrouded in darkness. In spite of his canonization, no biography or *vita* was written of him, except a short notice in the *Lectionary* (*Prolog*). The *Chronicles* are silent about him. This silence is appropriate to him, symbolizing the non-national, timeless character of his writings. All we know of his life is that, scion of a noble and rich family, he became a severely ascetic monk, a recluse, and that he was drawn from his cell in a "tower" by a local prince as a nominee for the bishop's see. He took some part in the ecclesiastical policies of his time, writing some epistles on Church affairs which have been lost. From his writings one receives the impression of a man who stands very remote from life, even from the moral needs of life, and who is entirely elevated to the sphere of religious worship and thought with its dogmatic or would-be dogmatic mysteries: he is a unique example of theological devotion in ancient Russia.

It is natural that his contemporaries were not much impressed by his unworldly personality. Nevertheless, they appreciated his works, and looked upon the most impersonal of ancient Russian authors as the expositor of Church tradition, along with the ancient Greek fathers.

Cyril's works fall into three groups: sermons, letters, and prayers. His sermons for the Paschal period, from Palm Sunday to Pentecost, are typical of Byzantine oratorical style; they are panegyrics, to glorify the dogmatic mysteries commemorated in the Church feasts. Most of them were incorporated into the official liturgical book called *Panegyricon* (*Torzhestvennik*), a collection of sermons of ancient fathers in the order of the Church calendar. Cyril's extant epistles are didactic and impersonal; they explain the significance of monastic life in an allegoric interpretation of Holy Scriptures, and contain some oriental parables. His prayers were designed for private use on every day of the week. Ancient Russia used this source of devotional inspiration together with official prayerbooks. Cyril's elevated style, which here was at its best, easily allowed their incorporation into the poetical store of prayers of the Eastern Church.

Cyril's high renown in ancient as well as in modern times was founded, however, not on his prayers or epistles, but on his sermons. He was one of the best orators of the Russian Church, second only to Hilarion. It must be acknowledged that he used the rhetorical devices of the Byzantine school to perfection. He followed freely and skillfully the great pattern of Chrysostom, of Gregory of Nazianzus, of Cyril of Alexandria. He was no more than a disciple and imitator; one looks in vain for a personal thought or an original expression. Yet he did not imitate in a servile way, and never literally copied his models. It could be said that Byzantine thinking and wording had penetrated his very blood.

Did he read Greek fathers in the original? It is generally so accepted, although he could have known them through

Slavonic translations as well. His theological wisdom, while of a good alloy, never exceeds the limits of the available Slavonic library of his time. As proof of his direct use of Greek sources some have referred to the close affinity of his Gospel exegesis to that of Theophylactes, Greek bishop of Bulgaria, his contemporary, who had not at that time been translated. Yet, as Theophylactes is only a compiler of ancient exegetes, mostly Chrysostom, there is not necessarily a direct influence of the Greek author upon the Russian.

Cyril never quotes his patristic sources, so we are unable to form an adequate idea of his learning. Striking is his Biblical erudition, particularly of the Old Testament. Certainly, he is the best Biblical scholar among ancient Russian writers. His quotations from the Old Testament flow in abundance to illustrate New Testament parallels—never to introduce us into an historic Hebrew situation. Considering Cyril's Biblical background, one is baffled by some of the deficiencies in his knowledge of the Gospels. Not only is he sometimes inexact in his New Testament quotations—he speaks of the miraculous feeding of the five *hundred* with five loaves, or of the healing of the lame (John 5) "in the midst of the Jewish feast" (John 7:14)—he even ascribes to Saint Matthew an oriental parable of "the blind and the lame." This ancient Indian tale, well known in all medieval literature, found its reception, through unexplained channels of tradition, into the Russian *Prolog,* the book of Church lections. Cyril commented upon it at length as a parable of the Gospels, insisting strongly and many times that he was treating the "doctrine of the Holy Scriptures," "the Gospel's words," and the "parable of our Lord which Matthew the Evangelist entrusted to the Church." The origin of his error is obvious. The beginning of the oriental tale reminds one strongly of Matthew 21:33: "There was a certain householder, who planted a vineyard." But the fact that this mistake passed unnoticed, together with the sermon of Cyril, even into the printed Russian *Panegyricon* (*Sobornik*) of the seventeenth century, throws a light upon the limitations of ancient Russian culture. Cyril of Turov was among the most learned. Yet even he was but a well-read man who, in all probability, used to read the Gospels not in context but in the "pericopes" arranged for Church reading, (*Evangelium Aprakos* from Greek Ἄπρακτος of Russian manuscripts).

As a writer and orator, Cyril is a true disciple of the late Hellenistic rhetoric, with all the exaggerations of the Byzantine age. His style is "high," solemn, poetic, closely approaching the language of Church hymns and never descending to colloquialism. He uses and abuses hyperbole, antithesis, and other figures of rhetoric. He likes to expound his ideas in the form of long speeches put in the mouths of Biblical characters. As his sermons are comments upon the Sunday lections of the Pentecostal season, and all these Sundays are consecrated to evangelical events, the Gospel narrative gives a natural frame for the preacher. Yet, the scriptural narration is drowned in a flood of quotations, of rhetorical development, of speeches and exegeses. At the end very little remains of the Gospel: it served only as a springboard for the liturgical theologian. Sometimes the very essence of the' historical event or even of its religious significance is obliterated. In vain one seeks in the Palm Sunday sermon for the messianic Advent or for a foreboding of the passions. One finds no Paschal joy in the Easter sermon nor Pentecostal grace on the Sunday of the Pentecost. Curiously enough, the Paschal sermon begins with the recollection of the Golgotha; it is only on the second Sunday after Easter when joy is expressed; the third returns us to the sufferings and entombment of Christ. A modern reader feels a lack of religious tact or sensibility.

More precisely, this oratorical manner must be characterized as passionless to the extreme; intellectual and not emotional; oriented towards the divine and not the human; seeking inspiration not in the Gospel but in the liturgical and theological tradition of the Church.

It is impossible to deny the aesthetic value of Cyril's achievements. However, it is an obvious mistake to endow him with an artistic sense of nature as do some Russian literary historians. Nothing is more remote from the Byzantine-Cyrillian art. The famous and frequently cited passage about the spring resurrection of nature (Sunday of Saint Thomas) was recently proved to be an imitation of the Paschal sermon of Saint Gregory. The few descriptive features lead us far from Russia into the late Hellenistic romanticism with its "new-born lambs leaping and returning to their mothers" and "shepherds playing on the flutes."

Cyril's theological method is allegorical. In many of his prologues he expresses awestricken admiration before the depths and heights of the divine mysteries, guarded in the Church treasure. The preacher is the exponent of these mysteries, proceeding not by his "poor reason" but according to the long tradition of the builders of the church. Here are some examples of his mysteries, taken from the first sermon on Palm Sunday. The "colt, the foal of the ass" is the people of the gentiles, the cloths put upon it by the apostles are the Christian virtues. Those "spreading their garments in the way" are rulers and grandees, those "cutting down branches" are common people. The "multitudes that went before" are prophets and apostles, those "that followed" are holy bishops and martyrs. Old men, adolescents, and infants (who are not mentioned in the Gospels) signify respectively the gentiles, monks, and Christians in general: "O, the revelation of mysteries and the solution of prophetic Scriptures!" After these examples one is not astonished to

read that Jerusalem itself is the "composition of our body."
All these ingenious and hair-splitting revelations the
Russian preacher received from the Greek. Yet it would be
unfair to deny to him any personal theological interest.
Among all these inherited traditional ideas there is one which
he pursued as the main line of his preaching. This is the
calling of the gentiles with the accompanying repudiation of
the Jews. Most of Cyril's themes give few, if any, occasion
for the development of this idea. But the ingeniousness of
the preacher, or his predecessors, triumphs over all obstacles.
We have seen how he transforms the Jewish crowd greeting
Christ into a symbol of the gentile Church. In the Gospel's
narrative of the Resurrection, he makes out of the two apostles coming to Christ's grave the image of the Old and the
New dispensations; Peter stands for the New as coming before John. The enemies of Jesus are commonly called
"Jews" in the Gospel of St. John, and this gives Cyril, in
commenting upon the healing of the lame and the blind, the
pretext for long invectives against the people of Israel. The
stiff-neckedness of Israel is vividly pictured and an immense
mass of Old Testament quotations are invoked to prove the
messianic fulfillment in Jesus. Indeed, this is not a secondary, but a main theme in most of Cyril's sermons. This emphasis is puzzling to us, but we remember the same predilection in Clement of Smolensk. We shall see it in Hilarion;
in short, in all the representatives of Russian Byzantinism.
Certainly this theme was inherited from the Byzantine and
ancient Christian theology. Nevertheless, its unique Russian
development still demands explanation.

The reverse side of this anti-Jewish theological attitude
is the unexpectedly liberal broadmindedness concerning the
salvation of the heathen. Christ, descending into hell, "con-
quered all the dark powers by the cross and rescued the all-
father Adam, together with all nations of mankind." In-

terpreting Isaiah 63:8, Cyril ventures: "He (Isaiah) calls *people* all the nations condemned to hell for their sins; and *children* he calls those who died under the Law." Now they all are liberated by the victory of Christ; the Law gives no privilege, and the "Heathen Church," together with the saints of the Old Testament, are gathered on the Mount of Olives to greet the ascending Christ.

The doctrine of salvation through Christ, though little developed, is the deepest aspect of Cyril's theology. It is by no means as naïve as many medieval theories of atonement, and it shows the Russian Byzantinism at its best. There is really a breath of grandeur, of the spirit of the ancient Greek fathers in passages like this:

I (it is Christ who is speaking) became man for thy sake, bountiful and merciful, and did not belie the promise of my incarnation: hast thou heard the prophet saying that a child will be born, the son of the Most High, and will be given us, and will bear our sorrows and our sicknesses? For thy sake, having abandoned the sceptre of the Kingdom above, I am wandering in the service of those below; for I came, not in order to be served, but to serve. For thy sake, being fleshless, I put on flesh to heal spiritual and bodily sicknesses of all. For thy sake, being invisible to angel hosts, I have appeared to all men: for I do not wish to despise my image lying in corruption, but I wish to save him and to lead him to the understanding of truth.

It is difficult to speak better of the mercy motive of God's redemptive work; even the "kenotic" side of incarnation is hinted at, though without any particular stress. The mystical significance of atonement is developed in the opposition of the two Adams of whom the second redeems the fall of the first.

I will tell you the mystery of the charitable love of God, who suffered for Adam, fallen into corruption. He came from heaven and was incarnate and made man in order to renew that which was corrupted and to raise it into heaven. The one, obeying the

enemy's advice, wanted to be God and was cursed; the other, obeying His Father, became God-man to destroy the serpent and to save
[var. deify] man. Adam stretched out his hands to the forbidden
tree, plucked the fatal fruit, and becoming the slave of sin, descended
from Eden to hell. Christ stretched out His hands on the cross and
liberated man from the condemnation of sin and death. Being
innocent, He was delivered up to rescue those, sold by sin, from
their slavery to the devil. He tasted vinegar and gall from the sponge
on the reed, to erase the manuscript of human offenses. He was
pierced with the spear in His ribs to remove the fiery sword forbidding men entry to Paradise. He shed his blood from his side by
which He purified all bodily stains and sanctified human souls. He
was fettered and crowned with thorns to loose men from the devil's
bonds and uproot the thorns of fiendish seduction . . .

So far, the quotation reveals itself as an organic blending
of the two great ideas of the Greek patristic thought: the
Athanasian doctrine of incarnation: "God became man to make
man divine," and the atonement or ransom theory of Gregory
of Nyssa (the so-called juridical theory) which also dominated the western Middle Ages. But, continuing to quote, one
is in the presence of another, third range of ideas, which can
be considered as a particularly oriental or Byzantine conception of the salvation through Christ. It is the conception
of Christ directly fighting against the demonic powers and
destroying or "harrowing" hell. Of course, this must be
considered as the final moment in the drama of redemption,
made possible only by the suffering and the death on the
cross. Yet, after the incarnation and the cross, Christ's triumph over Satan represents the decisive act of the drama.
In the popular theology of the East, as reflected by the
apocrypha and icon painting, the real victory of the Christ
is accomplished in Hades. The passage from Cyril quoted
above gives the story with all details as told in the apocryphal
Gospel of Nicodemus:

He darkened the sun and shook the earth and made lament all

the creatures, in order to destroy the hidden battlements of hell. The
souls abiding there saw the light and Eve's tears were turned into
joy. As dead, He was laid into the tomb to give life to those dead
from the beginning of time. He was pressed by the·sealed stone in
order to destroy from the fundaments the gates and the hinges of
hell. Watched visibly by the guards, invisibly He descended into
hell and fettered Satan. Angelic hosts, running with Him, exclaimed,
"Lift up your heads, O ye gates, and the King of glory shall come
in." And some, loosening the bound souls, liberated them from gaol;
others, tying the hostile powers, were saying, "Where is thy sting,
O Death; where is thy victory, O Hades?"

Wherever, in the concept of the redemption, the stress
is laid upon the divine power in its struggle against the powers of darkness, man's part in the redemptive work must
necessarily be limited. This fact is reflected, first of all, in
Christology—the nerve of all Christian theological thinking.
The main religious Christological interest of Byzantium is
in the divinity of Christ, not in His humanity. Therefore,
the balance of the Chalcedonian dogma is easily upset. This
is true in the case of Russian Cyril as it was of his great Alexandrine namesake. He might scrupulously try to preserve
Christ's humanity as it is revealed by the dogma of the
Church. His real religious experience is that of "man visible,
and God comprehensible," or of "God vested in flesh." This
makes Cyril very cautious in picturing Christ's kenosis. In the
Golgotha scene particularly striking is Cyril's care in emphasizing the triumphant divinity even on the cross. He could
not take seriously—indeed, he does not mention them—the
last words of Christ when in agony he felt abandoned by
His Father. More important for Cyril were the miracles
accompanying the death of the Son of God:

Our Lord Jesus Christ was crucified as man, and as God He
eclipsed the sun, and changed the moon into blood, and there was
darkness throughout all the earth. As man, He cried and yielded up
the ghost; but, as God, He did quake the earth, and the rocks rent.

As man, He was pierced in his side; but, as God, He rent in twain the veil of the first Law . . .

If Godhead on the cross is contemplated with more religious intensity than the manhood of Christ, this has as its consequence a remarkable shift in the conception of the Resurrection. The rising from the grave, the reappearance of the Lord to His disciples, can be central only for those having a paramount interest in His humanity and in the earthly destinies of human life. The personal victory of the human Jesus over death is the pledge of the universal resurrection to mankind. It is true for the ancient Church, as for the Christian West. But the Byzantine Greek was more interested in the life of God than of man, more in the events of the other world than of this earth. The resurrection of God is self-evident; in a sense, natural. Cyril, following Saint Gregory, tries to picture the joy of creation at the risen Lord. Yet, one must be aware that the Greek icon of the resurrection is not a vision of the rising Christ, or of the empty tomb: it is precisely the "Harrowing of Hell," so familiar to all students of Byzantine art. Here is Godhead in its supreme victorious action, and the fruits of this action are not for the living but for the dead, because the dead—true mankind—are so much more important than a handful of the living. Cyril never forgets, in speaking of the Resurrection, to mention the destruction of Hell. There is, however, an accidental circumstance which prevents him from developing this scene to its full length, with all the dramatic ornamentation of his style. The true date of this metaphysical event in the Church calendar is Good Saturday, and Cyril has composed his sermons for Sundays only. Thus the great oriental Resurrection idea looms only in the background overshadowing the joyful but less significant event at the sepulchre.

The full significance of Cyril's resurrection idea is

developed in his sermon on the Ascension. Theologically as
well as artistically it is the climax of all his oratory for the
Paschal-Pentecostal period. The triumph of Christ after
His victory over Satan can be consummated only in Heaven,
on His return to the Father. For all this grandiose scene
Cyril has practically no Biblical pattern. He is dependent
upon the apocrypha and, probably, on the imagination of
Greek homilists, although he, as usual, claims to speak
"according to apostolic and prophetic words."

Immediately after this promise, Cyril describes an amazing assembly on the Mount of Olives on the day of the
Ascension. Here Christ appears surrounded by the Church
of the saints, of both the Old and the New Testament, the
forefathers, patriarchs, prophets, apostles, the Seventy disciples—probably Cyril's interpretation of the Christ's appearance to more than five hundred brethren; mentioned by
Saint Paul in First Corinthians, 15:6. Saints of the Old
Testament belong, as it appears from other passages of Cyril,
to those raised from the dead on Good Friday. The
"heathen" Church is also present, as we have seen. But
there is more: the Church of mankind is side by side with
the heavenly powers: angels and archangels. In the universal exultation are drowned some all-too-human laments
of the heathen Church, "wounded by love," for the parting
bridegroom. Sitting on the throne of the Seraphim, surrounded by angels, Christ rises to heaven carrying with him
His human soul as gift to His Father. At the gates of
Heaven, the most dramatic scene is enacted. The guardians
of the gates did not recognize the Son of God in the "slave's
image" of man, vested in flesh. Only His voice reveals the
Godhead: "Open to me the gates of righteousness" (Psalm
118:19) which echoes His call in the underworld: "Lift up
your heads, O ye gates,"—as, indeed, the victory in Heaven
is the continuation and conclusion of the victory in hell.

It is then understandable why, for Cyril, "this feast is more venerable than the others," quite in conformity to the idea of Byzantine preachers (compare with the Pseudo-Epiphanius' homily on the Ascension). If this central position of the Ascension did not find its adequate expression in the Greek liturgy, where the ancient Paschal-Pentecostal tradition prevailed, at least it is reflected in the Byzantine and Russian iconography. The whole sacred painting of the Eastern temple, which was first the mosaic and fresco wall-painting and then the symbolic order of the iconostasis, is explained as the assembly of the celestial and earthly Church around the ascending Christ, whose medallion image looks severely from the dome.

What practical implications follow from Cyril's theological convictions? Perhaps the most significant point is that he is not much interested in practical implications. All Russian church and literary historians marked it Cyril's greatest defect as homilist that he does not offer his audience any moral or social teaching. Is it an art for art's sake, pure rhetoric, as Golubinsky seems to believe? Not only art, perhaps, but religious enthusiasm which finds its satisfaction in the contemplation of celestial things—the typical Byzantine attitude. In an exceptional case when Cyril concludes his sermon on Palm Sunday with some exhortations, they have an ascetic point: "Let us crucify ourselves for the struggle against sin, let us kill the lusts of flesh." Cyril lets it be known that he considers monastic life the only essentially Christian life. In another connection we shall study Cyril's conceptions of monastic calling: he consecrated to this subject all his didactic writings. At this point the only practical and social, if not moral, implication of Cyril's theology must be considered.

Out of the anti-humanistic Byzantine theology immediately follows the strictly hierarchical conception of society.

The ecclesiastical hierarchy corresponds to the celestial one, according to Pseudo-Dionysius, the ecclesiastical itself supported by the civil and political. That which is really striking in Cyril and typical, not of the doctrine but of the life in Byzantium, is the substitution of the ecclesiastical hierarchy for the celestial, and the claims of the civil to a place in the Kingdom of God.

When Cyril is speaking of the "builders of the Church," he is thinking not of the saints, but of the clergy: "patriarchs, metropolitans, bishops, abbots, priests, and all the teachers of the Church." Among the images of the Spring revival, he sees the clergy as an ecclesiastical chorus symbolized by the birds, as the monk is symbolized in the bee. In the hierarchy of saints, the holy bishops precede the martyrs; kings and princes go between martyrs and monks. But the most amazing thing is the difference in the ways of salvation for the great and the little of this world. All the difficulties are for the latter; the way of the former is easy:

A good and right way is Christ for the world-rulers and all the potentates. Spreading their alms and goodwill before Christ, they enter easily into the Kingdom of Heaven; those breaking branches from the trees are common people and sinners, who, easing their way with contrition of heart and moltenness of soul, with fast and prayer, come to God.

Here the speaker not only directly contradicts the evangelical saying on the salvation of the rich, but creates a group of sinners as a social category. "World rulers and sinners" is for him a usual subdivision of the Christian laity. With this class theory of salvation, Cyril stands quite isolated in ancient Russian literature.

In one respect, the sermons of Cyril can create a false impression in the understanding of his religious mind. Delivered on the occasion of great Church festivities, they are required to be the expression of spiritual joy. In them is

commemorated the victory of God and not the struggle of
man. Thus they may convey an illusion of Cyril's spiritual
optimism. Nothing would be further from the truth. One
must read the prayers composed by Cyril for private use in
the cell, to know his thought on man in relation to God, sin,
and salvation.

These prayers belong to the best in Cyril's works. They
lack artificial strain, and seem to flow naturally from a deeply
stirred heart. Withal, they have practically no personal
feature, but might be mistaken for a mere translation from
Greek. The nearest affinity to them is the prayers before
the Holy Communion.

The impersonal character of these prayers is reflected,
first of all, in their relation to the liturgical significance of the
particular week days. The Monday prayers are addressed
to the Angels, Tuesday's to Saint John the Baptist, Thursday's to the Apostles, Saturday's to Our Lady; the rest are
the prayers to Christ in remembrance of His betrayal, death,
and resurrection. The vivid sense of the celestial hierarchies
inspires the most intimate of religious emotions in Cyril.
Although the prayers may differ in their address or in the
holy persons receiving them, their content is the same. It is
a deep contrition of the soul conscious of its sinfulness. The
chief object is repentance and forgiveness. Even the day of
Resurrection brings no change. Immediately, after the recall of divine benefits, the prayers turn to man's indignity:

But I, wretched, having occupied my mind with love of the flesh,
have fallen into the stinking mud of sin and removed myself from
divine grace; being Thy son by birth from the spiritual fonts, I
became the slave of sin. Therefore, I am moaning from the depths
of my heart and am ill with spiritual disease; I contemplate the hour
of death and lose all my strength. Where shall I turn then, what
word say for my sins and what answer shall I hear from the Judge?
Where shall I hide the multitude of my iniquities? For there is
nobody to help me nor to rescue me . . .

These self-indictments extend for pages, reaching at times a terrifying and uncanny pitch.

When I remember the past times of my life I know myself a criminal, for I see that I have done more than any other man of the evil, perverse things, unpleasant to God, and I fear lest the fire descending from heaven shall burn me; or the precipice of the underworld shall swallow me. . . . Like Lamech, I confess my sins before all, but I never discard my bad habits. O woe unto me, the wretched, damned to all tortures.

One idea in particular haunts the sinful soul: that of sudden death:

I know my nature, corruptible and quickly perishing; what if I shall not survive until evening and my foe will rejoice over me!

Piercing as they are, these cries of the soul are certainly not the expression of despair. The gates of pardon remain open. The sinner has a multitude of celestial advocates: angels, saints, and, most of all, the Mother of God.

The most sinful of all, I dare not look up to Heaven, but prostrating before Thee I cry: "O Mother of God, the most immaculate! have mercy upon me and rescue me from eternal pain."

He even dares address himself immediately to Christ or to the Holy Trinity, hoping for Their mercy:

Thou art Christ, Son of God, giving prayer to the praying and receiving repentance of the penitents. Receive then my repentance, and release the iniquity of my heart and save me according to Thy mercy: for I am Thy slave, the son of Thy handmaid.

All these are common Christian, at least "catholic" feelings. What makes them so characteristic of the Byzantine devotion is their emphasis, appearing to obliterate all other elements of Christian faith, love, and hope. The onesidedness of these prayers represents this particular aspect of Russian high Byzantinism.

HILARION OF KIEV

Hilarion of Kiev is unanimously acknowledged the best theologian and preacher of all ancient Russia, the Muscovite period included. For this reason he must be considered as a kind of genius, the more striking against his background because he stands at the very beginning of the original literature of Russia. His exceptional position is emphasized by the fact that he was around 1051 the first, and for a century the only, Metropolitan of Kiev of Russian origin: all the others were Greeks. This detail almost exhausts all the biographical information concerning Hilarion. Even the attribution of his writings is based more upon scholarly considerations than upon tradition. The Russian Church has curiously neglected the memory of one of its first and most outstanding hierarchs. Looking for an explanation one finds only one plausible reason. The head of the Russian national party, Hilarion was elected uncanonically to the first see of Russia during the quarrel of Prince Iaroslav with Byzantium. Soon after he disappears from the pages of the *Chronicles*, a victim of the first national conflict within the Russian Church.

It could seem strange to consider this protagonist of the national Russian Church as the representative of Byzantinism. Indeed, we do it only with restrictions. Along with Byzantine trends, Hilarion, unlike Cyril of Turov, discloses some national Russian tendencies which will be the subject of later study. Now we shall examine Hilarion only as a disciple of the Greeks.

There are two works which are probably the most authentic and, at the same time, have the highest theological standard: his *Confession of Faith* and a sermon entitled *On Law and Grace*.

The *Confession* belongs to the category of theological developments of the Nicean Creed, well known in Byzantium, such as the Confession of Michael Syncellus of the ninth century. By definition it excludes original speculation, but tries to condense into short formulas the common dogmatic inheritance of the Church. Hilarion's *Confession* seems to be not a translation but a free adaptation of some Greek original. In its dogmatic terminology, precision, and sense of proportion, it bears witness to a thorough theological training. We quote some passages concerning the trinitarian and Christological dogmas.

[I believe] . . . in the Trinity consubstantial but dividing Itself into Persons, Trinity in name, but One God. I do not fuse distinctions nor divide unity: [The persons] are united without confusion and are separated unseparately. . . . [The Christ] . . . was a true man, not in appearance but truly in our flesh; perfect God and perfect man, in two natures and volitions. What He had been, He did not depose—His Deity—and assumed what He had not been—humanity. He suffered for me as man, but after Deity remained impassible as God. He died, being immortal, to revive me, who was dead. He descended into Hell to restore and deify my forefather Adam and to bind the devil. He revived as God; after three days he rose from the dead, as a victor, Christ my King . . .

Whereas in these Christological formulas a perfect balance between the two natures is preserved, one feature at the end of the *Confession* reveals a strong bias towards monophysitism. Hilarion is here speaking of the icon worship: "On Her holy icon [Our Lady's] I see the Lord as an infant in Her bosom, and I rejoice; I see Him crucified and I am glad." The perversity of this jubilation before the agony of the Cross indicates a lack of just appreciation of the humanity in Christ. Here, as with Cyril, one is in the presence of a practical rather than theoretical Docetism.

In his famous sermon on *Law and Grace*, Hilarion proves to be also a good theologian, but especially an orator of great style. Nowhere does he let us feel the pedantry of a schoolroom or the barren imitation of great patterns. He is always natural and strong, thoroughly on the level of his models—not, perhaps, of the highest but of the good Greek theologians. Their thought penetrated his blood, and one feels that he speaks out of his personal conviction in developing the main trend of his life.

This sermon, delivered between 1037 and 1051 in the presence of Prince Iaroslav and his court, is mainly devoted to a laudation of the prince's father, the great Vladimir, "Baptizer" of Russia. But this national theme is set into a grand world-historical frame of God's saving dispensation of mankind. The divine dispensation, which had elected and saved the Jewish people by the Law given to Moses, was revealed as Grace and Truth in Jesus Christ for all nations, including the last comers, the Russians. From this outlook, the conversion of Russia is moved into the midst of the historical situation represented in the New Testament. The preacher feels like a contemporary of Christ. A pentecostal spirit of joy permeates throughout this theological hymn of salvation.

The main theological idea is the comparison of the two dispensations given, respectively, to the Jews and to the gentiles. The latter are by far the more favored. This idea, found in both Cyril of Turov and Clement of Smolensk, is developed through the same allegorical Biblical exegesis. Only with Hilarion does it lose all traces of ridiculous minutiae. His explanation of the two dramatic episodes in the Bible in which the two elder sons were repudiated for the sake of the junior, very naturally are interpreted in the sense of the favored sonship of the gentile Church: Ishmael-Isaac, and Manasseh-Ephraim. The first image, which St. Paul uses, is especially precious to the preacher: "The image of Law and Grace is Hagar and Sarah, the servant, Hagar, and Sarah, the free; before the servant and after the free." This concept of the freedom of the Christian vocation as contrary

to the slavery of the Old Testament Law, is repeated again
and again, tempting us to suppose something like the Pauline
antinomism at the basis of Hilarion's theology. This sup-
position, however, would be false. The source of Hilarion's
theological ideas is not so much Pauline as Johannine. He
rarely uses the word "grace" without adding "truth," thus
referring us to John 1:14. His concept of salvation, expressed in the simple words "by baptism and good works" is as
anti-Pauline as possible. Hilarion does not, certainly, go so
far as to see a new Law in the Gospel, as did most of his
contemporaries. But the distinction between the two Testaments for him is gradual rather than revolutionary: a process
of deepening, of widening, of spiritualizing. In his own
words:

> Jews were justified by shadow and Law; Christians are not
> justified, but saved by Truth and Grace; for the Jews, justification
> is in this world; for us salvation in the age to come; the Jews re-
> joiced in earthly goods, but the Christians in heavenly; also, the
> Jewish justification was limited because of envy, for it did not extend
> to other peoples and remained in Judea alone, but the salvation of
> the Christians is liberal and bountiful, stretching to all the countries
> of the earth.

One sees otherworldiness and universality rather than
freedom from the law as the privilege of salvation through
Christ. Baptism is always emphasized as the means of salvation and, thus, Grace receives an exclusively sacramental
meaning.

Speaking of salvation through Christ, Hilarion dwells at
length upon the duality of the divine-human nature in Our
Lord as in his *Confession* or the aforementioned sermon of
Cyril of Turov. All these formulas are the bequest of the
Christological discussions of the ancient Church surviving in
Byzantium. In Hilarion perhaps the more perfect balance
between the two natures is achieved. In his brief hints at the

events of the Savior's earthly life, even Hilarion can not limit himself to the Gospel's narrative. The apocrypha furnish him with the legends of the Egyptian idols prostrating themselves before the infant Christ, and of the Jordan River running backwards during His baptism; both proofs of His divinity.

Yet the real core of Hilarion's thought is not theocentrical, like Cyril's, but rather anthropological. His main concern is with history, of course in its eschatological meaning. With great vividness and a feeling for historical truth he describes the clash between the messianic call of Christ, coming to His chosen people, and the stiff-neckedness of Israel rejecting his Savior. The destruction of Jerusalem, and the calling of the gentiles—last of all, of the Russian people— leads us into purely historical ground. The Christian philosophy of history is thus Hilarion's proper field. It is not simply a part of Greek tradition, since history is not a favored Greek approach to theology, particularly a national interpretation of history. Here Cyrillo-Methodian thought left its mark upon the Russian writer. But Hilarion embraces it with such freshness and vigor that it seems his own creation, a new spirit vivifying the Byzantine tradition. Later it will appear that this is the spirit not of Hilarion alone but of a new Russian Christianity as a whole.

We have seen that Hilarion stresses, against Judaism, the otherworldliness of Christianity. This otherworldliness, however, is not conceived in the light of spiritualistic immortality, but of the resurrection and life of a world to come. The present state of Grace and Truth is not a finite fulfillment; it is only the preparation for the eschatological end. Christ and the apostles themselves were the prophets of the future:

Law was precursor and servant to Grace and Truth, but Grace and Truth are servants to the world to come, to the incorrupted life

. . . Moses and the prophets had preached the Christ's coming. Christ and His apostles—the resurrection and the world to come.

With this positive eschatological trend, which becomes a common Russian feature, Hilarion is again further from the Greeks and nearer the Jews than he himself could guess.

A good insight into Hilarion's religious mind can be gained from his concluding prayer, so different in inspiration from the prayers of Cyril. It breathes with the spirit of joyful confidence in Christ, in the salvation by His grace and not by man's own works. Here Christ is called by Gospel names: "Good Shepherd, giving away Thy soul for Thy sheep. . ." A close tie exists between God and the new Christian people of Russia: "We are Thy people and the sheep of Thy flock. Our souls are in Thy hands, and our breath is in Thy will." Our sins are only natural: "Being earthly, we had been deviated to earthly things. . . . But if Thou rewardeth everyone according to his deeds who will be saved?" This truly Christian hope so encourages the preacher that he can end with "glad and joyful" doxology.

It is true that Cyril's prayers were designed for private use, and that Hilarion prayed for his nation: in fact, his prayer remained for centuries the national prayer of the Russian Church on the day of the New Year. The destiny of a nation can inspire more hope than the lot of an individual soul. Nevertheless, one cannot dismiss the impression that in Hilarion a different Christian attitude toward God and life is revealed than in Cyril. Between these two, we conclude, without hesitation, that Cyril, in his tragic asceticism, is nearer the Byzantine fathers than Hilarion in his optimistic, even triumphant theology of history.

To summarize the content of Russian theological Byzantinism is not an easy task. Of the three heads of this school the one, Clement, has left too few traces of his theological

thought, and the other, Hilarion, evinces besides traditional
features so strong a national Russian spirit that he cannot
be taken for a mere representative of Byzantium on the Russian soil. What is common to the three authors is their
education, and the use of literary and scholarly devices which
survived in Byzantium. These are: (1) the heritage of Hellenistic rhetoric with all its century-old store of figures,
tropes, and so on; (2) the allegorical exegesis of the Scriptures, moderate and balanced in Hilarion, and carried to a
ridiculous extreme in Cyril and Clement.

Is it possible to go beyond the cultural form to the common religious tenor? Of what would Russian-Byzantine
theology consist and, based upon it, the religious attitude
toward God and the world? It has been observed that Hilarion is unlike Cyril precisely in this last respect, although he
masters Byzantine theology as thoroughly as Cyril. Thus
we have to reconstruct the doctrine and mind of a group after
the isolated specimen Cyril, a daring undertaking. Yet, in
reality, it is not so venturesome as it appears. The Byzantine attitude which exhausts the thought and life of Cyril
extends, large and wide, through Russian Christianity. It
forms the background of every member of the Eastern
Orthodox churches without exception. It affected for centuries the Russian mind through personal contact with the
Greek Church and through the bulk of ecclesiastical literature. But mainly, it affected and continues to affect the Russian mind to the present day through the rich and en-
grossing liturgy of the Eastern Church.

The peculiarity of Cyril of Turov consists only in a
seemingly complete absence of the Russian national features.
He is nothing but an exponent of the Greek tradition on the
Russian soil. This tradition was denied by nobody but
modified by many: venerated, diluted or, sometimes, enriched by national creative spirit.

Abstracting from the national and personal gifts of Hilarion, one comes to the Byzantine religion of the Pantocrator, of the Heavenly King, Lawgiver, and Judge. The glory of God accumulates all positive, triumphant elements of religious emotions. Man dares approach his God only in awe and terror. The union between transcendent Godhead and fallen manhood is not fully restored by the incarnate Christ because His human features are not dwelled upon and, in the spirit of Alexandrine theology, are readily fused in His Godhead; the repenting humiliation of man forms the negative, but more practical side of religious life. Salvation is achieved in two ways: the way of sacraments and of ascetic purification. The consuming fire of the grim Godhead becomes tolerable through veils of the intermediary hierarchy of spiritual and heavenly worlds.

Russian Byzantinist writers have seldom the opportunity of plunging into high theology. They are more occupied with the problems of sacred history. And here we find, rather appallingly, that they are engrossed by the problem of Judaism. They live in the opposition of Old and New Testament, of Law and Grace, of the Jewish and gentile Church. It is the only theological subject which is treated by Russian authors at length, with never-tiring attention. The same interest in the Jewish problem will be evinced in many other Russian literary monuments.

Explaining this strange fact, many Russian and particularly Jewish historians point to the practical necessity of anti-Jewish polemics in ancient Russia, where the Jewish elements were extremely strong. The density of Jewish population in South Russia and its cultural influence are accounted for by the survivals of Khazar culture in these regions. As we have remarked, the Khazars, predecessors of the Russians in Kiev and in the southern steppes, were converted at least partly to Judaism.

Yet practical necessity can hardly explain the rich development of this subject by the scholarly writers addressing
the narrow circles of the Christian elite. The theme is miss-
ing in the sermons of those simple and popular preachers who
spoke to the half-converted masses to whom the warning
against the unchristian religious propaganda would be more
befitting.

The anti-Jewish theme was one of the traditional
elements of the Byzantine as well as ancient Christian theology. In Greece it was the product more of theoretical than
of practical concern. But, beyond doubt, in Russia, this partial theme acquired a dominating importance which it did not
have in Greece. If one may venture a conjecture, the reason
must be sought in the trends of the Russian religious mind,
apart from the Byzantine. The Russian approach to theology was primarily an historical one. Theological thought
was first awakened by meditation upon the religious destiny
of the nation. The late conversion of Russia and her glorious entry into the Church stirred speculation. Ancient Russia, so meagre in abstract thinking, was extremely gifted in
historical thinking of which the ancient *Annals* give such
eloquent evidence. However, the complete lack of Graeco-
Roman tradition precluded from the field of historical
knowledge all the ancient world except the Jewish as revealed through the Bible. Historico-theological thought
had hastened along the only channel open to it. The result
was that the Russian scholar stood before the Jewish problem usually, but not always, in a polemic attitude. Sometimes Judaism could even affect the Russian affirmatively,
seducing him as, for instance, in the story of the monk Nicetas
in the *Kievo-Pechersk Patericon*. During a part of his life
this future saint, seduced by the devil, so immersed himself
in the books of the Old Testament that he began to reject
the New. It was, of course, a rare instance. But, studying

the ancient Russian literature in general, one is amazed at the place held in it by the Old Testament. Its historical attractiveness gives one of the clues to this preference. Later we shall see the other motives tending in the same direction.

RUSSIAN KENOTICISM

*T*HE representatives of Byzantinism in ancient Russian literature belonged to the intellectual elite of Russian society. The Christian Middle Ages knew two kinds of spiritual elite: the cultural and the holy. Passing from the scholar's study to the cell of a saint, one breathes a different air. In spite of the unquestionable canon of holiness inherited from Byzantium, the portraits of Russian saints, so far as they are reflected in their rather conventional *Lives*, are much fresher and more national. Here one can find the religious ideal of the people expressed with maximum intensity. It must not be forgotten, however, that it is a necessarily Christian and ecclesiastical ideal: this means that it contains only those religious national features which would be acceptable to the judgment of the Church. Secondly, even the ecclesiastical ideal of holiness is not unique, but admits variations for which it is extremely important to search.

SAINTS BORIS AND GLEB—THE "SUFFERERS" OF NONRESISTANCE

It is, perhaps, no casual circumstance that the greatest among the ancient Russian saints and the first canonized by the Church, belong to a peculiar national type which can be designated by the name of "kenotic." Indeed, the princes Boris and Gleb, the sons of Vladimir, were the first saints canonized by the Russian Church after its foundation by their father. They became the first miracle-workers and celestial patrons to the "new Christian people." In the words of one of their biographers, they "took away ignominy from the sons of Russia" who so long had tarried in paganism. Their cult began soon after their death in 1015, before the ecclesiastical canonization. Moreover, this canonization was enacted, undoubtedly, not on the initiative of the supreme prelate, the Greek Metropolitan who nourished some doubt of the holiness of the new thaumaturges. Even in 1072, during the second translation of their relics, Metropolitan Georgius "did not believe in the holiness of the blessed ones." The firm belief of the Russian people in their new saints was needed to overcome the canonical scruples and resistance of the Greeks who were not at all inclined to favor the religious nationalism of a newly-converted country.

It must be confessed that the doubts of the Greeks were partly justified. Boris and Gleb were not martyrs for faith. They fell victims of a political crime in a feudal strife, as many before and after them. Their murderer, Sviatopolk, who began to slaughter his brothers in trying to establish a monarchy in Russia, only imitated his father, Vladimir, in the latter's heathen years. On the other hand, the Greek Church venerates very few laymen among its saints. Nearly all saints of the Greek calendar belong to the grade of martyrs for faith, of confessors (ascetic monks), and bishops. Laymen qualified as "just men" are extremely rare. This fact has to be kept in mind in order to appreciate the paradox that two princes killed in a feud were the first to be canonized by the new Church of a recently converted people.

The canonization of Boris and Gleb therefore raises a great problem: in what did the Russian Church and all the nation perceive the holiness of the princes and the meaning of their Christian achievement?

There exist three hagiographical works devoted to the
sainted princes which were composed in the first century after
their death; the detailed entry in the *Chronicle*, the so-
called *Lection* (*Chtenie*) of Nestor and the anonymous
Legend (*Skazanie*). The last document enjoyed by far the
greatest popularity among ancient Russian readers and therein particularly has to be sought the ecclesiastical as well as
popular conception of the holy "sufferers,"—such is the
liturgical title of Saint Boris and Saint Gleb.

Nestor alone, imitating the form of the Greek *bios*, reports some very scanty facts and features concerning the life
of the holy princes before their assassination. The absence
of all those facts in the widely-read *Legend* indicates that
not the lay piety of the princes but only their death remained
in the memory of the people. The *Legend* develops, in a
truly artistic way, the dramatic action and elaborates the lyric
prayers sometimes in the style of popular "lament." It is
a tale of the ruin of the innocent and, at the same time, a
religious interpretation of voluntary, sacrificial death.

The dry historical extract underlying all three documents
is the following:

The news of the death of Prince Vladimir reached his
son, Boris, while he was on his expedition against the nomad
tribe of Pechenegs. Without encountering enemies, or according to another version, after the victory, he started to
return to Kiev and on the road was informed of Sviatopolk's
plot to kill him. He decided not to resist his brother, in spite
of the advice of his warriors, who thereupon abandoned him.
The prince passed the night in prayer, waiting for his murderers. At dawn, Sviatopolk's henchmen broke into his tent
and pierced Boris with their spears. A loyal servant, attempting to cover Boris with his body, was killed upon his
master's breast. Wrapped in a rug, the body of Boris was
carried to Kiev in a cart. Approaching the city, the murder-

ers observed that he was still breathing and two Varangians
finished him with their swords.

Gleb, who was still a boy, was caught by the assassins on
the Dnieper River near Smolensk. A warning from his
other brother Iaroslav did not stop him. He could not believe in the wickedness of his senior brother, Sviatopolk. The
boat of the murderers met the boat of Gleb, who begged in
vain for mercy. Upon the order of the assassins, Gleb's
own cook cut his throat with his knife. The body was
thrown in the forest between two logs.

Passing from the facts to their motivation—the voluntary
yielding to death which at least in the case of Boris is obvious
—one finds two interpretations in the sources: one, moral-
political and the other, purely religious. The first, developed mostly by Nestor, is the duty of obedience to the senior
brother which, at the end of his work, the author uses to
convey a political lesson to his contemporaries:

> Do you see, brethren, how great is the obedience which the
> saints had to their senior brother . . .? If they had resisted him they
> hardly would have been granted such miraculous gifts. There are
> now many young princes who are not obedient to their seniors and
> oppose them; and they are killed, but they are not found worthy of
> such grace as those saints.

The memory of Boris and Gleb became the call to the
conscience in the feudal strife among the Russian princes
whose hierarchy was determined, not by constitutional law,
but only by clan or blood seniority. However, the very fact
of the later political importance of the "seniority" motive
must warn us against overestimating its religious implications.
Certainly, chroniclers and hagiographers had to emphasize it
as the only practical motive for imitation. Yet we do not
know how far the principle of seniority was efficient in the
world of princes and their Varangian warriors in the beginning of the eleventh century. Prince Vladimir transgressed

it. Boris is the first to formulate it, at least in the pages of the *Chronicle*. Perhaps he does not so much follow the tradition as inaugurate it, transferring his personal family feelings into the field of political relationships. At any rate, the authority of the senior brother, even of the father, was never extended, in ancient Russian usage, beyond morally justifiable limits. A criminal brother could not demand obedience to himself; resistance to him was always justified. Such was the just revenge carried out by Iaroslav against Sviatopolk, as reported in the same *Lives* of Boris and Gleb. On the other hand, the dynasties who were popular in Russia, and finally created the Russian monarchy, were, all of them, the lines of junior sons. It proves that the idea of seniority had no exclusive importance and was not understood by analogy with monarchical power. It is clear then that the voluntary death of the two—or at least one—of Vladimir's sons could not be considered as their political duty.

In Boris' meditations, as depicted in the *Legend*, other evangelical motives of his deed are given. The prince reminds himself of humility and love: "The Lord resists the proud, and gives His grace to the humble."

The ascetic idea is strongly emphasized: the vanity of the world and the senselessness of power.

If I go to the house of my father, many people will pervert my heart that I may expel my brother, as my father had done before the holy baptism, for the sake of glory and the kingdom of this world which passes away and is thinner than a cobweb . . . What had gained both my father's brothers and my father himself? Where are their lives and the glory of this world and the purple mantles and ornaments, silver and gold, wine and mead, tasty food and swift steeds, high and stately houses, many possessions and tributes and honor without measure and the pride of their boyars? All this, as if never existed for them, all has disappeared with them . . . Therefore, Solomon, having passed through all and acquired everything, said: vanity of vanities, all is vanity; the only help is from good works, from true faith and from sincere love.

In these meditations there is no allusion to the idea of political duty or the religious calling of a ruler. Even the reign of Vladimir has passed, as a drifting of vanities, without leaving any trace.

The thought of martyrdom dominates Boris most strongly. "If he sheds my blood I shall be a martyr to my Lord." These words are quoted twice in the *Legend*. On the night before his death Boris meditates upon the "sufferings and passions" of the holy martyrs Nicetas, Vaclav, and Barbara, who died by the hands of their fathers or brothers; and he finds comfort in these thoughts. Voluntary suffering is the imitation of Christ, the perfect fulfillment of the Gospel. On the morning of his death, Boris prays before the icon of the Savior. "O Lord Jesus Christ, who hast appeared on the earth in this image, who deigned to be nailed to the cross and accepted the passion for our sins! Vouchsafe me also to accept the passion." Tearfully he prepares for his bitter death, thanking God for allowing him to "suffer everything for the love of His word." His servants join their laments: "He did not wish to resist for the love of Christ—and how many warriors he held in his hand!" The assassins are already in the tent and the last words of Boris sound the same anthem:

Glory to Thee, for Thou hast vouchsafed me to flee the seductions of this deceptive life . . . For Thy sake, I am "murdered the whole day," they treated me like a lamb for consumption. Thou knowest, my Lord, that I do not resist, do not object.

It is noteworthy that the suffering of the holy princes lacks any kind of heroism. There is no stoical expectation of death, no provocation cast in the face of the powers of evil which is so often met in the passions of ancient martyrs. On the contrary, the *Legend*, as well as the *Chronicle*, employs no small art in painting the human weakness, the piteous helplessness of the princes. Bitterly weeps Boris for his dead father: "Woe unto me, O light of my eyes, the splendor and dawn of my face. . . My heart is burning, thought troubles my soul and I know not to whom to turn." Still more touching and heartbreaking is the lament of Gleb:

Alas, alas! I am weeping for my father, but still more I am weeping and despairing for you, Boris, my brother and my lord, how you are pierced, how you are mercilessly betrayed not by any foe but by your own brother . . . Better for me to die with you than to live in this life, lonely and orphaned without you!

To the departed father and brother, he addresses his agonized farewell. The love to one's own people, to one's blood, deprives the ascetic denial of the world of its severity. This renunciation is not monastic, it does not include the human world, especially beloved ones, tied by blood.

But the *Legend* goes still further. It depicts vividly the painful hardship of the break with life, the bitterness of the parting with this "delusive world." Not only for his father weeps Boris, but also for his own perishing beauty.

Walking along the road, he meditated on the fairness and beauty of his body and he was melted into tears; he wished to restrain himself but could not. And all people, seeing him, wept for his noble body and his precious spirit . . . Who would not weep at that cruel death . . . looking with the eyes of spirit at his sorrowful countenance and the contrition of his heart?

Such is also his mood in the last day before death which he spends abandoned by all, "in woe and sorrow, with an oppressed heart." In him the struggle is continuously waged between the two orders of emotions: pity for himself and the sublime participation in the sufferings of Christ. Unceasing tears are witness of this struggle. After the Vespers of the last night, "his dream was full of thoughts and sorrow, strong, heavy, and terrible." The prayer of the Matins fortifies him. The heart-rending psalms of the *Hexapsalmion* give vent to his despair. Already he implores Christ to let him "accept the passion." But hearing the whisperings about his tent, he "trembles" again although his prayer now is that of thanksgiving. After the first blows Boris finds in himself the strength to go out of the tent. Even here, he still beseeches the murderers: "My dear and beloved brethren, grant me a little time to pray to my God." Only after this last sacrificial prayer ("they treated me like a lamb for consumption") he is able to say to his butchers, though "melting into tears" as before: "My brethren, come and finish your task and peace be to Sviatopolk, my brother, and to you."

Still more striking in its tragic realism is the death of Gleb as described in the *Legend*. Here everything is said to let the heart of the reader bleed in acute pity as if to justify the words of Gleb himself: "It is not a murder but a butchery." A youth, almost a child, is trembling under the knife of his assassin, and almost to the end not one feature of a courageous reconciliation, of voluntary acceptance mitigates the horror of this slaughter. Gleb, before meeting his assassins, even after having deplored Boris' death, does not believe in Sviatopolk's cruel plot. Upon seeing the boats of the murderers, he "rejoiced in his soul, expecting greetings from them." The stronger then, is his despair, and the humbler are his entreaties:

Don't do me any harm, my dear brethren, please don't, I did you no evil . . . Have mercy on my youth, have mercy, my lords. You will be my lords, and I your slave. Do not reap me from my immature life, do not reap the unripe ear. Do not cut down the vine-shoot which is not yet grown up. . . .

However, this lament ends with the expression of a forgiving nonresistance. "If you wish to satiate yourselves with my blood, I am in your hands and in those of my brother, your prince." After the farewell to his departed father and brother, he prays and this prayer, starting with a bitter com-

plaint:— "Lo, I am being slain and I do not know what for"
—ends by expressing the conviction that he is dying for
Christ.

> Thou knowest, Lord, O my Lord. I know Thou hast said to
> Thy apostles: "For My name's sake they will lay their hands upon
> you and you will be betrayed by your relations and friends, and a
> brother will betray another to death."

One can express Gleb's idea in his agony in full accordance with the ancient hagiographer: every disciple of
Christ is left in the world to suffer, and all innocent and
voluntary suffering in the world is suffering in the name of
Christ. And the spirit of voluntary suffering—at least in the
form of nonresistance—triumphs even in Gleb over his
childlike weakness.

Nestor reduces to a minimum the presence of this human
weakness. He retains the tears but knows neither the laments
nor supplications addressed to the assassins. According to
him, Boris, after Matins and the parting with his friends,
bids the murderers "to accomplish the will of him who sent
you." Even Gleb does not exhibit any weakness before
death. Nestor tries to create an hagiographical portrait of
the martyrs as an object not of pity but of reverent admiration. Nevertheless, one finds in him the same motives of
conduct, with only a slightly different accentuation. The
author, obviously, is anxious to convey practical, edifying
lessons, derived from the action of the sufferers. He dwells
at length, as we have seen, on the idea of obedience to the
senior brother, and the charity for which the saints die is
understood in a utilitarian sense. The princes give up resisting lest they should occasion the destruction of their warriors. "It is better for me to die alone," Boris said, "than
so many souls." Gleb also, "chose to die alone for all, and
for this reason he dismissed them (his warriors)."

But the idea of sacrifice is present with Nestor as well. His Boris is "partaker of Christ's passion," and Gleb prays at the last hour: "Once Zacharias, on this day, was slain before Thy altar—so I am now slain before Thee, O Lord." Yet in the *Legend*, the idea of sacrifice, distinct from heroic martyrdom, stands out with particular force; here it is purified from all practical morality, even from the idea of the courageous fulfillment of duty; that is why it was necessary to emphasize the human weakness of the sufferers. Between these two interpretations of the holy sufferers, ancient Russia made its choice: the *Legend* overshadowed the *Lection* in popular favor.

Many liturgical offices composed in Russia in honour of the holy brothers hint at the same motives though they are diluted in a solemn rhetoric of Byzantine style.

You have forsaken the perishable glory of this world. Hating the kingdom of the world and loving purity, you have suffered the iniquitous murder in no way resisting your slayer brother . . . You were slain for the sake of the immaculate Lamb, the Savior of our Souls sacrificed for us.

Obvious as is the evangelical source of this idea—voluntary sacrifice for Christ's sake, though not for faith in Christ, it seems impossible to find for it hagiographical patterns. We read in Nestor that Boris and Gleb in their childhood were inspired by the passions of martyrs. The author of the *Legend* mentions the names of Saint Nicetas, Vaclav, Barbara; Nestor also of Saint Eustathius Placidas. Only Saint Vaclav, the Czech prince of the tenth century, murdered by his older brother, reminds us of the tragedy of Kiev. There is no doubt that the life and the death of this Czech prince were well known in Russia. Ancient Slavonic translations of his *Vita* are still preserved. Yet to mention the name of Saint Vaclav stresses a fundamental distinction. Saint Vaclav is a perfect and complete figure of a saint, even

without his violent death. His legend is a real *Vita*, the narration not only of his death but of his life. His death itself
can by no means be called a voluntary one. When his
brother rushes upon him with the sword Vaclav, as a warrior,
disarms him and throws him to the ground, and the other
conspirators, rushing up to aid the assassin, kill him on the
threshold of the Church. This comparison confirms our
impression: the act of nonresistance is a national Russian
feature, an authentic religious discovery of the newly-converted Russian Christians.

In his world-historical prologue to the *Lection*, Nestor
revives the whole history of the redemption of mankind in
order to introduce into the Church, "in the last days," the
Russian people as the "workers of the eleventh hour." These
workers were able, with the genius of childlike simplicity,
to be enthralled by the image of Christ and by the absolute
beauty of His way. The similar, though paler, reflection
of the evangelical light can be discerned in the pious doubts
of Prince Vladimir as to the legitimacy of the execution of robbers. The bishops who had effaced Vladimir's
scruples with the answer: "You must execute robbers," would
hardly have required from his sons a useless sacrificial death.
Boris and Gleb did what was not required of them by the
Church as the living Christian tradition which had long
since established truce with the world. But they did what
the Master of the vineyard expected of them and "took
away the ignominy from the sons of Russia." Through the
lives of the holy sufferers as through the Gospels, the image
of the meek and suffering Savior entered the heart of the
Russian nation as the most holy of its spiritual treasures.

Saints Boris and Gleb created in Russia a particular,
though liturgically not well defined, order of "sufferers,"
the most paradoxical order of the Russian saints. In it are
included some victims of political crimes among the princes

or simply victims of a violent death. Among them one finds many infants, the most famous, Prince Demetrius of Uglich in the sixteenth century,—in whom the idea of innocent death is blended with the idea of purity. In most cases it is difficult to speak of voluntary death; one is entitled to speak only of the nonresistance to death. Apparently, this nonresistance communicates the quality of voluntary sacrifice to death by violence and purifies the victim in those cases where, except for infants, the natural conditions of purity are lacking.

It is noteworthy that the Russian Church which loves the sufferers so much gives no outstanding place among her national saints to the martyrs who in the Greek, as well as in the Roman Church, always occupy first place both in the liturgical and popular cult. Most of the Russian martyrs for faith are forgotten by the Russian people. None among them ever could rival, in the veneration of the Church, Boris and Gleb, the sufferers. This means that the Russian Church, at least, did not discriminate between death for faith in Christ and death in following Christ, and even held the latter in special veneration.

Saints Boris and Gleb, immediately upon their death, became the patrons of Russia, heavenly defenders in the days of national danger, a dignity which they preserved to the threshold of the modern Russian Empire.

The impression made upon Russian society by the death of the princes Boris and Gleb, besides their canonization and the popularity of their cult, is demonstrated by the following fact. Each time the chroniclers relate the political murder of a prince, they hold the example of Boris and Gleb before their eyes. It means that the assassination is represented as a self-offering sacrifice, made for the atonement of sins. The voluntary character of the death is often contradicted by the circumstances related by the same author.

The first case is the assassination of Prince Iaropolk Iziaslavich in 1086. The motives of the crime and its secret instigators are not disclosed: "the instigation by the devil and by evil men" directed the sword of the murderer. The prince was slain while lying in a cart during a military expedition. Having drawn the sword out of his wound, Iaropolk shouted in a loud voice: "Oh, that enemy has destroyed me!" These words seem to indicate clearly enough that death came to the prince undesired. But in the posthumous eulogy the chronicler paints his portrait with the features of Saint Boris.

After suffering many misfortunes, expelled by his brothers without guilt, persecuted and spoliated, he ended with a bitter death, but was granted eternal life and rest. The blessed prince Iaropolk was calm, meek, humble, and loved his brethren. He gave each year a tithe of his property to the Holy Mother of God and always prayed to God: "O Lord my God! receive my prayer and grant me a death from another's hand, like that of my kinsmen Boris and Gleb, so that I may wash away all my sins with my blood and escape this vain and troubled world and the snares of the devil."

Although the chronicler calls Iaropolk blessed and is sure of his celestial reward, this prince, a victim of an unknown enemy, was never canonized. The two other princes, murdered in an open revolt or political plot, became the official saints of the Russian Church. Nothing but the circumstances of their tragic death earned for them this honorable place in the memory of the nation.

Prince Igor Olgovich was murdered by the Kievans in 1147. It was the time of the acute struggle for Kiev between the two princely lines: Monomachovichi and Olgovichi. Igor Olgovich was deposed from Kiev's throne after twelve days of rule. Thrown into prison, gravely ill, he expressed the desire to become a monk and after taking a monk's vows, was allowed to live in one of the Kiev monasteries. But, at a time of danger, the citizens remembered the presence in the town of a political enemy and eventual pretender to the throne; they held a meeting of the people and decided to kill Igor. In vain the Metropolitan, the prince, and the boyars tried to dissuade them. The mob broke into the monastery during the Mass and seized the monk-prince. Prince Vladimir and his brother freed him at the danger of their lives and sheltered him in the house of their mother. But the crowd broke into the courtyard and murdered Igor in the hall of the palace. After that they mutilated his body; they tied his feet with cords, dragged him all over the city, and, finally let him lie in the market place naked and bloody. But by that time the temper of the people began to change. Some pious men gathered his blood and pieces of his cloth, obviously considering him a holy martyr. A miracle confirmed them in this conviction.

In order to suggest or explain the holiness of the assassinated prince, the author of the narration inserted into the Ipatian Chronicle a long speech inspired by the Life of Saint Boris.

He wept and remembered all that had happened to Job, and meditated in his heart: "Such sufferings and various kinds of death occurred to the just." How holy prophets, apostles were crowned with martyrs and shed their blood for the Lord . . . and how holy orthodox kings shed their blood, suffering for their people, and also our Lord Jesus Christ redeemed the world from the temptation of the devil by His precious blood! . . .

Igor's contrition, humility, and sorrow before death are depicted as vividly as those of Saint Boris and even with the latter's words. The climax is his reconciliation to the idea of voluntary death:

I thank Thee, O Lord, that Thou hast humbled my soul. Grant me to transit into light from this dark, vain, and shortliving age . . . If they now shed my blood I shall be a martyr to my God.

The character of the Prince of Vladimir, Andrew
Bogoliubsky is least of all justified in its stylization after the
pattern of holy sufferers. Warlike, energetic, ambitious, he
left a bad memory, both in Novgorod which he sieged unsuccessfully and in Kiev which his troops captured and
sacked. Yet his political career was ended by a ghastly
death at the hands of the conspirators, his own servants, who
could not endure his despotism.

True, Andrew had, to his credit the building of the two
Churches of our Lady in his residences, Vladimir and
Bogolubov, which were famous for their beauty and richness of ornamentation. Yet, his devotion to the Church
was not a sufficient reason for considering him a saint. Only
the tragic circumstances of his death earned for him the
crown of the "sufferer." This event is related by a contemporary, who if not an eye-witness, probably was a Kievan
denizen who played an important part in burying the body
of the prince. But from his narrative it is clear that pity
for the helpless victim guided his pen and transformed the
scene of political crime into the Acts of Martyrdom.

On the eve of the Apostles' day, June 29, the conspirators, twenty in number, came like "wild beasts" to the
bedchamber where Andrew was sleeping alone without
guards. Even his sword was taken from him beforehand
by one of the murderers—"and this sword had once belonged
to Saint Boris." Nevertheless, after the doors were broken,
the prince defended himself fiercely. Covered with wounds,
he reproached his enemies: "Woe unto you, ungodly men,
who have become similar to Goriaser (one of the murderers
of Saint Gleb) . . . God and my bread will take vengeance
upon you." He was still far from the self-offering and the
forgiveness of a Boris. Considered dead, he was left by the
plotters who returned, however, upon hearing Andrew's
voice, to finish their bloody deed. It is in these last mo-

ments of his life, that the author lets Andrew utter the pious and kenotic meditations copied from Boris and Igor:

O Lord, look upon my infirmity and see my humility, my bitter sorrow and pains . . . I thank Thee, Lord, that thou hast humbled my soul . . . And now, O Lord, if they shed my blood, join me to the choirs of Thy holy martyrs.

This last whisper of the dying prince, unheard by anyone except God, is a literary device intending to transform a victim into a saint. One would be tempted to call it conventional but for the wholehearted sincerity of the author who is struck with terror and pity and obviously believes in the holiness of the victim. We emphasize this detail: the author is a Kievan in the service of the prince and his dramatic narrative is included in the Kievan chronicle. In Kiev, people had no reason to like the deceased prince. It was his violent death alone, particularly impressive in its dramatic setting, which started the posthumous veneration of him.

Certainly one is entitled to see in this development the degeneration of the idea of kenotic holiness. Particularly the mention of the "sword of Saint Boris," the victim of nonresistance,—the sword used as a weapon by his descendent—is religiously tactless. But here we are in the very core of the Russian religious world. Many a Russian saint was canonized for the only obvious reason: his violent death. Among them are found a boyar's wife, Iuliania of Viazma, victim of her persecuting prince-lover, a young salesman, killed by his cruel employer, Basil of Mangazeia, subsequently removed from the Church calendar, Demetrius, the infant prince, whose murder ended the dynasty of the Rurikovichi. Children are particularly numerous in this group, their natural innocence adding to the purification by blood. The underlying idea, evidently, is that of the redeeming and purifying merit of suffering and death. In

a correct, orthodox form, willing, self-offering nonresistance is needed to bring the victim into conformity with
the suffering kenotic Christ. In many cases, however, this
condition is simply hypothetical; in the case of infants, quite
unreal. Yet the Russian people hold to their favorite idea
of sanctifying suffering. They create saints from pity,
showing that pity is one of the strongest roots of their religious life. The last illegal offspring of this popular cult
of sufferers is the posthumous worship of Paul I. This
emperor, notorious for his despotism and whims, if not
for direct madness, was assassinated in 1801 by his courtiers
under circumstances not unlike the death of Andrew Bogoliubsky. This liberation from terror was welcomed with
joy by all educated and politically-minded Russia. But the
simple folk of the capital began to venerate Paul's memory,
praying at his tomb as at the shrine of a saint. This local
cult, not authorized by the Church, was alive and even re-
invigorated on the very eve of the Revolution.

SAINT THEODOSIUS—DISCIPLE OF THE HUMILIATED CHRIST

Saint Theodosius, together with his teacher, Saint Anthony, was the founder of the famous Pechersk or Caves
Monastery in Kiev and, therefore, of regular monasticism
in Russia. Very dissimilar was the posthumous destiny of
these two Russian ascetic leaders. When Anthony was canonized is uncertain. Since his ancient *Vita* was lost long
ago, some scholars doubt its very existence. Only con-
jectures can be made concerning the reasons for the oblivion
of Anthony's memory. A great unlikeness between the two
Fathers, even an antagonism in their spiritual ways, is hinted
at by the scanty evidence of our sources. Unlike were
their modes of life, unlike the ways of their respective
disciples, unlike even their political orientations in the
feudal troubles of their time. "Accustomed to live alone

and not bearing any troubles nor intercourse," as Nestor says, as soon as the novices began to gather around him, Anthony left them in the care of the new abbot whom he appointed, and secluded himself in an isolated cave, where he lived until his death. He was neither a spiritual father nor abbot of the community, except for the first few disciples, and his solitary ascetic feats did not attract much attention. Although he died only one or two years before Theodosius (d. 1074), at that time the latter was already the unique "shepherd of the rational sheep," an object of love and veneration, not only to members of his numerous flock, but of the whole of Kiev, if not all Russia. Some thirty years after his death he was solemnly canonized as the third saint of the Russian Church. This was ten years after Nestor had written his biography, large and rich in content—the best work of the chronicler.

There is no reason to surmise that the preference shown to Theodosius over Anthony was accidental. In the person of the former, ancient Russia found the ideal of the monastic saint to which she remained faithful for many centuries. Saint Theodosius is the father of Russian monasticism. All Russian monks are his children bearing his family features. Later on, new trends developed in Russian monasticism, but the image of Saint Theodosius will never tarnish. Nestor's work became the foundation of the whole Russian hagiography, inspiring and pointing to a normal Russian way of asceticism and, on the other hand, filling the gaps of biographical memory. Who of the holy Russian abbots does not repeat on his deathbed the last words of Saint Theodosius?

Nestor's *Vita* has exceptional value for the appreciation of the Russian type of ascetic life. Nestor, though a monk in the community of Theodosius, was not an eyewitness of his life. Having come to the monastery after his death, however, Nestor found an abundant and fresh tradition not yet dimmed by time or legend. He gives the names of his informants among the senior monks. The general impression of his work is that it is a reflection of life and not mere literature.

Life alone was not sufficient for creating the first Russian *Vita* of an ascetic saint. The literary tradition which had been fixed long before, in Greece, was a necessary component. Although Nestor likes to call himself "coarse and unlearned" he mastered this tradition perfectly. Studies by Russian scholars have clarified, in an exhaustive way, the problem of Nestor's sources. One is now able to discern the influence of his different models. We know the method of his work; we know that he used literal excerpts, sometimes rather long, from Greek *Vitae* familiar to him in Slavonic translations. However, in only a few cases is it legitimate to suppose that the literary pattern was deforming to the biographical structure of the *Vita*. In most instances the borrowed passages either have an ornamental character or point to the similarity of life, to the vital, and not literary, influence of the Christian tradition. The most interesting features have no Greek parallels at all: in them one is bound to see Theodosius' personal, or national, contribution to the Eastern tradition of spiritual life.

Among the Greek *Vitae* whose influence is reflected upon Nestor's work were singled out the *Vitae* of Saint Anthony, John Chrysostom, Theodore of Edessa, Theodore of Studion —all of them very popular and much read in Russia. Most influential of all, however, were the lives of the Palestinian saints of the fifth and sixth centuries: Euthymius the Great, Sabbas, Theodosius the Cenobiarch; John the Hesychast— the whole hagiographic cycle belonging to the pen of Cyril of Scythopolis. From Euthymius' and Sabbas' *Lives* chiefly, Nestor makes long and literal excerpts. He brings the

Kievan saint into direct connection with Sabbas the "Sanctified," especially for the years of the former's discipleship
with Anthony. This choice was not accidental and was not
conditioned by Nestor's personal estimation. It was the
estimation of all ancient Russia as well.

Reading closely the *Lives* of the Palestinian ascetics,
especially after the *Patericons* of Egypt and Syria, one is
struck by the affinity of the Palestinian ideal to the religious
life of Russia. Palestinian monasticism was a particularly
Russian school of salvation—that stem of Eastern monasticism from which the Russian branch sprouted. In the ancient
Russian hagiographical collections, the *Vitae* of Saint
Euthymius and Sabbas follow always that of Saint Anthony
the Great, the Egyptian founder of monasticism; but in
life they take precedence over him. The Russians possessed
in translations the full corpus of ancient *Patericons;* a great
number of ascetic *Vitae,* and ascetic treatises. Material for
the choice abounded in plenty and this choice was made in
full responsibility.

The ascetic feats of Egyptian and Syrian fathers are
amazing for their heroism, for their thaumaturgical gifts,
and the highly developed practice of contemplation. The
Palestinians are much more modest and less striking to an
onlooker. As compensation, they possess that gift which is,
after a saying of Anthony the Great, the first virtue of a
monk: discretion conceived as a sense of measure, as spiritual
tact. The Palestinian saints did not witness the first heroic
age of monasticism. They gathered ancient experience, but
expurgated the extremes. Their ideal, however severe, was
larger and more accessible. There was nothing superhuman
in it, although from the *Life* of Saint Sabbas (after Chrysostom), Russia borrowed its favorite qualification of a saint:
"The earthly angel and the heavenly man."

One may speak of the humanizing of the ascetic ideal in

Palestine and in Russia. The Palestinians neither invented nor practiced any artificial exercises for mortification. Their asceticism consisted of abstinence, fasting, and the restraint from sleep; and of manual work, concerning which the Egyptian fathers had many doubts. The life was divided between solitary prayer in a cell or in the desert, during Lent, and the spiritual fruits of community; liturgical prayer and the refectory united the brothers on Sunday. Palestine created predominantly the *Laura* (half-cenobitic) type of life along with the purely cenobitic one. The Palestinians also found time to serve the world. Saint Euthymius converted to Christianity a whole Arabic tribe; Saint Sabbas built many *xenodochia*, hospitals and hospices for pilgrims. They both took part in the ecclesiastical struggles of their age, supporting the campaigns against heresies in cities as well as in the Emperor's palace. Ancient Russia took this ideal for imitation and enriched it with some of her own spiritual gifts.

To organize the life in the Caves Monastery of Kiev, the cenobitic rule of Studion in Constantinople was taken which afterwards was theoretically accepted in Russia as a common norm. Personal connections, journeys, and pilgrimages also tied both Kiev and the north of Russia with Constantinople and Mount Athos. Nevertheless, ancient Russia learned most not from the Athonites nor Studites but from the Palestinians.

The influence of Palestinian monasticism was strongly enhanced by the spell of the Holy Land throughout the Christian world. This spell was overwhelming for Theodosius in his childhood. Seduced by the tales of pilgrims, the boy tried to flee to that land "where our Lord Jesus Christ was walking in the flesh." Later, if not at that time, the lives of Palestinian saints were superimposed in his mind upon the inspiring stories of the Gospels.

Theodosius' failure to escape to Palestine turns us back to the work of Nestor where this episode enters into the large frame of story of the saint's youth. It is Nestor's original and daring creation, without tradition or followers in Russia. Theodosius is the only saint of ancient Russia of whose childhood and youth a rich memory is preserved. The evidence for it is quite reliable, coming as it does from the mother of the saint who herself took the veil in Kiev after her son. Free from legendary influence, this story imparts to Theodosius' *Vita* the style of a biography, in a greater measure than is found in the *Lives* of any of the Russian saints.

The main theme of this youth history is Theodosius' strife with his mother over his religious calling; the cruel treatment he endured; and his threefold escape. Many scenes are painted with truly artistic skill, particularly the portrait sketched of the mother, with her passionate transitions from outbursts of anger to caresses, with her appearance of a virago: "She was strong in body, vigorous as a man: anybody who would not have seen her but only heard her voice would believe it was that of a man." Such details are not copied from books; they are life itself, as is the whole account of the saint and his mother.

In the childhood portrait of Theodosius there are of course some features which are not unique. When it is said that the boy, while going every day to the church, "did not approach playing children . . . and despised their games," one remembers having read this of the childhood of Anthony the Great. From Nestor's *Vita* this contempt of children's games will pass through all the Russian hagiography, becoming a commonplace designed to fill the gaps of tradition. Yet, even this image of a boy avoiding childish games suits his meekness and quietness, together with a certain innocent oddity of conduct, too well to be simply fictitious. But there are some details in Theodosius' childhood which have no model in the hagiographical tradition and which acquire full significance only in the light of Theodosius' peculiar religious trend. These stories about the child give the key to the man.

One reads in Nestor: "His garb was uncouth and patched." Many times his parents, who were well-to-do people, forced him to put on clean clothes and to play with other children; but although Theodosius was generally obedient, he "did not obey them." Later on as a young man serving in the house of the city governor, he was obliged to wear a "neat garment" presented to him; he walked in it "as if carrying a burden upon himself," and gave it to the beggars some days after. Theodosius' "uncouth garb" distinguishes him also in the years of his abbacy; it plays an outstanding part in his *Vita* and is the occasion of one of the most vivid scenes which pictures his humility. Even though "uncouth garb" occurs in ascetic literature, it is not found in childhood stories: besides, the attitude of the ancient fathers to this external display of humility is far from unanimous; many warn against it as a kind of vainglory.

Theodosius, from childhood, liked uncouth garb and bequeathed this predilection to the whole of Russian monasticism. But with him it was only a part of a total life orientation. After his father's death, he used "to go to the fields with the slaves and work humbly." In this social humiliation or degradation, and only in this, the ascetic inventiveness of the Russian saint manifested itself. In the peasant labor of her son, as later in his profession of baker of wafers, the mother of Theodosius was right to see a social degradation, a stain on the family honor. The saint, however, liked to be "as one of the poor" and persuaded his mother: "Listen, O mother, I implore, listen: our Lord and God, Jesus Christ, became poor and humiliated himself, giving us the example that we also should humiliate ourselves for His sake."

This self-impoverishment of Theodosius is nourished by the vivid contemplation of Christ's kenosis, of His "slave's form," and of His suffering body. One recalls in this connection Theodosius' attempt to escape to the Holy Land "where our Lord was walking in the flesh." Having chosen for himself the humble vocation of a wafer-baker, he justifies himself before his mother not on the ground of his love for the liturgy, but in regard to the body of Christ. With extraordinary force he expresses his religious attitude: "I ought to rejoice that the Lord has vouchsafed me to become maker of His flesh." These features, which have no Greek parallels, are evidence of Theodosius' strong religious intuition.

Only once in Theodosius' childhood does the cruel form of asceticism intrude into his meek and humble labors. It is the episode of the iron chains, hidden under his shirt which his mother discovered from the blood stains on the clothes. In Nestor's narration, the stress is laid not on the chains but on the clothes, the "uncouth garb." Nevertheless, this is one of the severest forms of Eastern mortification, suggested certainly neither by the Gospels nor by the Palestinian patterns. The chains were proper mainly to the Syrian ascetic circles, although they were extensively used throughout the Christian world. There is a great similarity between the chains of the boy Theodosius and the cord of the young Simeon, the Stylite, which, by the spots of blood, also betrayed to the abbot his self-willed zeal. In the latter parts of Nestor's work, one hears no more about the chains: apparently in Kiev the saint did not wear them. They were but a temporary device in his struggle with the passions of youth. More than once his biographer insists on the strength and vigor of his body. Nestor passed over in silence the carnal

temptations of the young Theodosius and this chaste silence
became a tradition of Russian hagiography. But a strong
body required taming; hence the chains which Theodosius
bequeathed, perhaps against his will if he really abandoned
them himself, to the later Russian asceticism.

The third and last escape of Theodosius from the tyrannical love of his mother brings him to Kiev, to the cave
of Anthony, the hermit. The dramatic interview with his
mother, who followed him there—for which there are many
oriental parallels—is full of conviction. The ancient *Patericons* offer many examples of the severity of a young monk
in refusing to see his mother, as Theodosius did. Yet, the
attitude of a Theodore, disciple of Egyptian Pachomius, has
nothing but superficial similarity to the conduct of the Russian Theodosius: both of them were persuaded by their abbots to change their minds. The apparent stubbornness of
the Russian saint has, however, quite another ground. It is
not severity but shyness, lack of confidence in the face of the
mighty despotism of maternal love. That Theodosius
eventually yielded to the mother's entreaties or menaces and
consented to see her, is typical of him. He is no radical, no
rigorist. For him the objective norm of conduct is sub-
ordinate to the law of love. Apparently defeated in this
struggle he is, in fact, the victor. It is not he who returns
to his mother but she who takes the veil in one of the Kievan
nunneries.

After this the years of monastic labors begin. Of Theodosius' deeds, of his asceticism, and of his spiritual character,
Nestor writes in a fragmentary way. He prefers to narrate
rather than to describe. Assembling all the scattered facts,
one may form an idea of the ascetic type of Theodosius.

The most cruel exploit of mortification is described in
the narration of the initial years of his life in the cave.
Naked to the waist, the saint offers his body to the stings of

the gnats while spinning wool at night, and singing psalms.
He was inspired, probably, in this deed by the pattern of Macarius of Egypt, and he left his example for imitation to
the North Russian anchorites. The wording of Nestor, "another time," seems to speak of a single action. Occurring in
the years of youth, this episode can be interpreted as an act
of struggle against the temptations of the flesh. In his later
years one does not discern the aspiration towards acute pain,
but only towards the emaciation of the body. He wears a
haircloth, covered by a mantle; he does not sleep "on his
ribs," but sitting on a chair; he "does not pour water upon
his body"—all oriental lessons of asceticism. Stale bread
and boiled vegetables without oil comprise his diet but, in the
refectory with his monks, he never loses a bright face. Typical of Theodosius is the secrecy about his ascetic exercises.
As he hides his haircloth, so hides he also his night waking.
One day, a monk, approaching his cell to receive his blessing
for the Matins bell, heard him "praying and weeping loudly
and beating the floor with his head." But hearing the noise
of footsteps, Theodosius feigned sleep and answered the
third call as though awakening from dreams.

The relatively moderate ascetic exercises of Theodosius
were supplemented by his continual labors. Strong and vigorous, like Saint Sabbas, Theodosius worked both for himself
and for others. Under the abbot Barlaam, he ground wheat
for all the brothers at night. After being elected abbot himself, he was always ready to take the ax and cut wood, or to
drag water from the well instead of sending one of the free
monks. "I am free," he said to the cellarer.

The pages of Theodosius' copious biography are filled
mainly by his labors. Yet the saint preserved the balance
of spiritual life and restored his forces in prayer. To prayers,
besides those canonically prescribed, his nights were consecrated. The saint spent the time of Lent in prayer when

he was accustomed to withdraw to the cave. Nestor, however, does not allow any conclusion either on the mystical quality of Theodosius' prayer, or on any higher degrees of contemplation. He prayed in tears, "often kneeling on the floor." Sometimes, we are told, his prayer had for its object the salvation of his flock. In his lonely dwelling in the cave he was frequently vexed by demons. This has the nature not of temptation, but only of intimidation. Ancient oriental features in these visions are intermingled with those purely Russian—"war chariots" with "fifes," the musical instruments of jugglers, which were loathsome to Theodosius. He himself told for the edification of the brothers, how long he was haunted in his prayers by a "black dog." By prayer and constancy he achieved a complete fearlessness before the dark powers and knew how to free his disciples from nocturnal obsessions. Some of the demonic infestations in the monastery take a typical Russian form of goblins' tricks, *domovoi* frolicking in the bakery or stable and "harming the cattle." Whatever place demonology may occupy in Nestor's work, it does not impart any particular severity or grimness to Theodosius' struggles.

In the spiritual life of Theodosius, of paramount significance is the fact that it was he who put an end to the cave life instituted by Anthony. If the abbot Barlaam built the first wooden chapel on the earth above the cave, Theodosius built the cells around it. The cave remained for Anthony and a few recluses. As the motive of Theodosius is described: "He saw the place depressive and narrow." The narrowness of the cave could easily be expanded, but the depressiveness evidently did not correspond to Theodosius' community ideal. No sooner had he built the monastery above than he sent a brother to Constantinople to fetch the Studion rule. He limited silence and contemplation for the sake of the working and communal life. Faithful to the

Palestinian spirit, he aspired after a certain harmony between the active and contemplative life.

Into this classical harmony of Eastern monasticism Theodosius brings a note of his own. Nearly on every page, Nestor emphasizes Theodosius' "humble mind and obedience," "humility and meekness." In spite of all the spiritual wisdom of Theodosius, Nestor points to a certain "simplicity" of his mind. The "uncouth garb" which he did not relinquish even as abbot, drew the raillery of the ignorant. A story of this kind had already circulated in oriental *Patericons,* which does not prevent its being also true in the life of Theodosius. The prince of Kiev sent his carriage to bring Theodosius to his palace. The driver, not recognizing the abbot and taking him for "one of the poor," because of his garb, compelled him to descend from the carriage and to ride on the horse. Social humiliation or degradation, approaching the "holy foolishness," remained from his childhood the most personal, and at the same time, the most national of his characteristics.

Elected head of the monastery, Theodosius did not change his temper: "He never was fretful or irascible or of wrathful glance, but always merciful and mild." With all this mildness and self-humiliation, he did not decline the duty of teaching. Nestor cites some fragments of his sermons. Several of Theodosius' short homilies are also preserved in ancient manuscripts. They manifest great similarity of form and content, together with a sincere warmth of emotions; we reserve them for a later examination. Yet, Nestor's stories contain much more personal material.

Having adopted the rule of the Studion, Theodosius endeavored to keep it in all the details of everyday life. With this Studion rule is connected the story of the nocturnal rounds of the abbot characteristic of ancient Russian cloisters in general. Listening outside the cells to some monks talking after

Compline, the abbot knocked at the door but it was only in the morning that, having summoned the guilty, he tried, by obscure "parables," to induce them to repentance. Without doubt, he appreciated the necessity of discipline: "He who is walking must hold his hands clasped on his breast." He desired that everything in the monastery be performed according to the rule and in the spirit of devotion. Yet, even though the saint advised "not to relax but be strong," he disliked recourse to punishments. His indulgence towards the deserters from his flock is appalling. He weeps for them and receives them with joy upon their return. There was a brother who "often used to flee the cloister," and every time he returned he found a glad welcome. The only field where the abbot's severity was displayed was the economic conditions of the community.

From a certain Theodore, the cellarer, Nestor heard many a story about how the saintly abbot, by his faith, used to save the monastery in its moments of need. The abbot's miracles, apart from the manifestations of foresight, are the only miracles that Theodosius worked; he did not heal the sick during his life. The Eastern hagiography offers models in abundance. The Palestinian *Vita* of another great Theodosius (the Cenobiarch) consists mainly of descriptions of pantries and cellars being miraculously filled. Most of the miracles of that kind in the Kievan Caves monastery were wrought in the natural order of things: it was sometimes a boyar, sometimes an unknown benefactor who sent to the monastery carts of bread or wine on the very day when the steward was already in despair how to cook dinner or find wine for the Mass. But through all the abbot's miracles runs a common thread: the saint's prohibition to "care about tomorrow," and his lavish charity which causes him to give the last drop of the cloister's wine to a poor priest for his church. This is in direct contrast to the economic efficiency and prudence of many later Russian monasteries. From Nestor's *Vita* it appears that the Caves cloister subsisted mainly by the alms of the world.

Most of all, the saint was zealous about the statutory poverty, taking away from the cells everything superfluous in vestments or food to be burned in a stove as "the devil's part." To "have no hope in property" was his principle in managing the goods of the monastery, although, thanks to the zeal of the devoted, it possessed some estates. When a too-prudent cellarer once spared for the morrow the "very neat breads" which the abbot had ordered to be given the brothers on Saint Demetrius day, Theodosius commanded the remainder to be thrown into the river. He always dealt in this way with anything "done without blessing" (permission). The meek and indulgent abbot became harsh when facing an act of disobedience which had sprung from economic calculation. It is noteworthy that even in this case, he did not punish the guilty but destroyed the material goods which became imbued with the demonic element of avarice and self-will.

Theodosius' bearing was always meek towards all. So is he towards the robbers who tried to plunder his monastery; so is he towards the sinners or weaklings among his monks. One is not particularly astonished to learn from Nestor that Theodosius many times "received blame and annoyance from his disciples." One also understands why, after Theodosius' death, the severe statutory life in the cloister did not last and the tradition of the early thirteenth century did not preserve the memory of the cenobitic (common) life.

Abbot Theodosius not only did not isolate his cloister from the world but he brought it into close relationship with the lay society. This was his testament to Russian monasticism. The very situation of the cloister in the neighboring outskirts of Kiev predestined it to be of social service.

Living on the alms of the world, the cloister gave back to the world out of its own abundance. Close to the monastery Theodosius built the house "for the beggars, the blind, the lame and the sick," and connected with it the church of Saint Stephen; one tenth of all monastic incomes was spent for running this hospice. Every Saturday Theodosius sent a cart of bread for the prisoners in the city jails. One of his sermons "On patience and love," was written as an admonition to the grumblers who were discontented with his immoderate charity: "It would be good for us to feed the poor and the wanderers with the fruit of our labors, and not to dwell in idleness strolling from cell to cell."

Saint Theodosius was the "spiritual father" of many laymen. Princes and boyars came to him to confess their sins. After his death the Abbot Stephen took his place among the Kievan boyars. Saint Theodosius thus started a long tradition: in ancient Russia, laymen mainly chose monks as their confessors or spiritual fathers. Penitence was one of the most powerful means of moral action upon secular society.

But Theodosius not only meets the world at the gates of his cloister; he himself goes into the world. One sees him in Kiev, at the prince's banquets, as guest of the boyars. He knew how to combine some mild warning with his visits. Everybody in Russia remembered his reproachful sigh upon listening to the music of jongleurs in the palace: "Will it go, prince, the same way in the future life?"

The mild preceptor could be stubborn and firm when the struggle for justice was in question. The last episode in the *Vita*, just before the death of the saint, deals with the protection of a wronged widow. This widow having once seen the abbot at work helping to build the new church, did not recognize him in his poor clothes and asked him:

"Monk, tell me, is your abbot at home?"—"What do you want from him? he is a sinner."—"Sinner or not, I do not know, I know only that he has rescued many from annoyance and misfortune. That is why I also come that he may help me; the judge has wronged me without justice."

Theodosius went to talk with the judge and restored the violated justice. "Our father Theodosius was intercessor for many before judges and princes, rescuing people; for it was impossible to disobey him."

Serving justice involved the saint in conflict not only with judges but also with princes. His struggle with Prince Sviatoslav, as it is described in the *Vita*, completes his moral portrait, and at the same time, illuminates the relationship of Church and State in ancient pre-Mongolian Russia. Iaroslav's sons, Sviatoslav and Vsevolod, had driven away their senior brother, Iziaslav, from the Kievan throne. Taking possession of Kiev, they sent for Theodosius to come to dinner. The saint answered sternly: "I will not go to the banquet of Jezebel nor communicate in viands full of blood and murder." From that day Theodosius did not cease to accuse Sviatoslav, who had usurped Kiev, that "he has done it against justice and sat on the throne against law." In this vein, he wrote epistles to him from which Nestor recalls a "very long one" containing the following words: "The voice of thy brother's blood cries to God against thee, as Abel's against Cain." This missive at last offended the prince and it was rumored that Theodosius was doomed to exile. He was glad to suffer for justice and redoubled his incriminations: for "he was very eager to go into exile." But Sviatoslav dared not raise his hand against the saintly man; the boyars and the monks implored the abbot to end the strife with the prince, and he, seeing the uselessness of words, changed his tactics: now he did not reproach the prince, but entreated him to return the throne to his brother. Sviatoslav rode to the cloister to make peace, displaying not a little humility. Theodosius explained the motives of his own conduct to the prince: "What success can our wrath have, my good lord, against your power? But we ought to admonish and speak that which is good for the salvation of souls, and you ought to hearken." Many times afterwards, in spite of the failure of his endeavors, Theodosius reminded the prince about the reconciliation with his brother. In the divine services at his cloister, he ordered the name of the legitimate, banished prince to be commemorated; upon the continuous entreaties of the monks, he consented, at last, to commemorate Sviatoslav as well, but only in the second place.

Obviously the saint did not consider secular and political affairs beyond his spiritual competence. In striving for justice he was ready to go into exile or to death. Yet he was no rigorist and, eventually, he subordinated the law of justice to the law of charity and to practical expediency. He believed his duty was to teach princes and theirs to listen to his admonitions. But he acted towards them not as one having authority but as the agent of the meek power of Christ.

Such was Theodosius—far removed from radicalism and onesidedness—sometimes even from consistency, but living a thorough Christian life. The image of Christ seemed to shine from inside his heart, gauging by the spirit of the Gospel the importance of external actions and virtues. He remained in the history of the Russian spiritual life as the teacher of spiritual plenitude, admitting only one infraction of the law of measure, deriving from the "foolishness" of humility, from the evangelical image of the humiliated Christ.

Reading the few authentic homilies of Theodosius confirms the general impression of his life, although he is a master not in words but in deeds. His homilies are as replete with quotations from the Scriptures as those of Cyril or Hilarion, with one great difference, however. All the stock of his quotations is derived, with a few exceptions, from the New Testament. The Gospel is his main source of inspiration. He uses touching and even stirring words when speaking of the love of Christ and of His gratuitous redeeming work:

> Does not our heart burn, hearing all these words?. . . What good have we done to Christ that He has chosen us, rescued us from this transitory life? Have we not, all of us, deviated and become useless for His service? . . . And He did not despise us who were in such evil, did not abhor our nature, but taking the form of a servant, became similar to us. (Philippians 2, 7).

And in another place:

> He sought us out, found and carried us on His shoulders and set us on the right hand of the Father: is He not merciful and loving-mankind? It was not we who sought Him, but He us. . . . No one is excluded from the love of Christ and His love is the model for our own: The Word of God descended upon earth, not for His own sake but for the sake of all; to suffer for all and to die.

In the vision to Saint Peter (Acts 10), God revealed that for Him nothing is unclean; therefore, we have not to discriminate in our love.

The distance of this Christology from that of the Byzantinists is obvious, even taking into consideration the predominance of practical interest in Theodosius and of the liturgical one in Cyril. Theodosius draws his main religious inspiration from the contemplation of the human nature of Christ (Cyril, the divine), of His descent to earth (not His ascension, as with Cyril). In the light of this Christology, one is fully entitled to term the spirituality of The-

odosius as "kenotic," using the Pauline word of "kenosis"
or "emptying" of Christ. As we have seen, Theodosius himself quotes the Epistle to the Philippians. His word to his
mother about Christ who "became poor for our sake," is
also Pauline (II Corinthians 8:9). Certainly many Greek
fathers used the last quotation before him as, for example,
Gregory of Nazianzus in Oration 1:5. Theodosius even
could hear it in the ancient ritual of monastic "tonsure." But
this does not diminish the new and creative character of his
religious attitude.

Theodosius found the kenotic idea practically lost in a
vast and complicated whole of ecclesiastical doctrine. He
made it the pivot of his spiritual life. For his daring he
had no teacher. It was not Anthony who initiated him into
evangelical kenosis. On the contrary, he probably had to
struggle for his ideal of life against his teacher, even as he
had struggled before against his mother.

Theodosius belonged to a newly-converted nation, hardly
to the second Christian generation in Russia. Boris and
Gleb belonged to the very first. This spiritual youth of
Russian Christianity turned out a great advantage rather
than a handicap. The old and ossified Byzantine tradition
had still little sway over Russian religious consciousness.
The shock of the Gospel was more immediate and overwhelming: it determined for all time the main Russian
approach to Christianity.

The kenotic idea has its practical expression with Theodosius in three Christian virtues: poverty, humility, and
love, in their complete unity as one inseparable whole.
Poverty and humility or obedience are virtues inherent in
monasticism from its very beginning. Here, however, their
meaning is changed. With Theodosius they are not ascetic
means for shaping Christian personality. They are rather
an end in themselves, expressing different sides of the same

personality: The incarnate Christ and His ideal disciple. Obedience is not an exercise for eradicating self-will and shaping another higher self. It is a direct way to Christ. With Theodosius it is better not to speak of obedience, but of humility. He was supremely and perfectly disobedient through all his life. But he remained humble even in his disobedience. Love is not the last and the most difficult degree of perfection, as it is with most of the Greek ascetic writers. It is a simple, immediate and self-evident implication of Christ's love to man. Love of one's fellowmen does not need to justify itself as if it were robbing something from the love of God. Indeed, Theodosius seems to ignore *Eros* in the sense of passionate and mystical love of God as celestial Beauty. *Agape* remained for him the only type of Christian love. That is why there is nothing mystical about him. Contemplation was not his business. When Nestor speaks of his secret prayers, they are not silent states of contemplation, but loud ejaculations with tears and violent gestures. In terms of Latin theology, it is *Oratio jaculatoria*, the expression of contrition, and not of beatifying vision. In this respect also Theodosius is the spokesman of ancient Russia. Mysticism is a rare flower on the Russian soil. Perhaps he even gives the key to his limitations. The terms in which he speaks, in his childhood, of his love for Christ, are quite remarkable: the Eucharistic bread and the land of Palestine speak to him not only of Christ, but especially of Christ's flesh. Theodosius' religion is not a kind of spiritualism, neither is Russian religion in general. The distance between the two worlds is not the gulf between flesh and spirit—as in Platonic mysticism— but between the fallen and the transfigured and deified flesh.

This lack of Eros, in the mystical as well as esthetic sense, constitutes the main difference between Theodosius and Francis of Assisi. Otherwise, the Russian apostle of

poverty and kenotic love has his nearest Western counterpart in the Umbrian Poverello. Theodosius, besides, is more
moderate and reserved. He shrinks from all external
gestures revealing his inner life. In this he is also typically
Russian. He did not seek new forms for the evangelical
ideal revealed to his intuition. Humbly, he tried to realize
it in the traditional forms of monasticism. If he failed,
Saint Francis failed also, and both were sublime in their
failure.

It is noteworthy that Saint Theodosius preceded Saint
Francis by some one hundred and fifty years. In the Western Catholic world, the revival of the Christ of the Gospel
was a great discovery of the twelfth century. Saint Francis
closed the movement, not as a precurser but as a fulfiller.
The Russian saint, alone, without any support of tradition,
himself began the tradition: not a fulfiller but a founder.

In connecting Theodosius, the monk, with Princes Boris
and Gleb under the heading of kenoticism, we do no violence
to their individual ways. The suffering of the princes is,
indeed, the expression of the same kenotic "following
Christ" (the Eastern Church does not like to speak of
"imitating" Christ). Boris and Gleb followed Christ in their
sacrificial deaths—the climax of His kenosis—as Theodosius
did in His poverty and humiliation. Humility and love,
if not poverty, are present also in the suffering of the
princes. We have seen their eloquent expression. Humility
and self-offering are the very core of Boris' action. His.
death is not the summit of a struggle, of an heroic action.
From the outside, it must give the impression of weakness
as Theodosius' poverty must appear foolish to the outsider.
Weak and foolish—such is Christ in His kenosis to the eyes
of a Nietzsche just as He was to the eyes of the ancient
pagan world. The semipagan Christian societies, such as
in Byzantium or the western Dark Ages, turned away with

fear and discomfort from the face of the humiliated God. Typical for the whole millenium is what Gregory of Tours in the sixth century tells about one of his contemporary bishops who ordered that the image of the nude Christ on the cross be hidden under a veil.   In the light of this, it is even more amazing and significant to view the great discovery of the first Christian generation in Russia: the kenotic Christ of the Russian saints.

V

ASCETIC IDEALS

THE HOMILIES OF THEODOSIUS

*A*s a basis for the foundation of a monastic community, the image of the humiliated Christ was not sufficient. There are some elements in which this conception may even produce a destructive effect upon a social organization: the humble and "foolish" superior lacks authority over a large body, beyond the narrow circle of his disciples. Theodosius, feeling the need of a strict order for his flock, fetched the Studion rule and tried seriously, although unsuccessfully, to enforce it upon his undisciplined family. As far as one can see, there was no spiritual affinity between the militant-zealot, Theodore of Studion, author of the famous rule, and the mild Kievan abbot. Yet Theodosius made great efforts to adapt himself and his community to Greek standards.

His homilies attest to this effort in the duality of his elevated, Christocentrical devotion, and his practical everyday exhortations. His basic theological premises have already been indicated; their application to monastic vows is simple and immediate. Christ has chosen us, who were perishing in our sins: He has already saved us without our merit. "His love is overflowing upon us, unworthy ones." We have only to answer this divine love by love. According to the Gospel, we must give up everything and follow

Christ. Loving Him, we must keep His commandments. But His commandments are the same works of love. In doing them we can glorify His father according to His words (John 15:8). "Who will not be amazed, my beloved, that God is glorified by our deeds?" In this state of mind there is no place for sadness or low spirits. We must rejoice and give thanks. Joyfully, we must go to church to pray. This spiritual joyfulness, however, does not exclude the spirit of repentance, the tears for our sins.

Christian love knows no limitations and demands active works to help the suffering. As Theodosius insists upon praying "for all the world, unceasingly" so he considers aid to the poor the first duty of monks. He is very far from his model, the author of the Studion rule, who had written as instruction to the future abbot:

Thou must not share thy soul nor thy heart with care for any others but those entrusted to thee by God, and given by me—thy spiritual sons and brethren. Never must thou use anything belonging to thy cloister for thy fellowmen by blood or thy relatives, friends, or companions; . . . for thou art not from this world, that thou mayst participate in the lot of those of this world.

Not so Theodosius, invested with divine, not human, authority, and using an unexpectedly peremptory tone in enjoining the precepts of charity:

Now I, unworthy, keeping in mind the commandment of the good Lord, declare to you: It would be good for us to feed the poor and the wanderers with the fruits of our labours and not to dwell in idleness, strolling from cell to cell. You have heard Paul saying: "neither did we eat bread for naught . . . but worked by night and preached by day" (II Thessalonians 3:8). And again: "If any will not work, neither let him eat." (II Thessalonians 3:10). We have done nothing of this kind. If the grace of God did not support and nourish us through poor men, what should we do with all our works?

Here the preacher forsakes the argument of praying

as a special vocation, of the spiritual division of labour, accepted so naturally in both the East and West: the laymen work, the monks pray. "For our singing, or fasting, or waking, they bring us everything, and for all who bring we prostrate (ourselves in prayer) many times." Theodosius would not hear of this too-easy doctrine and answers by the parable of the ten virgins in the interpretation of Chrysostom accepted by the Greek Church.

Why were they called foolish? Because they preserved the seal of virginity intact, thinned their flesh in fast, in waking and in prayer, but did not bring the oil of alms in the lamps of their souls and therefore were expelled from the wedding feast. (Matthew 25:1-13).

These ideals were obviously too high for the majority, or even for the average, of Theodosius' spiritual sons. His sermons attest to a deep and bitter disillusionment: "How many years have passed, and I see not one who would come to me and say: "What have I to do to save myself?" Laziness and the care for temporary goods, food, rest, clothes, occupy their minds. It obliges the father to descend from his spiritual heights and to insist upon a more modest virtue which evidently is most lacking. It is patience. All asceticism is included in this.

Let us remember our first entry when we came to the doors of the cloister: did we not promise to bear everything: blames, insults, humiliations, exile? . . . having called as witness the Lord God Himself, and saying: "here Christ stands invisible" . . .?

The memory of saints, of martyrs, of Job, must assist us in our firmness. We are soldiers of Christ: we ought not to sleep when the trumpet calls. Patience is the other side of Christian hope. Great is our reward, unlike that of the soldiers of this world.

But the spiritual soldiers do not hear the trumpet— or rather the bell—waking them early in the morning for the Matins. And Theodosius descends still another step to the earth and goes into the details of discipline: how to rise from bed at the first bell, how to enter and stand in the church—not leaning on walls and pillars—how to greet one another with deep inclinations, or how to keep the hands clasped together. Here, for the first time, one is confronted with the theme peculiar to Russian piety: the external, bodily aspect of worship. One must be cautious not to take Theodosius for a kind of ritualist. He was brought to this level by his bitter pedagogic experience. Those for whom spiritual achievement is inaccessible or too arduous must begin with the physical manifestations which stand under direct control of the will. The preacher is moved by the extremely dangerous situation and his own terrible responsibility. Even in this he shows nothing of the severe principal or pedantic schoolmaster. It is a spiritual call which he sounds, fraught with emotion;—not the stern call of a leader, but the humble and pathetic voice of a heartbroken father: "If it were possible I would speak to you every day, praying with tears and throwing myself at your knees that not one of you neglect an hour of prayer."

Theodosius in his monastic homilies is an example of the Russian kenotic ideal struggling desperately for social realization. But, as is easy to imagine, kenoticism was not the only basis for monastic or ascetic life. Its foundations in the East or in Greece were quite different. Since Russian monasticism was only a branch of the Greek institution, it must at least try to conform to it. Even Theodosius sought the Greek pattern in the Studion rule. In other Russian cloisters whose founders did not have so exceptional a personality, the Greek influence might be greater, extending not only to the external rules but to spiritual fundamentals as well.

Unfortunately, we have but few original Russian writings of this period which are concerned with ascetic life. Ancient Russia possessed a very rich library translated from the Eastern and Greek fathers. Among ascetic treatises the most influential must have been the corpus of Saint Basil the Great and the *Ladder* (*Climax*) of Saint John of Sinai, called "Climacus" after his work. Both works were recommended by Theodore of Studion in his *Testament*. The *Ladder* has been even to the present the most read and revered book on the spiritual life in Russia. One is not justified, however, in using Greek works for the study of Russian asceticism, for it is always uncertain in what measure they were really accepted and absorbed into Russian blood. Limiting the field to the rest of Russian literature, the student is dependent upon, besides Theodosius' *Homilies*, one doctrinal author and one hagiographical work. The single author is an old acquaintance—Cyril of Turov; the hagiographical work is the *Patericon* of the Kievan Caves Cloister.

THE ASCETIC WORKS OF CYRIL OF TUROV

Among the genuine writings of the Bishop of Turov, there are three works of didactic, nonpanegyric material which serve for the development of his ascetic ideas: two of them treat the monastic vocation directly, as is indicated by their titles, *The Tale of the Monastic Order* and *The Parable of the Laymen and the Monks;* the third is of a more general ethical interest, *The Parable of the Human Soul and the Body.* All three of them are written in the same allegorical method as his sermons, hence, the use of "parable" in his titles. The first tale is the quest for Christian monasticism in the Old Testament; the second is a Buddhist parable preserved in a Christianized *Life of Saint Barlaam and Joasaph.* The third deals likewise with an Indian tale, well-known in the medieval literatures of West and East— the parable of the blind and the lame. Curiously enough,

Cyril seeks for monastic patterns in Judaism and Hinduism, omitting the Gospels, the only source of Theodosius. It is true that Cyril takes, as we have seen, the Indian story for a chapter of the Gospel according to Saint Matthew, betraying his lack of feeling for both the style and spirit of the New Testament.

The idea of following Christ is not strange to Cyril; in one passage he even puts it explicitly; "Thou must heed the commandment and the life of Christ who suffered, from birth to death, annoyances, calumnies, insults, and wounds for thy sake."

But the motive of following Christ is of secondary importance to Cyril. Enumerating the reasons for embracing monastic life, he does not mention the Christological motive at all: "Whether you want the promised Kingdom, or dislike the sinful work of the devil; whether you detest worldly care . . . or are worried by your wife and children. . ." All these motives are legitimate, and apparently, exhaustive.

The greatest motivation is the evil of the world and the practical impossibility of being saved within the world. "The whole world lies in evil," as Paul says. All worldly vocations are infected with inherent sin:

> Every government is connected with sin: as for the merchants, wherever a purchase is made there is a sin committed, and all other worldly things, in poverty and in wealth, like family or home, are obstacles to salvation.

Here Cyril the ascetic comes to drastic contradiction with Cyril the panegyrist. In his sermons, speaking to laymen, he stressed, as we have seen, the easy ways to salvation open to princes and wealthy men. In the parables, he makes no difference between rich and poor either, but this contradiction is characteristic not only of Cyril; it is a fundamental contradiction within Byzantine Christianity: between the Church of the Desert and the Church of the Empire. For the ascetic radicals of the desert all the secular world is doomed to perdition. For the optimistic exponents of the imperial Church, this Church is already the Kingdom of Heaven on earth. This opposition is ingenuously expressed by Cyril in the image taken from the Song of Solomon: " 'Black and beautiful is the King's daughter' (1:5)—black is she from her world-ruling power, beautiful from her monastic veil."

If the world contains nothing but sin, monastic life is not one Christian call among others, it is the only Christian call. "Every Christian is compelled to bear the yoke of the Lord," that is, to take upon himself the monastic *schema*. If Cyril does not speak plainly of the damnation awaiting the laymen (he calls them by the Greek word "the cosmic") this idea is implied in the following exegesis of the prayer of Christ in John 17:9: "Jesus Christ, who gratuitously saves the monastic order, Himself prays for us saying, Holy Father, I pray not for the world but only for them."

According to Cyril, conversion begins with "sadness of mind" and "memory of death"—a more Hindu than Greek motive of world pessimism. The "sadness" brings man to the gates of the cloister; the memory of death, which does not abandon him there, is symbolized as "his inseparable wife who sings to him a sweet song." The song is sweet because joy awaits the just in another world.

The life in a cloister means "fasting, prayer, tears, abstinence, and bodily purity." Yet, the struggle against body is but a secondary motive. True, "spirit is eager and prompt for all virtues, but flesh is weak," yet it is rather amazing how mild are Cyril's incriminations against the flesh. In his interpretation of the oriental parable of *The Blind and the Lame*, he even takes a neutral stand in the struggle between spirit and flesh. The blind is spirit, and the lame is flesh. They, both, joining their maimed forces, committed the sin of robbing the orchard of the Lord. In vain they tried to cast the blame upon each other. The Lord condemned both; and they shall pay a common toll of pain after the resurrection of the body.

Quite consistently, therefore, Cyril does not emphasize bodily asceticism. He never goes beyond the general and unavoidable fasting. He goes even as far as to call monastic life an "easy life" in a comparison with Eden—and he defines it as the absence of labor: "Take easy bread, like manna, out of the cellarer's hand and be nourished."

This bodily easiness of the cloistered life is very delusive because it entails more severe demands upon the spirit: a complete sacrifice of self, a destruction of the ego which is the root of all sin. The monk "has made himself a victim, according to the Old Testament, like the lambs slain in the desert for God in the time of the Passover." This mortification, the most painful of all, is performed through the mediation of man—an abbot or a *starets* (spiritual father). "Offer yourself to him like Caleb to Joshua, cast away all your will." Cyril is eloquent and terrifying when he speaks on obedience, which is for him the supreme monastic virtue.

You are a candle: only up to the church doors may you be under your own will, do not examine how and what you are made of; you are a cloth, and you may be conscious of yourself until someone takes you in his hand; do not worry if you willl be torn for footwear . . . only up to the cloister you may have your will; but after receiving the *schema*, throw yourself entirely into submission, do not hide even the least self-will in your heart, that you may not die in your soul like Ananias.

Obedience is so high a virtue that it constitutes an affinity between monks and angels: "All service is common to angels and monks for they have abandoned all their will." Theo-

dosius, too, tried to inculcate obedience to the monastic rule.
But for him the primary virtue was humility, obedience being
its external or social implication. These two virtues are
closely connected in all ascetic community programs. But
it is important to be careful in discerning the main stress.
Humility is a peculiarly Christian ideal, a reflection of the
kenotic vision of Christ. Obedience can be pagan—Spartan,
Roman, or Stoic. As an ascetic device it is a means of training for eradicating the will, whereas humility aims at the
transformation of heart. In the case of Cyril of Turov,
there is no doubt about the religious function of obedience,
the destruction of sinful self. As for humility, he hardly
mentions it. He can even see a new advantage in the monastic state because "the great ones of this world bow their
heads before the monks, as before the saints of God." One
feels that this is worlds away from the kenotic ideal of
monasticism.

That disobedience is the essence of original sin is a common doctrine of the Church. But Cyril, in his allegorical
and free interpretation of Genesis, makes his interpretation
still more drastic by considering the fruit of the Tree of
Knowledge as a spiritual good in itself. The sinfulness of
Adam's deed was in the self-will manifested in worship:
"The tree of the Knowledge of Good and Evil is a rational
sin and the wilful action of piety." According to his
apocryphal exegesis, Adam was placed by God in Eden and
not in Paradise, which differs from the former as the Most
Holy differs from the Church. But Adam "dared enter
into the Holy before consecration,—from Eden into Paradise." This conception seems to preclude mysticism from
Christian life as a daring transgression of established
boundaries.

And, indeed, Cyril permits the monk little, if any,
spiritual joy. Very significant is his attitude toward the

Holy Eucharist. In one of his oriental parables Christ offers the monk the cup with wine but the monk declines it—"conscience restraining him . . . let us not crucify Christ by unworthily communicating." This warning is not counterbalanced by any positive call to the Eucharistic chalice.

Instead of joy, the spiritual atmosphere in which Cyril's monk abides is that of fear. Cyril invokes this atmosphere by drawing some of his best allegories from the Old Testament. He says, "You encircled yourself more than the mountain of Sinai by the fire of the fear of God," at the taking of monastic vows, and "Smoke then, as that mountain, with sighs over your sins. . . By this fear, as the prophet said, the earth shakes, the stones crack, the animals tremble, the mountains smoke . . . the stars serve like slaves." Cyril does not spare threats of hell; he knows how to describe in detail the tortures of the future life awaiting the monk in case of his "weakening." Obedience, patience, and effort constitute the whole of monastic life which is only mildly lightened by the transcendent hope of death.

The transcendence, or "numinousness" of God is so necessary to Cyril's spiritual world-outlook that he even finds offense in the idea of man's being created after the image of God. "Man has no similarity to God." Confronted with the Biblical doctrine of the image of God in man, he evades a direct interpretation but emphasizes the dangers of its heretical misuse in the sect of the anthropomorphists. No doubt Cyril was too much a theologian to deny the dogmas of the Church. But he feels obviously uneasy when faced by the humanity of Christ. Nothing then would be more strange to him than to dwell upon the humiliations of Christ or to lay at the base of his ascetic doctrine the idea of following Christ. Instead, he remains true to himself, the author of theological homilies and prayers of compunction.

THE SAINTS OF THE KIEVAN CAVES PATERICON

In the two ascetic ideals—Theodosius' and Cyril's—
there are no close parallels. On one side we possess an excellent and detailed biography, interpreted by some authentic
sermons; on the other side, only treatises without any biographical illustrations. In the case of Cyril, it can only be
surmised how life would have been organized in a cloister
established according to his principles. One can well imagine
the negative side: no exaggerated physical asceticism, no
mysticism, no social work. The rayer and discipline which
remains is really too general and too vague. It is known
that the author himself lived temporarily as a recluse. This
obviously gives opportunity for prayers; but less obviously
for discipline.

Theodosius and Cyril do not exhaust all the ascetic currents in ancient Russian monasticism. That which remains
for study is supplied by hagiographical material. As is not
the case with Cyril, here we have idealized portraits and
pictures from life without any doctrinal background.

One literary monument is particularly valuable for
this kind of study. It is the *Kievan Caves Patericon* already
mentioned. It contains about thirty short portraits of local
saints in the great cloister founded by Anthony and Theodosius. In most cases those represented are the direct or
indirect disciples of the two founders. It is interesting to
observe what happened to the spiritual family of Theodosius
in the course of time.

Still more promising is the study of the line of Anthony's
disciples. Since his own ancient *Vita* was lost, the reconstruction of his asceticism can be attempted only through
its survival in his followers.

Unfortunately, this literary monument consists of many
heterogeneous parts. Some of it had been written in the

eleventh century, but the bulk belongs to the thirteenth. On the whole, there are more legends here than biographical sketches. Indeed, some stories are far removed from reality. Yet for the main purpose of this investigation, the study of the spiritual trends of ancient Russia sometimes finds no less significance in the legends than in reality itself. The Kievan *Patericon* is the richest, even unique mine of information for one particular current of Russian spiritual life; we may designate this particular trend the school of Anthony.

In spite of the levelling work of legend, there are two currents, clearly distinguishable, which can be legitimately attributed to the great names of the founders. In most cases, the spiritual affinity is corroborated by a clear indication of discipleship: that of Anthony or Theodosius. One feels, however, that for the authors of the thirteenth century, the line of Theodosius is somewhat eclipsed to the advantage of his rival.

The general impression of the *Patericon* is that quite another spirit is breathing here than in the *Life* of Theodosius. Theodosius' connection with these inmates of his cloister seems almost inconceivable. Everything here is grim, excessive; full of thaumaturgy and demonology. The social service of monasticism is relegated into the background. Besides, community life has apparently gone out of existence. Wealth and poverty live side by side. The greatest achievements of the holy few stand out sharply against the licentiousness and insubordination of the others. It is not accidental that the most vivid and impressive portraits of the *Patericon* are those of the recluses.

It would be more expedient, however, to begin with the spiritual family of Theodosius. His spirit still walks in his cloister. Faithful to him in his humble labors is Nicholas Sviatosha, one of the princes of Chernigov, the

first princely monk in Russia. He took the habit in 1106
and for three years served for obedience in the kitchen,
to the great indignation of his brother-princes. Afterwards,
he became a gate-keeper until, forced by the abbot, he settled
in his own cell. No one saw him idle; his work in the
vegetable garden or in making clothes was accompanied by
the unceasing recitation of the so-called Jesus prayer (a short
praying formula used continuously by the Eastern monks).
He disposed of his personal fortune, which was not small,
for the assistance of the poor and for the "church building";
he gave many of his books to the monastery. After his
death, his brother, Iziaslav, having been healed by Nicholas'
sack cloth, always wore it in battles.

A peculiar service to the world was performed by Prochorus, nicknamed Pigweed-eater, who took the monastic
vow at the end of the eleventh century. His nickname was
derived from a form of fasting which he invented. He
never took other bread than that which was prepared from
pigweed which he himself had collected. It is remarkable,
however, that the author of his life emphasizes a peculiar
"lightness" in his ways of life, as if embodying the poverty
of Christ: "he was wandering lightly along his way . . . his
life was like that of a bird . . . his food came from the non-
sowed grass on nonploughed land." In a time of famine,
the ascetic diet of the saint was transformed into a source
of charity. He baked his pigweed bread for the many
people who came to him, and the bitter bread turned miraculously sweet. But the loaves which were stolen from
him became bitter as wormwood. When there was a disastrous want of salt because of the war, Prochorus distributed
ashes which turned into salt. This brought him into conflict first with the merchants and speculators of Kiev and
then with Prince Sviatopolk himself who, for profits sake,
did not abstain from robbing the store of salt belonging to

the saint. The salt, of course, turned back into ashes, and the avaricious prince had to become reconciled with Prochorus and the abbot.

Along with the true disciples of Theodosius can be counted a humble wafer-maker, Spyridon, who, "ignorant in word, not in mind," with reverence performed his given task, reciting ceaselessly the Psalter which he "had learned by ear." This first group of saints of the *Patericon*, the nearest in spirit to Theodosius lived the life of poverty, charity, and humility and were never severe to the sinners and evil-doers of this world. But in the portrait's of Agapit and Gregory, both closely related to Theodosius, some new features already appear. Their charity, discriminating and mingled with severity, was overshadowed by other merely ascetic virtues.

Agapit, a "disinterested physician," or "healer," devoted himself to nursing and healing the sick, by prayers and vegetables instead of by medical plants;—the latter only for the sake of appearance, as the author affirms, these vegetables being his own diet. His life was thus consecrated to charity but his story in the *Patericon* is exclusively that of his struggle against the secular medicine of an Armenian physician. In this struggle the saint triumphed and the Armenian finally became a monk in the Caves Cloister. Nevertheless, victory was achieved by the power of miracles and not by meekness. The saint was rather severe to his opponent. He addressed him "with wrath" and, being informed of his heterodoxy, upbraided him: "How did you dare come in and profane my cell and hold my sinful hand? Go away from me, infidel and impious man."

Gregory had learned from Theodosius himself "the monastic life, the love of poverty, humility, and obedience." He embraced poverty so eagerly that he even sold his books to give money to the poor, after thieves had taught him the

precariousness of earthly goods. But his main concern was
prayer. By continuously reciting "exorcising prayers" he
gained a peculiar power over demons, and developed his
thaumaturgical gift. He used to pray in a cellar, imitating
to some extent the life of a recluse. His three meetings
with robbers may be compared with similar episodes in the
life of Theodosius. The robbers who tried to plunder the
Church were not punished by Theodosius but converted
to the way of virtue. Gregory also converts, but by punishment. The thieves who attempted to steal his books fell
into a dead sleep lasting five days as a result of the saint's
prayers; upon awakening they languished with hunger.
This chastisement was sufficient for them. Having learned
that the governor of the town had ordered them to be
tortured, Gregory redeemed them from the execution. He
treated other thieves who robbed his kitchen garden more
severely. For three days they implored him for pardon,
rooted to the spot; finally he delivered the following verdict:
"Since you have remained idle all your life robbing the
fruits of other people's labours and not wishing to work
yourselves, stand here, idle for the rest of your days."
Nevertheless, their tearful entreaties and promises of repentance won for them a conditional amnesty. The saint
condemned them to labor for life in the monastery. He
took the same attitude with a third group of thieves; one
of whom, however, perished by a terrible death, hanging
from a tree. The saint did not sentence him to this death,
but he forecast it. Perhaps the criminals themselves provoked this death by trying to deceive the saint. But the
severity of the punishment remains. A grim foreboding of
a similar kind caused the violent death of the saint himself.
Having been insulted on the river bank by the servants of
Prince Rostislav, he predicted: "All of you, together with
your prince, shall die in water." The cruel prince had the

saint drowned, but afterwards met his own well-deserved end. How differently Theodosius would have acted, who was never guided in his relations with people by the law of retaliation!

The portraits of the saints given above depend, in different degrees, on the ethical pattern of Theodosius. The recluses lead us into an entirely different world. The life of the recluse Isaac belongs to those composed by an eyewitness in the eleventh century; the lives of Nicetas and Lawrence are written in the thirteenth; but they depict the same social and religious setting. In the stories of the recluses the distinction between the two spiritual schools in the monastery appears in full relief.

Isaac was a novice and disciple of Anthony himself. "Having chosen an extravagant way of life," he was not contented with a sackcloth but put on a raw goatskin, and never took it off, until it dried up and stuck forever to his body. Anthony shut him in a cave four cubits long, and passed him, through a narrow aperture, his scanty food: one wafer-bread every two days. No wonder that he became mad. The demons haunted him and drove him to a heavy fall. Appearing to him in the guise of angels of light, they induced him at last to adore a demon as Christ. Consequently he was in their power for years; he lost his wits, faculties, almost his life. He narrowly escaped being buried alive. It was Theodosius, not Anthony, who helped him on the road to recovery by nursing him and accustoming him to food. After two years, having returned to health, he "takes again to the atrocious life," but this time not in reclusion; "You have seduced me already, devils, while I sat in one spot. Hereafter, I will not shut myself in a cave." He is the first Russian to take upon himself the sham folly of a Greek *salos*,—the "holy fool in Christ." At the beginning this foolishness finds its expression only in self-

humiliation and in some eccentricities which are perhaps the
aftermath of his years of real madness. Isaac served in the
kitchen where he was the object of mockery. One day,
obeying the command of the mockers, he caught a raven
with his hands after which (a miracle!) the brothers begin
to venerate him as a saint. This was the occasion for his
assuming the part of a fool. "Not wanting human glory
he began to do foolish things and to annoy, now the abbot,
now the brothers." He walked outside the cloister and,
gathering some children together played monks with them.
For this he was beaten by the abbot Nicon. At the end of
his life, he won a complete victory over the demons who
acknowledged their impotence. The contrast in his life
between reclusion and the humility of a fool for Christ's sake
clearly connects itself with both the name of Anthony and
of Theodosius.

The dislike of reclusion marks the first generation of
Theodosius' disciples. Abbot Nicon persistently dissuaded
Nicetas from reclusion. True, Nicetas was young and
possessed of the thirst for human glory. But the abbot cited
the example of Isaac. Nicetas wilfully shut himself up and
also fell. His temptation was much more cunning and
sophisticated. A demon in angel's disguise suggested reading books instead of praying, and he became well-read in
the Old Testament. His extraordinary knowledge of the
Bible and his demon-sent clairvoyance attracted laymen
to the recluse. But the senior monks disclosed the fiend's
influence: "Nicetas knew all the Jewish books well," but as
to the Gospel, he wished neither to see, nor hear, nor read
it. The demon was expelled; and together with him, the
sham wisdom of Nicetas disappeared.

After these disastrous experiences Lawrence was simply
forbidden by the seniors, without any particular motivation,
to shut himself in a cave. He had to satisfy his taste for

silence and meditation in another cloister of Kiev. His
life ran without incidents; he did not achieve, however, the
grace of exorcising demons which was proper to the best
"thirty" old men of the Cave cloister.

This fear of the dangers of seclusion, which the "seniors"
held at the end of the eleventh century, entirely disappeared.
In the twelfth century, there lived the recluses Athanasius,
John, Theophilus, and others who achieved a high degree of
perfection. One does not hear that they had any particular
temptations; temptations visited other brothers too. Moreover, their portraits are set in the very center of the
Patericon. It is they who illuminate with their livid cave-
light the whole century of cloister history.

If the personal influence of Anthony is strongly felt
early in recluse life, in the later parts of the *Patericon* belonging to the thirteenth century, his personality, previously
overshadowed by Theodosius, grows into a larger stature.
His name is often mentioned, always before Theodosius,'
and sometimes without it. There are frequent quotations
from his lost *Life*. In an atmosphere of sensual temptations, crude demonology, and atrocious sufferings the amazing deeds of Anthony's posthumous disciples are performed.

Here is John, the "Much suffering," who spent thirty
years in seclusion wearing "Heavy irons" on his body. He
had suffered much from the temptations of the flesh in his
youth, and, praying at Anthony's grave, heard his voice
commanding him to shut himself up in a cave. He went his
way of salvation, naked, in chains, "emaciated by cold and
iron." Not contented wtih these tortures once, during the
Lenten time, he dug himself into the earth up to the breast.
But, even so, he was not relieved. He felt a dreadful heat
in his legs as from fire; his veins were twisted and his bones
cracked. Over his head he saw the mouth of a horrible
serpent belching flames. When the paschal night came, the

serpent took the recluse's head and arms into its mouth and
scorched his hair. Out of the serpent's mouth John cried
to God, and the fiend disappeared.

The strength of temptations and the perils of hell are
illustrated in the *Patericon* by numerous stories of the fall
and sins of the saints. The priest Titus lived in hatred and
enmity with a deacon Evagrius. Theophilus, by one movement of vainglory and anger, was brought to the brink
of perdition, in death without repentance. Erasmus, who
had given all his fortune to the Church, began to live "most
negligently and disorderly." Arethas is greedy and merciless: "he never gave one penny to the poor"; he even sues
innocent people and unjustly torments them. Theodore
was seduced by avarice; having found a hidden treasure in
his cave, he planned to leave the cloister in secret. He was
saved by his friend, Basil, as were others by the heavenly
intercession of Saint Anthony and Theodosius, or even Our
Lady.

The demons appear as instruments of temptations and
intimidations. They play a much more tremendous role in
the *Patericon* than in the life of Theodosius. Sometimes they
assumed a human appearance—as when, in the form of Basil,
they lured Theodore—sometimes an angelic one, as when
they seduced the recluses. In the church Matthew saw a
demon in Polish dress, throwing flowers at the monks which
made them relax in their prayers. Another time, Matthew
saw a whole herd of demons astride pigs, riding "to get
Michael Tobolkovich," a certain monk who dared go out
of the cloister's precincts. Demonology is characteristic of
the Kievan *Patericon* to the same degree as it is in the
Patericons of Egypt.

The acuteness of the temptations and the intensity of
the struggle against them account for the high valuation of
suffering and of its purifying effect. The strongest expres-

sion of this idea is found in the life of Pimen, "Much-sick-ly." Ill from birth, the youth had no desire to be healed: "He prayed not for health, but for an aggravation of illness." This prayer proved more powerful than those of all the monks in the cloister who prayed for his recovery. Having received monastic consecration from the angels—"the bright eunuchs" of his miraculous vision—he remained for the rest of his life lying in a state of incurable disease which evoked the disgust of the nursing brothers. But, significant for the Anthonian school, this voluntary sufferer also possessed punitive power. He made negligent monks ordered to nurse him fall ill. After twenty years of pain, on the day of his death, he rose from bed, and passing through all the cells, venerated the sepulchre of Anthony in the Church, as if pointing to his teacher.

The life of Moses the Hungarian is the tale of the endless sufferings of a war prisoner in Poland who defended his chastity against the amorous attacks of a noble widow. Eustratius, also a war prisoner, who was crucified by a Jew in Crimea—apparently because of his refusal to accept the law of Moses—is a martyr for the Christian faith. But Nicon the Dry, during his long captivity among the Polovtsi, simply refused to pay ransom and submitted to various tortures, confident in the will of God. Kuksha, the missionary among the Viatichi murdered by the heathens; Gregory, Theodore, and Basil, killed by Russian princes, all filled the role of sufferers and martyrs, voluntary and involuntary, listed among the many other saints of the Kievan *Patericon.* But here it is the expression of an extreme ascetic attitude rather than the kenotic conception of following Christ in self-offering love.

It is worthwhile to examine more closely the character of ascetic suffering in the *Patericon.* This is not peculiar to Kiev or even to the Russian school of spiritual life. It belongs to a common and perpetual tradition of the Christian East as distinct therein from the Catholic West. However terrible and inhuman ascetic tortures may be in the East, they never consist in the direct, active infliction of acute pain or wounds. There is no flagellation, no bloodshed. In western Europe flagellation acquired great popularity since the Italian "eremitic" movement of the tenth and eleventh centuries. As early as the fifth century young Benedict of Nursia used to throw himself with naked breast against thornbushes in order to suppress temptations of the flesh. This is also the main purpose of Eastern asceticism, but the means are different. Flesh must be macerated, emaciated, must lose as much as possible of its vital strength. Technically, it is spoken of as "withering," "drying up," or mortification in a terrifyingly literal sense. Life ought to be a continual dying of the body to release the life of the spirit; a perfect monk is a living corpse. That is why in the East the ascetic saint is always thought of as a *starets*, or old man (*geron*). "Fast" or "labor" are often used as general synonyms for asceticism, especially in old Russian or old Slavonic where the Greek term of *ascesis* was not adopted. Upon deeper examination of the religious background, it appears that the idea of crucifixion determines, only in a small degree, the Eastern way of asceticism. The imitation of Christ stops before His passions, avoiding through religious awe the contemplation of His wounds. When spoken of in ascetic context, crucifixion preserves only the same moral meaning which it has with Saint Paul: "crucified flesh with its passions and lusts." Not the cross of Christ but the coffin, his own, not Christ's, is the sensual image of the ascetic. Very often a real coffin is put in the cell of a monk. It illustrates "the memory of death" of Cyril of Turov. The cave life of the Kievan recluses was peculiarly suitable for these sepulchral meditations.

Nowhere in the Kievan *Patericon* is any trace of mystical life to be found. The recluses with whom one is tempted to suppose a contemplative turn of mind seem to be wholly occupied by the negative ascetic struggle against demonic powers. If there were a mystical or even purely contemplative life somewhere in Kiev, it found no author to reveal it. It would be misleading to infer the existence of mystical prayer from the so-called Jesus prayer recommended by Theodosius and practiced by Nicholas Sviatosha: "O Lord, Jesus Christ, Son of God, have mercy upon me, a sinner." In fact, in later Russian mysticism, since the fourteenth century, this prayer was the starting point for the achievement of the highest mystical states. Yet, in all times, even up to the present, it is used in the Eastern Church by simple devotees, even by lay people in everyday life to keep one's mind from distraction. It would be absurd to ascribe mystical intent to Nicholas. His is a very active nature, devoted to continual work and humble service.

This negative observation, drawn from but one literary monument, can be enlarged. In none of the writings or traditions of pre-Mongolian Russia are mystical traces to be found. This fact is indirectly confirmed by the absence of translations from the Greek mystical literature which rose in the eleventh century. The greatest of the Greek mystics, Simeon a monk of Constantinople, called the New Theologian, lived at the time of the conversion of Russia. His works left no traces in ancient Russia before the fourteenth century, in spite of the frequent intercourse between the cloisters of Kiev and Greece.

Thus, upon closer examination, two currents of spiritual life are disclosed in the monastery of Saint Anthony and Theodosius: one subterranean, ascetico-heroic, connected with cave-reclusion; the other "superterranean"—humble, obedient, charitable. The Anthony type dominates in the *Pa-*

tericon. The separation of the two kinds of life is not always possible, as many of the cited portraits show; their contrast, however, remains. In the realm of legend they are perhaps best embodied in two legendary figures: Mark, the Cave-dweller, and Alypius, the Icon-painter.

One is a grim old man who spent all his life under the earth in the service of grave-digging, in an odd familiarity with death; he brings the dead to life for a few hours until the grave is prepared; he makes them turn over in order to fit the dimensions of the tomb. Severe to the living, he is quick in punishing them for one evil movement of heart and shows them the way of tears and repentance.

The other is a bright artist, a man of labor, giving no rest to his hand; a disinterested worker distributing his gain to the poor; caluminated, persecuted by the monks, but always meek, punishing nobody and putting his hope in celestial powers. His miraculous pigments heal a leper; and angels, visible, paint icons for him.

It would be interesting to trace these two lines of spiritual life still farther, beyond the two founders of the Kievan cloister, to the very soil of Eastern Christianity. As to Theodosius, his affinity to, and even direct dependence upon the Palestinian type of asceticism has already been established. Saint Sabbas is his nearest oriental model. The Palestinian tradition—a harmony of prayer, labor, and charitable work—had passed through the Studion rule, and was there enriched by the strict community organization, before reaching Theodosius. The last Studite element of order and organization was followed in Russia in but very limited measure. In the Kievan cloister after Theodosius, no survival of it is found. All the more strong was the third element—the personal impact of Theodosius and his kenotic vision of Christianity.

The genealogy of Anthony is not so clear. He obviously

considered himself a disciple of the Greek anchorites of
Mount Athos. In fact he spent some years of his life there,
and one of our sources (the *Chronicle*) ties the history of
the Kievan cloister with the "Holy Mountain." "The Blessing of the Holy Mountain" is mentioned many times by
Anthony. Now the Russian Anthony school has very little
in common with the classical Greek tradition as represented
by Studion. Athos always held an exceptional place in Greek
monasticism: a place of the severest ascetic exploits and
lonely contemplative life. Unfortunately, the conditions of
life on the mountain during the sojourn of Anthony in the
first half of the eleventh century are little known.

The nearest literary pattern for Anthony's school is
found not in Greece but in ancient Syria of the fifth century,
reflected in the hagiographic work of Theodoret, the *His-
toria Religiosa*. The Syrian ascetic saints were well known
in Russia because all the chapters of Theodoret's book had
entered into the Slavonic *Prolog* (*Lectionary*). Whether
through literary channels or through the mediation of Athos,
the Syrian pattern of life is easily recognizable in Kiev. It
is a cruel, almost superhuman bodily asceticism with the spirit
of perpetual repentance: a visible sign is the gift of tears.
There are no mystics, no contemplative states. There is,
however, a great external difference of habits between Syria
and Russia. Most of the Syrian anchorites lived on
the hilltops: this fact is connected with the ancient Syrian,
and also Biblical cult of sacred mountains. The cave-life
of Anthony's disciples, though not unknown in Syria, finds
a nearer parallel in Palestine where it had, however, quite
a different meaning. The cave in Palestine, open to the
fresh air and to the sight of nature, is simply a shelter from
the sun—a "God-built" (*theoktistos*) house. The Kievan
caves, on the other hand, were subterranean catacombs, dark
and humid—very "depressing" as Theodosius found them,

and thus they became a supplementary form of ascetic torture. So far, we can state that the school of Anthony represents, in Russia, the Syrian tradition, just as the Theodosian school represents that of Palestine, both having passed through the Greek mediation of Studion and Athos.

The destiny of these two spiritual schools on the Russian soil was not identical. The Anthonian line was unquestionably less efficient and less lasting. In this respect the impression made by the Kievan *Patericon* can be erroneous. Anthony left some personal disciples, devoted to the recluse life, whose extraordinary exploits strike our imagination as they struck the authors of the thirteenth century. But the Patericon itself gives evidence of their limited influence. Anthony's disciples were outnumbered and sometimes even neglected by the school of Theodosius. To the latter belonged the authoritative "seniors" of the monastery, strong not only by their high standing but also by the holiness of their lives. Their open dislike of Anthony's methods apparently prevented his canonization until an uncertain date. The composers of the *Patericon* bear witness that in their time (the thirteenth century) the *Vita* of Anthony was little known. One of the motives for their literary work can be seen in the intention to revive and reinvigorate the Anthonian tradition.

Among the hundreds of Russian saints of later times, no one can be considered a follower of the Kievan Cave tradition. In most of them the influence of Theodosius is obvious. At least the literary dependence of their *Vitae* upon the *Vita* of Theodosius indicates his religious influence. In modern times Kiev became the holy city of Russia, the center of popular pilgrimages. The hundreds of mummified bodies in the Catacombs have attracted people who saw in their incorruptibility the sign of sanctity. Yet, even though they venerated the bodies of ancient recluses and read of their terrifying achievements, people were not allured to imitate them.

One can consider the Anthonian school as the first, unsuccessful attempt of the newly-born Russian monasticism to imitate the Oriental patterns in their most severe expression. It bears evidence of the radicalism, or thoroughness of the Russian approach to religion. Certainly the Anthonian tradition did not expire without leaving any traces. At all times one will find the severe, ascetic type of religion side-by-side with the kenotic or caritative one. Yet, its forms and even its religious background will be found different. Little is known about the life in the pre-Mongolian monastic communities, but all of them, at least those which can be located, were built in the immediate outskirts of towns. This points to their interdependence with the life of the world, of the same kind as was observed in Kiev. The cloisters were dependent upon the material support of the laity which they partly repaid for in charitable work. Many cloisters were built by princes as the repositories for themselves and their families, where perpetual prayers were said for the souls of the departed. Spiritually, the monasteries were to the lay world the refuges of prayer and religious guidance. The layman chose, from preference, his confessor among the monks. Had the monks sought isolation from the world, they could have found it in the forests, as in fact they did in the later Mongolian period when the contemplative spirit was born.

RUSSIAN ESCHATOLOGY

SAINT ABRAHAM OF SMOLENSK

*T*HE two spiritual currents which we have traced through the literary works that issued from the Caves Cloister in Kiev obviously do not exhaust all the varieties of ancient Russian monasticism. Our sources are scanty but it is perhaps significant that the only detailed *Vita* of a pre-Mongolian saint, besides that of Theodosius, leads into quite a new spiritual atmosphere. Saint Abraham of Smolensk stands apart not only among the pre-Mongolian saints but among all the Russian saints in general. His type of temperament is very rare among the select in the Russian Church: his restless, dynamic, prophetic figure reminds one of Savonarola. But the contents of his teaching, which was for him a personal religious call, is very Russian. Because of his unique character Abraham is usually omitted or even forgotten in the general outlines of Russian spiritual life. But the historian of pre-Mongolian spirituality ought not to pass him by. His eschatology remains, for all time, an outstanding feature of the Russian religious mind. But even his severe militant spirit will later revive in Avvakum, the founder of the Russian Old Believers schism, as well as in some Church leaders of modern times.

Although his biography is a very sober, reliable document written by his disciple Ephrem, it contains some interesting points which, so far, have defied all efforts at historical interpretation.

Saint Abraham of Smolensk was not only venerated in his own town after his decease at the beginning of the thirteenth century but was canonized by one of the councils of Moscow, probably in 1549. His disciple, Ephrem, was also venerated in Smolensk as a local saint. In spite of the numerous literary influences upon Ephrem's work, *The Life and Patience of Saint Abraham*, it gives an impressive portrait, full of original features.

The *Life* tells little about the childhood and youth of the holy man. After the death of his parents, he, refusing marriage, distributed his property among the poor and put on the "uncouth garb," just as Theodosius before him: "walking as one of the beggars and taking upon himself sham folly." This temporary "sham folly," of which no details are related consisted perhaps in social humiliation, similar to the youthful exploits of Saint Theodosius. Soon the youth was tonsured under the name of Abraham, in a suburban monastery of Smolensk. Persevering in vigilance and fasting day and night, Abraham zealously devoted himself to the perusal of books. Studying the fathers of the Church and the *Lives* of the Saints, he assembled the whole library, "copying one with his own hand, another with the aid of several copyists." Among the Fathers John Chrysostom and Ephrem the Syrian were his favorite authors.

It is known that Smolensk of the twelfth century was one of the centers of Russian culture. From there came the second Kievan Metropolitan of Russian origin, Clement Smoliatich, of whom the Chronicler says that there had not yet been such a "scholar and philosopher in the Russian land." The epistle of Clement to Thomas, a priest of Smolensk, bears witness that there was in that city a circle of men capable at least of discussing theological problems in connection with Biblical exegesis. In this setting the erudition of the monk Abraham is not surprising; "his abbot also was learned in divine books." This erudition of Abraham distinguished him from the simple Theodosius, but the life of Abraham stands in closest literary dependence upon the life of Theodosius. In his youth Abraham undoubtedly went through the school of Theodosius and imitated him. Like Theodosius, the *Lives* of the Palestinian saints made up his favorite reading. Nevertheless, his portrait stands out sharply and originally against the Palestinian-Kievan background. As we know, Theodosius frequented the prince-ly banquets, although he sighed while listening to the music of the jongleurs. Abraham never went to the banquets "be-cause of frequent altercations from the struggle for prece-dence"—a motive which ought to justify his deviation from his prototype. Abraham kept Theodosius' "uncouth garb" even in his mature years. But in sketching the portrait of his saintly hero at the acme of his spiritual forces and during the decisive struggles of his life, Ephrem reveals under the humble garments of Theodosius quite a different, severely ascetic figure.

The face of the saint and his body were emaciated, one could count his bones and joints; the brightness of his face had a pallor from the great labors and abstinence and vigilance and from much speaking.

The tradition of the bodily strength and joyful serenity of the holy man was established by Cyril of Scythopolis in the sixth century in his *Life of Saint Sabbas*, and this ideal was bequeathed to Russia. The pale and emaciated ascetic from Smolensk does not fit into this tradition. And yet, the author consciously tries to draw the portrait of a militant ascetic; he depicts a middle-aged and not an old man—and this after fifty years of ascetic life. "His image and likeness (iconographic type) is after Basil the Great: he had a black beard, only his head was bald."

This ascetic leanness, this abstinence from food and sleep, is in conformity with the quality of his prayer.

By night, he took but little sleep; he used to bend his knees and shed abundant tears unceasingly: beating his chest and shouting to God, he implored the Lord to have mercy upon his people and to avert His wrath.

This gloom and sorrow of repentance does not abandon the saint even at the threshold of death:

Since then the blessed Abraham redoubled his efforts, in great humility and sorrow of heart, with sighs and moans, reminding himself of the separation of the soul from the body.

Perhaps together with this new trend of spiritual life— we could term it "metanoetic"—the caritative aspect of Abraham's life was but slightly expressed, compared with Theodosius. Ephrem mentions his giving alms, but it was not compassion for human infirmities which brought the stern ascetic out of his cell; he came out with a word of admonition, and his otherworldly and probably terrifying teaching filled the hearts of his hearers with trepidation. In Abraham this particular "gift of, and labor over, the divine Scriptures" took the place of the gift and labor of caritative service, without which one can hardly imagine a saint of ancient Russia.

Abraham is closer to the Russian tradition in his attitude to Church devotion, to the beauty of liturgy and ritual. Expelled from his cloister, Abraham took refuge in the monastery of the Holy Cross, also in Smolensk. He did here as in his last monastery, in the house of Our Lady: "he adorned it like a beautiful bride . . . with icons, veils, and candles." He is especially exacting in the matter of the Church devotion: "He strictly prohibited speaking in the Church, particularly during the Mass." Apparently his attitude toward the Eucharist was quite peculiar and personal. He did not omit for a single day, since the day of his ordination, the "bloodless sacrifice"; thus, his suspen-

sion from the celebration was for him a particularly painful
ordeal.

Out of these scanty and scattered characteristics we can
discern the figure, unusual in Russia, of an ascetic with a
tense inner life, with restlessness and vehemence, breaking
out in stirring emotional prayer, with a grim penitential
idea of human destiny; not an oil-pouring healer but a
severe accuser, moved by a kind of prophetic inspiration. If
a spiritual school is to be sought in which such a type of
Russian asceticism could be found, it would be in monastic
Syria, although not in the Syria of Theodoret, but that of
Saint Ephrem. It can hardly be considered a casual fact
that his disciple and biographer took the monastic name of
Ephrem.

The "gift of teaching" occasioned ruthless persecutions
against Abraham and became the source of his "patience,"
and the main virtue of his life. These persecutions raise a
series of insoluble problems.

The monastic cell of Abraham became a center of attraction in Smolensk; many laymen came to him from the
city for the "comfort of the holy books." On the contrary,
the priests and monks rose against the saint because of his
teaching. After theological disputes with the clergy of the
city, the abbot, who had formerly held the saint under his
protection, now forbade him: "I am responsible for you
before God—cease teaching."

The saint, after having suffered "many annoyances,"
left his cloister and moved to Smolensk. Here, in the monastery of the Holy Cross, he continued his preaching activity. His numerous followers provided him with the
means for helping the poor and adorning the Church. But
the enemies of Abraham succeeded in instigating almost the
entire city against him:

All our city assembled, from boys to adults, against him; some suggested deportation for him; some, to affix him with nails to a wall and set it afire; others, to lead him through all the city and to drown him.

In the description of these sorrowful events the pen of a contemporary witness can be discerned:

The servants sent to arrest him have dragged him like a criminal; some scolded him, others railed at him and hurled scurrilous words; all the city in the market and on the streets, everywhere the crowd of people, men and women and children; it was a grave shame to see.

In the bishop's courtyard were assembled for the trial not only bishop Ignatius with the clergy but also the prince with his boyars. The laymen's verdict, however, proclaimed him not guilty; and the bishop, retaining him under arrest together with two of his disciples, the next day convoked a purely ecclesiastical tribunal of abbots and priests. Ephrem, the biographer, does not cite the verdict of this tribunal but wishes to stress its happy issue: "He did not suffer any evil." Nevertheless, Abraham was relegated to his previous cloister in Selishche, and, as is clear from the subsequent narration, he was forbidden to celebrate the Mass. Two just men prophesied to the bishop the wrath of God upon the city of Smolensk for the persecution of the saint: "A great punishment will be upon this city, if you do not repent." The bishop is said "to have sent to all abbots and priests instructions to abstain from all evil-speaking against the blessed Abraham." And yet the saint remained under suspension. The promised punishment arrived in the form of an unusual drought. The prayers of the bishop and all the people remained unheard. Then, upon the advice of a priest, Ignatius invited Abraham, reëxamined the incriminations against him, "and, having verified that all was a lie," pardoned him and bade him pray for the suffering city. God heard the prayer of the saint: "He did not even reach his cell when

God sent rain upon the earth." Since then the veneration of Abraham revived, as well as the confidence of the people towards him.

The last years of the saint were passed in peace, in the dignified role of an abbot of a new cloister, the third of his monasteries. This small cloister of Our Lady, where a few old men were nourished with the bishop's alms, apparently did not enjoy a very good reputation. There were no volunteers to become its abbot. "After the lapse of much time," Ignatius called Abraham and gave him the blessing (mission) of the house of Our Lady. Abraham gladly accepted the abbacy, "continuing his first mission" of teaching and being spiritual father to his fellow citizens. Enjoying general love and veneration, the saint survived his bishop and died after fifty years of ascetic life.

The unusual type of Abraham's mission and of the persecutions suffered by him, raises the question as to their real cause. His biographer emphasizes many times that the saint became a victim of the clergy of Smolensk. His erudition and pastoral gifts are contrasted with the deficiency of "ignorant people taking the order of priesthood." During his trial "God softened the hearts of the prince and the rulers, but the abbots and popes would be glad to devour him alive." Therefore the punishment of God personally strikes the priests and abbots. The subsequent reconciliation of Abraham with the bishop Ignatius induces the author to reduce as much as possible the part of the bishop in this ill-fated trial; Ignatius is represented as victim and dupe of the priests and abbots. But the author did not wish to conceal the acute conflict between his saint and the overwhelming majority of the clergy; he dramatically developed this conflict into the form of a traditional "passion." Which motives does he suppose to be dominant with the adverse party?

Some of the alleged motives are of a petty human character. Crowds of people streamed to Abraham from the city; he was a "spiritual father" to many. Thus the complaints of the priests became understandable: "Already he has drawn all our spiritual children." Upon this ground grows a slander: "Some accused him on account of women." More important and more interesting, however, is another group of charges: "Some called him heretic, others said he read 'glubinnyia' books,—others called him a prophet." Heretic, prophet, reader of prohibited books,—these incriminations touched the very tenets of his teaching. They disturbed even his abbot, a learned man, formerly so favorable to him.

The tenor of his unusual, troubling doctrine can only be guessed from the brief allusions in the *Life*. It certainly was concerned with salvation; Abraham preached repentance, and that with much success. "Many came (to him) from the city—passing from sins to repentance." But spiritual guidance or moral admonitions alone could not, of course, bring upon Abraham the charge of heresy.

Ephrem more than once speaks of "the gifts of the Word of God granted to Saint Abraham . . . The Grace of God was given to him not only to read but to interpret, so that nothing in the divine writings could be secret to him." In the realm of exegesis of the Holy Scriptures, or of its obscure, mysterious passages, there were dangers for the audacious theologian. For this exegetic preaching he, according to his own word, "during five years, suffered temptations, and was insulted and dishonored like a malefactor."

Ephrem offers a hint towards Abraham's fundamental theological interest. The saint of Smolensk was not only an erudite scholar but also a painter. His biographer speaks, obviously not without purpose, about the two icons from Abraham's brush. "He painted two icons: one, the Terrible Judgment of the Second Coming; the other, the trial in the aerial "toll-houses." The recollection of these icons brings to the author's mind the memory of that terrible day, "from which there is no escape: lo, the river of fire is running before the tribunal, and the books are opened, and the Judge is sitting, and the works of all are manifest. If it is gruesome to hear about it, brethren, more gruesome it will be to see for ourselves." In similar thought and mood, the saint awaits his hour of death.

> The blessed Abraham often brought to his mind how the soul would be extracted by the angels who will come for it; how it would be tried in the air at the demonic toll-houses; how it would stand before God and give account of everything; into what place it would be led and how it had to appear at the Second Coming before the tribunal of the terrifying God; what answer will be heard from the Judge; and how the river of fire would run, consuming all. . . .

Striking is the vividness of detail in these images, the artistic plasticity of the visions. Their inner kinship with the "metanoetic" type of asceticism is not to be denied. The details of these visions are not found in the Apocalypse of Saint John, nor in the book of Daniel. They are all taken from the vast patristic and apocryphal literature on eschatological subjects. For instance, all the details of the Terrible Judgment are contained in the famous sermon of Ephrem the Syrian *On the coming of the Lord, the end of the world and the coming of the Antichrist.* The classical source for the "toll-houses" was the Greek *Vita* of Saint Basil the Younger with "the visions of Theodora" for its appendix. But then, whence the persecutions against Abraham, whence the charges of heresy?

Why they derisively call him a prophet is easily understood. The eschatological interest directed to the approaching end of the world tears away the veil from the mystery which makes a prophet. But this other accusation that "he reads glubinnyia books" indicates that the very source of these prophecies was under suspicion: perhaps, the Greek eschatological tradition itself, not without some ground.

It is well known how the authentic eschatological works of the fathers, that is, of Hippolytus and Ephrem, became overgrown with pseudepigraphs and inspired anonymous apocrypha. In the vast apocryphal literature the eschatological themes dominate. In the Greek and, afterwards, in the Russian Church there were in circulation the indexes of prohibited books. But such lists had a private character, contradicted one another, and were little complied with, as is evidenced by the fact of numerous apocryphal manuscripts preserved in cloister libraries. The absence of critical training and philological culture made the task of separating the apocrypha from the authentic heritage of the fathers quite impracticable.

What "glubinnyia" books are we do not know. The Slavonic word "glubina" means depth, profundity. Among the gnostic literature of early Christian times existed a book called *Bathos* (the *Depth*). There are no traces of its survival in the later Byzantine period, still less of its Slavonic translation. But the title could either survive the work or else be the label for some later apocrypha or the whole apocryphal literature in general. This name in Russia is sonorous and tempting, conveying the idea of secret, profound knowledge. Among Russian religious songs there is one consecrated to the "Golubinaia" book, which is considered to contain the answers to all questions of cosmology and eschatology. A slight change of spelling, "golubinaia" instead of "glubinnayia," produced a new symbolical meaning: that of the *Book of Dove*. That the primitive form was "Glubinnaia"—the *Book of Depth*—is accepted by most of the Russian literary historians.

Returning to the enigmatic "glubinnyia" books of Abraham's Life, it is possible to see in them cosmological works

of the Bogomilian literature. In the Middle Ages Bogomilism (a revived Manicheism, called Catharism in the
West) was wide-spread over all the Slavic countries of the
Balkans: Bulgaria, Serbia, Bosnia. Russia, which had borrowed from the southern Slavs nearly all her ecclesiastical
literature, could not help borrowing something from the
heretics as well. Not one frankly Bogomilian work was discovered in Russian libraries, but some Bogomilian motives
are reflected in Russian folklore: legends, tales, and religious songs.

A concrete and very serious accusation was thus raised
against Abraham, one wonders with what degree of probability. There are no traces of Manicheism in his life;
it is impossible to take for such the severe otherworldly
asceticism which is often observed in the orthodox monasticism. If Abraham read Bogomilian books, it was through
sincere error, just as other orthodox Russian readers, who
possessed no criteria for recognizing them. But perhaps his
biographer was right in judging the enemies of his spiritual
father severely. Abraham's ordeal is the first conflict in
the history of Russia between free theological thought and
the obscurantism of ignorant mobs, the mobs in this case
represented by the clergy and the free theologian supported
by the laity.

We are at a loss to determine what party in this conflict
was theologically right or, at least, represented a higher
level of theological culture. As we have pointed out,
Smolensk, in the middle of the twelfth century and in its
second half, under the rule of prince Roman (1161-1180),
into which falls the life of Abraham, is justly treated as
one of the most flourishing centers of Russian culture. But
comparing the dominant interests of Abraham's thought
with those of Clement one is struck by their divergence.
Clement, as a disciple of Byzantium, is fond of exegetic

speculations for their own sake; no vital idea particularly dear to him can be discovered. Abraham's interest is purely vital: repentance, salvation, and eschatology as a bridge between theological gnosis (rather than speculation) and practical life, oriented towards death. In this respect Abraham's attitude is truly Russian. In this tendency he presages one of the dominant streams in the religious thought of Russia. Not very successful in theology, ancient Russia, out of all theological themes clung with preference to the eschatological one, although she developed it more in the creations of folklore than in written literature.

THE SERMON OF THE CELESTIAL POWERS

An excellent illustration of the Life of Saint Abraham can be supplied by the anonymous eschatological *Sermon of the Celestial powers*, included sometimes among the works of Cyril of Turov but attributed by some critics to Abraham of Smolensk. Nothing in its style or vocabulary recalls Cyril's solemn eloquence. Besides, it contradicts Cyril in one essential eschatological point: the torments of the sinners begin, according to the anonymous author, immediately after death, which we had seen was denied by Cyril. The sermon is rather an artless and naïve compilation, not, however, without a claim to occult wisdom, as is manifest from the start: "This mystery was not revealed to all and is not known to many. . ." The author is convinced that "ignorance is worse than sin," a sentence current in the ancient Russian literature but arguing here a gnostic savor. The "divine writings," the ignorance of which is the source of all errors, are not the Holy Scriptures. Although the author does not disclose either names or titles, it is not difficult to identify his sources among the popular works of Greek eschatology. The *Vision of Theodora* and the sermons of Saint Ephrem the Syrian are his chief fountain-heads. There is, in fact, no obstacle to the assignment of this early Russian sermon to the gnostic saint of Smolensk. If it does not belong to his pen it fits perfectly well into the frame of his thought. Built entirely of Greek elements, it represents the canon of eschatological beliefs held by the Russian people for many centuries as the dogmatic doctrine of the Church. Ecclesiastical art and popular poetry drew their inspiration abundantly from this source. Thus, it can justly be considered truly Russian, reflecting the deepest tendencies of the Russian religious mind.

Three groups of problems, or myths, compose the circle of the Graeco-Russian eschatology: the destiny of an individual soul after death; the end of history or the reign of the Antichrist; and the Last Judgment in which the individual and cosmic destinies find their solution in the final triumph of God over His adversaries. The first, the individual cycle can be termed a "small eschatology," as distinct from the last two which represent the "great" or proper eschatology as the prophetic doctrine of the "last things."

Ancient Christianity, as well as Judaism, was interested not so much in the immortality of the soul as in the resurrection of both soul and body. The "great eschatology" is the content of the Judaeo-Christian apocalyptic literature. The "small eschatology," though not entirely strange to the spirit of the New Testament—as witness the parable of the Dives and Lazarus—, was nourished mainly on Hellenistic and Oriental popular gnosticism. In Byzantine and Russian religious thought both branches of eschatology are kept in balance, as in many other spheres of Eastern Orthodoxy, Jewish and Hellenistic elements are organically intertwined.

The Russian sermon begins its eschatological plot with a kind of prologue which gives the mythical substance of man's earthly life. Behind its visible course runs the invisible but essential chain of events. Every man receives from childhood

two angels, one of God and another of Satan, who guide his
soul towards good and evil and keep an account of his deeds.
The action of superhuman powers is described in such a manner as not to destroy the freedom of man. "When man begins to dwell in justice, then the angel of God has the upper-
hand over him." The "dwelling in evil things" gives over
the power and superiority to the angel of Satan. When one
or the other provisionally takes the lead, the other has but
to weep. Yet both accounts are cautiously guarded until the
posthumous clearing.

Terrible and pathetic appears the death of man, even of
a just man. The first trial awaiting him is the separation of
soul and body. It is the most picturesque moment of the
drama.

First, the demons appear and present all the sinful deeds of the
soul which it had wrought from youth to old age; they unroll the
parchment scrolls and begin to accuse the soul, revealing its sins . . .
"Hast thou forgotten the sins that thou hast sinned during all thy
life? But we did not forget and have them clearly written!" Then,
two angels appear, sent by God for the soul. As soon as the soul
has seen them, it will be horrified; all its image and beauty and face
will change; feet and hands will be torpid, and the hearing as well;
the tongue will be chained by silence; and man will be all sorrowful
and invalid and woeful; and afterwards, appears death. And then,
with a terrible pain the soul will issue from the body and stand looking at its body, as someone who has taken off his vestment and
stands looking at it. . . .

The last striking image, familiar in Russian poetry from
the religious folk songs to Tutchev, originates in Plato.

Taken by the angels the soul is borne to the heavenly
spheres where the second trial awaits it: the twenty aerial
"toll-houses" (*mytarstva*). For this part the Russian author
is entirely dependent upon the vision of Theodora which has
popularized the doctrine of celestial *theloneia* (toll-houses).
The primitive idea is, obviously, that of octrois or custom-

houses where the wandering soul, on his way to heaven, has to pay toll for every sin committed on earth. These tolls must have been some expiatory pains. But already in the *Vision of Theodora*, as well as in all Russian texts, *theloneia-mytarstva* are the places of judgment or reckoning, not of punishment. Here again, demons show lists of all the sins committed by the soul under a particular rubric of vice, and angels counterbalance them by the corresponding virtues or good deeds. The whole procedure reminds one of bank-clearing, except for the terrible import of the balance. If an overdraft of sins is the result of the trial, the soul is given into the power of demons for eternal torments. Successfully overcoming one theloneion, the soul rises to the next. Each of the twenty trials is assigned to one particular sin, beginning with envy and ending with avarice (or mercilessness). There is no attempt to a graduation or systematic order. Most of the twenty sins are misdeeds against fellow men, disclosing thus no monastic preoccupation. Several of them, on the other hand, contain indications of some specific Russian customs. Under the seventh *mytarstvo*, which is "shameless speech" are cited, besides obscene words, also dances "at banquets, weddings, evening-gatherings, game-places, and in the streets." Under heresy are referred popular superstitions such as the beliefs in "occurence, sneezing, bird cries, and spells . . . and also, telling tales and playing *gusli* (guitars)." The last vice, mercilessness, is obviously considered the most grievous:

Here, the demons accuse the soul, if we have harmed our brother or a beggar, or expelled him from our house, or threatened somebody. . . . Even if we have fulfilled all the commandments of God, but are pitiless and not merciful towards the poor or our servants, not giving them sufficient clothes or food, injuring them by deeds or other grievances, all will be questioned by the aerial demons.

This passage has specific bearing on Russian lay ethics.

The soul which overcame all twenty trials rises to the throne of the Almighty and, after having adored Him, is led by Michael for forty days through Paradise and Hell. This last voyage, however, presents no danger to it, serving only for the satisfaction of its curiosity. Returning to Paradise the soul receives its "place of rest" until the last resurrection.

The souls of manifest sinners are not admitted even to the first *mytarstvo*, but immediately after death are captured by the demons. The latter, however, act strictly according to justice, showing all the sins written upon their scrolls with exact indication of place and time. From the vague narrative of the sermon it is not clear who is admitted to the aerial trials. Taken literally, it can be understood as the just souls alone. The sermon's particular trait is strict legalism; the acts and not the quality of soul are judged. Good works can outnumber and outweigh sins. In this moral arithmetic there is but little place for the Christian idea of redemption. One gets the impression that the soul saves itself, or perishes on its own merit or guilt. Only in one instance are the moral accounts crossed by supramoral religious Grace: this point is repentance. Repentance alone can erase the sins marked on the demons' scrolls, but only under certain conditions. Sins have to be forgiven at the sacrament of Penitence, provided the spiritual father imposes upon the penitent a due amount of expiating works (*epitimia*). Otherwise both father and son are damned forever. So even repentance requires for its validity a due equivalent of good works, and the only point where the breakthrough of Grace would be conceivable is closed again by moralism. It is the complete triumph of Pelagianism.

From the small to the great eschatology the distance is short. In the view of the author "the end of the world is near, little remains of our life and age." All historical tribulations, wars, and riots predicted in the Gospel are being fulfilled. The author finds even some colorful additions to the words of our Lord: "There will arise prince against prince, bishop against bishop, monk against monk." The Antichrist will come three years before the seven-thousandth year from the creation, and will reign during these three years. But our author is very meager in details concerning the historical apocalypse. In some Byzantine apocrypha this subject was treated at length in connection with the historical destinies of the Empire. But the Russian author speeds to the cosmological end.

For the picturesque details of this end, Ephrem the Syrian and a Byzantine writer known by the name of Palladius convey all the necessary colors. The Gospel, and even the Apocalypse of Saint John, have little to do with this picture. The Last, or Terrible Judgment is only mentioned; indeed, it has hardly any meaning after all the posthumous trials of the soul. Here the Hellenistic myth of *theloneia* obviously replaces the Judaeo-Messianic Judgment. But the fiery consumption and the renewal of earth and heaven (II Peter 3:10-13) are narrated at length.

At the sound of the trumpets blown by Michael and Gabriel, all the dead arise.

> Then undying fire will flow from the East to the West, devouring mountains, stones, trees, and the sea. The firmament will be dried up and turned like birch bast, and all existing things, except men, will melt like wax by the rage of the fire. All the earth will be burned; and through this undying fire all mankind has to pass. There will be no place to run and hide oneself; it will be woe and pain without comfort, particularly for unrepenting sinners. They will see the anger of God, full of rage and wrath, bearing the woe of revenge.

All mankind has to go through this fire: but for the just it will mean purification; for the sinners, "singeing and darkening of their bodies." After the passing of mankind, the flaming river will gather into a fiery lake for the eternal torture of the sinners.

Afterwards, the earth will be new and flat (the ideal antique landscape) as it was in the beginning, and whiter than snow; it will be changed by the order of God, and will be like gold; there will grow upon it various grasses and flowers, never fading, because spiritual; and trees will come forth, not similar to those visible now; their height, beauty, and splendor the lips of men are unable to express, because they are spiritual.

The eschatology ends upon this cosmological triumph. Full of ecstasy before the transfiguration of nature, the author forgets to mention the bliss of the saints upon the new earth. In this, he is supremely Russian. Slavishly following his Greek pattern throughout his patchwork, at the very end he is truly enraptured by the eschatological vision of the transfigured earth. In the light of the whole Russian religious experience, we are entitled to emphasize this attitude. The purely Russian idea of Redemption is the redemption of Mother Earth.

The Ordinary Christian

THE RITUALISM OF THE CLERGY

*D*OCUMENTS of Canon Law seem to be the least
promising source for revealing the religious mind of
a nation. In their body they belong to the Church Universal, being a juridical instrument for shaping the multiformity
of life into the unity of a supernational society. Indeed,
Graeco-Byzantine Canon Law claimed and gained unlimited
authority in ancient Russia. The codes of this Law, the so-
called "Nomocanons" in several versions written in the sixth
and ninth centuries, have been accepted to the present day
in the Russian Church as the unquestionable norm. But the
Russians, or their ecclesiastical leaders, could not always find
in the sacred codes the answers to the complicated problems
of their lives, remote from the Mediterranean patterns; consequently they tried to fill in the gaps with their own additions. These Russian canonical supplements, official or private, even though conceived in the spirit of literal fidelity
to the Greek Law cannot help reflecting Russian religious
needs and the Russian state of mind.

Among Russian canonical literature the first place belongs
to the ecclesiastical statutes of Russian princes, Vladimir,
Iaroslav, and others who had to determine the competence
and the extent of the jurisdiction of the ecclesiastical courts.
There is then a group of canonical questions and answers in
which some ecclesiastic authority—a bishop or metropolitan
—gives his solution of the difficult practical problems pre-

179

sented to him. Finally, we possess a mass of formless anonymous or pseudonymous literature in which some canons of the Greek Church, some Russian constitutions and customs, and some inventions of private canonical zeal are united. These compositions, long and short, are divided into separate items or canons, without any attempt at systematic treatment. Several items repeat the sound valid canonic norms, others are outstanding for their fantastic extravagance and were, even in ancient times, considered by the experts as belonging to the "bad Nomocanons" (canonical apocrypha). Generally, however, ancient Russia, unable to draw the line between the right and the wrong canons, lived in the confusion of many contradictory norms. A "bad" and obviously spurious canonic norm could gain, in the course of centuries, indisputable authority and deeply influence the life of the Russian people. As in other anonymous Russian writings it is not easy to distinguish the Russian production from the translated Greek or the imported Bulgarian. In this domain, however, much has been done by Smirnov, the last student and publisher of the Russian "penitential" documents.

The best known and the most embracing of the question and answer compositions belong to a group of Novgorodian priests in the middle of the twelfth century, among whom Kirik takes first place. The answers are given by the bishop Niphont and other prelates. The questions and answers are reflections and sometimes verbatim reports of real conversations between the bishop and the priests who come to him, canonic collections in hand, to solve their practical difficulties.

The main body of Kirik's questions are concerned with sacramental and ritual details of the Church service which have, naturally, a permanent professional interest for an Eastern Orthodox priest. But many other items pertain to the ritual obligations of laymen, Kirik's spiritual sons and daughters. Their moral sins and the corresponding *epitimia*

constitute the third group of questions connecting Kirik's
work with "penitential ordinances" in the strict sense.

Of the same mixed content are the two other monuments
preserved from pre-Mongolian times: *The Canonical Answers of Metropolitan John II* of Kiev (1080-89) and the
so-called *Precept of the Holy Fathers to the Confessing Sons
and Daughters*.* The documents, with some others of
minor size and importance, will help us to control Kirik and
discern the general features from his personal prejudices and
concerns.

If a priest consults his bishop about the complicated detail
of the ritual only recently adopted in a newly-converted
country, it is in itself no indication of his ritualistic tendencies. It is simply a part of his professional training. The
more devotional awe one has towards the sacraments of the
altar, the more significance do the tiniest details of the ritual
acquire. It is but natural that Kirik wishes to know how to
perform correctly the ritual of baptism and how to administer
the sacrament to the dying; what are the religious and moral
obstacles which exclude one from Communion, or what are
the dietetic and other conditions of a true fast. But even in
this liturgical interest Kirik goes beyond the limits of reason,
revealing a spirit of narrow bigotry and ritualism in a pejora-
tive sense; many times he deserves the rebuke of his somewhat more broadminded bishop. The main point is, however, the relation of ritualistic questions to the whole of the
composition. Kirik does not limit his inquiry to the problems
of ritual. Using the knowledge and authority of bishop
Niphont he raises the problems of the most various content
which troubled him in his practice as priest and spiritual
father. Among his hundred and one items can be marked
two exegetical, two historical, and about a dozen moral ques-

---

*In quotations the three documents are distinguished by these letters:
Kirik—K, John—J, Precept—P.

tions. All the rest concern the ritual or the rites in a larger
sense. The proportion of ritualistic questions is a striking
proof of the direction of his religious interests.

Among Kirik's hundred and one questions, one finds the
following ones:

1. (What is the penance) if a man vomits after communion?
2. Is it fitting to read the prayer upon the defiled vessel if it is earth-
   en, or only upon the wooden, and should all others be broken?
59. (Is it a sin) if a man strikes an egg against his teeth before the
   Mass, especially before the Easter Mass?
65. Is it a sin to tread upon written letters?

It must be understood that these examples are chosen
from among the extremes. Since they are well known to all
students of Russian culture they generally serve to create a
caricatured impression of the Russian clergy. As a matter
of fact, they are only an abnormal outgrowth of a sense of
professional scrupulousness in a rather narrow mind.

Trying to orient oneself in this maze of ritual casuistics,
one can easily discover the basic leaning of the Novgorod
priest. It is not a simple search for canonic exactness, precision, or *acribia*—to use this favorite word of the Greek
Canon Law. The concern with *acribia* is undeniable and
natural for any primitive mind, taking conscientiously upon
itself the complicated law of a higher culture. We might
cite the famous questions addressed by the Bulgarian King
Boris to the Pope Nicholas I. But Kirik's desire for *acribia*
is overshadowed by another motive: the fear of ritual impurity understood almost exclusively in the physical, or
physiological sense. In this regard Kirik stands on the same
ground as the primitive religion of Israel which is reflected
in the ancient parts of the Bible. Kirik's mind could thus be
defined as Judaistic, except that it lacks the prophetic spirit of
Israel. The source of impurity is the human body with all
its organic functions; impure are all secretions of this body,

with the exception, perhaps, of tears. Nutrition and sexual
life are the main channels of ritual sin.

The very first question put by Kirik reveals his fundamental preoccupation, when the basest physiological uncleanness is brought into connection with the highest of sacred
things: the natural result is "physiological" sin. Question 1
is—[What is the penance] "if a man vomits after Communion?" The penance varies according to the reasons for the
sin, but even an ordinary illness is not exempt from the
penance.

The preparation for the Holy Sacrament by fasting and
the absolute prohibition of eating anything in the morning
before the Communion (or even the Mass in general) can be
understood on ascetic grounds. But of purely physiological
consideration are the doubts as to the admissibility to the
Communion if "a man has a sore from which pus is sup-
purating" (K 61) or "if blood is oozing from his teeth."
(K 62). Analogous preoccupations find expression in the
prohibition to rinse the mouth before the Communion—lest
some water penetrate the stomach, or to eat garlic the day
before. (P 25).

Not only the Holy Communion but also the kissing of
the Cross raises the same question of ritual unworthiness and
uncleanness. The tendency of our sources is here more liberal: sinners and unclean persons in most, if not all cases,
are admitted to the Cross-kissing. But "after having kissed
the precious Cross it is prohibited to eat meat or cheese"
(P 41).

The last prescription overlaps the extremely complicated
regulations of fasting. The ecclesiastical fast has, first of
all, an ascetic meaning of mortification, of weakening bodily,
primarily sexual, energies, and subduing the will to the guidance of the Church. The fast regulations of the Eastern
Church are much stricter than of the Roman Church, even

as they stood at the high age of medieval asceticism. All Wednesdays and Fridays are fast days; three long annual periods (four since the fourteenth century); and some separate feast days,—more than half a year altogether. On all these days not only meat but even eggs, milk, and all dairy products are excluded from the table. In Lent even fish is prohibited, and during certain weeks or days, only dry, unboiled vegetable food is allowed. The details of these regulations give occasion to endless comments and explanations. As the stress is laid upon a particular kind of food and not upon its quantity the primary ascetic meaning of fasting shifts into ritualistic taboos or prohibitions. In ancient Russian canons newly born infants were allowed to suck the mother's breasts only during the first two fast periods. They were obliged to be participants in the third fast, although they were less than one year old (P 55). If this can still be understood as the irrational extension of ascetic practice another group of food taboos escapes all ascetic interpretations.

As a remainder of Mosaic ritual law the primitive Church retained the ban on consuming blood and "things strangled" (Acts 15:29). This so-called canon of the Apostles' council was repeated by the Constantinople or Trullan council of 680 (67). It never was abrogated officially, but was dropped in the West sometime during the Middle Ages. In Russia it was in force until the end of the Muscovite Tsardom about 1700. With a characteristic inexactitude in quoting the Holy Scripture, this rule was used in enlarged form: "James, the brother of the Lord, forbade nothing except fornications, sacrificial meats, strangled things, blood, [animals] eaten by beasts, and dead ones." (K 88).

The Novgorod priest and his bishop are cautious in the application of this rule: they do not go beyond the Greek canons in this enlarged form. The main practical question in Russia was offered by the general use of traps and clap nets by hunters. Birds and small game caught in this way were strangled and consequently not fit for food. Of the Bishop Niphont the following anecdote is narrated: "A grouse once was brought to him at a banquet; and he ordered it to be thrown over the fence, saying: 'He who would eat it is not worthy even to communicate.'" (K 88).

The prohibition against consuming blood led to many casuistic problems solved in different ways by the bishop of Novgorod. He sees "no harm" in eating the blood of fish (K 86) but objects to the drinking of milk of a newly-delivered cow," "because, it is with blood." On the other hand, Niphont is against the discrimination of clean and unclean animals which already had taken root in certain ecclesiastical circles in Russia. Both points of view, strict and "liberal," are reflected in the question of Kirik and its solution by the bishop: "I asked in behalf of the peasants . . . some of whom eat squirrels and the like." "It is a great sin to eat the strangled things but if they eat squirrels or other animals which are not strangled there is no harm." (K 89). But the stricter attitude soon prevailed in Russia. A canonical monument, so-called *The canon about the Believers in the Reptiles* of the fourteenth century contains a long list of the unclean and prohibited animals:

Those who eat wolf, fox, she-bear, dog, hedge-hog, marten, squirrel, and others which are unclean, turtle and each beast, small or big, or horses, or donkeys, and those from wild or domesticated animals which the law of God (Mosaic?) called unclean, if they will be found eating by their own will and wish, shall repent for four years. (16).

Another canon concerning the prohibited birds completes this list. (15).

After the Mongolian conquest ritualism became a power-

ful current in Russia. The relatively liberal point of view
of Niphont was changed to the stricter one in all canonical
documents. In many cases the scarcity of our sources makes
one uncertain which of the canonic institutions or customs
go back to the Kievan period. It seems probable that the
bishops at that time did not recommend the Mosaic prohibitions. But many priests did, guided perhaps, not so much
by Biblical reminiscences as by a very strong feeling of
physiological repulsion in connection with their idea of holiness. *Precept to the Confessing Sons and Daughters* is undoubtedly a pre-Mongolian canonical collection, although
private, and not attributable to the Metropolitan George II
as Golubinsky wrongly surmised. The anonymous Russian
canonist considers it a positive sin to consume, even unawares,
the food defiled by insects or unclean animals: "If a dog
licks food or if a cricket or a centipede, or a toad, or a mouse
fall into it, only say a prayer; if a mouse or a toad rots there,
do not eat. If somebody eats of it unawares he shall fast
for eight days." (P 80). An unavoidable conclusion is that
if an unclean animal falling into food defiles it religiously,
it must be the more unfitting for food itself.

A further corollary was to suspect the uncleanness of
the skins or furs of such animals. Logically, it would exclude almost all furs from Orthodox costumes. Yet, this
conclusion was energetically rejected by Bishop Niphont,
and in this point, at least, posterity followed him: "As for
vestments, there is no harm in wearing anything you like,
even bearskins." (P 91).

A particular problem of conscience, sometimes a tragic
one for ancient Russia, was the question of eating together
with pagans, Jews, or even Western Christians.

The canons of the Ancient Church forbade eating with
heretics. Their aim was, obviously, to prevent the community of life with heretics and the danger of their influence

upon the orthodox. Such or similar canons were enforced
in Russia because of the heathen who were numerous within
as well as outside the country. This prohibition was of the
most practical importance for the relations with the Polovtsi
and other nomads of the steppes with whom the Russians had
to live sometimes in intimate relations as merchant-guests,
military allies, or war prisoners. Among the very authoritative canons of Metropolitan John II (1080-89), there is
canon 19, defining: "Whoever eats with the heathen unawares must accept the prayer prescribed for defiling and
thus he is worthy to be accepted (in the Church)." In the
case of the willing transgression of this canon other canonical
collections assign as *epitimia* three to nine days of fast. The
punishment is not grave, probably, because the sin was, in
many cases, unavoidable. The Metropolitan is more severe
to the merchants: "Great are the sins of those who for the
sake of property or riches defile themselves with the
heathen." Although he does not find canons excommun-
icating them, he insists upon cleansing with prayers (J 28).

In the last canon the sin of the merchants is defined exactly as "going to the heathen and eating the unclean food."
The ancient meaning of prohibition, namely, spiritual danger, is forgotten: the ritualistic-dietetic sense is in the foreground.

Why the food of the heathen is unclean can be explained
either by the spiritual uncleanness of heathendom infecting
even their bodies and all bodily life, or—and this is the more
relevant point—by the uncleanness of their food itself. Indeed, the Russian authors like to expatiate about the indis-
criminate diet of the heathen which inspires their disgust.
When the Russian chroniclers start describing the heathen
life of their forefathers, the indiscrimination of food together with sexual disorders or barbarous wedding customs
characterize the very essence of paganism. Speaking of dif-

ferent tribes of the eastern Slavs the author of the *Primary Chronicle* writes:

> The Drevlians lived in bestial fashion, and were like cattle. They killed one another, ate every impure thing, and there was no marriage among them, but instead they seized maidens by capture. The Radimichi, the Viatichi, and the Severians had the same customs. They lived in the forest like any wild beast, and ate every unclean thing (141-2).

On another page, while tracing the genealogy of the Pechenegs, Polovtsi, and other nomad enemies of Russia, the chronicler speaks of the legendary nations shut up in the mountains by Alexander the Great. His source is the apocryphal Methodius of Patara:

> He (Alexander) penetrated the eastern countries as far as the sea called the Land of the Sun, and he saw there unclean peoples of the race of Japhet. When he beheld their uncleanness, he marveled. They ate every nauseous thing, such as gnats, flies, cats, and serpents. They did not bury their dead, but ate them, along with the fruits of abortion and all sorts of impure beasts. On beholding this, Alexander was afraid lest, as they multiplied, they might corrupt the earth (1096).

These unclean races who obviously embody the extreme degree of devilish wickedness, are kept in the Ural mountains from where they will be released by the wrath of God before his Last Judgment.

As one of the reasons for the canonical prohibition to have intercourse with Roman Catholics, a Greek Metropolitan of Kiev cites their food indiscrimination. The separation of the West and the East had been of recent date (1054); dogmatic heresies were but secondary in the lists of Roman abuses. For John II the Roman sins are as follows: "They celebrate with unleavened bread, eat meat in the week before Lent and [eat] blood and strangled things." (J 4). The Metropolitan does not go so far as to prohibit entirely eating with Catholics as he does in the case of heathens. He allows this food communion "in case of need, for the love of Christ." But we are only in the beginning of the process which culminated in the Muscovite period in a complete breakage of personal intercourse with all foreigners except the Orthodox of the East. In the Kievan period there was no political or psychological reason for such nationalistic seclusion. Russia was open both to the West and the East. Matrimonial connections of Russian princes with Catholic royal and princely houses were very common, in spite of the canonical prohibitions, such as J. 13. In Novgorod of the twelfth century, women used to bring their children to Varangian (Catholic) priests for prayer (K 18)— as, in cases of sickness, they brought them also to the pagan *volkhvi* (K 18). Kievan Russia was remote from religious fanaticism. Yet food discrimination already existed, and out of it the process of nationalistic seclusion was gradually developing. At its source one finds not a dogmatic or theological aversion but rather a physiological one, sublimated into the realm of ritual or sacred taboos.

Another and still more dangerous source of ritual uncleanness is sex and all its functions. We are not speaking here of sexual sins, adultery, fornication and sins against nature, which occupy a large place in the canonical collections. Even an honorable marriage, consecrated by the Church, is looked upon as the root of continual ritual troubles. Here, ecclesiastical conscience is divided between the Biblical recognition of the sanctity of marriage and the distrust of every act of sexual life, even in marriage, as the source of sin. Uncleanness is a better word than sin in this relation. It becomes sin when put in contact with sacred things, and a complicated system of precautions is enacted in order to purge and restrain this dangerous element.

In ancient Russia the Church attempted to regulate sex-

ual life as strictly as it did nutrition. The modes and times
of the marital act were prescribed by the canons. It is noteworthy that copulation is prohibited not only, or not so much,
on the fast days as on the feast days. It means that the original motive is not ascetic abstinence but ritual cleanness.
Bishop Niphont cites an ancient canon of Patriarch Timothy,
which was read to all newly-wedded couples and which prohibited copulation on Saturdays and Sundays. Very soon
Friday was added to these days. The *Precept to the Confessing* enjoins this prohibition with a curious warning: the
child conceived during these three days risks becoming "thief,
or robber, or fornicator," and then his parents have to do a
penance (P 108). The liberal Niphont is indignant about
these superstitious exaggerations. When referred by Kirik
to this, or similar, canonical authority he gives his opinion:
"Those books are fit for burning" (K 74). Nevertheless,
the prescription of "those books" prevailed, and the superstitious view rejected by Kirik became a general belief of the
Russian people.

The *Precept* won over Niphont's judgment also in another point: in the extension of sexual prohibition to all feast
days and to Lent. This seems to be the practice of the Novgorod priests, which angered Niphont. "Do you teach abstinence from wives during Lent? You sin in this" (K 57).
Obviously, the Bishop considered this abstinence beyond the
capacity of laymen. The *Precept* insists upon abstinence, at
least, during the first and the last weeks of Lent (P 64).
The canons of the Muscovite period are more intransigent in
this point as in many others.

The abstinence of Lent undoubtedly has ascetic-sacrificial
character. It allows no inference as to the moral and religious quality of the sexual life itself. The most significant
indication in this respect is given by the general canonic prohibition to the priest of the Eastern Church against celebrating

the Mass the morning after coitus with his wife. It is the Eastern correspondence to the Roman celibacy—somewhat mitigated on one hand, but on the other, emphasizing more strongly the religious meaning of the prohibition. The celibacy of the priest has practical and social purpose, besides the sacramental one: it makes the minister of the Church more independent of the ties of this world. Socially, and economically, the Eastern priest is entirely within the world, burdened with his duties of family life; so the prohibition of the canons has in view only the uncleanness of sexual act making man unfit for sacral actions. Many embarrassments of Kirik are connected with this point: which sacramental actions, and under what conditions, are allowed or prohibited after coition. That uncleanness is taken in a physical, or rather in a physical-religious nonmoral sense follows from the canonic obligation of washing in prescribed ways. "A priest who has been with his wife, may read the Gospel outside the Sanctuary and eat the blessed bread." (K 27). "A secular priest (not a monk) who was with his wife during the day before the celebration, may celebrate after having washed himself up to the waist, without prostrations and without bathing." (K 28).

Similar injunctions are given to the laymen: "One may kiss the relics of the saints after having been with one's wife without bathing, but having washed oneself up to the waist, even after having eaten and drunk" (K 26). A particular case of conscience was the perplexity of "being with one's wife" in the presence of icons or of the holy cross. From the context it can be inferred that in Kievan Russia, unlike during the Muscovite period, the icons were not kept in inhabited heated chambers but in separate cold rooms. But these rooms could also be used as bedrooms. This explains the question: "If one keeps icons or the precious Cross in a room (*klet'*), is it lawful to be with one's wife?" Niphont is as liberal and peremptory as usual: "The wife is not given to one for sin. . . Do you take off your cross when you are with your wife?" (K-Sabbas 4). In this last point the bishop is second-ed by the *Precept*: "A layman must keep the cross upon him-self if lying with his wife." (P 43). The Muscovites were of another opinion. But the fact that such questions were raised in the earliest times is evidence of the widespread view that all sexual life was unclean. The pre-Mongolian Church tried to oppose this conviction by stressing the sanctity of marriage. But the dual attitude toward sex was too deeply rooted in the Christian past. The ancient canons bear wit-ness of it; and it was only natural that one of these cur-rents, the negative one, should start a new development in Russia.

The uncleanness of sexual life finds its expression in the ritual uncleanness of woman after childbearing or during her menstruations. Following the example of the Old Testament and of the purification of Mary as described in Luke 2:22, the Church considers the woman unclean for forty days after childbearing. On the fortieth day the mother and the child must be presented in the Church where they receive a special prayer of purification. "The mother after the birth shall not enter the church for forty days," confirms Kirik (K 42). "When a woman gives birth to a child it is forbidden for others to eat with her," cautions the *Precept* (P 62). The house (or the room) where the mother gives birth is unclean; it is forbidden to enter it for three days; afterward it is purified by the same prayer that is said over an unclean vessel (K 46). If the mother is unclean how can the child suck her breast? The question was natural and it was offered to the Metropolitan John II. The answer was liberal but provisional: "If there is no wet-nurse during the forty days when the mother is unclean, may the infant suck its mother so that it may not die without food? Better

is it to keep it alive than to kill it by exaggerated abstinence."
(J 2)

Menstruation makes the woman unworthy not only to communicate (this canon is so well known that it is not even mentioned in Russian questions), but even to eat blessed bread (*antidor*), to kiss the Gospels, or to enter the Church (K-Sabbas 23).

More indulgent is the Russian practice toward the woman suffering from "whites" (leucorrhoea). As the disease is a lasting one, the strictness of ritual canons would condemn an innocent woman to a complete separation from the Church. All sacred acts forbidden to women for certain days each month are permitted to the ill one, even participation in the Holy Communion if the illness has lasted "one year or half a year." (K 45)

In the matters of physiological uncleanness woman is at such a disadvantage compared with man that the corollary was always tempting to consider her a being naturally unclean. Reading Russian canonical documents one comes to the surmise that the famous belief in the inferiority of woman was gradually developed in Russia more out of the idea of ritual uncleanness than out of the considerations of her moral weakness. One of the most famous questions of Sabbas, the Novgorod priest, has this general idea for its premise: "If a piece of woman's cloth happens to be sewed into the vestment of a priest, is it legitimate to celebrate in this vestment?" The witty bishop answers with a cross-question: "Is woman impure?" Here Niphont hits exactly the underlying idea of his priest.

The sexual uncleanness which is merely physical in later cases has a moral aspect as well; having wide implications, it can easily be regarded as morally impure. Very often we are not able to discriminate which side, physical or moral, is uppermost. The Russian priests treat young unmarried men with particular suspicion. Chastity for them is out of the question. The canonical writer silently assumes that they are living in a state of incontinence. For this reason they ask the questions that are puzzling for a modern reader: whether bachelors may enter the Church, kiss the Gospel, and so on. Niphont orders that they are not to be removed from the common worship and even allows them to communicate at Easter, provided they have practiced abstinence during the whole period of Lent (K 67, 63). There is, however, some disagreement among the manuscripts on this point (K-Sabbas 5). The later copyists or redactors felt more scruples in exposing the Holy Cross and other sacred things to the kiss of the impure lips.

Merely physical, however, is the uncleanness resulting from disease or wounds, such as blood flowing from the teeth or a malodorous sore. It is noteworthy that the bishop admits a man with sores to the communion with wise discrimination: "It is not fetidness which separates man from the Holy, nor that which issues out of the mouth of certain people, but the fetidness of sins" (K 64). Yet, the same Niphont excludes from the Chalice the laymen (not the priests) with blood running from the teeth, "that they should not be too negligent" (K 62).

Quite apart from the ritual prescriptions connected with the cultual worship stands out a strange canon of the *Precept:* "If anyone urinates towards the East [the penance is] three hundred prostrations" (P 115). Here, without any Christian disguise, we have an ancient Pythagorean rule with the East taking the place of the Sun. The sense of the previous rule, reverence for the Sun (Helios), now becomes generalized. The East is considered as the side of God or Christ who was so often identified with the Sun as the "Sun of Justice." Ritual prescription in this case preserves its natural, pre-Christian character.

It is difficult to exhaust all the rich ritualistic content of the Russian canonical documents. Yet, before drawing any premature conclusions as to the national religious attitude which they are supposed to reflect, we are obliged to make some critical remarks. The tendency to gross exaggeration in the matters of ritual purity is obvious on the part of the Novgorod priests, and the anonymous authors of the *Precept* and other "bad Nomocanons." This tendency is restrained by the bishops of Novgorod and Kiev. The bishops themselves are not quite free from ritualistic preoccupations, but they sharply oppose unjustified local customs. The metropolitan of Kiev is a Greek; the bishop of Novgorod is a man well acquainted with the Greek ecclesiastical customs and he himself refers to them (K-Sabbas 4). Their ritualism is that of the Byzantine Church. They insist strongly upon the practice of the Great, that is, the Constantinopolitan Church. They forbid, for example, the eating of strangled things, but make no discrimination between the clean and the unclean animals. One is forced, therefore, to acknowledge in all the elaborate accretions of purity laws a specific Russian development.

Does it mean that it was the influence of the masses of the Russian folk, of the newly-converted Slavs and Finns who did not yet abandon their pagan manner of life? The answer would be negative. In forbidding them to eat the meats of animals killed by beasts rather than by man, Metropolitan John II enjoins: "Follow the [canon] law rather than the custom of the country" (J 3). Indiscrimination in eating food was, then, the custom in Russia. It is also hardly thinkable, and contradicts all the evidence of our sources, that the heathen Russian had a chaste abhorrence of the acts of sex. But then it means that the ritualism of purity could not be the creation of the Russian people in general, or reflect their national trend in religion. The only possible conclusion is that it was the creation of a particular class of people which defended and developed it: the middle clergy, the priests,— in particular those of the priests who bore the duty of penitential guidance under the name of "spiritual or penitential fathers" (*dukhovnik* or *pokayanny otets*). They represented the most zealous, though not always the most learned, part of the clergy. They accepted with enthusiasm the teaching of the Greek Mother Church, represented in Russia by the translated Canon Law and by some Greek prelates at the Russian bishops' sees. The tendency of overrating the ritual side of religion, common to any semibarbarian society, was sharpened for them by the necessity of the continuous war against the pagan customs and survivals. Theology and moral instruction were not the most effective weapons in this war. Custom against custom, rite against rite, the line between Christianity and heathendom had constantly to be distinguished. Behind the religious fears of impurity proper to Russian canonists the acuity of their struggles and of their polemics can be felt.

Nevertheless, being Russian themselves, bearing in their blood the religious instincts of their nation, they could not help undergoing the impact of the national religious mind. This impact is seen in the very choice of the objects of their negation. What they have in common with their people whom they oppose is the physiological approach to religion. While it is unbelievable that the heathen Slav could have the same religious aversion against bodily uncleanness, one can guess that he sought the approach to the divine through sensual functions. Sexual life must have been the most sacred sphere for him. Coming from hypotheses to historical facts we find that from early Christian times to the present, the Russian has been finding his way to God through the bodily senses, all five of them; not only through sight by means of icons, and hearing by means of the Church chant, but also through touch by kissing, smell by means of incense, cypress, and mother-of-thyme, and taste by sacred bread, water, and all kinds of consecrated food. In all these things the Hellenistic-Byzantine tradition was greatly enriched and developed in Russia, particularly since the Mongolian conquest. The awareness of the divine in consecrated sensual objects has its negative correlate in the acute sense of the desecration of impurity. The negative side of the Russian physiological religion was expressed earlier in historical documents, and probably in the Church life itself. The positive practices developed gradually without drawing much attention, because they met with no protest.

The influence of the clergy upon the newly-converted people was not limited to the lessons of ritualism. In his preaching and through the sacrament of penance, in his role of "spiritual father," the priest had to inculcate the general Christian virtues, the chief among them being charity, though with what success he taught them is another question which we reserve for one of our subsequent chapters. Dwelling now on the problem of religious ritualism we have to search our sources to acquire the clearest possible idea to what extent the lessons of ritualism were assimilated by the lay society in Kievan Russia. Here an important distinction must be made between high society and the masses.

For the masses which lived with half-pagan customs and world-outlook, any kind of Christian ritualism is out of the question. They did not observe the minimum of rites which would be held necessary in any Christian society. The same Metropolitan John II who insisting upon the prohibition against unclean food called the eating of the unclean food "the custom of the country" (J 3), bears witness that the ecclesiastical blessing of marriage was not in use among the simple folk: "You say the marriages of the simple folk are not blessed nor wed, but only boyars and princes are wed, and the simple people take their wives like concubines with dances, music, and noise." The Metropolitan considers such marriages as fornication, and prescribes a corresponding penance (J 30). This was, of course, a pious wish. Were it to be followed, the result would be the exclusion from the Church sacraments of the overwhelming mass of the Russian people. We know that the situation disclosed by John lasted until the sixteenth century. In the extreme north of Russia where churches and priests were rare, the peasants used to live without the sacramental wedding even in the twentieth century. In the eleventh century even bigamy existed as a remnant of heathen times (J 6).

Concerning the sacrament of the Communion and the observation of fasts, John's inquirer complains that "there are people in the border lands of Russia who do not communicate and who eat meat in Lent and unclean food" (J 5). John orders them to be removed from the Holy Communion—an act, which obviously only perpetuates the existing conditions, and proclaims them "adversaries of our faith." Even the usual attendance of Church on Sundays and feast days was not a general rule then as it became in a later period. Some preachers complain that the churches are empty; that, instead of going to the service, people hurry to their amusements, preferring to dance or watch, or listen to jugglers and minstrels (*skomorokhi*).

Not only in the borderlands but even in Novgorod, the second largest city of Russia, women did not shrink, as we know, from bearing their sick children to a heathen volkhv or to a Roman priest. All these facts entirely exclude the possibility of viewing the religion of simple folk in Kievan Russia in the light of later Muscovite ritualism.

High society in Kiev was certainly devoted to the Church and manifested its sincere Christian mind on every possible

occasion. The chronicles of this period witness the piety of
the princes and their boyars. Most of them had their private
or palace chaplains or chose as their spiritual father some
abbot known for the holiness of his life. But in this completely Christianized society one cannot find any trace of the
exaggerated ritualism of Kirik's type. Prince Vladimir
Monomach, of whose profound devotion to the Church there
is no doubt, in the *Admonition* to his sons does not give any
suggestion of a ritualistic kind: he does not even expect from
his sons the daily attendance of Church service, and for their
domestic devotion he gives them not the obligatory patterns
of the prayer book but short prayers of his own inspiration.

As we know, the intermarriage of the Russian princes
with the princely families of western Europe, forbidden by
the Metropolitan John II and other canonists, was extremely
frequent in that period. Less frequent, but not rare, were
marriages with daughters of the heathen Polovtsian khans.
In the last case the baptism of the bride was, of course, a
preliminary condition. But these friendly relations with the
Polovtsi required social intercourse, including the common
banqueting which is, in fact, confirmed by the evidence in the
Chronicles.

There are, however, some signs that the lessons of ritual
ism gradually began to find a more open ear in the princely
circles of Kievan Russia. Such a sign is the part taken by some
Russian princes in the disputes concerning fast days that
troubled the Russian Church in the second half of the twelfth
century. The issue, in itself, seems of small importance.
The Russians wondered whether they had to fast on Wednesdays and Fridays when these days fell on great Church
festivities, Christmas, Epiphany, and so on. In the Greek
Church, unfortunately, the local practice varied, and the
Russian clergy had to go their own way. The general Russian custom in the twelfth century was more "liberal" than

the Greek: in Russia the fast was abolished on all great feast days. Two Russian bishops, both of the city of Rostov, undertook the reform of these fast rules. One of them, Nestor, wished to bring his diocese nearer the Greek practice; Leo, going beyond that, required the strict fast on every Wednesday and Friday, regardless of what feast might fall on them. In the eyes of the chronicler who dislikes Bishop Leo for the spoliation of the clergy, this was the "Leonian heresy." Prince Andrew Bogoliubsky, probably stimulated by the clergy, proceeded very energetically against his bishops. He removed Nestor, although the patriarch of Constantinople took the side of the latter. Leo was condemned in Greece; his removal from his see by the prince is less surprising. For the same reason, and at the same time, in 1168, the prince of Chernigov deposed his bishop Anthony, who "forbade the prince to eat meat at the dominical feasts."

In all these cases the opinion of the Russian clergy and of the chroniclers supports the drastic action of the princes. How fanatically these issues were considered by the Russian clergy is shown by the events in Kiev. Metropolitan Constantine II, the Greek, confined the abbot Polycarp of the Cave Cloister in 1167 for following the Russian fast practice. The next year when Kiev underwent the ghastly sack by the troops of Prince Andrew, the chronicler explains this disaster as the punishment "for our sins and for the Metropolitan's injustice," which he finds in the suspension of the Abbot Polycarp (Lavr. 1168). Under these circumstances the actions of the princes, far from being the evidence of their ritualism, could be understood as a concession to the national clergy against the Greek prelates or the Greek practice.

A curious reflection, not exactly of ritualism, but of the physiological religious approach, can be found in the canonical ordinance of Prince Vladimir I. Among the transgres-

sions which are attributed to the jurisdiction of the ecclesiastical courts is one, called in Russian *zuboiazha*. The literal
meaning of this word is "tooth eating" or biting. The crime
consists in biting a man in anger or in fighting. Why, of all
kinds of physical injuries this one is selected as a religious sin
becomes clear from the point of view of food impurity. Biting human flesh approaches cannibalism. Of all kinds of
prohibited meats human flesh is, certainly, the most defiling.
Biting is not eating; but if the striking of eggs against the
teeth is equivalent to breaking the fast, then biting may be
punished as though it were eating.

That this ritualistic refinement could find its place in the
law of the first Christian prince is rather astonishing. But
the origin of Vladimir's ordinance is much disputed. Most
of the scholars of the nineteenth century denied its belonging
to the time of Vladimir. In spite of Professor Iushkov's
recent attempt to defend this dating, the later origin of this
particular item, if not of the ordinance itself, appears more
likely.

VIII

THE RELIGION OF THE LAITY: THE TRANSLATED COLLECTIONS

*T*HE types of Russian piety which have been examined thus far belong to the religion of the spiritual elite and the clergy. Monasticism, in spite of its liability for moral degeneration, reflects the radical religious ideal, the attempt to achieve Christian perfection at the price of total sacrifice. But what was the way of salvation for the multitude, the mass of sincere but nonheroic Christians who had to combine their loyalty to Christ and the Church with loyalty to family, state, and society?

The average man under discussion is not necessarily a middle-class man; his definition has to do with spiritual and not with social characteristics. As a matter of fact, the average Christian available for this kind of investigation is for the most part one of the upper class. Christianity in Kievan Russia was spreading among the people from above, downward from princes' palaces and boyars' houses. The sons of the nobles, we are told, were the first pupils in Prince Vladimir's schools; the boyars were the first readers of ecclesiastical literature, the first audience of the Church preachers. Underneath, Christianity was still struggling with paganism or its remains. On the top of society its victory was secured and it could promulgate its demands upon the individual morals and ways of life.

As sources for the investigation of this middle religious standard we can use: 1) numerous short admonitions which

fill the content of the so-called *Isborniki* (collections);
2) sermons or epistles designed for the laymen; 3) a few
works by lay authors; 4) the *Chronicles*.

Isborniki or collections of short "articles" and excerpts of
various content, constituted at all times a favorite reading of
ancient Russia. Satisfying the practical religious needs of
the readers, they served more for edification than for theoretical knowledge. Their content was not fixed; their
authorship uncertain. Most of the articles were ascribed to
great church fathers—John Chrysostom, Basil, Gregory, and
others. In many cases these venerable names were but a
covering for unknown Slavic or Russian compilers. The de-
limitation of Greek, Slavonic (Old Bulgarian or Moravian),
and Russian contributions is a difficult, though very important, task. Only in rare cases the Greek originals can be
determined. As a rule, even this part belongs either to the
anonymous or to the *spuria* department of the Patrology.
Very often this literature was inspired by the great authors
or represented popular restatements of their work. The
exposition is usually sustained at such a low level that it is impossible to distinguish Greek translations from Russian
originals by their contents, especially if the third element,
the Old Bulgarian one, is a possible source. After a century
of philological research very little progress has been made
in the distinction between Greek, Bulgarian, and Russian
contributions within this anonymous literature.

Under such conditions it seems daring to use these
Isborniki as a source for the study of the Russian mind.
Certainly in the course of time all this material, whatever
its origin, was russified. It went into the blood of the Russian people; it shaped their moral and religious life in the
Muscovite period. But during the Kievan period one can
not be so dogmatic. Undoubtedly this literature represented
a challenge to the young Christian society in Russia. But

challenge is not a response. This material can therefore be used only as a background for purely Russian productions, depending upon the delicate task of distinguishing the slight nuances between the Greek and the Russian lines of thought.

Dealing with the authentic Russian documents, one is pleasantly struck by an emotional energy behind the poor theological frame; by vital religious power; sometimes by a picturesque expression. But these Russian works of religious content are very scanty. Besides those already examined, only one pre-Mongolian sermon by Lucas Zhidiata is preserved, plus a few letters by monks and bishops to their spiritual sons: the letter of James to Prince Demetrius, of George of Zaruba to an unknown; also two letters or written sermons by the Metropolitan Nicephorus, who was a Greek. In this group of popular clerical authors can be included Daniel the abbot, author of an interesting description of a pilgrimage to the Holy Land. He is the representative of an average, although not strictly laic, religious mind.

Aside from the famous *Tale of Prince Igor,* two secular authors are known of this age: Prince Vladimir Monomach and a certain Daniel nicknamed the "Exiled." The first, one of the most worthy and powerful among Iaroslav's descendents, left to his sons a religious and political testament, a kind of Russian *Mirror for Princes,* rich in concrete rules of conduct and full of emotional overtones. Daniel wrote to his prince pleading for his benevolence a long missive full of bookish "wisdom" of a rather satirical tendency. Lighthearted as he is, he plays with the same Graeco-oriental maxims of life which had for others an extremely serious salvation value.

Finally, the Russian *Chronicles,* although composed mostly by the clergy have, with their rich political experience and documentation, a double value for the research of our kind. First, they reflect the religious and moral ideal of the

Russian Church as applied to the political life in an inevitable moderation or laicization of its standards; and second, they show in what measure the life—at least of high society—conformed to the standards.

Finding a way through the confused literature of admonitions, exhortations, and so on, one is at first quite lost among the commonplaces piled up without any visible system or central idea. Yet, reading over and over again one begins to grasp the thread. All the detailed rules and prescriptions can be divided into a few general categories. The so-called *Hundred Chapters* of Pseudo-Gennadius might serve as a general introduction. It is a pseudepigraph of unknown origin, which was the favorite religious compendium (a *Summa* in a dozen pages) in Russia until the breakdown of the old Muscovite civilization. Though I believe this work is Greek in origin, it began its Russian career very early, as is proved by its preserved copy dating from the eleventh century and an abridgement from the twelfth century. Far from considering it as the expression of Russian Christianity at this time we rather see in it the challenge, the standard of the Greek Church and its clergy in Russia, offered to the Russian layman.

It starts with a summary of dogmatic doctrine in eleven articles which has very little in common either with the Nicene creed or with theological confessions of high Byzantinism of Hilarion's type. The two first articles deal with the mysteries of the Trinity and Incarnation. But, instead of passing over to the redemptive work of Christ, Gennadius enumerates the other objects of veneration: the Mother of God, the Cross of Christ, the icons, the saints, the relics, and the Eucharist. This is logical, because the accent is not upon a doctrinal but upon a practical religious attitude—not "I believe" but in imperative form: "believe" (thou must believe), "invoke," "venerate," "pray," "kiss," "commun-

icate." Coming to the Nicene symbol in the last article—
the Resurrection of the dead—Gennadius is not contented
with simply describing it, but enlarges it with the idea of the
Last Judgment: "Remember the Judgment; expect to answer and receive retribution according to thy deeds; and believe that it will be so." One feels that this is the most vital
part of the dogmatic creed.

Yet this creed is only an introduction to the practical code
of Christian life which is the main content of the *Hundred
Chapters.* There is a certain order in their arrangement and,
trying to discover it, one comes to a very important conclusion. All the multifarious religious and moral precepts
of this booklet can be summarized under two great headings:
the Fear of God and Love. What is still more important,
one draws the same general observation from the study of
hundreds of short treatises or fragments which constitute the
main bulk of Russian literature. Be they of Greek, Slavic
(Bulgarian), or Russian origin, they are centered around
these two ideas: *Phobos* and *Agape*, fear and love. In many
a treatise a third element may be added which follows an extensive development on Russian soil, the liturgy and ritual.
But even this group of precepts, from the theoretical point of
view, can be conceived as the extension of the fear of God
to the practical sphere of worship. Fear and love, always
together, regulate the religious life of the average Christian
in Russia, though in an unequal measure. The preponderance
of either of them gives the best gauge for classification of
the material, the simplest and most obvious demarcation between the different currents of Russian religious life and
mind lies here. In many cases, however, the bias is too slight
to justify a definite choice. One can say that the equipoise
of fear and love is, in itself, the characteristic of ancient
Russian Christianity up to the Muscovite period. If all the
literary material had already been sifted with regard to its

national origin and its chronological data, the history of the Russian religious mind would be an easier task. Thus far only a general impression can be communicated that in monuments of Russian (or Bulgarian) origin, love is more emphasized than in Greek-Byzantine literature, where fear more often dominates. One must not overgeneralize this observation, nor forget Saint John Chrysostom on the Greek side and Cyril of Turov on the Russian.

Returning to the *Hundred Chapters* of Pseudo-Gennadius, it is obvious that here the idea of fear dominates, although love, in the detailed caritative rules, occupies no small place. Nearer to fear than to love, it gives to love enough place to have become a kind of practical catechism in Russia for seven centuries.

Gennadius begins his moral catechism in chapters twelve and thirteen with the double evangelical commandment: the love of God and of one's neighbor. One often finds this commandment, as is natural, at the threshold of such expositions. But the author cannot proceed further after the principle of love towards God and in the fourteenth chapter he substitutes fear of God for love of Him. The reason is obvious: love towards God in Christian ethics can have only two meanings: either the mystical Eros, in the Platonic-Augustinian sense, or the love for Christ, as God-man or Jesus. The first idea is rare in Byzantium and quite unknown in pre-Mongolian Russia; the second is the spiritual property of the few, such as Theodosius. For the average man the fear of God is the only possible attitude towards Him. Fear can immediately become the cornerstone of ethics as in the fifteenth chapter of Gennadius: "With the fear of God, as with a bridle, restrain your mind, keeping a watch on yourself every hour." As love cannot exist except totally and the love of men is the necessary corollary of the love of God, so is it with fear, inasmuch as fear becomes the basic principle of

religion. The fear of men arises immediately out of the
fear of God, and the author continues in sixteen, without
transition: "Bow your head to everybody senior to you . . .;
fear the prince with all your power . . . from him you will
learn how to fear God . . . Who does not fear the earthly
lord how will he fear Him whom he does not see?" This
is an obvious hint to and distortion of the Johannine doctrine
of love (I John: 4, 20). Descending to a still lower level
in twenty-two: "A pupil fears the master's cudgel more than
the master himself," with the tacit implication that the tsar
is naturally more feared than God. It is not only the tsar or
prince to whom one owes the salutary fear, but all higher
members of the social hierarchy. "After them, bow your
head with humility before every rich man." "Those who
have received power and fortune from their tsar require
glory also from their friends and demand veneration from
minors" (23). It is obvious that this conception of fear has
nothing in common with the Old-Testament idea of God's
fear. In the prophetic religion of Israel fear of God frees
one from the fear of man. Neither Judaistic nor Evangelical, this conception is purely Byzantine. It presupposes
harmonious correspondence between the Kingdom of God
and the kingdom of this world. One could conceive of it as
the social extension of the dogma of icon-veneration which is
so essential to Byzantine piety. The tsar is, as it were, the
living icon of God, just as the whole orthodox Empire is the
icon of the heavenly world. This is the idea underlying
Eastern theocracy.

It is true that this whole theocratic monism is contradicted
by another mighty religious idea: the ascetic negation of the
world. In the same *Hundred Chapters* of Pseudo-Gennadius there are six chapters treating secular glory: "Do not
wish secular glory in anything. . . . If the glory of this world

were near the glory of heaven the sons of this world would
not have crucified the Lord of Glory; what slave will dare
dwell in that house where his Lord was not acknowledged?"
And even more: "Thou must like dishonor as the cup of
wormwood. . . . Whoever holds the faith loves dishonor."
Here Desert and Empire are in the sharpest collision in the
pages of the same moral catechism. Of this the author was
hardly aware, writing as he did by the method of excerpts.
In the practice of Byzantium, as well as of Russia, the reconciliation was not too difficult. One was not to love the world
with its glory, but, once having entered the world, one had
to accept all its hierarchical structure. Radical asceticism does
not try to change the world, it simply flees from it. As to
the love of humiliation, it is for heroic saints ("holy fools").
An average Christian did not have to bother about this paradoxical ideal. The author himself could not take it very
seriously.

The fear of God specified and qualified embraces one
dark hemisphere of Christian virtues: obedience, humility,
repentance, and mortification. But one must be cautious in
this classification. The same virtue can have quite a different
religious and moral value; all depends on the general context and motivation.

As for obedience, Gennadius has no special chapters on
it because he covers it under the rubric of fear. It occurs to
the student of ancient Russian literature at every step, very
often in a strengthened or redoubled form, as "obedience
and submission." Some of the students even saw in this
emphasis, quite wrongly, the characteristics of the most ancient period of Russian Christianity. In fact, obedience is
much more stressed in later periods, beginning with the fourteenth century. With Theodosius, with Boris and Gleb, it
has a different meaning. At first, it is the extension of love:

"love and obey each other." Both Theodosius and Prince Boris in his obedience to his senior brother repeat: "There is no fear in love: for the perfect love casteth out fear." (I John 4:16) Secondly, obedience in the same saints has the kenotic value of the imitation of Christ who was "obedient even unto death" (Philippians 2:8).

Humility, the most ambiguous among Christian virtues, has the same double value. The consciousness of one's sins is common both to the religion of fear and the religion of kenosis. But in the first it is enhanced by the feeling of the abysmal distance between God and man; in the second it is, on the contrary, an expression of nearness to the incarnate God. Kenoticism lightens the consciousness of sin and makes it bright and sweet as the yoke of Christ. Socially, in kenoticism, humility means a kind of descending love; in the *Phobos* religion humility very often means an interested attitude of self-preservation or, at its highest, an ascetic self-denial. In the eclectic Gennadius one finds all these motivations: "A worm is very humble and base, and you are glorious and proud; but if you are sensible, you yourself should humiliate your pride by meditating: 'my strength and my force become a shelter for worms' " (57): the worm's distance from man symbolizes man's abysmal distance from God. "Meekness means not to annoy anyone either in words or deeds or commands, but to please every man by one's behavior" (32): that is, social adaptation or servility. "Do not say, 'I am the son of a rich man and poverty is a shame for me'; nobody is richer than Christ, your heavenly Father, who begot you in the holy fonts and had walked in poverty with nowhere to incline His head" (25): in other words, kenoticism.

The social projection of humility is emphasized in external behavior, in a system of gestures ranging from reserve to abjectness, and which constitute the true Byzantine ideal of social decency. "Have a meek gait, a meek sitting, a meek glance" (31), demands the Pseudo-Gennadius; and the Pseudo-Basilius joins him in an exhortation, always very popular in Russia, for "the lowering of the voice, the eating and drinking without shouting and with moderation, silence before old people . . . not to argue in speaking, not to laugh easily . . . to hold the eyes low and the soul high." A certain father, whom some erroneously believe to be a Russian author, writes in a still more popular admonition to his son, "My son, be low of head but high in spirit, hold your eyes to the earth and your spirit to heaven, your lips closed, but your heart crying always to God, your feet walking slowly, but your spiritual steps running fast to the gate of heaven." . . . Here the ideal of social manners is deepened into a spiritual conception.

The monastic origin of this educational standard is obvious. Yet in Byzantium as well as in later, Muscovite Russia, it was imposed upon the laity with some success. The Byzantine standard of decency has maintained its sway in Orthodox Russia up to the present day. It is clear how dangerous this standard of social humiliation without true humility may become. Hypocrisy and abjectness install themselves immediately in the empty place. On the other hand, one is not justified in supposing hypocrisy wherever exterior humbleness is found. It would be particularly unfair to ancient Russia which took humility quite seriously.

Equally serious was the need of mortification, particularly in the *Phobos* religion. In the tracts designed for laymen the only generally enforced kind of asceticism is fasting. Its chief aim is the taming of flesh and the killing of will, as in Pseudo-Gennadius: "Inasmuch as you do harm to your body you tame it, and you build grace in your soul." (41) "Dry up your blood with dry food" (42) is a familiar ascetic ideal,

now offered as an aim for every layman. The motivation
vacillates. The same author on the same page advances, side
by side, as the grounds for fasting, first the will of Christ,
then the imitation of martyrs; and, more naturally, the two
ideas based on the fear-complex: "The heavenly Judge will
retribute what one has suffered for him" (41). The heavenly King likewise expects from man a clean house: "You know
that those who invite the Emperor [to visit them] clean their
home. So you, if you want to introduce God into your bodily
home for illuminating your life, must sanctify your body by
fast; exhaust it by thirst . . ." The roots of Christian asceticism are multifarious, especially as developed in monastic
spirituality. But for the laity the Judge and King motives
are predominant and even sufficient.

Repentance, like humility, can have a double origin: fear
and the love of perfection. Both motives can coincide, and
do coincide, in practically any man's life which does not exclude the predominance of either. In all its nuances, repentance is one of the mightiest forces of Russian devotion, even
as it was with the Byzantine Greeks. For monks it could be
considered the main purpose of their vocation.

Repentance motivated by fear often involves the idea
of death. The remembrance of death is considered of great
educational value. The anonymous "father" writing to his
son insists: "My child, recollect death always, and death will
teach you all the good, [and] how you are to live in this short
space of life." The Pseudo-Gennadius even suggests visiting of the dying as a practical way to repentance: "It is a very
profitable means for repentance and tears—visiting the dying. Who would not have compunction seeing his own nature descend into the grave and his name become extinct and
the glory of the rich turned into putrescence?" The short-
ness of life and the corruption of all things is naturally one

of the frequent themes of admonitions. The "father" begins his introduction with this theme: "Let us think a little, my son, what a multitude of men have lived on earth from Adam, our forefather, up to our age,—and all of them died and are forgotten . . ." Of the saints alone is memory preserved in glory.

That fear is not the only fountainhead of repentance is proved by the insistence on tears. Since the end of the fourth century in Egypt, and particularly in Syria, tears of repentance and of prayer were considered a much-appreciated *charisma*. The grace of tears is a sign of inward contrition and of warm and sincere prayer. In the course of ages this ascetic grace became generalized and was considered an element necessary to every prayer. Pseudo-Gennadius, writing for the laymen, holds tears an obvious condition of repentance and gives practical suggestions for acquiring this grace:

> If you have no tears, do not despair; sigh frequently and heavily from all the heart: for tears are the gift of God, and by and by, with sighs and prayers you will obtain them from God . . . (50) Having found a secluded place, sit down and meekly remember your sin and your desertion of the Kingdom, enter into contrition of heart and mind and body; bow your head and speak with moaning: "Woe is to me, that my exile has been prolonged . . . Who will give water to my head and tears to my eyes?" (49) Having found tears, preserve them with all your strength. (51)

Tears must accompany not only the private home prayers. The "father" recommends them also in the church. "Every day go to church; fall down before the most High; shed tears; cover the ground with your face; and force Him to have mercy upon you."

The admonitions concerning prayer, in general, exclude every idea of a mechanical performance. Fear is no adequate motive of prayer, although it can be an initial phase. Gennadius discloses a deep understanding of prayer as a spiritual nourishment, as the condition of spiritual life.

> The praying spirit is the light of the soul. . . . Do not refuse prayer—food of the soul. As the body suffers and grows weak deprived of food so the soul, deprived of the sweetness of prayer, approaches its spiritual death.

Prayer itself leads to practical worship and cult regulations. In the religion of the fear of God, ritual law is bound to claim primary importance. Worship is the active practical expression of the devotion toward God and the more this devotion bears the "numinous" character, based upon the fear before the Transcendent and Unfathomable, the more meticulous and zealous is man in conforming to the imposed rules in his intercourse with this transcendent God. The rules of worship represent a special group of counsels in the literature of the *Collections*. They represent ecclesiastical requirements addressed by the Church to the new Christian society in Russia. They insist upon continual attendance of Church; Xenophon requires three times a day: in the morning, at noon, and in the evening. Theodora suggests prayers at the third, sixth, and ninth hours, besides Matins and Vespers, but this can be understood as home prayers. The tendency is clear—to impose upon laymen the full monastic circle of prayer. The Greek Church, indeed, in the course of centuries, extended the monastic liturgy to all the laity. The Russian *Euchologion* (Prayerbook) became the most common book to every one who was initiated into the art of reading, whereas the corresponding *Breviary* of the Roman Church remained limited to monastic and priestly use.

The *Hundred Chapters* contain no liturgical precepts. But consistent with their general authoritative trend, they conclude with injunctions of reverence towards the clergy:

bishops, priests, even deacons and minor clerics. Especially recommended for such observance are the monks: one is instructed to salute every monk on the road, to visit convents —even those afar, "situated on mountains"—and to bring them material provision in exchange for spiritual food (98-99). The acquaintance with their "order and statute" can help one in improving his own life. The same reverence for monks is enjoined by nearly all the authors of admonitions. It must be admitted that the foundation of it is not merely liturgical (as with clerics), but spiritual and moral. Especially in the *Admonition of the Father to his Son* the monastery is described as the home of spiritual refuge and monks as the best spiritual advisers.

I show you, my son, true refuges—monasteries, the houses of the saints: have recourse to them and they will comfort you; shed your sorrows before them and you will be gladdened: for they are sons of sorrowlessness and know how to comfort you, sorrowing one . . . In the city where you are living or in other neighboring towns seek a God-fearing man—and serve him with all your strength. Having found such a man, you need grieve no more; you have found the key to the Kingdom of Heaven; adhere to him with soul and body; observe his life, his walking, sitting, looking, eating, and examine all his habits; first of all, my son, keep his words, do not let one of them fall to the ground; they are more precious than pearls— the words of the saints.

Here one can grasp the origin of the institution of the monastic "spiritual fathers" for the laity which is so common in Russia. At the same time this fragment shows how akin was the layman's religious and moral ideal in Byzantium to that of the monk. The difference is in quantity rather than quality: the layman is a Christian of a second sort.

Fear and love are not mutually exchangeable; they are simply juxtaposed in moral treatises. In Pseudo-Gennadius caritative prescriptions occupy the second part of the work. The author's fine feeling for systematizing accounts for his attempt to connect these two religious orders by beginning the love duties not with those toward the living but toward the dead. In fact, his first precept of love is to follow any funeral procession one encounters to the grave. The doubly meritorious character of this act is explained: "You will receive two benefits: recalling on the occasion of his death the necessity of your own dying you will humble yourself, and, on the other hand, having pitied his body and entrusted it to the grave you yourself will be pitied." (59) This rule, strange as a precept of love, found a large response among the people of ancient Russia, to whom the duty of burying the poor was always one of the first moral commandments.

The other rules of Gennadius repeat, more or less, the commandments of the Gospels. In great detail he enumerates the duties towards the sick, the poor, prisoners, and wanderers. A particular virtue of persons of the upper class is shown in intercession for the innocent and the oppressed before the princes and judges, which in Russia was a duty and a privilege of the clergy. What is most important, the caritative ideal requires not merely the acts of charity, but also the corresponding state of mind—compassionate love. One is obliged not only to visit and to care for the sick: "when he is moaning from pain you must shed tears of compassion and sigh towards God about his woe." (61) The same is suggested by the "father" who is more concise in his caritative admonitions: "Feed the hungry . . . visit the sick and the imprisoned . . . and sigh seeing their distress . . ." Especially touching and picturesque are the social contrasts Gennadius used as stimuli to compassion:

When you are sitting at the manifold viands remember those eating stale bread not being able to fetch water because of their illness. . . . Enjoying various beverages, remember him who drinks warm water, heated by the sun and mixed with dust. . . . Lying on the downy bed and stretching your limbs, remember him lying on the bare earth under his rags not daring to move his leg because of the cold. . . .

It is a real litany of mercy worthy of Chrysostom, though its nearest literary source is to be sought in the life of Saint John Eleemosynarius, the patriarch of Alexandria (d. 619).

There are some Byzantine treatises in which charity obviously outweighs fear: such are the short admonitions under the names of Xenophon and Theodora to their sons. Both works extend the meaning of charity: it is not only compassion for the suffering, but love for all; peace with all men; the pardon of wrongdoers; the overcoming of envy. One is forbidden to enter the church if one bears wrath in his heart, still less to approach the Holy Communion, placing love, and the love to men, above the duty of worship, or supreme to one's duty towards God. This is a purely evangelic idea, shifting the scale of values based on fear.

The group of admonitions supposed to have a "father" or "parents" as their authors and addressed to the "sons," are the richest in formulating the concrete duties of family and social life. Here we find the rules for the education of children and the treatment of servants. It is interesting that the first are enjoined to be treated with more severity than the latter. The need of punishment, and especially of corporal punishment of one's sons, is emphasized as strongly as the need of mildness and carefulness towards slaves and serfs. The author takes into account the natural feelings of the paterfamilias and tries to check his weak points. But certain authors, like Xenophon, go so far as to recommend the liberation of the old slaves: "Love those who are in slavery; be merciful to the young and grant freedom to the old servants, giving them food until their death." Such counsels as this must have been very appropriate for a young Russian society living under the conditions of a slave economy. These domes-

tic admonitions, thanks to their practical character, enjoyed a
particular favor in Russia and gave birth to an original Russian literature of House or Father's Wisdom.

Among the ancient sermons in Russian literature a particular place belongs to the homilies for the Lenten period.
They served not for private but liturgical use, to be read
from the church chair, and maintained this authority for
seven centuries. They are transmitted under the name of
Chrysostom and are not unworthy of his inspiration. In fact,
they are most probably of Slavonic, Old Bulgarian, origin.
It is remarkable that, in spite of their Lenten designation
which would justify a more severe ascetic trend, they breathe
the spirit of love. The Gospel parables of the Pharisee and
the Publican, of the Prodigal Son, speak of the God of mercy.
The parable of the Last Judgment itself is menacing only to
the transgressors of the law of mercy. The last Sunday before Lent is dedicated in the Eastern Church to mutual pardon as a condition of the pardon of God. Even while pointing to the ascetic abstinence of food, the preacher goes immediately to the caritative precept:

Relieve your neighbor of his sorrow and forgive him his debt;
take no delight in suits and quarrels. Are you abstaining from meat,
but not from quarrel; have you given up supper but sit late at talk
blaming everybody?—No such fast have I chosen, says the Lord.

The false attribution of these Slavonic homilies to John
Chrysostom is not accidental. His name more frequently than
any other adorned native productions of the Russian or Slavic
pen.

This reduction of Christian lay ethics to the two categories of fear and love may appear somewhat artificial.
Actually, it corresponds to the fundamental dualism of
traditional Christian ethics. Fear and charity are the
two focal points of religious life. Between them is al-

ways a certain tension, an inward struggle of tendencies, each trying to incline the balance on its side. When the balance is broken, one of the two tries not to eliminate the other, but to interpret it in terms of itself. Thus, charity can be conceived merely as a command of divine law taken for granted without an inner understanding. In this instance charity is often degraded to alms, having in common with fasting the virtue of expiating sin. On the other hand, charity can also exploit fear to its own benefit. The example of Chrysostom is significant. He is far from the all-pardoning meekness or benevolence to all men. Being a radical moralist, he blends the preaching of charity to the poor with severe condemnation of the rich. This double tendency has its source in the Gospel itself where the parables of Dives and Lazarus and that of the Last Judgment are terrifying to the violators of love. Both parables, partly through Greek homilies, often under the same name of Chrysostom, made a deep impression in Russia and became later the most popular subjects of folksongs.

Our dualistic scheme is capable of removing humility into second place. That is why we have to emphasize its central position in the Byzantine and Russian religion. Situated, as it were, in the midst of fear and love, equidistant from both, it undergoes attraction from both sides and, consequently, may change its religious and moral meaning. It can be tinctured in colors of fear or love, but in moral implications the differences are leveled and the two kinds of humility support each other without even coming to a consciousness of their different origins.

Taking into consideration the general affinity of all Christian ethical systems, it sometimes is not only in the presence but also in the absence of certain elements that one can find specific characteristics of any one system. In our field the more neglected among Byzantine virtues are precisely those which are the most honored in the modern Anglo-Saxon world: purity and justice.

Some chapters in Gennadius on truth and on fasting, far from exhausting the content of these virtues, touch them only at the periphery. Suggesting that one must always speak the truth before the prince, Gennadius has in view the practical consequences of conduct rather than the love of truth for itself. Truth and justice are not identical, even though the Russian language, knowing how to differentiate them, possesses a common name for them (*pravda*) and likes to use it with an intuition of their essential unity, especially on the higher level of religious thought. No trace of this development is to be found in translated Greek treatises.

Since purity is essential as a condition of mystical contemplation, it was the main object of asceticism in the schools of Eastern platonizing monasticism. Without this relation to the mystical it loses its interest in Oriental ethics. The absence of mystical elements in ancient Russia corresponds to the underdevelopment of the purity-ethics in the translated literature as well.

Further on we shall see what aspects of these two feeble shoots took root on Russian soil. Here it is important to emphasize that the purity as well as the justice in their one-sided growth are often stained by pride. English puritanism gives a modern confirmation to the experience, well-known to the ancient Church. "Justice falls by arrogance; sin is destroyed by humility," is the sentence of Pseudo-Chrysostom, commenting upon the parable of the Pharisee and Publican. The religious system which considers pride as the supreme evil (Eastern Christianity) is naturally very cautious towards the virtues which can be the reverse of this worst vice. But, justice and purity alike have a great social value; even their partial neglect means a serious lack in social ethics which cannot be filled by charity alone. This was, in fact, the case in Byzantium and, in a lesser degree, in Russia. Yet one dares not forget that the depreciation of these Old-Testament values begins already in the Gospel with its severe polemics against the Pharisee—the just and pure one.

In contrast to what is generally said about Eastern Christianity, all these treatises and sermons are penetrated by a very active, practical spirit. They are designed for conduct, and not for edification alone; in that respect they remind one of moral codes rather than of meditations. In their Russian imitations these features are stressed still more. The awkward preachers preferred to give simple catalogues of vices and virtues rather than to omit some of them in developing general ideas. So this ethical ideal is, first of all, vital and practical. Whether it is true of Byzantium in the same measure as of Russia, is questionable. I rather doubt it, but in their choice within the Byzantine legacy, the Slavic and Russian translators manifested their practical world-outlook. The fear of God is embodied and shaped in meticulous precepts of worship and ascetic duties; the love of neighbors, in a detailed program of private and social charity. "Faith, apart from works, is dead." This remark of Saint James (2:26) runs through all of Russian religious literature and can be chosen as its motto.

This raises before us a problem, perhaps the greatest problem of Christian anthropology. How far was the might of sin and the need of grace for salvation realized by the Greeks and Russians? Here we can give no more than a hint to the problem, since we are studying it only in the frame of Russian literature. Nowhere in our sources is it treated systematically, but there are general theological premises which throw light upon the practical meaning of the doctrine of sin and grace in the religious and moral life.

One must keep in mind that the Augustinian doctrine

of the original fall which has determined the whole theological development of the Christian West, remained completely strange to and ignored by the Christian East. Not
one work of Augustine was translated in Greek. The Byzantine Church lived by the tradition of the ancient Greek
fathers, who saw the fatal consequence of Adam's fall in
his mortality and corruptibility rather than in the radical
moral depravation of human nature. Treating the issue
of the freedom of will, so essential in the apologetics against
gnosticism, the ancient fathers silently presupposed that
mankind is still preserving the same freedom of choice between good and evil that the first man possessed. That is
the viewpoint of Methodius of Olympus whose treatise
Περὶ αὐτοξουσίου —*On Freedom of Will* was translated
into Slavonic, together with the rest of the Corpus Methodia-
num. One cannot credit ancient Russia with a widespread
knowledge of this philosophical work, since it exists in only
one manuscript. But every Russian scholar knew and repeated
that man is "free" or "master of himself," *samovlasten,*
which is the Slavonic equivalent of αὐτοξούσιος. An exposition of faith, of Greek origin, preserved in a Russian
manuscript of the twelfth or thirteenth century, gives the
doctrine of the fall and redemption as follows: "Man was
created in the image of God, that is, free for better or worse."
As a consequence of his sin, "he was exiled from the richest
glory and paradisiac life; became subject to death and corruption and slave of the apostate (Satan)." After dwelling
at length on the mystery of incarnation and the two natures
in Christ, this creed very briefly describes the fulfillment of
Christ's redemptive work: "He was crucified and tasted
death, being sinless, and rose again; having not seen the corruption of His own flesh, He made mankind free from corruption, resuscitated it for immortality and raised it to
heaven."

It is obvious that the author of this confession saw re-demption in the first place as salvation from death and not from sin. Not only Saint Augustine remained unknown in Russia but even the Pauline theology of the Epistle to the Romans seems to have left no traces in Russian thought. At any rate, Saint Paul was not cited to counterbalance Saint James, with the latter's emphasis on good works. In this respect Russian theological outlook was perhaps still more moralizing and anti-Pauline than the Greek. There is one curious evidence of it. The *Questions and Answers* of Ana-stasius Sinaitas, very popular in Russia, begin with: "What is the sign of the true Christian?" The Slavonic translation gives a direct answer: "Orthodox faith and pious works." Now, looking at the original, one sees that the Greek father had some doubts concerning such a simple formula. The Greek text reads:

Some people say: the orthodox faith and pious works. But Jesus does not define a true Christian in this way. For a person can have both faith and good works, but can become elated by them and then not be a perfect Christian. For the Christian is the true home of Christ built with good works and pious dogmas.

Simplifying this passage the Slavonic translator does not betray the thought of the Greek author. In the last anal-ysis, faith and good works alone are essential to Anastasius also; and faith is understood as dogmas or beliefs. He does not introduce the idea of grace in his definition of the perfect Christian. He only wishes to prevent the classical formula from Pharisaic abuse. In this purpose the Slavic disciple stood on the same ground with his teacher. But he could not understand the theological scruples of the Greek and for practical reasons preferred the ambiguous formula, which indeed became a theological axiom in ancient Russia.

The western theologian is accustomed to style all anti-Augustinian theology as Pelagianism or semi-Pelagianism, charging it with religious shallowness and moral pride. Primitive Russian theology may indeed have been shallow, but the religious life was not; as to pride, it has already been remarked how far Eastern Christianity is from this danger. With humility as the central virtue and pride the supreme vice, the East escaped the potential dangers of the theology of free will. There has never been any noticeable difference between West and East in the evaluation of the sinful burden of mankind. Monastic asceticism in the East is by no means more optimistic than in the West. But the Eastern Christian's sins are entirely his own. He ascribes them to his own evil but free will, and does not impute them to fatal inheritance. This outlook is capable rather of increasing his sense of personal guilt and the acuteness of his repentance. He is aware of his ability not to sin and, at the same time, of his perpetual sinning. As to grace, he contemplates it, primarily, as the gift of divine pardon. Without this pardon he feels himself doomed forever. He hopes to obtain pardon by two ways: by his own prayers, his own pardoning or charity to other men; and by the sacraments of the Church which he considers mainly from this point of view. This means that the two leading sacraments for him are baptism and penance—not the Eucharist.

One can notice, besides, that the word "grace" in ancient Russian had no technical theological meaning, but was used rather in the sense of the general gifts of God. We have seen already that the greatest of Russian theological writers, Hilarion, employed this word not in the Pauline but in the Johannine sense. As to grace in the meaning of aid or assistance of God, it was believed not to be refused to anybody because the salvation "economy" of God embraces the whole of mankind. The idea of special vocation and of particular gifts was developed in Russia, as will be seen further on, in connection with the national rather than the personal life.

This system of Christian ethics for the use of laymen, as expounded in these Graeco-Slavonic treatises, admits of different levels of depths and different degrees of radicalism. Sometimes the moral precepts are given with a paradoxical point which springs from their evangelical or ascetic sources. The monastic inspiration is manifest in the *Hundred Chapters*. Such pointed form gives a "spiritual salt," even to common Christian commandments. Yet the same paradox of form lessens its practicability for average use, especially of a newly-converted barbarian nation. Therefore in Russian collections the plain, simple, and clear articles were generally preferred to the witty or profound ones. The commonplace subject matter was an advantage. Ancient Russia revelled in commonplaces, in the literature of adages which must have appeared to her as wisdom itself, not only far from boring but quite new and stimulating.

At this point an interesting observation may be made. The ethics of fear and love, purified of its paradoxical Christian refinements, is easily reduced to the Old-Testament level, not of the prophetic religion of Israel but of the so-called "Wisdom literature," which includes The Proverbs, Ecclesiastes, The Wisdom of Solomon, and The Wisdom of Joshua the son of Sirach. The last two are deutero-canonical books belonging to the later Hellenistic Judaism and not included in the Hebrew canon. But the Greek Church, as well as the Roman, did not make any difference between canonical and deutero-canonical books of the Old Testament. And thus, one observes in many a Slavic treatise on ethics the Old Testament or Sirach savor. Among the books of the Bible (the New Testament included) the most popular and most frequently quoted, after the Psalter, was the book of Sirach. Looking through some of the old

Russian collections, like that of Sviatoslav around 1076, one has a general impression of a predominant Old-Testament atmosphere. The Christian influence is manifested mainly in a particularly strong presentation of such virtues as humility and love. But as soon as the writer, teacher, or preacher tries to abbreviate or simplify his doctrine he reduces it to the Jewish measure: fear of God and love of neighbors. The "Wisdom" quotations confirm this "Wisdom" standpoint.

This taste for moral commonplaces, so strong in the ancient Russian society—found further spiritual food in a Byzantine anthology of moral quotations known under the title of *Bee* (Μέλισσα). Here the verses of the Bible which were predominant, were accompanied by sentences of the Fathers and, in conclusion, by a few quotations from Philo, Plato, Aristotle, and the Greek poets. The latter were the main source for the knowledge of the classical culture in ancient Russia. But it was quite natural that in order to bring forth unity out of this heterogeneous material, it had to be leveled to the common measure. And this measure was that of practical religious common sense as best embodied in the Wisdom literature.

It is unexpected and rather painful to discover that ancient Russia in its moral and social ideology was dependent more on Jesus Sirach than on Jesus Christ. But that is a general destiny of the Christian society. It cannot base its relative moral values on the absolute ideals of the Gospel and needs other norms of conduct, be it Aristotle, some other ancient "pagan" philosophy, or the Bible of the Jews. The book of Sirach (or Ecclesiasticus) was also popular in the Christian West. No lesser one than Saint Augustine made a larger use of it than of the Gospels in his Biblical excerpts for popular use (*Speculum*). The Gospel is too high for the ethics of this world. Yet it was not com-

pletely lost to ancient Russia. We have seen that it inspired the lives of the heroic few. Through their lives, and
more indirectly and obscurely, hidden as it were under the
liturgical veil, the Gospel really influenced and transformed
the life of society itself. But one is obliged to acknowledge
the very limited place of the Gospel among the teaching
literature, among what could be considered, in Russia, if
Russia knew this term, as *magisterium Ecclesiae.*

IX

THE RELIGION OF THE LAITY: THE RUSSIAN ADMONITIONS

*P*ASSING from the Byzantine patterns to their Russian imitations one is prepared to find the same fundamental rubrics. In fact, to the superficial glance original Russian works are little distinguished from the Greek. Fear of God and charity are still the two focal points. Yet closer examination, based on the general impression of the whole literary material, reveals the differences. They are differences in emphasis, in degrees rather than in ideas, but they are essential. They could be summarized under three headings: a certain warmth of tone, the predominance of the *Agape* motive over *Phobos*, and the greater development of liturgical and ritual prescriptions. Certainly there are different types on this lower religious level, corresponding to those, already studied, on the higher. But this is the general impression and, unfortunately, it must remain an impression only, lacking strict scientific proof until the whole of Russian manuscript literature is sifted and separated from the overwhelming mass of translations and Bulgarian works.

The significance of this impression is far-reaching. The warmth of tone is evidence of the deep sincerity of the reception of the new religion by the recently heathen people. Christianity speaks in them from heart and not from lips, not as a foreign book wisdom. The predominance of charity proves that Russia embraced Christianity, first of all, as a religion of love and not of law corroborated by threats.

228

That law was not absent is proved by a certain ritualistic trend, which is, however, much less developed than in the canonical documents concerning the clergy.

Let us now take for analysis, one after another, some ancient monuments of admonition literature.

THE SERMON OF LUCAS ZHIDIATA, BISHOP OF NOVGOROD

Lucas was the second bishop of Novgorod since 1036, and the first bishop of Russian origin in this city; some scholars have supposed him Jewish. His short and artless sermon belongs to the most ancient relics of Russian literature. On a single page the preacher endeavors to fix in the memory of his listeners or readers all the tenets of the Christian religion. No wonder his sermon becomes mostly a dry catalogue of precepts and prohibitions; what is amazing is that he sometimes succeeds in introducing a personal and even touching note.

He begins with the trinitarian confession of faith, referring to the Nicene creed which is supposed to be familiar to his listeners. Then immediately come the liturgical and prayer precepts: "Do not shirk going to Church for Matins, Mass, and Vespers." Having spoken about private prayer by night and about the fitting attitude for prayer in church, the preacher emphasizes charity and dwells on its specifications in most of his sermon. Here he is more personal and inventive. His idea of charity is much more than alms-giving or even compassion. "To have love towards every man" means also "to rejoice with the rejoicing" and to be sincere: "Be not one in heart and another in lips." The negative "not to condemn" finds its rather unexpected reverse in: "Praise one another that God also may praise you." It is only after these commands concerning charity that Lucas comes to speak about fear: "Remember that tomorrow thou willst be stench, pus, and worms." Among the rather confused list of commandments based upon the Decalogue with which the preacher hastens to the conclusion, one might notice: "Judge the judgments aright," addressed to the governors; and the ritualistic prescription: "Do not eat anything unclean."

If one is justified in drawing any conclusions out of so short a page, one may define Lucas' religious trend as based on charity, in its deep and serious meaning, with a slight but noticeable coloring of ritualism. It was observed by the literary historians that his style in its artlessness was typical of the northern, especially Novgorod Russia, as distinct from the richer, more cultivated and rhetorical South. Concerning Lucas' religious style, one cannot help regarding him as typical of the average Russian Christian in general. In Kiev we will find similar features.

THE MISSIVE OF THE MONK JAMES TO HIS SPIRITUAL SON DEMETRIUS

The date of this work as well as the person of the addressee are uncertain. Whereas most of the historians saw in him the prince Iziaslav Demetrius of Kiev (d. 1078), the last investigator, S. I. Smirnov, considers him a prince of Rostov of the thirteenth century. The style of the missive is marked by a rather severe tone and some attempts at a theological founding of morals. James writes to a repenting sinner, to a prince who, after some unknown transgression, proved his desire for reconciliation with his spiritual father by a humble and even pathetic letter. Unfortunately, the prince's letter is lost. His guide tries to use the favorable situation to enforce upon the sinner the precepts of Christian law without any indulgences or mitigations. "All angels in heaven rejoice in the repentance of one single man. ... But if the sin is overcome does it mean that we can be weaker now?" This is the main theme. Half of the epistle is an invective against carnal sins and the dangers of lascivious women, indicating the kind of sin or habitual weakness of the prince. The psychology of lust, which begins with an unclean imagination, is depicted with real penetration, giving evidence of the author's acquaintance with ascetic literature and practice. The personal character of this kind of admonition is confirmed by the fact of its rarity in Russian literature. The accusations against women in general, "evil women," belong, on the contrary, to the common subjects inherited from the Byzantine tradition. Pseudo-Chrysostom's sermon on *Good and Evil Women* was the source of numerous Russian imitations.

The counsels of charity as well as the classical New Testament texts on love are not lacking in James' letter. Yet one feels that they are not at the center of his thought. The most striking and really inspired use of the Gospel is made in connection with patience, not with charity. Patience, after chastity, is for James the greatest virtue. He gives "a wonderful indication" of how sublime it is:

The Almighty, borne by Cherubim, is now led in bonds by soldiers; sitting at the right hand of the Father, He stands in the tribunal before the archpriest and Pilate . . . The face, shining more brightly than the sun, is beaten and spit upon by the ungodly.

Here the kenoticism of Christ is used as the pattern of patience, not of self-humiliating love. Its tragic greatness is immediately obliterated by the arguments of commonsense, taken partly from Solomon: "One little word brings forth wrath and by little sorrows great ones are avoided. . . Said Solomon: the patient is better than the strong as far as possessing his own soul." Proverbs and Wisdom quotations elsewhere punctuate, somewhat inconsistently, the author's high-flown subject matter. For his own religious ideal no aim is high enough. We can rival apostles and martyrs.

If you wish to imitate the miracles of the apostles, it is also pos-

sible; they made the lame walk and healed the dry-hands; and thou
—teach the lame in faith and turn the feet, walking to spectacles,
back to the church; make the hands, dried up from avarice, expand
for giving to the poor.

As to the martyrs, "they endured fire, beasts, sharp
swords; thou endure inflaming lust and bestial thoughts
arising within, and the tongues of malicious men. . . That is
why Paul orders us to be ever in arms." Such a high ambition accounts for the high evaluation of man's freedom.
"Freedom (self-ruling) is God's imprescriptible gift to
man." The whole epistle is written in a courageous, almost military spirit. One looks in vain for the humility
so dear to the Russian heart. It is, at best, mentioned in a
few words; the militant exuberance overthrows it. Yet
there is no trace of optimism either. Death and Judgment
are the great finale.

Nobody knows about the secret judgments of God concerning
him; we all must tremble . . . everything is thinner than a shadow;
see God already coming from the heavens for the Judgment . . .
Thou must know that fire awaits us; by fire shall we be tried; by
fire is our life covered . . . live as if you are already in Gehenna.

Some loving and encouraging words in conclusion soften
the terrifying impression of this prospect. After the exaggerated expressions of his own unworthiness, the author
ends by a new poetical transport—this time glorifying the
law of God and active moral life.

Neither in heaven above nor on the earth beneath is there anything higher than to know the Lord, to obey His right hand and to
keep His commandments; for the great name will not lead into the
kingdom of Heaven nor the word without deed help the listener;
but the word confirmed by deeds makes itself worthy of faith.

If one were to seek among the ancient Russian religious
writings a reflection of the Pelagian spirit, this magnificent
piece of spiritual eloquence would come nearest the pat-

tern. It is a call for the heroic moral struggle intensified
by an apprehension of perils but, at the same time, by the
consciousness of human freedom and its great possibilities.
In all these qualities it is by no means representative of
Russian piety. Nor can it be considered as an expression
of the average lay ideal. The wish of the "spiritual father"
to conform to the needs of his son is obvious. For him he
chooses the main virtues: chastity and patience; for him he
makes his selection of the common-sense adages. But it is
clear that his own spiritual world is too distant from the
worldly mediocrity to allow an efficient adaptation. His
heroic Christianity is not for the weakling prince. A real
"average" religion must be sought elsewhere.

THE ADMONITION OF THE MONK GEORGIUS OF THE
ZARUB CAVE

Here the situation is the same as with James and Demetrius: a spiritual father, a monk, admonishes his son, a layman. The latter's name as well as the date are unknown, but
the monastic origin is easily perceived. But Georgius achieves
a greater adaptation to the laic moral world. The whole
atmosphere is quite Russian, though not yet laic. The
great simplicity of thought and verbal expression sharply
contrasts with the theological depth and acuteness of James.

Nearly one half of the short epistle emphasizes one's
duty to stay with one's spiritual father, freely chosen, and
not to exchange him for another guide. "Do not seek another teacher besides me, ignorant one. For my ignorance
is sufficient to tell you by what you can be saved." To prove
the high rank of the monks and the necessity of venerating
them Georgius tells an apocryphal story about Christ.
Coming from heaven to earth,

He did not wish to bow before the King, being Himself the
King of kings . . . nor before anybody . . . but having heard of an

old man, poor and strange to those parts, starving from hunger, naked, wearing a cloth only up to his knees . . . He came to him and inclined His immaculate head, giving an example to you.

It must be left undecided how far this introductory praise of the monastic order reflects the personal interest of the "spiritual father" rather than his sincere and high idea of ascetic vocation and of the value of obedience.

For Georgius, too, the two great pivots of practical religion are the fear of God and charity. But fear is the primary motive. He is not harsh in expressions; he tries to be mild and even caressing in his approach to his son. "My beloved child—my sweetest child," always are on his lips. Yet, the first thing that his son must keep in mind is:

Remember always the ferocious death, its suddenness, how many it ravishes without letting them say one single word. And what after? Is it not the terrible Judgment and various torments, cruel, endless . . . and the thrones of glory and the crowns in heaven ready for the righteous? . . . Bear the fear of God in your heart and a great love toward Him.

Here follow short precepts of charity of a common pattern. But, in conclusion, the father dwells at length upon a particular precept which has great weight in his opinion and which is very typical of his spiritual tendency. Undoubtedly, it is connected with the Phobos religion: "Avoid evil laughter, do not let jugglers, buffoons, and musicians for amusement into your home. It is a pagan custom, not Christian. Whoever like these amusements are heathens." The condemnation of laughter comes from the Byzantine ideal of decency. The prohibition of secular music and all kinds of entertainments is a specific Russian feature. Many sermons are preserved which contain this unreserved condemnation of musical and vocal arts, the relics of paganism. The Russian Church without doubt viewed the folk art which had originated in pre-Christian times, as the artistic expression of paganism and condemned it all without discrimination. In this respect no difference of attitude can be stated between various authors and spiritual trends. In the struggle against folk art all were united.

The meek Theodosius gave the meekest expression to this general clerical feeling. We remember him sighing at a prince's banquet with musical entertainment: "Will it be so, my prince, in the other world?" Ever after, the prince, when inviting Theodosius, removed the musicians.

As this example shows, the struggle of the clergy against folk music was not successful. The Russian people fortunately have preserved its rich treasure of folk songs. However, the condemnation of the Church prevented the ancient poetic tradition of the people from being written down and cultivated by the upper classes. No one piece of Russian poetry was preserved in writing up to the seventeenth century. This loss of poetry is an enormous and irreparable damage to Russian culture.

As a compensation for folk music Georgius offers to his son the spiritual poetry of the Psalter.

> This is our 'gusli' by which we must always rejoice before God . . . This is our precious merriment, our glorious song uniting us with angels . . . And if you are looking for amusements and entertainments—read the stories, words and deeds, and passions of the saints.

The suggestion was not bad and not devoid of clearsightedness. The Psalter and the lives of saints became, indeed, the favorite reading of the Russian people and gratified not only the religious but also the artistic needs of the Russian soul.

In all his positive and negative injunctions, as well as in his own idiom, Georgius is very Russian—reflecting one religious trend common in ancient Russia, but only one, and this neither the most profound nor the most widespread.

THE RUSSIAN PENITENTIALS

The last two literary documents under examination belong to the group of instructions addressed by "spiritual fathers" to their sons. The written intercourse between spiritual fathers and sons is rather an exceptional form of communication. The oral word was the main vehicle of influence, and its focal point was the sacrament of penance. This leads us to the question, of what quality and of what strength was the influence of the clergy upon the Russian laity through the penitential administration of the Church. At the time of the conversion of Russia, the secret confession had probably almost supplanted the ancient institution of public penitence. The origins of this development in the Greek church are the same as in the West; since the sixth century the monastic practice had spread throughout the lay world. The confession, now secret, became more frequent and extended to all kinds of sins, even the most insignificant. Gradually, the sacrament of penance became a necessary condition to the partaking of the Eucharist. This meant, as a consequence, the end of the frequent weekly communion as practiced by the ancient Church. We do not know if this process was completed in the eleventh century when the young Russian Church began to build its life after the Greek pattern. The canonical documents, translated from Greek or originated among the Balkan Slavs, which were accepted as authority in Russia drastically contradict each other in this respect. At any rate, in the twelfth century the development was at an end: there was no communion without confession; no absolution without penance.

That the sway of the penitence over ancient Russia was far from the light formality of recent times is clear. The

absolution of sins was granted only under the condition of
definite penalties or *epitimia*, and these spiritual penalties
were very heavy. They included additional fasting, numerous prostrations, and excommunication from the Eucharist
for periods lasting months, years, and for some heavy sins,
even decades of years. On the other hand, the Church suggested, though did not compell every laymen to choose one
priest as his spiritual father and not to change him in any
case except with his consent. It completely tied the moral
life of the layman to the guidance of a priest, though he
chose freely. This priest, as a rule, was a monk. The high
esteem for the monastic state and the relatively low level of
the secular clergy made it preferable for the believer to submit his will to a worthier representative of the Church, that
is, to the monk. Such could be found in a neighboring cloister
or even in a common parish church. In ancient Russia a great
number of parishes were entrusted to the care of monks.

Considering the tremendous responsibility of personal
guidance through the sacrament of penance the Church
tried to create general norms for both the confessor and the
penitent. In addition to the liturgical text of the Sacrament,
special lists were put into circulation containing the enumeration of sins with the required satisfactions or *epitimia* for
each. The most ancient of those lists was attributed to John
the Faster, a patriarch of Constantinople of the sixth century.
The original text of his penitential canon, if John really was
the author, has not been preserved. The Church never
came to accept one obligatory penitential canon. Such canons
were left to the initiative of private compilers who em-
broided the given patterns with their own details. In principle, the priest was free both in his inquiry into the moral
state of his spiritual son and in distributing "spiritual medicine" of penances. In practice, an average priest must always conform to the written text of canons after having

made his choice between different versions at his disposal. As original texts were very brief, a large field for supplements was open. In Slavic countries and in Russia, anonymous writers continued this branch of ecclesiastical literature, extremely important for shaping the religious life of the people. In Russia national canons were found in circulation together with Bulgarian and Greek. The national origin of many of them is not yet determined with a sufficient degree of certainty, in spite of extensive research done by Almazov, Smirnov, and others. Until all this material is critically sifted and chronologically ordered one cannot make proper use of it in studying the spiritual history of Russia.

Since its origin one common feature runs through all this literature, instilled by the Greek ascetic mind: the predominance of sexual over all other moral subject matter. Most of the Greek canons begin with the question: "How did you break your virginity, with your wife or another woman?" And so it goes on, passing in review all the dark realms of vice, natural and unnatural, with disgusting details, as if the seventh commandment were the only one in the Decalogue. Murder and theft are barely mentioned. Many Russian canons follow this pattern; only ritual transgressions of the kind we are already acquainted with occupy still more space than sensual sins. One would venture to say that for a Russian confessor sexual transgressions lay on the same level as other transgressions of ritual purity; that is, that physical, objective impurity weighs more heavily than the moral side of the sin. One might also observe that the sins against fellowmen, or against charity, take more place in Russian canons than in the Greek. Here a greater differentiation of detail is observed and even a certain refinement of moral sense in matters of social charity. In spite of these examples of a refined social ethics, one re-

mains in doubt as to the moral value of all penitential literature and, consequently, of the medieval confession itself.
The lessons of ritualism misled religious orientation; the
emphasis on sex perverted imagination. The latter consequence was realized finally at the time of the great reforms of Peter I, and since the outset of the eighteenth
century sexual details have been dropped from penitential
canons pending the future obliteration of the penitential
books altogether.

Our negative impression is mitigated by the study of
some Russian documents connected with the administration
of the Penance, other than the penitential canons in the
proper sense. Such are the two undoubtedly pre-Mongolian admonitions published by A. S. Pavlov. The first is
the *Admonition of a Spiritual Father to a Penitent*; the second, under the title of the *Preface to the Penitence*, is the
general instruction addressed both to the priest and the
penitent. Both are very serious and pertinent to the practical needs of Russian society; they are completely lacking
in ritualistic trifles or obscene details. They are able to give
one a higher idea of the moral standard of the teachers of
the Russian Church.

The first document is more severe and nearer to the
Byzantine ethical precepts. Nevertheless, it begins with
words of encouragement to the layman who had already
confessed his sins. "My son, you have disclosed a very
grave sickness, not easy to be healed after the sense of men;
but, confronted with the mercy of God, it is nothing at all."
After having vividly depicted the strife of two angels, good
and evil, for the soul of man, the author suggests "to
close the doors of the heart to the demon and not to give
him place within oneself," but "to open them to the good
angel and receive him." God helps the sinner in this struggle by sending pains to convert him to repentance. What

is true repentance? "Nothing but sighing, and tears, and labor, watching oneself and taming one's soul with fast, vigilance, and prayer." The temporary excommunication, prohibiting entrance to the Church, serves the same end.

The penitence is the beginning of a new, better life and on its threshold the spiritual father gives his son a series of counsels for practical conduct. His duties towards God consist in constant prostrations with short ejaculatory prayers of the type: "I have sinned, pardon me, O Lord." The food is strictly regulated not only during fast days, but on all days of the year. The father considers this dietetic norm easy, fit only for the beginner. With his spiritual progress the son would add to it himself.

For moral life the point of departure is classical: the fear of God. "This is the purification of sins. And from fear, go to love, for upon it depend the Law and the prophets." Fear and love are due to earthly authorities. "Do not dare say: they are men, the same as we. . . Every power is from God; give honor to all according to their rank: love your equal and have mercy upon the lower." This Byzantine canon is concluded with a rather long precept of charity which already shows some Russian developments. Here are mentioned foreigners and beggars, orphans, widows, and servants.

> Teach them the good not with fury, but as your own children. . . . Do not blame others . . . but hold yourself the greatest sinner beneath all . . . Give a tithe of your fortune to God—to the poor and the clergy . . . Restrain your hands from unjust grabbing; better a small lot earned justly.

But the end is the climax of this practical ideal:

> Toward every man have this consideration: he is a man, created after the image of God, being flesh like me, having a soul, similar to me in all—therefore, what you like him to do, do unto him your-

self. This is agreeable to God and to men. Both the Old and the New Laws teach this.

The Preface to Repentance is marked by the largeness of its views and evangelical spirit. In these qualities it represents another tendency in the penitential discipline. To begin with, this document puts the greatest emphasis upon the wisdom and the moral level of the confessor; upon these depend the efficiency of the confession itself. It raises the question: "Is it useful to confess one's sins to spiritual fathers?" The answer is: "Yes, good and useful, but only to those [fathers] having experience. . . If the priest is rude, or ignorant, a drunkard or a proud man, he will make yourself wicked, negligent, loose, and lazy." For the author of the *Preface* "ignorance is worse than sin because the sinners who repent sincerely are saved but the senseless, falling into heresies, are damned." The layman, therefore, must carefully seek a wise spiritual father and, having found such a one, obey him in all. Especially, he must not look for a priest "after his heart, indulgent and teaching weakly, who does not bind with *epitimia;* if the priest will not bind, eternal bonds await us." As is evident from the subsequent exposition penances are needed, not for the redemption of past sins but for the renewal of the moral life. Indeed, the main concern of the author is the real improvement of life, not the administration of the sacrament. Besides wisdom, a true confessor must possess fearlessness before every worldly power:

Do not fear, nor hesitate, nor be ashamed before the face of man, be it tsar, prince, judge, or warrior: thou art appointed by God; thou art the slave of God and the servant of Christ, and thou shall work with daring the commandment of God.

In the second part, the *Preface* goes into details dramatizing the conversation of an ideal confessor with his son. Before the confession in the proper sense, the priest, sitting with his son, "in a secret and neat place" (not necessarily in a Church), has to be convinced of the purity of the latter's intentions: "whether he repents from all his heart . . . and is willing to receive the commandments of God and to work what is ordered by thee, with a glad and joyful heart." The inquiry itself must also proceed in the form of a kindly conversation: with "mild face and meek and joyful heart." The result, nevertheless, determines whether the confessor accepts the penitent or sends him away. The first confessional question put to a worthy penitent is: "What is your rank, your work, and what do you do?" In sharp contrast to the sexual curiosity of the Byzantine penitentials, the *Preface* begins with the query about the professional state. Professional ethics, social caritative obligations stand in the foreground. The questioning itself is not developed—obviously because it depends entirely upon the class and rank differentiations. The author goes immediately to the injunctions of the priest which, for him, take the place of traditional *epitimia*: "Renounce drunkenness, not drink; renounce gluttony, not food; renounce profligacy, not marriage; renounce lawless possessions, do not hide rightful property, nor spare it in distributing to the poor." Coming to this point, the author, assuming here the style of preacher, continues upon this subject, the denunciation of acquisitiveness in all forms of social injustice. He denounces usury, the keeping of taverns, acquisition by calumny, by bribing the courts, by false oath, and by open robbery. He treats one kind of social oppression in particular detail: the profit gained from the emancipation of slaves. The master can require from his slave no money beyond the amount paid for his purchase. The preacher does not spare threats for this abject sin: "They sell innocent blood and the account for this blood will be exacted by God, at His Terrible Judgment: better for them not to be born."

What is most amazing is the practical conclusion. If the penitent is guilty of unjust acquisitions, immediately— within one hour—he must go and return the money to those wronged by him. "Then come back for a pure repentance, and God will pardon all your sins; and I will accept you as your father and teacher." Otherwise, he can look for another confessor, an "indulger, after his heart and pleasure"; and both may enjoy the life in this world and shall pay in the future.

The *Preface* is by no means an easier guide to repentance than the first admonition and its Greek pattern. But the emphasis is here put on the other category of sins as well as the remedies; not upon personal purity and redeeming ascetic exercises, but upon social charity and justice; the only redemption provided here is restitution. The other sins, except the above cited, are not mentioned. We must realize, however, that the *Preface* is an instruction aiming to be an addition to the Penitential lists, and not replacing them. It is also striking how little the sacramental moment of the Penance is stressed. The father says to his son: "Jesus Christ, who takes away the sins of the whole world will also take yours, if you repent with all your heart and begin to fulfill His will." But even here, the pardon is conditioned not by priestly absolution but by the moral state of the sinner. We dare not, however, exaggerate this point. Hardly any Russian priest or layman would deny the sacramental significance of the Penance. Yet, on the other hand, all canonists and preachers condition the efficacy of the sacrament by the active efforts of the penitent: some putting the stress upon the fulfillment of fixed *epitimia,* others upon the improvement of moral life.

At the end of this short inquiry one is still uncertain as to a final judgment of the good or evil effects of the penitential practice in ancient Russia. A wise, enlightened father

could do as much good to his sons as a narrow ritualist conforming to the written penitentials could do harm to the
young and naïve Christian consciousness. Since the wise
are always in the minority our conclusion seems to be rather
negative. One must keep in mind, however, that the practice of Confession, as well as Communion, was far from
being general at that time. The canonists point to people
who never take part in the sacraments of the Church. These
nonconformists must be sought mainly in rural districts. We
do not know whether they constituted the majority of the
population. If such nominal or half-educated Christians
missed the religious and moral profit afforded by the sacrament of Penance, they were free on the other hand from
the perversion and misguidance of narrow or ignorant confessors.

THE ADMONITION OF PRINCE VLADIMIR MONOMACH

With Vladimir Monomach (d. 1125) one finds the Russian lay religion at its best. This admonition is written by a
layman for laymen, by a prince for his sons, but also with
other aims. The author, undoubtedly the best political
ruler and leader among Iaroslav's descendents, was quite
serious in the purpose of his writing. It is no literary exercise or reflection of book wisdom. However deeply it is
impregnated by the influence of the Greek Church and its
moral tradition, the *Admonition* is, in the first place, based
on the experience of personal life, and aims at helping the
author's sons in their practical life, in the performance of
their vocational duties as Christians and princes. Originating
in Byzantine patterns of similar paternal admonitions, it is
the first purely Russian prince's *Mirror* which thanks to a
great simplicity of life can be, to a great extent, adapted to
other social classes as well.

The practical, vital character of the *Admonition* is linked

with a high appreciation of active life. "Do not be idle, do
work. Laziness is the mother of all (evil)," such expressions run through the entire *Admonition* from beginning to
end. The author believes that even purely religious exercises, such as prayer, are primarily the issue of labor, of
work. In this, one of his main emphases, he represents an
important attitude of the average Russian religious mind.
The Epistle of Saint James stands at the source of this Russian ethical trend.

At first glance, one is tempted to classify Vladimir's
piety as part of the Phobos religion. In fact he begins with
the classical introduction: "First of all, for the sake of God
and your souls, have the fear of God in your heart and give
generous alms"—a sentence which recurs once more. Yet
upon closer examination of the prince's attitude toward
God one is convinced that fear is not the appropriate term
for it. Vladimir gives us sufficient material for judging his
religion. Far from being a theologian, abstaining from
all doctrinal statements about God, he betrays the quality
of his faith by his choice of quotations. He was accustomed
to keep a notebook in which he wrote down the most striking
or the most gratifying sentences which he came upon in his
reading. With these excerpts he filled his admonition; while
his practical counsels spring from his own experience, the
general motives are the fruit of his learning. Chosen from
his life's studies, the pages of quotations cannot be irrelevant
or accidental. At the same time they give one the opportunity to gauge the extent of a laymen's reading in ancient
Russia—at least of a layman of the highest educational
standard.

Most of the quotations derive from the Psalms. The
Psalter was the most familiar book to Vladimir. He has
it at hand even in travelling and he tells us what use he
makes of it. Once, on a journey, when he was depressed

and disgusted with political intrigues, he opened the Psalter "with sorrow" and looked at "what turned up." It is a kind of religious divination; we know that the Psalter was actually used in Russia for purposes of divination. After the Psalter came the prayers of the Church, especially penitential prayers of the Lenten time. The Bible also yields a few sentences from Isaiah and Solomon, but practically nothing from the New Testament. The fathers are represented by Saint Basil: two excerpts from his ascetic sermons which occur in many Russian collections and perhaps the *Hexameron,* though the latter comes into consideration only as a source of inspiration, for there are no direct quotations.

Three aspects of God are revealed as particularly dear to the Russian prince. God is just and does not let the righteous perish. All the quotations from the Psalms, without exception, describe the hope or reward of the righteous and the punishment of the ungodly (Psalms 42, 37, 56, 58, 59, 63, 64, 84). This judgment of God is accomplished during this earthly life and is not relegated to the eschatological future. With full confidence Vladimir repeats the Old Testament proclamations: "I have not seen the righteous forsaken nor his seed begging bread . . . Verily there is a reward for the righteous; verily there is a God that judgeth on the earth."

The righteous God is also a merciful father to the repentant sinner and for this New-Testament idea, Vladimir uses no quotation, but expresses it in the words of his own coinage:

Verily, my sons, understand how merciful and overmerciful is the loving God; we, men, being sinful and mortal, if someone wrongs us, wish to lacerate him and shed his blood; but our Lord, master of life and death, endures our sins which are above our head, over and over, until the end of our life, as a father, who loves his child, beats it but draws it to him again.

The third aspect of God as the wise and good creator is revealed to Vladimir in the contemplation of nature. In this passage where the historians saw an influence of Basil's *Hexameron* (it is nearer to the *Prologue* of the *Hexameron* of John, the Exarch of Bulgaria), one could find the reflexion of psalmodic poetry as well. Yet here also Vladimir speaks mostly out of his own, or from the Russian national feeling with regard to the religious value of nature. Here his diction is at the peak of poetical inspiration:

Who would not praise, not glorify Thy might and Thy great wonders and beauties found in this world? how the sky is ordered; how the sun, moon and stars, darkness and light, and the earth laid upon waters, O Lord, by Thy providence! various animals, and birds and fishes adorned by Thy providence, O Lord! And this wonder we admire: how Thou created man out of dust and how various are the images in human faces; let us gather the whole world, there are none of the same image but everyone by God's wisdom has his own image. Let us also wonder how the birds of the skies go from their paradise, fall into our hands but stay not in one country but go, strong and weak alike, over all countries, by order of God, to all forests and fields. And all this God has given for the use of man, for his food and joy . . . And those birds of the skies are taught by Thee, O Lord; when Thou commandest, they sing and delight men for Thy sake; and when Thou dost not command they are dumb though having tongue.

Certainly Saint Basil is not responsible for the whole of this piece of "natural philosophy." The old Slavic mythology has its part in it. The Slavic or Russian religion of nature softens the severe moralism of the Hebrew religion, accepted by Byzantium, with some esthetic features; faith becomes emotional and even enthusiastic; it is a faith which sings, the faith fructifying artistic creation. With Vladimir we trace the first signs of this extremely important element of Russian religious feeling.

God just, kind, and wise cannot inspire with fear a man

of goodwill; and Vladimir, while speaking by habit and tradition of the fear of God, is practically free from fear. He does not stress hell and eternal torments, and he teaches his sons not to fear death, the menace of which so many ascetic writers put at the base of Christian ethics:

> Do not fear death, my sons—neither war nor wild beast—but do the manly work as God will allot you . . . no one can harm or kill you, unless ordered by God; and if death comes from God, neither father, nor mother, nor brothers can rescue you; but, if it is fitting to be on one's guard, the guard of God is better than that of man.

It is characteristic of Vladimir that he suggests the memory of death not as the menace of punishment but as medicine against greed. Not death but mortality is what he insists upon. Being mortal, man has no profit in accumulating riches: "We are mortal—to-day alive, to-morrow in the coffin; everything that Thou has given us is not ours but Thine; Thou has committed it to us for a few days." The practical corollary is given: "Do not bury (treasures) in the earth; it is a great sin." In a letter to Prince Oleg, which is partly preserved, together with his *Admonition*, speaking to a different type of man, aggressive and rancorous, Vladimir sees fit to emphasize the memory of death, but with the same ethical implication: "What are we? men, sinful and evil, today living, tomorrow senseless, in a coffin, and other people will divide our treasures." On this occasion there was a particular reason for sorrowful thoughts: Vladimir's son had just been killed in a feud on behalf of his father. Perhaps, in his connection one must appreciate the single mention of the "Terrible Judge" Vladimir makes, conscious of his part of sin in the fratricidal war:

> O me, sorrow-stricken and sad! Much dost thou struggle, my soul, with my heart; and thou overcomest my heart because, being corrupt, I think how I may stand before the terrible Judge, for we

did not show repentance and humility toward one another. And if someone says: I love God and do not love my brother, it is a lie. . . . If you forgive not trespasses to your brother, your heavenly Father will not forgive them to you.

We should notice here the purely evangelical connection between the idea of the Judgment and the lack of love. Suffice it to say that this gloomy contemplation was a passing mood in Vladimir's life. His ordinary relation to God is based not on fear but on hope: it is a calm, firm confidence in the "guardianship of God which is better than man's." Upon this hopeful confidence a whole practical, active ethics can be built.

Yet, between God and man's action stands man's sin. It would be an unfair simplification of Vladimir's religion and ethics to represent him as a moralist of the good Pharisee type. His philosophy is much deeper than that. He does not believe that man is saved by his own deeds. He needs the pardon of the merciful God, and it is not a formal thing, so that repentance becomes one of the outstanding traits of his religious mind. "By three good works one gets rid of the enemy (devil) and vanquishes him: repentance, tears, and alms." It is obvious that repentance and tears mean the same thing. Thus Vladimir's formula of salvation is: repentance and charity, which better expresses his personal religion than fear and charity. How seriously he takes repentance is attested by the whole content of the *Admonition* which is filled by prayers for Lent, that is, of penitence. A literary historian has spent much wit trying to date the manuscript from these Lenten quotations. Whether Vladimir composed or began to compose his *Admonition* during Lent is a secondary question. What has more importance is the fact that out of his notebook representing the recollections of his whole life, he chose these excerpts for posterity. It means he had a predilection for the prayers of Lent, a preference which has always been shared by the Russian people.

In the prayers of Vladimir a living and personal relationship to God is colored strongly by repentance or contrition. The long prayer with which the *Admonition* closes is taken from the Lenten liturgy, especially from the "canon" of Andrew of Crete, with its refrain: "All-merciful, have mercy upon me, fallen one." "Start up, my soul, and meditate on thy deeds, bring them before thine eyes, shed drops of tears, tell thy deeds and thoughts to Christ and cleanse thyself." Vladmir gives the following suggestion concerning prayer to his sons: "If God softens your hearts, shed tears because of your sins, saying: 'As Thou pardoned the harlot, the robber, and the publican, likewise pardon us sinners.' Do it in the church and upon going to bed." Vladimir's instructions on prayer disclose a practical but deeply serious religious mind. He does not insist on frequent church-going—two or three times a day—although from his own everyday order it is probable that he began his day by Matins. What he insists upon is a short prayer at morning and at night. For the first he offers formulas that seem to be of his own creation: "Enlighten my eyes, O Christ-God, who gave me Thy beautiful light," and another one: "Add to me, O Lord, year to years that I may praise God, having repented of my sins and justified my life." For the night prayer he limits his counsels to one prostration only, but to three, "if an illness begins": "do not neglect it; be not lazy; by this night prostration and singing (psalms?), man overcomes the devil; by this means man rids himself of what he has sinned by day." In compensation for the brevities of the daily prayers, he suggests: "When you are riding on horse and have no business conversation with anyone, if you know no other prayers, call 'Lord, have mercy' unceasingly and secretly: that prayer is best of all, better than thinking of nonsense while riding." Vladimir seems not to be fond of long prayers or of the mechanical repetition of canons. He values more the inner and emotional efficiency of prayer as is shown by his appreciation of tears.

This gift of tears, so highly esteemed by the Eastern Christians, Vladimir himself possessed to a remarkable degree. It was noted by the chronicler in his panegyrical obituary at the year of his death: "And he received such a gift from God, that when he came to a church and heard the singing he instantly shed tears and thus he offered his prayers to the Lord Christ with tears." We shall have further opportunity to analyze this Russian gift of tears more closely, especially in its difference from the Oriental monastic charism. Here it is enough to say that this emotionalism in prayer, this gift of tears, obviously had no enervating influence upon Vladimir's active life. He has nothing sentimental or effeminate in him. The transition from the energetic tension of everyday life to the moments of contrition must have been very definitely marked, so that tears really meant purification, *catharsis*, and not poisoning or weakening moral character.

Repentance as the main way of salvation presupposes humility. Pride makes repentance impossible or vain. Vladimir is perfectly conscious of this fact: "First of all, have no pride in your hearts." To the Holy Virgin he addresses this particular prayer: 'O Our Lady, Mother of God! Take away from my poor heart pride and fierceness that I may not be elated with the vanity of this world." Trying to break his natural pride, he goes into the school of the Church and finds monastic rules and forms expressing the hard virtue of humility. From the very first words of the *Admonition* the reader is astonished by his exaggerated terms of self-humiliation, appropriate more to an abbot than to a prince. He calls himself "bad" or miserable. He admits that his

epistle may displease his readers and he himself suggests
to his critics the disparaging sentence: "Upon a long journey,
and sitting on the sledge you have told nonsense"—for which
the most probable interpretation would be: "the old man
is out of his wits."

But on the other hand in the course of his *Admonition*
the prince speaks with a self-conscious authority and sets
himself, very naturally and in agreement with the Byzantine
pattern, as an example to his sons. For this purpose he
enumerates his expeditions; he tells of the labors and good
habits of his life. This exemplary autobiography occupies
more than one third of the *Admonition*: therefore the author can not be quite serious in his expressions of self-con-
tempt.

It would be unfair, however, to dismiss these utterances
as purely formal, or as the requirements of a Byzantine good
style. If a Russian prince adopts them, it is something more.
It is a serious attempt at bringing himself under the monastic rule of behavior. In this point, in humility, Vladimir,
as the Eastern church in general, made no distinction between monastic and common Christian virtue, although in
external forms and verbal expressions the Byzantine rule
of humility is not Biblical. Neither the Gospels nor the Old
Testament know such refinements of self-humiliation. The
danger of this cultivation of humility is obvious: to put it
in one word, it may be hypocrisy. A man says not what he
feels but what he believes he ought to feel; or, what is
worse, that which is imposed upon him by the standard of
social decency. As this standard is patterned upon the exceptional achievements of ascetic saints, the discrepancy
between form and content must be fairly general. Yet to
term that virtue hypocrisy even though it may be a
source of hypocrisy, would be unfair. In many cases it is a
school, a training, and an endeavor. Training often begins

with the external, with word and gesture, in order to produce corresponding spiritual content. Such is, for instance, the general ecclesiastical doctrine of prayer.

That Vladimir was serious in his training for humility and made a remarkable progress in fighting his pride is proved best of all by the military autobiography concluding his *Admonition.* It is a list of seventy-eight expeditions over a period of about forty-six years, with an appendix of the prince's hunting experiences,—"my toil which I have toiled, journeying and hunting since my thirteenth year." The heading is as striking as the narration itself. Vladimir calls his expeditions "journeys," most of which were real wars against both external and internal enemies; he unites them with his hunting under the rubric "toils," or labors. In fact, he never speaks of victories nor mentions his skill or courage. In cases of evident success, he simply writes: "God helped us." A peaceful but protracted journey, very tiring under the conditions of the time, is put on the same level as a glorious battle: as a labor, a work, a part of princely duty. No idea of glory or personal achievement enters the commentary of his military career by the prince who remained for posterity the most glorious political figure of two centuries of Russian history. He is also a strange hunter, for he does not boast of the number of his trophies, but on the contrary tells of the wounds inflicted upon him by beasts: "Two aurochs threw me with their horns, me and my horse; one stag gored me and two elks," and so on. The nearest he comes to boasting is in his account of capturing wild horses—"I tied them up, alive, with my own hands."

He tries to bequeath to his sons one main example out of his experience—his endurance and his indefatigability in labors. It can be taught, assimilated, trained; that is why the father dwells at length upon it. If he boasts, it is boasting in the sense of Saint Paul, of sufferings and labors, not of achievements.

In spite of his monastic conception of humility, Vladimir is conscious of the radical difference between monastic and lay ethics. In this insight he was not unique, although the exclusively monastic view was also represented in Russia. Vladimir does not wish to impose upon his sons an unbearable burden of asceticism. He insists upon the three virtuous deeds: "repentance, tears, and alms. . . They are not heavy. It is not the solitude nor monasticism nor hunger which are endured by other good people; but with a small deed you can win the grace of God."

By sketching in detail the program of secular ethics, Vladimir feels obliged to offer his sons a portrait of Byzantine good manners as painted by Saint Basil in popular excerpts. We know this Byzantine ideal: "Clean, unspoiled souls; emaciated bodies; meek and moderate conversation; the word of God; eating and drinking without a noise; to have the eyes toward the ground and the soul towards heaven. . ." A significant misunderstanding is connected with these excerpts of Basil. They belong to his ascetic sermons designed for the monks. In the Byzantine or Slavic tradition they turned into admonitions for laymen. The former heading: "How a monk must behave" was changed into "How a man must behave." The confusion between monastic and lay ethics finds its most drastic expression here. Vladimir was misled by the Slavonic title. To this he added a second mistake (whether induced by the false title is uncertain) in taking this excerpt for Basil's famous admonition addressed especially to youth. He certainly had no objection against the ideal of dignified decency. He copies it obediently as the voice of the Church father for the edification of his sons. Yet, he certainly does not expect them to follow these counsels literally. What was convenient in the Byzantine or later Muscovite palace was certainly unthinkable in the life of a medieval prince, agile, energetic, necessarily boisterous, living amidst banquets and military expeditions.

As a matter of fact, Basil's excerpts find their place among other Biblical and liturgical quotations. They belong to the general introduction. When Vladimir descends to the practical level he begins with the suggestions for prayer already examined, and comes directly to the commandments of charity:

First of all, do not forget the poor; but in the measure of your possibilities feed them and make presents to the orphan; give justice to the widow and do not permit the mighty to ruin any man. . . . Visit the sick, walk behind the dead, for we all are mortal; do not pass a man without greeting, say a kind word to him.

These are not general words nor Biblical quotations. Vladimir does not despise the suggestions of common sense supporting the ideal norms:

Love your wives but do not give them power over yourselves. . . Wherever you go on your way, do not let your men harm anybody, neither your own people nor aliens, neither in the township nor in the fields that they may not curse you. . . . Most of all, honor a guest from wherever he comes, whether he be a simple man, or a noble, or an envoy; if you cannot give him presents, give food and drink; for they, passing by, will create fame for a man, for good or evil.

Vladimir does not reject the motive of interest in ethics because he wishes its rules to be fulfilled. All the more striking then appears the following rule, addressed, one must remember, to the princes: "Do not kill either the just or the guilty; do not order a man to be killed; even if deserving death, do not destroy any Christian life."

The aversion of Vladimir Monomach to capital punishment, like that of his great namesake, Saint Vladimir, is a sign of an evangelical conception of Christianity. It is true that Russian law, like ancient Teutonic laws (*Leges barbarorum*) did not use the death punishment for common crimes: the penal system was based on fines replacing the previous blood revenge. Yet, the chronicles give enough evidence to the effect that Russian princes did not shrink from killing either their personal political enemies or criminals, a procedure which was considered their natural right as rulers. Monomach's conscience does not allow him to acquiesce in this order. His abhorrence of capital punishment has nothing to do with ecclesiastical influence. When Vladimir I, the "Baptizer" of Russia, decided not to execute robbers, it was the bishops who dissuaded him, stating the principle: "It is just to execute robbers." The Church itself lived according to the Byzantine law and was accustomed to its cruel criminal system. It is interesting to notice that the only known sentences of cruel mutilations in Russia were passed by the ecclesiastical courts. These mutilations in Byzantium were considered, not without a great deal of hypocrisy, as mitigation of the death punishment. In fact, they were often aggravating forms of it as in the terrible trial by the Kievan metropolitan of Theodore, bishop of Rostov, in 1169. Theodore, himself a cruel tyrant in his own diocese, was condemned by the Greek hierarch to have "his tongue cut off, his right hand hewn, and his eyes ripped out." This treatment finds the complete and even enthusiastic approval of the chronicler as an act of justice, which it was. Certainly, the Church was not more humane than the State in its courts. Thus Vladimir's humanitarian aversion to capital punishment was not suggested to him by his spiritual counsellors: it was an inspiration of his own.

One would be mistaken in regarding Vladimir as a too tender nature whose evangelical charity reaches otherworldiness. Suffice it to read the memoir of his military activities

to be sobered in this respect. It even can afford a real dis-
appointment. Indeed, it is a very sad list of devastations,
burned towns, captured populations, and so on. Not only
"pagans" such as the Polovtsi, appear as victims, but often
the Russian subjects of hostile princes. Typical is the lot
of a town, Minsk, that was taken by Vladimir with the aid
of Chernigov's prince and the Polovtsian allies: "We
stormed the town and left neither slave nor cattle." All
this is told in a most objective tone; Vladimir neither glorifies
his deeds nor repents of them. He considers them, as we
have seen, as a part of his "labors." In military methods
he simply conforms to the practice of his age. He probably
could not help conforming. But in exercising justice and
in civil administration, he finds he can inaugurate a new
practice which does not contradict the letter of the ancient
law.

The most important question in connection with Vladimir's ideal of charity is this: are his ethics primarily charity
ethics? However strong may be the impact of Christian
charity upon him, the general impression of his work, all
the practical details with which it is replete, point to another
guiding principle. Charity is to him the highest virtue, but
everyday life is based not on it, but on the conscientious performance of one's duty. The main interest of Vladimir's *Admonition* lies in its being the first and, for a long time, the only
attempt at secular vocational ethics, although penetrated by
otherworldly aspects. General injunctions are given: do
not idle, do everything by yourselves, be cautious, study,
labor. The counsels about private life are blended with
those concerning princely duties, military and civil. The
religious background of practical ethics is the faith in the
God of justice, not the God of love; the hope and confidence
in God's reward, even in this earthly life.

It is rather disappointing to see how few political principles Vladimir included in the *Admonition* designed to be his Testament. Some political rules are simple applications of the general moral law: especially, the insistence upon faithfulness to treaties ("cross-kissing"). In the *Chronicles*, which are full of admiration for him, one sees the great outlines of Vladimir's policies: the pacification of the Russian lands by a system of nonaggression pacts, the loyalty to the traditional "feudal" order, and the united defense against the nomadic Polovtsi and their ceaseless forays.

One document exemplifies these policies in a particular case and at the same time allows a more precise and deeper insight into the moral character of Vladimir. It is the letter to Prince Oleg, written after the death of Vladimir's son, Iziaslav. This young son was involved in a conflict with Oleg, his uncle, and was killed in battle against him. Vladimir writes immediately upon the tragic event not to threaten his enemy, but to offer reconciliation over the body of his son. He does not wish revenge or bloodshedding: "Let us not ruin the Russian land." The strife for possession of towns and lands can be settled by agreements. Although Vladimir cannot abstain from bitter reproaches, he does not hold himself or his clan blameless. This unfortunate son was wrong: "He should not have sought another's goods, nor bring upon me shame and sorrow: some young men had advised him." Vladimir also was not always right in his previous feuds with Oleg: "If I, when I was young, had sinned against you at Chernigov because of the pagans, I repent it. . . . I am but a man."

This concrete acknowledgment of one's wrongs is, certainly, more difficult and more valuable than a general confession of sins—humble utterances which can be taken as stylistic formulae. The death of his son had stricken Vladimir deeply. One sees it from his heartfelt, troubled speech, written as if through tears.

When my son—and yours—was killed before your eyes, you should, at the sight of his blood and body faded like a flower recently blossomed, slain like a lamb, you should, standing over him, have taken heed of the thoughts of your soul and said: "Alas, what have I done?" . . . You should have repented before God, have written me a letter of comfort and sent my daughter-in-law to me (the widow of the killed son), because there is neither good nor evil in her, in order that I may embrace her and comfort her with dirges for her husband rather than with wedding songs: for I had not witnessed her joy nor her wedding because of my sins; for God's sake, let her be sent to me with the first envoy, I shall cease my tears; let her sit down like a turtledove wailing on a dried tree, and I shall be comforted in God.

Such a language speaks for itself. One sees how serious humility was for a Russian prince at his best; and what kind of humility: contrition, the melted heart, the pardon through tears in a consciousness of common guilt. One believes in his absolute sincerity in citing the humiliated Christ as the example of human humility: "Our Lord is not man, but God of the universe, who works in a twinkling of an eye everything He wishes and lo, He suffered insults and spitting and blows and was given to death, being Himself Master of life and death, and we—what are we? . . ." Thus, in his profoundest religious moment Vladimir finds comfort and inspiration in the kenosis of Christ, the highest expression of the Russian religious soul.

In his *Admonition*, written in a calmer state of mind, Vladimir is sparing in his quotations from the Gospel. The Psalter, and not the Gospel, is his preferred book. How can we explain this?

In our opinion Vladimir, the man of practical ethics, looks for religious writings which could guide him in life. The Gospel, with its paradoxical rejection of all earthly values is puzzling to the social mind. A complicated and not always honest exegesis is required for the practical use

260 THE RUSSIAN RELIGIOUS MIND

of the Gospel in everyday life. Vladimir was too sincere
and perhaps too little trained theologically for such an
exegesis. The Old Testament was more useful for his purpose, as a guide for life. The same is true, of course, for
most Christians. The religious superiority of Vladimir over
many of his contemporaries is evident from his preferring
the Psalms to the Wisdom-books. The common sense of
the "Wisdom" was too low and the absoluteness of the
Gospel too high for him though his aversion for capital
punishment is quite evangelical. The Psalms and the
Prophets, especially Isaiah were at his level. This indicates
that his level was rather high. Vladimir's religious ethics
moves just at the border line between the Old and New
Testament. It is always illuminated by some softened rays
falling from the Gospel; and in rare, sublime moments he
dares see Christ, the humiliated Lord, face to face.

THE SUPPLICATION OF DANIEL THE EXILE

Daniel is the second, and the last, lay author of a didactic epistle in pre-Mongolian Russia. He remains a rather
enigmatic character, the more so since his work reached us
in numerous later transformations and revisions which bear
the stamp of different ages. Recent critics hopelessly dis-
agree as to the date of Daniel's life, shifting the period between the twelfth and the thirteenth centuries. His work
is a supplication to a prince in whose service Daniel previously had fallen into disgrace. In order to regain his
liberty and to insinuate himself again into the prince's grace,
Daniel makes a sparkling display of his erudition derived
from different books of gnomic and "Wisdom" literature:
Solomon, Sirach, the Bee (*Melissa*), *Hundred Chapters*, and
so on. The whole composition is a tissue of proverbs, similes,
apophthegms, some of which may be Daniel's own creation;
he is undoubtedly an able stylist. As far as literary form

is concerned, the *Supplication* belongs to the genre of admonitions; its author claims to be a teacher of moral and practical wisdom. Yet, at the same time, unmistakable also is his intention to please, to play with words, to perform the part of a prince's fool. The prince, if not impressed by his wisdom, certainly would be provoked to smile by the witty, sarcastic *mots* of the exile. This is the idea underlying his peculiar literary production. Modern literary historians, who gladly welcome in Daniel the representative of a secular trend, have termed him the first Russian humorist, the partisan of a social protest, a kind of revolutionary prophet. Indeed, he can be considered a sort of nihilist before the time. But, on the other hand, he is a flatterer and a courtier. His moral attitude is merely negative, his religious background extremely vague and shallow. He could easily be passed over in the history of the religious mind were it not for his negative value: he reveals religious and moral weaknesses inherent in the "Wisdom" religion so popular in Russia and thus he becomes a warning against the overevaluation of the religious element in Russian culture. Let us try to extract the little which constitutes Daniel's religious and moral background.

This teacher of wisdom is by no means humble in the appreciation of his own wisdom. With his very first words he poses like David or Solomon reincarnate: "Let us blow the golden trumpets and strike the silvery organs of our reason." Or, "Put earthen bowls under the streams flowing from my tongue, that sweetest honey may be trickled to you with the words of my lips." Less pretentious and nearer to the truth is the following acknowledgment:

I, O prince, my lord, neither went beyond seas nor learned from philosophers: but I was like a bee which flits from flower to flower, gathering honey: I, likewise, gathered from many books the sweetness and sense of words and absorbed them as a goatskin does the

water of the sea; and that not from my reason but from God's
providence.

"The sweetness and sense of words," a purely literary
culture, is Daniel's idea of wisdom. This wisdom he puts
above military valor, the professional virtue of the class
to which Daniel obviously belongs. "A valiant man, prince,
you could procure easily, but a wise one is expensive." He
confesses to not possessing military virtue himelf, but bears
it lightly: "If I am not very valiant in battles, I am strong
in words." He even holds his case as typical and affirms
the incompatibility of wisdom and valor. "A wise man usually is not very valiant in battles, but strong in his purpose."
It has been suggested, with a great degree of probability,
that cowardice was the main reason for Daniel's disgrace.
Belonging to the military class of society, Daniel by these
avowals disqualifies himself socially. On the other hand,
he has no taste for monastic life. Declining both holiness
and valor, he stands for reason understood as skill in using
witty and "sweet" or beautiful words. It makes him the
first or rather the only known intellectual of ancient Russia,
similar to the type of medieval cleric vagrant in the Catholic
West. He also shares the moral weaknesses common to this
social group.

The original vice of gnomic wisdom is its lack of any
straight direction as soon as it leaves the trodden paths of
commonplaces. In popular proverbs and apophthegms one
can find maxims for justifying quite opposite ways of conduct. If, in addition, they aim not at moral propriety but
at wit, the clash of contradictory precepts of the wisdom is
inavoidable. Let us take, for instance, Daniel's attitude
toward poverty. At present he is poor in his disgrace, but
he endeavors to free himself from this miserable condition.
In the double range of sentences concerning poverty and
wealth Daniel has a rich choice of adages for his invective

against the rich. Wisdom and poverty can live well together: "A wise beggar is like gold in a dirty vessel. I am
poor in garb but rich in sense. . . I am soaring on my
thought as an eagle in air. . ." Suffering is a good school for
perfection: "Gold is tested by fire and man by tribulations.
In sorrow man finds the perfect mind." Yet, on the same
page one reads: "As tin perishes when often melted, so also
man, oppressed by many needs. No one can eat salt and
preserve his sense in sorrows." Daniel can even go so far
in repudiation of poverty (which, after all, is a natural
attitude) as to affirm: "Better for me to die than to continue
life in misery."

Another series of contradictions which is less pertinent
to us is offered in his appreciation of the monarchical authority of a prince. A bounteous boyar is praised highly;
but, generally, this class of high counsellors and vassals of
the prince is one of the main targets of Daniel's satire. Another target, for some unknown reason, is the class of
"malicious wives." Here, indeed, Daniel is inexhaustible.
He became a classic of anti-feminism in Russia.

A very interesting piece of satire concerns monastic life:

Many people having secluded themselves from the world and become monks, return to secular life as a dog to its vomit and . . . walk
around villages and manors of the great of this world, like begging
dogs. Wherever weddings and banquets are, there monks and nuns
will be found . . . having an angel's image and a harlot's manners, a
father's dignity and a fornicator's habits.

These incriminations, though proclaimed in the name
of the ascetic ideal, the angel's life, can deceive no one.
Daniel uses this unpleasant picture of monastic decadence
as the pretext for his declining the monastic vocation. His
lack of any serious religious interest would in itself be a
sufficient reason.

The most striking feature about this strange man is

his posthumous appreciation. Daniel's work was very popular in ancient Russia and was handed down to modern times in numerous manuscripts. The fact is the more remarkable since the *Admonition* of Vladimir and the *Tale of Prince Igor's Expedition*—the pearls of ancient Russian literature —were each preserved from oblivion by only one manuscript. Thus pious Russia in neglecting and allowing these monuments of secular spirit or provenience to perish, carefully and devotedly preserved the work of her earliest humorist. It can be accounted for by the well-known preference of ancient Russia for Wisdom literature. As the example of Daniel teaches us, they often sought not wisdom but simply wit in this literary branch. Despite the pious exclusiveness in her literature, Russia possessed, most naturally, human and secular interests which needed for their satisfactions the stamp of "holy writings." The Biblical Wisdom books and the *Bee* or other gnomic collections possessed this divine sanction under cover of which some most undivine and worldly motives could find vent.

THE ANCIENT CHRONICLERS

*T*HE Russian *Chronicles* or *Annals*, rich in historical material and often very picturesque in their narrative, are unfortunately all anonymous. Recent historians, including Shakhmatov and his school, have attempted with an amazing amount of critical penetration to single out the different hands which had worked on the Russian *Chronicles*. The results, although very valuable, are still hypothetical. It is clear, however, that most of the *Chronicles* belong to the pens of monks or priests, with the exception perhaps of the Galich *Chronicle* of the thirteenth century, which betrays a secular hand. Large as is the place which ecclesiastical affairs hold in the historical entries of the annalists, the main subject matter of the *Chronicles* is the contemporary political history of the Russian principalities. In them secular Russian society finds its reflection, at least, in the person of its leaders, princes, and boyars.

Passing through the medium of clerical writing, the secular mind and moral standards had to undergo a certain refraction. One must expect a monkish or, at least, ecclesiastical idealization of some popular figures, and, at the same time, a condemnation of others according to standards foreign to their social setting. As a matter of fact, the disfiguration resulting from this quality of moral standards is not very great. The distance between lay and ecclesiastical standards was real but not large, not nearly so large as in the western Middle Ages. Most of the laymen of the upper classes wholeheartedly accepted the moral law of the Church. Vladimir Monomach is an eloquent proof of it, although his Christian learning and training may not have been in line with that of his enemy, the proud and aggressive Oleg Sviatoslavich or, in general, the dynasty of Chernigov princes. On the other hand, a monk who dedicates himself for years to the work of political records, acquires an amount of experience in state affairs which brings him to mitigate or change his ethical criteria when passing judgment in the secular and military field.

Russia had no purely monastic chronicles which aimed at the history of a single religious institution. Even the chronicler affiliated with a particular cloister, connected in most cases with a particular princely family, marks the events of the whole Russian nation or, primarily, of a particular "land" or principality. In recent times critics have emphasized the contradictory political tendencies of the different authors. Their partisanship, however, has been much exaggerated. In this respect there is a steady decline from the eleventh to thirteenth century. The interests of the Russian land as a whole prevailed in ancient times; but local and dynastic allegiances dominated in the late twelfth and the next century. But in both cases, national or local, it was the secular and political viewpoint that moderated and sometimes supplanted the ecclesiastical outlook.

Sometimes, but not very often, the reader is in the presence of a clash between the two standards. The chronicler may picture the state of mind of a prince in order to condemn it. He also may do so without any moralizing intent. He likes to record in short pointed sentences, in which the historical actor himself gives the motivation of his conduct. These winged phrases, corresponding to the long speeches of classic historians, are not necessarily fictitious. But even those that are fictitious must be typical, psychologically suitable, and were probably created by folk tradition and not by the writer himeslf. Here the laymen's standpoint is not always a profane one: it can be religious, Christian, but of another species than the generally accepted ascetic doctrine of the teaching Church.

Let us begin with a general idealized portrait of a Christian prince often given by the chronicler when he mourns the death of a popular or virtuous prince. Unpleasant characteristics are absent in these obituaries: for a bad or hostile prince the chronicler contents himself with a short factual entry of his death. The blame can be laid, sometimes very outspokenly, in depicting the actions of the living. These princely obituaries are stereotyped, obviously copied from one another, but in their monotony they reflect one ideal type. In its shortest form, condensing all essential features, the first icon-portrait occurs in the year 1056, the death of Rostislav Vladimirovich: "Rostislav was a man good for war, of a stately stature and a handsome face, and merciful toward the poor." In 1078: "Gleb was merciful toward the poor and hospitable, zealous to churches, warm in faith and meek, handsome of face." And at the same date (1078). "Iziaslav was a man, handsome of face and big in body, mild of habits, detesting wrong, loving right; he had no perfidy nor fraud, but he was simple in mind, not rendering evil for evil." And so it goes on, without marked changes, for centuries.

Curiously enough, the mention of physical beauty is never lacking. Together with mercy and almsgiving, this is the only constant feature of an ideal prince. Military valor is present in most cases, but it can be lacking, obviously in correspondence with real life. Of the famous prince of Galich, Iaroslav (Osmomysl 1187), the chronicler remarks that "he did not go himself with his hosts but sent them with his captains." But generally in the twelfth century military valor is more appreciated than in the earlier chronicles. The thirteenth century is opened, in the Galich *Chronicle*, with an epic, completely secular, praise of the prince Roman: "He was grim like a lynx, he would rush upon the heathen like a lion, and killed them like a crocodile, and crossed their country like an eagle. His valor was like that of an aurochs."

Military valor and physical beauty constitute a purely secular ideal of dignity. Ascetic features are not found, as a rule, in this portrait. In the exceptional cases when they are mentioned they must have been genuine, as in this very modest characterization of Vsevolod Iaroslavich: "He himself abstained from drunkenness and lust" (1093). With Vsevolod, the Graecophile, husband of a Byzantine princess and father of Vladimir Monomach, a certain abstinence or, at least, external correctness of conduct was very natural. Probably, it was rare in other princes. At any rate, the eulogy of "bodily purity" is found only in reference to one other prince, Sviatoslav Vsevolodovich (1194).

Christian coloring is given to the portrait not by asceticism but by two other characteristics: love of the Church or churches and love for the poor or almsgiving. The first includes not only piety or strictness in discharging ecclesiastical duties in worship and rituals, but also the love for the persons of clergy who are on these occasions enumerated in detail: bishops, monks, priests, and so forth. As the main expression of this love is the lavish bestowing of donations to the clergy, this virtue is confused with charity toward widows, orphans, and the poor. Mercy to the poor is never absent in the obituaries along with the handsome appearance of the prince. It is mentioned concerning princes whose temperament was far from mild, but who, for some reason, deserved a favorable obituary. Upon the general observation of this trait, as well as from the study of Russian sermons and admonitions, one is led to a legitimate conclusion: charity, or, at least, the giving of alms, was considered in Russia as the first and the last virtue of the layman.

Generosity towards the clergy had, of course, still another powerful motive. It is a well-known fact that in the Christian Middle Ages both in the West and the East, the laity felt dependent upon the clergy's prayers for salvation. The praying order of society, particularly the monks, had to be supported by the fighting and working classes, if society was to stand at all. The prayers of the clergy saved the people as individuals and nations from the ever-imminent wrath of God. For this reason alms or generosity to the clergy was not so much the mark of charity as the fulfillment of a social contract. To what extent emphasis upon this direction of princely munificence must be attributed to the clerical class feelings of the chroniclers themselves cannot be decided.

There are, however, cases where princely generosity, praised by the chronicler, takes a different, unclerical direction; towards the military companions of the prince, the *druzhina,* thanes, or retainers. One would rather expect a natural jealousy or competition between the military and the clerical friends of a prince. In western Europe, the antagonism dividing feudal and ecclesiastical society was sharply expressed. In ancient Russia there are no traces preserved of this conflict. The chronicler may or may not have belonged to the military class before his ordination or tonsure. At any rate, he is able to enter completely into the interest of the class of retainers, and considers the lavishness of a prince towards his druzhina as a military and political duty. Prince Rostislav Sviatoslavich "honored his druzhina and did not spare his fortune nor collect gold and silver, but used to give it to the druzhina or to the clergy for the care of his soul" (1172). The same is almost literally repeated on behalf of Prince Vladimir Glebovich (1187) with the following comment: "For he was a good prince and strong in war and marked by a firm courage." The first quotation seems to imply, that the author made a difference between the secular and clerical munificence: one is needed for the success in this world (in wars) and the other for the "care of the soul."

These citations all belong to the later Kiev *Chronicle* of the twelfth century. The primitive chronicles of the eleventh century are more expressly imbued with the monastic spirit. Yet the same appreciation of a prince's lavishness is found in them. Such is the tradition of Saint Vladimir's relations to his druzhina (*anno* 996).

> Having drunk a little they began to grumble against the prince: "It is shame on our heads to eat with wooden spoons instead of silver." Vladimir, overhearing this, had silver spoons forged for his druzhina, saying: "With silver and gold I cannot find druzhina, but with druzhina I shall find silver and gold, as did my grandfather and my father!" For Vladimir loved his druzhina.

These secular and practical considerations receive even a Biblical foundation, after an apocryphal source, in the story of Prince Sviatoslav Iaroslavich (1075).

> There came envoys from Germany to Sviatoslav. Sviatoslav, boasting, showed them his wealth; but they, after having seen the immense hoard of gold, silver and silk, said to him: This is of no use, it lies as if dead; knights are better than this, for vassals will acquire still more. In the same way boasted Hezekiah, king of Judah before the envoys of the king of Assyria; and all his wealth was taken to Babylon: likewise, after the death of Sviatoslav all his fortune was dissipated.

In the eternal strife between gold and sword the Russian chronicler takes the side of the sword. He strongly dislikes every accumulation of wealth. Fortune is good only to be given out. The best investments are the poor;

then come the people of the Church, monks, priests, and vassals. Greed and stinginess are often blamed, but never prodigality. It is interesting to note that the sinful son of the Gospel parable is called not "prodigal" but "profligate" in Slavonic. Such, at least, is the moral attitude of the southern pre-Mongolian writers.

The social expression of charitable prodigality is the banquet. It is striking how often the chronicler mentions princes' banquets, and with what warmth of feeling. He obviously sees in them the expression of friendliness, of mutual love, almost as if it were the matter of the old Christian *agape*. "The brothers dined all together, everyone with his boyars, in great love." (1072) The banquets are often mentioned on the occasion of an ecclesiastical festivity: "And they were joyful at the feast of the prince—the clergy and the citizens of Kiev." (1183) A real orgy of banquets in and around Kiev is described in 1195 on the occasion of the meeting of the two princely brothers for political parleys. The chronicler does not fail to emphasize the moral significance of these festivities:

David departed from Smolensk in boats with Smolenskians and came to Vyshgorod on Wednesday after Trinity; and Rurik invited him to dinner. David came to Rurik for dinner, and they were in great love and extreme joy. Rurik presented him with many gifts and saw him off. After that his nephew Rostislav Rurikovich invited him to dinner in Belgorod. David went to Belgorod and there they dwelled in great joy and love; Rostislav presented him many gifts and saw him off. David also invited for dinner the great prince Rurik, his brother and his sons, and they dwelled in joy and great love, and David presented to his brother Rurik many gifts and let him go. Then David invited all the monks for dinner and was joyful with them and distributed rich alms to them and to the poor and let them go. And then David invited all the Black Hoods (a Turkish tribe), and all the Black Hoods drank with him; he bestowed many gifts upon them and let them go. The citizens of Kiev began to invite David for feasts affording him great honor and many gifts;

and David invited the citizens for dinner and dwelled with them in extreme joy and great love and let them go.

One sees joy and love are inseparable; and thus, worldly entertainment is raised to the dignity of a Christian virtue.

The presence of the clergy at a banquet after the consecration of a new church or on some other ecclesiastical occasion has nothing unnatural in it. But one sees that their presence is rather the rule than the exception. When the town Belgorod is assailed by the enemies the prince "Boris was drinking in the hall with his druzhina and with priests of Belgorod" (1150). Entertaining the clergy, particularly the monks in one's house was considered a godly work, a form of charity. The pious prince Rostislav Mstislavich "also established this virtuous custom: at the time of Lent, every Saturday and Sunday, he invited twelve monks to dinner, the thirteenth Polycarp the abbot; and thus, having fed them, dismissed them not with empty hands" (1168). The period of Lent seems hardly to be fitting for banqueting, especially for monks. Yet from the point of view of the secular prince this most unascetic custom was an act of charity and a social form of almsgiving. The clergy approved it and probably insisted upon it, with a few exceptions. Saint Abraham of Smolensk never went to the banquets of laymen, but Abraham was known for his severity as a preacher of repentance. The great Saint Theodosius did not decline invitations to princely tables. We have already seen how he tried to preserve his monastic decorum on these occasions. His example became a rule but probably without his restrictions. Among Russian sermons, including one in a twelfth century manuscript, are preserved some picturesque descriptions of drunkenness during the banquets, where "popes" (priests) are included among the drunken guests.

As the poor received their part on the occasion of these festivities it was easy to represent a banquet as a work of charity. The most significant precedent was established by Saint Vladimir whose famous banquets were celebrated in chronicles, in *Lives*, in panegyrics, and even in folk poetry. In his account the chronicler introduces a series of Biblical quotations on charity which must have impressed Vladimir after his conversion.

Hearing it he ordered every poor man and every beggar to come to the prince's courtyard and receive all kinds of provision, drink and food, and some furs (old Russian money). Also he established this custom, saying: "The invalid and the sick cannot reach my court." And he ordered carts to be brought and, loading them with bread, meat, fish, various vegetables, mead and *kvas* (drink), he sent them through the town calling: "Where is anyone sick or poor, not able to walk?" and he ordered the provisions distributed according to their needs. And this again he did for his own men: every Sunday he ordered a banquet to be prepared in the hall of his court and invited boyars and druzhina, hundredsmen and tensmen and other distinguished persons, whether the prince was present or not (996).

The picture of carts laden with provisions and sent through the town is literally repeated in the panegyric to Prince Andrew Bogoliubsky (1175), and so it seems to have become a custom. But the Russian epic that makes Vladimir the center of a large cycle of songs recalls only his banquets. Nearly all of these songs begin with the description of Vladimir's feasts. Since Vladimir was a canonized saint it would be natural to embroider his biography with the traits of asceticism, but this was not done. Besides his great deed, the "baptism" of Russia, and the general Christian change of his life which was formerly debauched and cruel, his charitable banquets are the only preserved detail of his Christian virtues.

We insist so much on the detail of the banquets because

it throws some light on the very important question of
whether ancient Russia knew the distinction between lay and
monastic Christian ethics. After so many examples of laymen's unascetic virtues, the answer seems to be positive. The
way of charity can lead to the same high degrees of perfection as the way of renunciation. This conclusion is all
the more weighty because Byzantium did not know, or knew
little of, this ethical dualism. For her the only true perfection was to be found in a monk's cell. The layman must
follow the monk as far as he can without hope of equalling
him. This was the prevailing, although not exclusive,
doctrine of the Greek Middle Ages. How did ancient
Russia dare to set her own standard against the teaching of
the Greek mother church? Tension was inevitable. We
have found monastic exclusiveness of the most drastic kind,
expressed by Cyril of Turov. This point of view could
impress many layman, even in a princely palace. The attraction of monastic life must have been strong to the most
pious and church-devoted princes. There are, indeed, some
cases of princes taking the monastic tonsure, but they are
not numerous. Only one of the prince-monks, Nicholas
Sviatosha, marked his way by high ascetic achievements.
Most of the princely tonsures were taken under political
duress.

The Ipatiev *Chronicle* (1168) preserved a very interesting dialogue between a prince of Kiev and an abbot
which reflects the conflict of the two ethics. Strangely
enough, the monastic life is defended and sought by the
prince; the abbot shows the way of salvation within the
world. Prince Rostislav had dreamed for a long time of
monastic life. He always used to say to the abbot: "Build
me, Abbot, a nice cell; I fear sudden death." Polycarp the
abbot replied: "God commanded you to live in this way: do
right in this world, give just verdicts in courts and stand

firm on the cross-kissing." Then Rostislav: "My father! princedom and the world cannot be without sin; and I have been living a long time in this world." The prince longed to imitate the "orthodox emperors," the martyrs, and holy fathers. Polycarp replied: "If you desire it, my prince, the will of God be done!"

Rostislav procrastinated his renunciation until his death in 1168. Within the next generation a compromise between the two viewpoints was found or, rather, was accepted by ecclesiastical opinion. Princes began to take monastic vows on the deathbed. This custom had long been rejected and refuted by the best spokesmen of monastic tradition: it was justly considered as a last-minute attempt to cheat God. But since the act of monastic consecration or tonsure was looked upon as a sacrament erasing all the sins of the previous life, the temptation to use the benefits of this "second baptism" was too strong for those laymen powerful enough to break the opposition of the Church. After the end of the twelfth century the tonsure of dying princes became very common in Russia. One is not justified, however, to see in it the triumph of the monastic idea. On the contrary, it reveals rather a relaxation of ancient ascetic standards. It is natural that, at the approach of death, the mood of repentance and the disgust with worldly illusions becomes overwhelming and lends a certain sincerity to belated monastic conversions. The chronicler, in the more or less fictitious prayers of a dying prince tries to describe his new ascetic piety, his monklike humility, his renunciation of the world.

Prayers of this kind are ascribed to the dying David of Smolensk, whom we have seen banqueting in Kiev and who became monk before his death two years afterwards in 1197. Yet it is remarkable that after two ascetic prayers accompanying his tonsure, at the very last moment of his earthly life, he uttered quite a different, entirely unascetic prayer, reminding one of Vladimir Monomach's hymn of creation:

God immortal! I praise Thee for all. Thou art the only King of all, giving all riches for the delectation of Thy creatures. Having created this world Thou guardest it, awaiting the souls sent by Thee; Thou wilt honor with divine grace those who have a good life and those who did not submit to Thy commandments Thou wilt bring to judgment. For all Thy judgments are just; without end is Thy life; Thy grace Thou bestowest to all having recourse to Thee.

There is an undeniable connection between the legitimate "delectation" of earthly goods and the banquets of the prince's past. His last prayer, like Monomach's, is the expression of Christian hope, and not of fear. Thus, in spite of his newly invested monastic garment he dies as a pious layman.

As to the acceptance of double Christian ethics, the Russian Church stood by it as before. The best evidence of this can be found in the great number of the lay-saints in its calender, composing about a quarter of the galaxy of the Russian saints, a proportion impossible in Greece or in the Latin West. But if one examines the Russian entries in the so-called *Prolog*, a service book which contains edifying lectures for every day of the year, then this proportion becomes still more striking: the laymen are in majority among the Russian saints of the *Prolog*. And most of them belong properly to the class of princes. Later on we shall see where the holiness of the canonized princes lies. Now let us return to the *Chronicles* with their realistic appreciation of good and bad rulers.

The chronicler is not inclined to make any distinction between the private and public or political virtues of a prince. His charity, meekness, and even his humility are praised in both his private life and his political career. One has only to be cautious in the determination of the degree of this meekness and humility. Here they are measured on general Christian and not monastic standards.

Although some Russian princes—the most glorious among them—are adorned by the chroniclers with the title *tsar* which can be translated by both king and emperor; their portraits are far beneath the highness of a Byzantine *basileus*. Highness and majesty never appear as attributes of a Russian prince. He is called to serve the country and not to dominate it. In 1185 "Good Vladimir [Glebovich], sorely wounded, wiped his sweat valiantly [shed] for his father's land." In 1178 Mstislav Rostislavich "wished with his whole heart to suffer for his land." The same Mstislav "always endeavored to die for the Russian land and for the Christians and would fight with whole heart for his country— and all the Russian land, being unable to forget his valor, mourned him, and all the Black Hoods could not forget his kindness."

This was the ideal relationship between the prince and the country, his own princedom or the whole Russian land. The prince was not so much a ruler as a defender and warrior. But he was a judge as well and this part of his service is often referred to by the chroniclers in speaking of his "justice." We have already seen these remarks in the characteristics of the good princes; we noticed also that they can be absent. It is very important to stress the role of princely "justice" in pre-Mongolian Russia. After the Tartar invasion, from the thirteenth up to the middle of the nineteenth century, the injustice of Russian courts was considered by the people as a constant and, as it were, normal fact. Russian folklore is replete in "unjust judges," but it has preserved not one name of a prince famous for his justice. There are no Russian parallels to the legends of the justice of Charlemagne or Saint Louis of France or Harun-al-Rashid. In Kievan Russia the part of justice was, certainly, more advantageous. The ecclesiastical sermons, the *Chronicles* often speak of it and try to give good examples for imitation. Such is Prince Vsevolod Iurievich, "in tribunal giving a true and not a hypocritical justice" (1212). Yet one must confess that these indications are very brief and never illustrated by any concrete or anecdotal features. And at an early date a cynical note is already audible among the pious Biblical praises of justice. After the murder of Prince Andrew Bogoliubsky in 1175, the citizens began to sack the houses of his *tiuns* (officials), who were obviously detested by the people for their oppression. The chronicler, as a zealous partisan of the assassinated prince, tries to clear his memory by this remark: "they ignored the fact that, where there is law, there are also many outrages."

On the other hand, justice as an extolled virtue is rarely separated from mercy. Sometimes one gets the impression that only such justice is salutary and Christian which gives support to the weak and poor. In a well-known treaty on "Chastisements of God" included in the *Chronicles* (1068), the author calls for repentance: "Seek justice, rescue the offended." One remembers Monomach suggesting to his sons: "You yourselves mete justice to the widow and do not let the mighty ruin a man." This emphasis upon a charitable justice is certainly a part of the Biblical, prophetic tradition. One cannot avoid the impression, however, that in ancient Russia, unlike the Old-Testament pattern, charity tended to envelop justice, to absorb it completely until its specific function was atrophied. We are speaking, of course, of ideals and norms. In life, justice must have been violated more often by self-interest or indifference than by charity. But here we touch the very core of the ethics so fatal to Russia's civic development. The Russian is either above law or below it—never, or rarely, capable of appreciating law for its own value as an ethical minimum, or as a necessary mediation between the kingdom of God and the animal struggle for life.

In the first century of Russian historiography meekness and humility are often praised as high princely virtues. They have to be interpreted mainly in the sense of peaceful and friendly relations both to fellow-princes, and to their subjects. It is natural that these virtues are mentioned for the most part on account of unhappy, or weak princes, who fell victims to their foes. "Meek and humble and brother-loving" was Iaropolk Iziaslavich, "who suffered many calamities, was expelled without guilt, was harmed by his brothers, plundered and, finally, died a bitter death" (1086). The same ill fate beset his father Iziaslav who was "harmless by mind . . . not paying evil for evil. How much wrong was wrought him by the citizens of Kiev: they expelled him and plundered his house, and he did not render evil for it" (1078). If meekness toward rebels is praised, it is legitimate to suppose by implication it was recommended in rendering justice as well. We remember Saint Vladimir's unwillingness to execute robbers and Monomach's *Admonition* to his sons: "Do not kill anybody either right or wrong."

It ought to be noticed, however, that at the end of the twelfth century, the idea of justice seems to have changed; its double-edged character is more stressed. The first Russian prince to state this Biblical duty of severity is Vladimir of Galich: "God has created us as governors, for revenge to the evil-doers and for benefit to the pious" (1149). It is perhaps not without relevance that this justification of the avenging sword is put into the mouth of an unscrupulous politician, whose death is represented by the annalist as a divine punishment for blasphemy. But in 1197 it is said of the pious David of Smolensk in his panegyrical obituary: "He loved his druzhina and punished the evil-doers as it suits the kings to do." In 1212 died Vsevolod, the great prince, grandson of Monomach, one of the most powerful princes of northeastern (Suzdal) Russia. "He was adorned with all good virtues, chastising the evil-doers, and pitying the virtuous, for the prince beareth not the sword in vain, for revenge to evil-doers and for praise to those who do good." Although Vsevolod's panegyric is copied partly from that of Vladimir Monomach's, in the same chronicle, the passage of Monomach's meekness and of his pardoning his enemies is omitted. The times have changed. It is not meekness but severity that marks the junior line of Monomach's descendants: Iury, Andrew, Vsevolod, the builders of a powerful state, far from the ancient center of Russian lands. The annalist, a churchman (probably a secular priest), shares in this new political conception. And yet the panegyric of Vsevolod's son Constantine, written by another hand, brings us back to the early times of the Russian annalists. "Constantine has acquired eternal life by his alms and exceeding loving-kindness . . . He was righteous, bounteous, meek, humble, merciful to all . . . he never afflicted anybody . . . did not render evil for evil." (1218)

If meekness or charity prevails in the administration of private justice, the attempt was made very early and sustained for long, in spite of historical failure, to base political relations between Russian princes upon the same lofty ethical principle. Speaking roughly, not law but love was supposed to govern the interstate (if not international) affairs of Russian lands. These affairs were extremely complicated and confused. All Russian principalities were completely independent but ruled by one family, the descendants of Saint Vladimir, the Rurikovichi. The prince of Kiev had only honorable precedence and no legal power over his brother-princes who were not his vassals. The most astonishing feature of the ancient constitution of Russia was the continuous moving of princes from town to town. In theory a prince was not connected for life with any particular territory, but the whole of Russia belonged to one princely family which continually shared and reshared their common possessions according to varying standards of right and power.

The most ancient and venerable of these principles was that of clan seniority. All degrees of kinship were classified according to seniority, and the eldest in the family had the right to the best, that is, the richest principality. Such was the "legal" order under Iaroslav's sons and grandsons. In the twelfth century this principle of seniority was combined with and gradually supplanted by the principle of inheritance from father to son. Clan yielded to family, in the modern sense. Moreover, other principles and forces were at work: personal pacts between princes, the will of the people in the election or "invitation" of the prince, or simple power politics. No wonder that almost continuous war resulted from this confusion, not dissimilar to the feudal wars of contemporary western Europe. The main distinction between Russia and the West lies in the direction of interest: in Russia it was not the extension or strengthening of one's heritage, but the exchange for a more profitable one.

This chaos of interests and juridicial principles the Church or Christian conscience tried to check and to order by charity—charity, however, of quite a peculiar kind. It was charity within kindred, based on common blood. All princes of Russia were brothers or cousins in different degrees and actually felt their blood ties. Although these ties were covered by the name of "brotherly love" and thus brought under a general Christian virtue (corresponding to 'philadelphia'), it is easy to distinguish in it a pre-Christian stratum, an ethics of clan. The heathen Slavic ethics was sublimated and received a Christian sanctification; but it preserved a physical, fleshly, or bloodly character remote from the spirituality of universal evangelical charity.

In the mouth of the dying Iaroslav (1054), the *Chronicle* puts the following political testament to his sons:

My sons: have love between you, because you are brothers of the same father and mother; if you have love between yourselves God will be in you and subject your enemies under you and you will live in peace; and if you live in hatred, in quarrels and altercations, you yourselves will perish and ruin the land of your fathers and grandfathers which they had acquired with great labours; dwell then in peace, obedient one brother to another.

The eldest, Iziaslav, receives Kiev: "Obey him, as you have obeyed me, he is in the relation to you that I was." Such was an ideal moral and social order, probably written down in the light of princely quarrels and usurpations which had already begun under Iaroslav's sons. At the end of the pre-Mongolian period one finds the same idea of blood charity expressed in the testament of Prince Vsevolod Iurievich (1212), but narrowed in its extension from the whole Russia of Iaroslav to the political possessions of Vsevolod:—"You must be to them as their father," says Vsevolod to his eldest son: "treat them as I have treated them; you ought not to fight one another; but if some other prince rises against you, all together you shall be against him and God will be your aid and the Holy Mother of God and the prayer of your grandfather George and your great-grandfather Vladimir, and I then shall bless you."

The political idea of a firm union among brothers as a guaranty of peace and order is incorporated into the sphere of the highest Christian virtue. Prince Iziaslav fell in battle while coming to aid his brother against their nephews around 1078. This sad episode of what could be considered at the time as inter-family feud was transformed into an act of supreme ˰crifice of love. "He took upon himself the sorrow of his ʰer revealing a great love.—Truly, if he had done any transgression in this world it will be forgiven him because he has laid down his life for his brother . . ." And then follows a hymn in honor of love, composed of the most elevated quotations from Saint John. The end is, perhaps, the oratorical climax of the Russian writer himself: "In love everything is effected; for love's sake even sins are erased; for love's sake our Lord descended upon the earth and was crucified for us sinners, taking our sins upon him . . ." This, which can perhaps be considered the most beautiful expression of the Russian conception of Christ's redemptive work is here uttered by a politically-minded annalist in connection with a common and ambiguous military enterprise. True, Iziaslav deserved the praise of the chronicler for his forgiveness of all previous misdeeds of his brother Vsevolod against him. Even his taking part in the fatal expedition was in accordance with his father's political testament.

The ties of blood kinship and clan charity were not limited to the brothers in a strict sense. All Russian princes belonging to the same generation were considered as brothers and their peaceful relations as the expression of "brotherly love." Andrew Bogoliubsky is praised by his partisans as being "merciful to his *rod* and, generally, to the Christians" (1149).

An amazing example of the strength of this clan feeling is the pact between Prince Iziaslav and his uncle Viacheslav (1150) by which the former recognized his uncle as his father and restored to him Kiev whose possession had been the source of strife. Iziaslav let his envoys declare:

Father! I salute you; God had taken my father Mstislav and you are become my father. I now incline my head, I have sinned against you [There follows the enumeration of his misdeeds] . . . Now, father, I repent all this before God and you; if you, father, will forgive me, God will forgive me also. And now, father, I give you Kiev; come, sit down upon the throne of your grandfather and father.

Viacheslav was touched and thankful,—the political situation was not at all favorable to him. He answered: "You have no father and I have no son; you are my son and you are my brother too." And they kissed the cross that they should not separate either in good or bad times but should stand together. Since then, both princes held Kiev together as would be natural between a father and his son—the younger having the real power and carrying the burden; the elder, the honor and profit of the high title.

Taking into consideration that the whole history of ancient Russia is a never-ceasing war between related princes, the conclusion is tempting that blood ties were weak and the "brotherly love" belonged rather to the province of political rhetorics than to reality. This conclusion, however, would be erroneous. There is at least one example of the real inplications of clan relationship.

The interprincely wars and feuds in ancient Russia were a cruel reality. They were accompanied by the capture, sack, and burning of towns and villages, by the killing and enslaving of whole populations. Among all these bloody exploits one fact is striking—the death of a prince in battle was considered a calamity, an unexpected blow which stroke not only his druzhina and friends but also his foes. In the epistle of Monomach to Oleg on the occasion of the death of his son we have already read what line of conduct he expected from his enemy-cousin. In the year 1151 a great battle between two coalitions of princes took place which ended with the victory of Iziaslav's allies. He himself was heavily wounded, but among the defeated one prince, Vladimir Davidovich, was killed.

Iziaslav Mstisalvich was fainting from his wounds, having lost much blood; but he heard another Iziaslav (Davidovich) lamenting over his brother Vladimir and so he overlooked his own sickness. He was helped to horse and went thither and wept over him as if he

were his brother. Long he wept and said to Iziaslav: "We cannot resuscitate him any more. . . ."

The kinship between Iziaslav and Vladimir was very remote; but the consciousness of belonging to a common clan made Iziaslav weep over his dead enemy.

It follows, then, that the aim of a feud was never the killing of one's rival, and that a duel between Russian princes was unthinkable. After having defeated the hostile army and taking hold of the enemy, the victor either concluded a pact by kissing the cross with him, or held him imprisoned until the change of the political situation. We know other cases of cruel treatment: the blinding, after the Byzantine pattern, or even the treacherous murder of the princes. But this was considered a monstrous crime worthy of Cain and Judas, and the aversion of the chronicler to the authors of these abominations seems to have been shared by all Russia. Nevertheless, a gradual lowering in moral reaction can be stated. The blinding of Vasilko (1096) raised the coalition of princes in his defense which ended with his rehabilitation. But the blinding of two princes of Riazan' imprisoned by Vsevolod of Vladimir in 1177 had but little repercussion. Local chroniclers try to mitigate the responsibility of Vsevolod by throwing the blame on the populace of the city of Vladimir or even simply by passing over the cruel deed in silence. Sviatopolk, Saint Vladimir's son who murdered his three brothers in 1015, lost Kiev and met some mysterious and inglorious end outside Russia's frontiers. The surname of "Cursed" remained attached to him forever. Two hundred years later in 1217, Gleb of Riazan', who insidiously assassinated his six princely cousins at one of his banquets, was compared by the chronicler to Sviatopolk the classic villain of Russian history, but he was disturbed by nobody in consequence of his crime.

In the aversion to the killing of princes the general Chris-

tian motives of charity were supported by the strong sense
of blood bonds. Before the stark fact of war, however,
Christian charity was badly armed. Yet, it waged its generous though unsuccessful war against war for centuries. The
Church considered it her duty to preach peace and to secure
it by all the spiritual and diplomatic means at her disposal.
"Prince," said the Metropolitan Nicephorus to Rurik in
1195, "we are charged by God in the Russian land to restrain
you from bloodshedding." This duty of peace is stressed on
every page of the chronicles. Many times the seventh beati-
tude is quoted in old Slavonic translation where the word
"peacemakers" is equivalent to "those who humiliate themselves," as in Slavonic "humility" *smirenie* derives from
"peace" *mir*: "Blessed are they who reconcile themselves
with one another (or humiliate themselves) for they shall
be called the sons of God."

The chronicles give praise to every prince who yields to
his rival, even to the point of giving up his obvious right in
order to "avoid bloodshedding." In 1138 or 1140 Vsevolod
Olgovich assaulted the prince of Kiev, Viacheslav, without
any other ground except his desire of possessing the city. He
sent to Viacheslav this brief message: "Go from Kiev with
your skin safe." Viacheslav "not wishing to shed blood, did
not fight against him." The Metropolitan "pacifies" them
and "confirms it by the precious cross." The usurpation is
tolerated from a love of peace. At least, this is the public
side of the story; the weakness of Viacheslav was probably
the real reason for his pacifism. Sometimes the slowness or
caution of military operations may have been justified by the
cover of peacefulness. In 1180 Vsevolod of Suzdal and
Sviatoslav of Kiev stood against each other, divided by a
small river. Slight skirmishes continued for two weeks, and
Vsevolod's druzhina insisted on a general assault. "But
Vsevolod, being merciful, did not wish bloodshedding and

did not ride against Sviatoslav." From subsequent events, one sees that Vsevolod simply preferred to fight his enemy with the arms of his allies, the princes of Riazan'.

Certainly such examples hit beyond the target. Here peacefulness becomes a screen for lower and even very base motives. But, as in all cases, hypocrisy is a proof of the esteem paid to virtue, in this case the virtue of peace.

There was a kind of war which was not only accepted but insisted upon and glorified: that was war against the heathens, chiefly against the nomads of the steppes who never ceased to harass the Russian boundaries. Here the Church was the first instigator and inspirer of both defensive and aggressive operations. "In 1170 God put into the heart of Mstislav Iziaslavich a good thought about the Russian land because he wished good for it from all his heart." It was a common expedition against the Polovtsi: "Would it not be good, brothers, looking to God's help and with the prayer of the Holy Mother of God to seek the ways of our fathers and grandfathers and our own honor?" The answer of his brother princes was enthusiastic: "Grant us, God, to lay down our lives for the Christians and for the Russian land and be numbered with the martyrs."

The nomads of the steppes were a terrible foe to Russia. It looks sometimes as if all bonds of moral law were abolished in the struggle against this enemy. Yet in the most treacherous act of these campaigns, in the murder of the Polovtsian chief Itlar with his men, a moral scruple is uttered by Monomach. Itlar and his men came to the Russian town of Pereiaslavl to conclude peace. During these negotiations they were perfidiously assassinated. Vladimir Monomach bears full responsibility for this act. Yet, the chronicler assigns the initiative to the druzhina and lets Vladimir object: "How can I do it after having taken an oath with them?" The druzhina dissipate his doubts:

"Prince, there is no sin in it; God has led them into your hands; they also, always taking oaths with you, destroy the Russian land and continually shed Christian blood." Vladimir consents and although the chronicler describes the ghastly deed very objectively without any comment, the reader cannot help feeling that Vladimir is not quite in peace with his conscience. Otherwise, Vladimir's first reaction could be covered by silence. Certainly, the validity of moral obligations in ancient Russia, as elsewhere, had its limits in national and religious barriers. But they were not infringeable, even in the case of the heathen.

The wars of Russian princes against the pagan Lithuanians (Iatviagi) were deprived of every sanction of a Christian crusade. The narrative of them is as dry as could be: "Roman Mstislavich went to the Iatviagi to avenge himself; for they had devastated his land" (1196).

As to the Catholic neighbours of the West, Poles, Czechs, and Hungarians, they certainly stood with the Russians in the moral community which shunned in principle the state of war between them. Vladimir the Saint is praised explicitly for living in peace with his "neighboring princes": Boleslav of Poland, Stephen of Hungary, "Andrich" (Oldrich) of Bohemia; "there was peace and love between them" (996). The chronicler of Galich in the thirteenth century treats the Hungarians and the Poles, with whom the western Russian principalities live in an inextricable community of interests, on the same level as the Russian princes; only in the case of a foreign aggression something like national reaction is felt.

Despite this readily accepted duty of peace, Russia lived in a constant state of intestine wars which a modern reader would be inclined to consider civil wars. The ancient chronicler saw in these feuds (kotory is the old Russian word for them) the main reason for the decay of the land and for the success of the heathen. These feuds, however, could not be avoided. They could not even always be considered sinful. War itself was one of the pillars of political order in feudal times. Ancient Russia was aware of the eternal conflict between peace and justice and experienced it with the same poignancy as we have in our own time.

The Russian land consisted of dozens of independent principalities held together only by a princely clan without any supreme arbiter. There was no king in Russia, no organ in charge of the common well-being. The community of princes as a whole had to guard order and justice, not unlike the amphictyony of ancient Greece. A sword drawn in defense of justice under these conditions meant necessarily the sword of war. Returning to the famous political testament of Iaroslav (1054), which marks the birth of feudal Russia, one finds the precept of a just war in the prince's words to his eldest son Iziaslav: "If anyone wishes to wrong his own brother you must aid him who is wronged." Even applying the highest Christian standards the chronicler may approve a prince who, for the love of peace, renounces his own rights, but not him who tolerates an injury or oppression of another, his "brother" in a larger sense. Thus Iziaslav, we have seen, was praised as a victim of supreme charity when he fell in battle aiding his brother in strict obedience to his late father's will.

The very complicated juridical claims among Iaroslav's descendants needed continual corroboration in private pacts between princes who obliged themselves to fight against a law-breaker. The classic example of these pacts is that of Lubech (1097) on the initiative of Monomach: the princes promised to keep the possessions of their respective fathers— a new anti-clan principle. "And they kissed the cross so that, if one should assault another, they all shall be against him, they and the most precious Cross. And they said: 'The Cross

shall be against him and the whole Russian land.'" Thus
the principle of a just war was introduced into the political
ethics of Russia, based primarily on charity. Between justice and charity the moral judgment of the chronicler is continually wavering, reflecting the moral struggles of Russian
society itself.

Unfortunately the confusion of juridical principles prevailing in ancient Russia permitted the claim of any prince
to find a legitimate foundation. The strife of the interests
always took the form of conflicting juridical and moral
claims. That is mainly the reason why all juridical pretences
had to be covered by the religious sanction of "cross-kissing."
The chronicler speaks seldom of the justice or injustice of
the particular claims, but more often of the fidelity to or
breaking of the "cross-kissing." And thus the general conflict between peace and justice takes a religious form of conflict between the evangelical command of peace and the in-
vincible power of the Cross.

The *Chronicles* give rich evidence of the gravity of the
oath upon the Holy Cross. In 1067 the three sons of Iaroslav lured the Prince Vseslav of Polotsk by breaking their
oath:

> They kissed the precious cross, telling Vseslav: "Come to us, we
> shall do you no harm;" confiding in the kissing of the cross, he
> passed over the Dnieper in a boat . . . and they captured Vseslav, . . .
> transgressing the cross. Iziaslav brought Vseslav to Kiev and put
> him in prison with two of his sons.

It was the first political oathbreaking in Russia connected
with the profanation of the Cross. The punishment was
terrible and immediate. The next year, in 1068, a new and
mighty enemy, the Polovtsi, invaded Russia and defeated
the Russian princes. As a result of this catastrophe the
population in Kiev revolted, rescued Vseslav from prison,
and raised him to the Kievan throne. The chronicler, in

spite of his firm loyalty to Iaroslav's sons, sees the hand of God in the succession of these events:

> Lo, God revealed the power of the cross, for Iziaslav had kissed the cross but captured him; for this God launched the heathens. And Vseslav was rescued by the precious Cross. On the day of the Exaltation of the Cross, he sighed and said: "O precious Cross! because I believed in thee, deliver me from this prison." And God revealed the power of the Cross to teach the Russian land that they should not transgress the precious Cross after having kissed it.

The lesson was never forgotten. "We have kissed to Iziaslav Mstislavich,—say the brothers Davidovichi to the Prince Iury—and now we wish to be with him, we can not play with our souls" (1149). Three years before, one of these Davidovichi departed for a campaign to help Prince Igor with whom he was tied by sacred oath. The bishop of Chernigov provided him with the following sermon in the guise of viaticum: "If any one forsakes the cross-kissing he shall be cursed by the twelve Dominical Feasts." The power of the cross itself, however, was mightier than all the Dominical Feasts together. It brings vengeance at once on the breaker of oaths and the mocker at its holy power. Such was the lot of Vladimir, the mighty prince of Galich. The envoy of Iziaslav reminded him of his promise to return him certain towns: "Prince, you have kissed the cross to the king (of Hungary) and to your brother Iziaslav."—Vladimir's answer is blasphemy: "What, this little cross?" The envoy had an advantageous role to play in preaching the theology of the cross: "Prince, if the cross is small, great is its power in heaven and on earth; the king brought you a fragment of that precious Cross, upon which God, by His will, had spread His arms. . . . If you forsake it you will not live." The same day, upon leaving the chapel of his castle Vladimir had a stroke and died before nightfall (1152).

A grave conflict could arise when the cross required participation in war and conscience or the voice of the Church reminded one of the duty of peace. In this conflict the Russian conscience was hopelessly divided. Even bishops and monks hesitated as to what was the primary virtue of a Christian prince. That the breaking of an oath was a sin was beyond doubt. But the Church or the clergy could, if not release the prince from his sacred obligation, at least take the sin upon themselves. Metropolitan Nicephorus (1195) solved the hesitation of Rurik between his obligation toward a prince and the fear of war that would spring out of this act in this way: "You have given a land to a younger prince and have kissed the cross to the scandal of a senior one; but if blood has to be shed in the Russian land I take from you the cross-kissing and take it upon myself." True, in this case the bishop only met with Rurik's own desire. But the bishop of Chernigov quoted above would perhaps have refused to act in this way, preposterous to the sanctity of the cross.

The same religious conflict, in its drastic form, is described in 1127. In that year the old prince Iaroslav Sviatoslavich became victim of aggression by his nephew Vsevolod, who expelled him from Chernigov. Mstislav, son of Monomach, prince of Kiev, promised to aid Iaroslav, his uncle, to restore his right. But his cousin, the aggressor, tried by presents and entreaties to avert the expedition against him. The wronged Iaroslav reminded the Kievan prince of his cross-kissing. Under these circumstances the Kievan clergy had to pronounce their judgment. The Metropolitan was absent; the majority stood for peace. Among them there was a certain Gregory, the abbot of Saint Andrew's monastery, "who was loved by (the late) Vladimir, honored by Mstislav, and by all the people." This influential personality told the prince: "That sin will be on me if you transgress the cross-kissing; it is better than to shed Christian blood."

The whole assembly of priests took this viewpoint: "This
sin shall be on us; make the peace." Mstislav "did their will
and transgressed the cross to Iaroslav and repented it all the
days of his life." Here the chronicler and the prince obviously stand on other ground than the Kievan clergy: the
sanctity of the oath prevails over the virtue of peace-
making.

If these scanty facts authorize some general conclusion,
we could venture that in conflicts between peace and the
cross (or peace and justice) the clergy stood mostly for
peace; for the princes the cross had a greater value. This
attitude is, perhaps, accounted for by the natural love for
military exploits in the feudal class and the natural aversion
to bloodshedding among the clergy. It can be said that
the first attitude represented, in a limited sense, the defense
of the political order, the second that of the welfare of the
common, civilian population.

Political cross-kissing opened the door to the conception
of a just Christian war. This conception obviously prevails
in the twelfth century among the feudal class when peace-
making became the duty of the clergy. Princes go to war
for the judgment of God who will, by the issue of battle,
punish the wrongdoer. With or without cross-kissing, war
is judgment, like death, as the latter is called in Slavonic and
Old Russian. "The judgment came to my brother," writes
Monomach's son informing his father of his brother's death
on the battlefield in 1096.

In a difficult situation between two mighty adversaries
in 1150, Prince Iziaslav speaks to his druzhina: "Either I
shall lose my head or find my father's land and your goods
... And with him [the foe] I look for the judgment of God
—how God will judge between us." In 1180 Sviatoslav and
Vsevolod stand with their armies on both banks of a river.
Vsevolod is more cautious, whereas Sviatoslav seeks the

earliest occasion for battle. He sends to his enemy the request to retreat from the river and let him cross or vice versa: "cross to this side, and here God will judge between us." In this case there is no mention of any cross-kissing; it is a naked struggle for possession. Every kind of war is thus considered under the aspect of judgment. Every party takes a risk which can be expressed in this way: "I believe I am right; if I am wrong God will punish me." At the news of the death of Iury Dolgoruky in 1158, his ancient enemy Iziaslav cannot restrain joyful tears: "Blessed be Thou, O Lord, that Thou hast judged between us by this death and not by bloodshedding."

With this conception prevailing, every war or feud could be invested with a sacred character. The heavenly powers always are active on the battlefield and give victory to the right side. It would be interesting to trace what specific powers were thought of as the masters of battles. The name of God is seldom mentioned alone in this connection: Prince Rurik (1180) "looked upon God and drove against them [the foes]." In practically all cases God is named together with other celestial powers, or else these powers act alone. Often the powers are simply manifestations of God, but they can obtain a certain mythological independence in the minds of people.

The first power held for lord of battles is the Cross. Since on most occasions the belligerents appealed to the Cross as the warrant of their oaths, it was natural to consider it the arbiter in battles. The blinded Vasilko, after all his misfortunes, is attacked by Sviatopolk of Kiev who had just kissed the cross to him "to have with him peace and love." On the battlefield Vasilko raised the cross saying: "You have kissed it; first, you have taken the light from my eyes; and now, you wish to take my soul; let this cross be between us." During the battle, which was victorious for Vasilko, "many

Orthodox people saw a Cross on high above the warriors of Vasilko."

Even in cases where no breaking of oaths was involved and the holiness of the Cross had not been insulted, the Cross is believed to be a victory-giving divine power. This concept of the Cross as the giver of victory is not a Russian innovation. Since the conversion of Constantine it had become a prevailing Byzantine idea which had found a rich liturgical expression. The feast of the Exaltation on the fourteenth of September and its *troparion* (main hymn) praise the Cross not as a tree of redeeming death but as a symbol of political might of the Orthodox Empire. There is nothing astonishing then in the fact that "God and the Cross" or the "power of the Cross" alone, became a current formula for the Heavenly Lord of battles. "And thus, God and the power of the Cross turned them to flight" (1147).

But the Cross was not the only victory-giving power. Side by side with it are mentioned the Mother of God, Archangel Michael, and various saints: Boris and Gleb, Theodosius, Nicholas, Theodore. With some of them, as with Michael and Theodore, their warlike attributes were attested to in their legends and iconography. The other saints were local patrons of Russian cities. It was natural for a pious citizen of Kiev to think that the Polovtsi menacing the city were defeated "by the prayers of the Holy Mother of God and our holy father, Theodosius" (1107). Prince Andrew in battle calls for aid upon the martyr Theodore, "because there was a commemoration of Saint Theodore that day . . . and for his faith, God and Saint Theodore rescued him without any harm" (1149). For the cities, like Kiev and Novgorod, where the Cathedrals were dedicated to Saint Sophia, this divine entity is the natural protector—or protectress—in battle. "God stands for our prince and Saint Sophia" said the citizens of Kiev in 1147. In Novgorod, Sophia became the symbol and incarnation of the republic.

Churches to the Mother of God existed, probably, in all Russian towns; in many of them, the cathedral was dedicated to her. Besides, the role of Nike, military patron of the city, was inherited by her from Byzantium: the liturgy was rich in hymns describing poetically the delivery of her city (Constantinople) by the heavenly queen. Ὑπέρμαχος στρατηγός dux propugnatrix is the title and the beginning of a hymn which is sung daily at the prayers of the prime. Another circumstance comes to enhance the military dignity of Mary. The oath corroborating public pacts was often sworn not upon the Cross but upon the icons of the Holy Virgin or Christ. Thus, in many cases Mary was a guarantor of pacts and, consequently, avenger for their break. "We shall kiss the Holy Mother of God that we shall not seize you," promised the princes Davidovichi in 1146. In 1172, the victory over the Polovtsi is assigned by the Kievan chronicler to the "Holy Mother of God of the Tithe" (that was the name of the eldest Maria's church in Kiev), probably, because the Polovtsi, by having plundered an estate belonging to this church, attracted upon themselves the wrath of its heavenly proprietress. The success of a northern expedition in 1164 against the Volga-Bulgars and the escape of the Russian army from the Bulgars in 1173 (a victory was out of the question) were attributed to our Lady: "Manifestly, they were protected from the heathen by the Mother of God and the prayers of Christians" (1172). In this case, the protection of the Holy Virgin is explained by the fact that the expeditions were sent by the prince of Vladimir. This city stood under her special patronage since Prince Andrew had transported there the famous Byzantine icon from Kiev— one of many attributed to the hand of Saint Luke—which afterwards received the surname "Our Lady of Vladimir." Since then, all military expeditions of the principality of Suzdal-Vladimir have enjoyed her mighty protection. Her name constantly recurs in the chronicles of the city of Vladimir. All the political successes of Vladimir are counted so many "new miracles" of Our Lady.

Vladimir and its offspring, Moscow, had a great historical future before it. Yet, it had not only victories to score. Among its reverses there was one famous in the annals of the Russian Church. In 1169 the allied armies of "all Russian" princes sent by the same Andrew of Vladimir against Novgorod underwent a resounding defeat under the walls of that city. This victory was ascribed by the Novgorodians to the miraculous intervention of their icon of Our Lady, which recieved from that time the surname of "the Sign" or "the Miracle." As Vladimir's army stood, as usual, under the protection of Our Lady of Vladimir, it looks as if, to the naïve imagination of the Middle Ages, Our Lady of Vladimir must have been defeated by Our Lady of Novgorod. Yet, it is important for the fair appreciation of Russian religion, that no trace of such a pagan idea can be found. This time the chronicler of Vladimir keeps silence about the heavenly protectress of his city and frankly acknowledges the miracle of our Lady of Novgorod. In his variant of the legend "In three churches of Novgorod on her three icons the holy Mother of God had wept, imploring Her Son with tears that He should not destroy the Novgorodians for their sins." The Vladimirian chronicler does not admit the justice of the Novgorodians' cause. They are sinners and were moderately punished by that war and by its devastation. But the mercy of God's Mother saved them from final destruction. On the other hand, the citizens of Vladimir were also punished "for our sins" which are not specified, unlike those of Novgorod. In that skillful and pious manner, the chronicler achieves a smooth reconciliation of his local patriotism with the idea of the universal Providence manifesting itself on the battlefields.

Coming back to the question of the heavenly powers as masters of victory, one can observe a double tendency since about the middle of the twelfth century: first, the Cross gradually retreats into the background before Our Lady and the Saints; and second, there is an ever-increasing trend to multiply and combine the names of heavenly protectors, the beginning of which goes back to very ancient times.

We have already seen the Mother of God in association with Saint Theodosius and the Holy Cross. In 1146 the victory of Iziaslav over the Olgovichi is won "by the aid of God, and the power of the Holy Cross and the intercession of Saint Michael and the prayer of the Holy Mother of God." In the same year, the young Prince Andrew goes to battle, confident in "the aid of God and the power of the Cross and the prayers of his grandfather." With the "prayers of the grandfather" quite a new element comes into the traditional formula. Its uniqueness is stressed by the fact that only one manuscript of the chronicle has these last words. But soon they became frequent and common under the pen of the Vladimirian chroniclers. In 1151, the same Andrew is "preserved without harm by God and the prayer of his parents." In 1171 "God and the prayer of their father and grandfather" helped Michael and Vsevolod, Andrew's brothers, against the heathen. Neither their father nor grandfather was canonized as a saint; they never were considered saintly—least of all the father, Iury, who had no mark of piety about him—but they represented a powerful family line. The grandfather was Vladimir Monomach himself. Iury was nearest, for a time, to being the actual ruler of the whole Russia. The city of Vladimir, which was the heritage of this line of Monomachovichi, felt strong by the protection of these ancestors now in heaven. Subtracting the political part of the story there is a remainder which brings us to the religious meaning of the clan in Russia. The prayers of the grandfathers in Christian times had replaced the protection of the ancestors' spirits in pagan times. In Novgorod which had no princely dynasty of its own, the same tendency expressed itself in a formula like this: "Novgorod was saved by the great Catholic and Apostolic church of the Saint Sophia and the Saint Cyril and the prayer of the holy archbishops and the orthodox princes and holy monks of the priestly assembly" (1238). Deceased princes and bishops, together with pious monks protect their beloved city by their prayers from heaven.

We shall later discuss the religious meaning of the recession of the Cross into background and the emergence of human, even nonholy, heavenly patrons in battles. Let us return once more to the Cross as the symbol and arbiter of just war.

The conception of war as the judgment of God obviously met insurmountable difficulties. Victory too often crowns an unworthy head. There must be found some other corrective to save the faith in God's immediate providence. This corrective was found by the first monastic chroniclers in the antithesis "pride-humility" as supplementing "wrong-right." A just cause can be lost by the human pride of its advocates. "God resisteth the proud but giveth grace to the humble." (James 4:6) These and similar quotations from the Bible occur on every page. If there was a revolting case of oppressed and injured innocence, it was the blinding of Vasilko in 1096. All the Russian land was deeply stirred by this crime. Vasilko himself, in his depression, meditated upon his sins which could inflict upon him such punishment of God. (We know about his state of mind through the words of his spiritual father). His sin he found in his pride: "God has punished me for my elation." He had dreamed of glory; nothing seemed impossible to him. "I thought: I shall invade the Polish land . . . and after, I wished to seize

the Danube Bulgars and transplant them to my land; and
then . . . to go against the Polovtsi, that I might either acquire glory or lay down my life for the Russian land."
There was nothing sinful in these dreams except their human, too human, pride.

Without any doubt, Prince Iziaslav Mstislavich enjoyed
the sympathy of the Kievan chronicler of his time. He was
defeated in a battle for Kiev in 1149 by his uncle Iury, who
was loathesome to the citizens. A delicate indication of the
religious ground of the catastrophe is sketched in this tale.
Before the battle Iziaslav attended the Mass in the cathedral
of Pereiaslavl.

> The bishop Euthymius shed tears and implored him: Prince,
> reconcile yourself with your uncle; you will receive much grace from
> God and deliver your land from great distress. But he did not agree,
> confident in the multitude of his warriors; he said: I have won Kiev
> and Pereiaslavl with my blood.

This is the hero's tragic guilt, his *hybris,* attracting upon
him the wrath of God. If the friendly princes are punished
for their self-confidence, so much more are their adversaries;
thus is described the end of Iaroslav Sviatopolchich, enemy
of the popular Monomach. With a great military force he
was besieging the town Vladimir which was held by young
Andrew, Monomach's son. "Elated with pride, confident
in the multitude of warriors" he boasted to Andrew and the
besieged citizens: "This is my town; if you don't open and
come out in subjection you will see: tomorrow I shall storm
and take the town." All of a sudden, he was assassinated by
two murderers in ambuscade. "And thus, Iaroslav died
alone at the head of such an army, because of his great pride;
for he did not hope in God but in his multitude of warriors."
His proud conduct contrasts with the humility of Andrew
and his father (1123). Boasting alone is sufficient to ruin

a good cause, as in the famous Prince Igor's expedition of 1185, in the eyes of the Vladimir chronicler.

One is not obliged to accept at face value the moral judgments of the chroniclers, since they were often guided by partisanship. Thus pride is often, but not always, an easy expedient with which to charge one's adversary or to explain his defeat; humility is, on the contrary, a complementary virtue for a successful and popular prince. Both can be listed among the characteristics of the same person by different writers. That the young Andrew Bogoliubsky "was not boastful of warlike deeds but sought praise from God alone" is told in the description of his exploits in a battle in 1149. The same Andrew, many years after, collected a great army against the Rostislavichi with whom the chronicler was, obviously, partisan. "Andrew was full of conceit and pride, confident in the force of flesh and protected by the multitude of warriors" (1174). After having told of the failure of this undertaking, the chronicler concludes: "Prince Andrew, so clever and courageous in all his affairs, spoiled his character by immoderation and fury; for he uttered words of boasting. Boasting and pride are shame and disgust before God."

The argument from pride and humility possessed its full weight in the eleventh century and the beginning of the twelfth when the *Chronicles* were composed by pious monks, and when political morality was more deeply determined by Church standards than in the subsequent period. Since the middle of the twelfth century it is useless to look for a serious moral meaning behind similar concepts in the political sphere. They became slogans to cloak mere partisanship. In fact, of all Christian moral categories applied to politics and to the life of the warlike feudal class, humility is the hardest for and most foreign to human nature. That a serious effort was made by the Christian elite like Monomach to conform to this ideal is beyond doubt. For the majority, however, as for the upper classes of all times, it is either empty words or superficial behavior. Reading through the Russian *Chronicles*, one sees at every step the clash between the Christian ideal of humility and the aristocratic ideal of honor. The search for glory which is sinful pride for a monk is a natural or even virtuous attitude in a prince.

It often was maintained that honor was specifically a western idea, alien to ancient Russia. If ancient Russia is understood as Kievan, pre-Mongolian Russia, this assertion is certainly wrong. Yet, the aristocratic idea of honor had more difficulties in asserting itself against the Christian standard of values in the Byzantine East than in the Roman West. During the first century of the Russian historiography, the chroniclers were reluctant to attribute the secular search for honor and glory to Christian princes while freely, and not without a certain national sympathy, speaking of honor in the pagan past. To Sviatoslav, the pagan, father of Saint Vladimir, a proud sentence is ascribed: "Let us here lay down our bones, for the dead have no shame" (971). Yet, one hears nothing of this kind about Vladimir, Iaroslav, or his sons and grandsons.

In the first half of the twelfth century the chroniclers are full of praise for the princes, even the weak princes, who give up their legal rights for the sake of peace. That the same conduct was looked upon with contempt by the feudal class itself is clear from the narrative of the events of the year 1136: "Iaropolk (Monomach's son) . . . did not go against them (the Olgovichi); did not commit bloodshedding; but feared the Lord's judgment and made himself the least among them, taking upon himself blame and reproach from his brothers and everybody" (1136). That means a serious conflict of standards between ecclesiastical and secular ethics. Four years later the same expression "did not wish bloodshedding but made himself the least" is used, probably by the same author, of the weak prince Viacheslav who gave up Kiev to his rivals the Olgovichi (1140). At this time, however, we approach a great change. Secular values begin to appeal to the chronicler. Curiously enough, in the same year, 1140, he notes the proud and provocative reply of the young Prince Andrew Vladimir-ovich, brother of both Iaropolk and Viacheslav: "Better death for me with my druzhina in my father's and grand-father's land than the princedom of Kursk. . . . I will not go alive from my land." Andrew was challenged by the same enemy as his brother's to hand over his city Pereiaslavl. His refusal led to a feud in which Andrew got the upper hand. Andrew is one of the favourite heroes of the chronicler. His victory is granted to him by God: "God helped the men of Andrew"; and his proud words are quoted with obvious satisfaction.

It is probable that the passage on Andrew belongs to an-other pen than the two notices above on Monomach's sons. But since the middle of the twelfth century the words "honor" and "glory" occur frequently in the mouth of princes without incurring any blame from the chroniclers. In the long struggle for Kiev between the son and the grand-son of Monomach, both adversaries, Iury and Iziaslav, ap-peal to their honor. Says Iury in 1149: "I shall either blot out my shame and avenge my country or find my honor, even if I lay down my head." And Iziaslav in 1150: "I can not be insulted. . . . Better, my brothers, let us die here than take this shame upon us . . ." And thanking his brother Vladimir: "God help you because you have labored for the sake of my honor and your own." The honor is assigned as well to the Russian land, not on the occasion of a national war but of a common feud, which the same Iziaslav was carrying on as an ally of the Hungarian king: "Brothers and druzhina!

God never left the Russian land or Russian sons in dishonor; everywhere they used to win their honor. And now, brothers, let us be zealous for it; in these lands and before strangers may God let us gain our honor" (1152). Even usual expeditions against the Polovtsi, justification of which was always sought in the defense of the Russian land, begin to appear as the cause of honor. This motive is blended with others in a pious invitation of Mstislav: "It would be right, brothers, looking to God's assistance and the prayer of His Holy Mother, to seek the way of our fathers and grandfather, and *our honor*" (1170).

It is but natural that the motive of honor continues to appear in the Galich *Chronicle* of the thirteenth century. The principality of Galich lived in continuous intercourse with its western neighbors, Hungarians and Poles, and underwent a strong impact of western ways of life. On the other hand it is important to state that in the Russian northeast (Suzdal-Vladimir) one hardly meets in the chronicles the emphasis on honor. That the ground is not to be sought in a pure Christian attitude of the northern chroniclers or their princes we shall see later.

Closely linked with the longing for honor is the motive of revenge. Its un-Christian character is even more obvious. The ancient chroniclers, narrating at length the legends of the revenge of a pagan princess, Olga, could not tolerate it in a Christian prince, even for a just cause. The unfortunate Vasilko, if anybody, had the right to avenge the terrible crime against himself. And he actually took his revenge on his foes, once burning the town of his enemy, and another time, having his archers shoot two of the boyars whom he considered as main instigators. Both acts attracted the blame of the chronicler who was, however, full of compassion with his woes: "Vasilko took revenge on innocent people and shed innocent blood," speaking of the burned town; and on the execution of the guilty ones; "This was the second revenge taken by him, which was not good to take that God might be the avenger" (1096).

It may be said that the moral demand in this case was too high for political application. Half a century later, together with the rehabilitation of honor, vengeance too comes into its own. In the year 1151 Iziaslav says to the king of Hungary, his son-in-law and ally: "Vladimir of Galich has killed my men and yours; may God not let it be borne by us but may God allow us to avenge our druzhina." And the same Vladimir of Galich, his enemy, proudly declares: "If I live I will either lay down my head or avenge myself" (1152). True, this time his pride, leading him to blasphemy, is punished, and does not meet the sympathy of the chronicler. But vengeance, once freed from Christian restraint, remains as a legitimate political motive. In 1196 Rurik, of whom the Kievan chronicler is an obvious partisan sends such a message to his ally Vsevolod: "Let us meet somewhere in order to avenge our outrage and shame, rescue our nephew and retrieve our right." In the next generation Mstislav the Bold (Udaloy), one of the last chivalrous princes, very popular at the time of the first Mongolian invasion, declares: "I will go to seek the Polovtsi and to avenge my dishonor" (1213). At that time the expeditions against the heathen are naturally and frankly treated as the revenge for harm inflicted. The chronicler qualifies in factual style: "Roman Mstislavich went against the Iatviagi (Lithuanians) to avenge himself" (1196).

The breaking through of secularism, with its aristocratic morals of honor, is one of the marked features of the southern (Kiev and Galich) chronicles since the middle of the twelfth century. Another development of a more ambiguous character can be observed in the chronicles of Vladimir (northern or Suzdalsky). Here ecclesiastical phraseology goes hand in hand with the loss of Christian moral standards in politics. Not chivalrous honor but local interests and the struggle for power among the territorial princes appear to be the leading motives of the clerical writers. To appreciate fully the meaning of this change one has to glance at the whole development of the Russian annals from this point of view: religious judgment versus partisanship.

Recently much has been written about the partisanship of Russian chroniclers since the very beginning of Russian historiography. Undoubtedly any monk holding the pen in the eleventh and twelfth centuries had his own favored princes. Yet, the question is on what is this preference based: on the local interest of a certain monastic institution, on the dynastic loyalty, or on moral and general grounds —the qualities of the respective princes, or the justice of their political claims? In our opinion, the second, the moral and general motives, prevailed up to the death of Monomach in 1125. The Kievan chronicler liked Iziaslav because of the legitimacy of his power (as eldest son of Iaroslav) and the undeserved outrage from the hand of his brothers; he liked Monomach because of his great abilities and high character. This is proved by the freedom of moral judgment of the chronicler towards even his favorite princes. We have seen some instances of this critical independence. The chronicler condemned the perfidious capture of Vseslav of Polotsk by Iaroslav's sons (Iziaslav among them), and attributed to this crime the invasion of the Polovtsi. He went so far as to justify the popular rebellion in Kiev which sent into exile his beloved Iziaslav. We have seen how severely the unhappy Vasilko is judged, in spite of all sympathy and compassion he enjoys from the chronicler. Even in regard to Monomach, the great hero, the chronicler is not yet disarmed in his moral judgment. Few princes stood in such bad repute for aggressiveness and association with the Polovtsi as Oleg of Chernigov, Monomach's cousin and enemy. And yet, the chronicler acknowledges expressly at least one of the claims of this prince against Monomach, the claim to Murom, his father's town: "Oleg was confident of his right, for he was right in this" (1096). This was also the conviction of Vladimir's son Mstislav, who wrote to his father upon the death of his brother Iziaslav, killed in this feud for Murom: "For my brother came the judgment; be not the avenger of him" (1096).

After Monomach's time one does not meet such a disinterested and generous political attitude. The chroniclers became more partisan. On the one hand, the consciousness of the unity of the Russian land was dimmed by its division into separate territories, each with its particular local interests and patriotism. Besides, the continuous state of inter-princely wars demoralized the mind of the chroniclers. While not giving up the pretense of moral appreciation, speaking constantly of cross-kissing and its breach, between the clashing moral and legal claims they made a choice which was convenient to their local or dynastic feelings.

There is eloquent evidence, however, that in exceptional cases, the Kievan chronicler could put religious and moral values above his local patriotism. The editor of the Kievan *Chronicle* at the end of the twelfth century, included in his work two obituaries in pure hagiographical style, of the two murdered princes, Igor in 1147 and Andrew in 1175. Both were in disfavor in Kiev, belonging to unpopular dynastic lines; the latter was even guilty of the terrible sack of the city in 1169. But the circumstances of their death, inflicted either by the mob or by treacherous servants, deeply stirred the moral sense of the contemporaries. Both princes were considered as martyrs and venerated by the church. The Kievan chronicler did more than an act of official reverence. The Kievan narrative of Andrew's death is much more em-

phatic and panegyrical than that of the northern chronicler
who was, however, a legal subject and political partisan of
the prince. By that time, even the northern (Vladimir)
chronicler could acknowledge the protection of an enemy
city, Novgorod, by the Mother of God, though unwilling to
acknowledge the "justice" of Novgorod.

Since the end of the twelfth century, one observes a further change for the worse. We do not possess the continuation of the Kievan *Chronicle* after 1200. The *Chronicle*
of Galich in southern Russia has more secular character and
reflects the political viewpoints of Galich princes. The attempts at religious and moral judgment in politics are very
few.

It is otherwise in Vladimir. Here the religious outlook
prevailed, but it seems to have been separated from the moral
one, presaging the future Muscovite development. The
Vladimirian chronicler believed firmly in the protection of
the divine powers as if the cause were independent of justice.
As early as 1168, he dares ascribe such an unheard of deed
as the sack of Kiev by the army of Andrew to divine assistance.

God and the Holy Mother of God, and the father's and grandfather's prayer helped prince Mstislav Andreevich and his brothers;
they stormed Kiev, which never had happened before . . . and the
whole of Kiev, its churches and monasteries, was plundered for
three days, icons were taken, books, and vestments. This was done
because of their sins.

The will of the prince of Vladimir becomes a supreme
criterion, taking the place of justice and the Cross. "At this
year (1174) the Rostislavichi became insubordinate to prince
Andrew and were not walking in his will." We understand
now why the power of the Cross almost disappears from the
annals of Vladimir, giving place to the local Palladium: the
Mother of God of Vladimir. The Cross was too much linked

with the idea of political justice in the keeping of pacts. The icon of Vladimir was merely the local patron of the city.

The whole political philosophy of Vladimirian patriots is expressed in the *Chronicle* on the occasion of the local and civil wars following the death of Andrew in 1176. Vladimir, a young foundation but the residential town since the time of Prince Andrew, felt outraged by the ancient cities of northeastern Russia, Rostov and Suzdal. The citizens of Vladimir rebelled against the princes of Rostov and Suzdal, elected a prince of their own, and in the ensuing war defeated the ancient cities and their princes. In this conflict, the traditional right was on the side of their adversaries. The chronicler of Vladimir accepts it; but opposes to the "justice" of Rostov and Suzdal the new "justice" of Vladimir which is, at the same time, "that of God and of the Mother of God." He cites from the ancient *Chronicle* the custom that "from the beginning the ancient cities used to meet in councils called *veche*, and what the ancients decided, that the suburbs (the younger towns) stood upon." In this case the old towns are Rostov and Suzdal, and all their boyars "wished to do their justice—resisting God, the holy Mother of God and God's justice."

Why the right of Vladimir is God's justice is not explained except by the statement of facts and claims: "This city (Vladimir) was founded by the great Vladimir (Monomach) . . . and this Michael (the prince elected in Vladimir) was chosen by the Holy Mother of God." The inhabitants of Vladimir are "minor" people; but in the Gospel is said "what is hidden from the wise is revealed to the infants." The citizens of Vladimir

understood and firmly seized their justice and said to themselves: Either we shall have Prince Michael or we shall lay down our heads for the Holy Mother of God and the prince. And they were comforted by God and the holy wonder-working Mother of God of

Vladimir. . . . Those of Vladimir are glorified by God all over the world for their justice.

Justice is here equivalent to the particular rights or privileges of Vladimir; the Mother of God, to Vladimir itself; and God's assistance is equivalent to virtual power. In the annalistic entry of the next year (1177) this political philosophy is completed by the sentence: "God gives power to whom he wishes; for king and prince are created by the Most High." In the context of the Vladimirian civil wars, it means only that no legal claims have a place in politics. Only power decides; and power is the sign of God's will. One is tempted to say that the possession of the miraculous icon of Our Lady had a destructive influence on political morals in Vladimir.

It is not astonishing then that meekness and mercy in politics find little favor with the Vladimirian chronicler. Telling of the punitive expedition of 1178 against Torzhok, a frontier town belonging to Novgorod, the chronicler relates the dissension between Prince Vsevolod and his druzhina. Vsevolod "did not wish to storm the town because its inhabitants had promised to give tribute to him." The druzhina were for sacking the town with cynical motivation: "We have not come to kiss them." The town was taken and burned; all the population, women and children, captured and enslaved, "for the iniquity of Novgorod." The chronicler is satisfied with that act of "justice" and quotes abundantly from an Old-Testament prophet threatening the wicked with terrible plagues.

We have already seen that in the panegyric obituaries of Vladimirian princes a new feature appears: the severity toward evil-doers. The northern chroniclers do not go so far as to justify Vsevolod's blinding two captured princes of Riazan'. They either silence the cruel deed or transfer responsibility to the mob. A sincere condemnation in the style of Nestor of the eleventh century is out of the question.

Hand in hand with political opportunism goes a new attitude toward war and peace. Peace ceases to be a good in itself and is judged by its expediency. A good war is openly preferred to a bad peace. In 1187 the Vladimirian chronicler tells of an unsuccessful (in his eyes perfidious) peace-making between Vladimir and Riazan'. The bishops of the hostile cities are working in the traditional manner as intermediaries between the princes. As Riazan' did not conform to the demands of Vladimir, its bishop Porphyrius is treated by the chronicler as an "intriguer and liar," and on this occasion a justification of war is given by a Biblical quotation. "As the wise Solomon says: Wrath tamed by lying produces quarrels, and war waged not up to the end sheds blood; a glorious war is better than a shameful peace; those living in a false peace do great harm to the people." However much can be said for this principle from the point of view of *Realpolitik* it contrasts strongly with the attitude of the Russian Church and Russian chroniclers of the eleventh and twelfth centuries. The quotation is, probably, taken from *The Bee*, a moral anthology, translated from the Greek, and it appears on a page of the Russian chronicles for the first time at this date (1187) in the Vladimir annals. Since then the quotation had a dashing career: one finds it commonly used in the thirteenth century, around 1234 in the Galich *Chronicle*. Northeastern Russia precedes, at least by one generation, the general decadence of political morality.

The ·same development can be observed in the Novgorodian chronicles, although belatedly; it can even be said that here it never reached the same level of political cynicism.

The chronicles of Novgorod are marked by brevity and matter-of-factness of their entries. Nevertheless moral

appreciation is rarely absent. The love of peace and horror
of war is clearly seen in sentences like these: "God, by his
mercy, did not shed any more Christian blood" (1180), or
"God did not let Christian blood be shed among them"
(1198). This reflection is proverbially applied to the conflicts with other Russian lands in which Novgorod was involved. In the case of Novgorod's setbacks a laconic statement is used in 1195: "God helped those of Chernigov"
(the enemies). The famous battle of Lipetsk in 1216,
where the host of Novgorod fought on the side of the anti-
Vladimir coalition, is preceded by a somewhat naïve ex-
clamation of horror: "Alas, a terrific and amazing wonder,
my brothers, son went against father, brother against brother,
lord against slave, slave against lord." Some Novgorodian
citizens fought on the side of the enemy. Certainly, the
final victory was hailed as the manifestation of divine powers: "O, how great, brothers, is the providence of God! Those
of Iury were defeated. . ."

Civil wars, or wars among Christians were waged in Novgorod not only against hostile Russian princes but also between the struggling parties of its own citizenry. There is
no democracy without struggle. These civil wars are related with horror by the Novgorodian chroniclers as the
work of the devil. Not that the writers are always above
partisanship but they certainly do not favor the shedding
of blood. Typical is the appreciation of the revolt in 1218.
The Mayor Tverdislav accepts the fight as the judgment of
God: "If I am guilty, let me be dead; if I am right, give
justice to me, O Lord." It is quite the style of Russian
princes of the eleventh and twelfth centuries. But the
chronicler, whose sympathy is with Tverdislav, cannot
restrain a sigh: "What a great wonder the cursed devil
wrought! At the time when they ought to fight against the
heathens they began to fight one another." The end of the

feud is hailed: "The devil was trampled by God and Saint Sophia; the Cross was magnified."

But civil riots in Novgorod were as frequent as inter-princely feuds, and by their frequency demoralized the political conscience. The chronicler is still able to see in natural calamities such as famines the wrath of God provoked by hatred among citizens (1230), yet at the same time, having related the murder of some boyars by the opposing party, he makes this reflection concerning their plundered fortune: "They had labored and gathered, and the others enjoyed the fruit of their labor; of such the Holy Ghost said: 'You gather, and do not know for whom you gather.'" Here the blame seems to be turned against the victims instead of the assassins. It is imposible not to see here the victory of partisanship over the moral conscience. But one has to reach the eve of the Mongolian conquest (1238) to see the decline of the old Christian spirit in Novgorodian historiography. In Vladimir it could be observed some sixty years before.

In order to preserve a true perspective it is necessary to recall that the degradation of political morals did not yet destroy the standards of pre-Mongolian Russia in purely personal ethics. The same chronicler of Vladimir who reveals himself merciless toward the enemies of his city confesses to kenotic Christianity when speaking of an ideal bishop. In the portrait of bishop Lucas of Vladimir (in 1185), the prelate is praised for his mercy and kindness, meekness and humility: "Bearing upon himself the humiliation of Christ, not having a city here but seeking a future one." Still more interesting is the portrait of a layman, the Prince Sviatoslav Iurievich whom a heavy illness prevented from ruling and participating in all secular activities. This handicap is considered a great spiritual gain:

This prince was God's elect; from his birth until the close of his manhood he was afflicted by a bad illness; such illness was asked for of God by holy apostles and holy fathers; whosoever suffers from this kind of illness, as the books say, his body is tortured, but his soul saved. Thus, this Sviatoslav, in truth a holy man, God's saint chosen among princes—God did not let him reign on earth, but gave him the kingdom of heaven (1174).

This contradiction between personal and social ethics is typical of many epochs of Russian, and in general, Eastern Orthodox life. The most striking example is given later in the nineteenth century. It must be emphasized that this was not typical of Kievan Russia; it appears at the end of its best period and at the beginning of the disintegration of its culture.

THE TALE OF IGOR'S CAMPAIGN

*T*HE *Tale of Igor's Campaign* stands unique in ancient Russian literature. It is the only work of purely secular content and of intentionally artistic form. It could be styled a poem and would deserve the title but for its external form which reads like rhythmic prose rather than verse. In artistic value it looms like a mountain over the flat plain of contemporary literature. The anonymous author, living at the end of the twelfth century, was undoubtedly a poet of genius. One has to wait until the nineteenth century, until Pushkin, to find his equal. In western poetry the *Tale* can be compared to the *Chanson de Roland* and the *Niebelungenlied;* to the Russian taste it might even excel these in poetic value.

Ancient Russia, however, was severe towards her best literary creation. Although read and imitated by some authors up to the fifteenth century, *Igor's Tale* came down to us in only one manuscript which was unfortunately burnt during the Moscow fire of 1812. The obvious neglect of this masterpiece on the part of medieval readers can be explained by its purely secular—in fact, somewhat pagan—content and form. It was too much for the pious Muscovites.

Whether *Igor's Tale* was always unique in Russian literature or rather belonged to a literary species which had flourished in its time but had disappeared completely from the monastic libraries, the only stores that transmitted the

315

ancient documents, is hard to decide. The author himself
invokes an old poetic tradition which is embodied for him
in the person of Boyan, a poet, apparently at the end of the
eleventh century. Yet, after what is told of Boyan in
Igor's Tale—our only source of information concerning this
person—Boyan was both a poet and singer who accompanied
his songs on a musical instrument. The author of *Igor's
Tale* is a writer, a literary man who combines the epic tradition of Boyan with the historic style of the Byzantine
chronicles. He is well-read in the Russian chronicles as
well. In this double stylistic form, in the attempt to merge
the oral Russian poetic tradition with the written Greek one,
the *Tale* was perhaps unique. The blending of the two
heterogeneous forms was carried out with an amazing perfection: the reader is never shocked by, and seldom aware of,
the duality of style.

The subject matter of the *Tale* is an episode of the age-
long struggle of the Russian princes with the Polovtsi, the
nomads of the southern steppes. Historically exact, the
narrative deals with an event of little importance and of
dubious renown. Igor, the prince of a small southern town
of Novgorod-Seversk, undertook this expedition with his
brother Vsevolod, his son and nephew. They were defeated and taken prisoners by the foes. After some time
Igor managed to flee from his capturers. This is the historical content of the *Tale*. The author must have belonged
to the intimate circle of the druzhina or retinue of Prince
Igor to find in this inglorious adventure matter for his
grand epic. The main lyrical strain is the threnos or lament
over the fallen Russian warriors and over the whole Russian land torn by the inroads of the nomads and feuds of her
own princes. These princes are called upon to speed aid
and to efface the outrage to Igor. The end resolves the
tragic tension in joy and jubilation.

In analyzing the religious tenor of *Igor's Tale* one must keep in mind its stylistic form. The tale deals with the same feudal society as the contemporary chronicles, but it belongs to quite a different literary school. Stepping from the ecclesiastical air of the chronicles—not to speak of the rest of contemporary literature—into the secular and even slightly heathen world of *Igor's Tale* is no little surprise. Without its miraculous preservation, one would have quite a different idea of the strength of the Christian and Byzantine impact upon the pre-Mongolian Russia.

With regard to the religious and moral world-outlook of *Igor's Tale,* three strata can be discerned in its artistic tissue: Christian, heathen, and purely secular. Measured by mere verbal criteria, the Christian element is the scantiest of all. There are, all in all, four sentences which give unmistakable evidence of the author's Christian faith. Even those four sentences are, all of them, but formal expressions which do not disclose any profound conviction. One is a gnomic quotation from Boyan: "Neither a clever nor a skillful one can escape the judgment of God." Speaking of Igor's escape from captivity, the author says: "God shows the way to Prince Igor." Having reached Kiev the happy prince is "riding up Borichev hill to the Holy Mother of God Pirogoshchaia," the name of a venerated icon, brought from Constantinople. The word "Christians" appears in the penultimate sentence: "Hail to the princes and warriors fighting for the Christians against the pagan hosts." These are all the positive expressions of the author's Christianity. Two indirect expressions can be added: the insulting denotation of the Polovtsi as "pagan" which is used throughout, and once as "demon's sons." On the other hand, one cannot be quite sure of the religious meaning of the Russian word *pogany* (derived from Latin *paganus*) in *Igor's Tale.* In the Russian language, this foreign word changed its original sense of "heathen" into "unclean," "impure," in the physical or physiological sense. Examining the usage of the word in *Igor's Tale*, one wonders whether one is present at the beginning of this evolution which also occurs in Kirik's canons, a generation earlier. In most cases this word seems to have the meaning of a simple insult, as in such phrases: "*pogany* slave," "*pogany* heads of the Polovtsi" or "thou, black raven, *pogany* Polovets." If the religious sense of *pogany* were always present in the author's mind it would be the more striking that Russian warriors were not called "Christians" except in the concluding sentence; they are designated simply by the national name: Russians or "Rusichi," that is, "Russian sons."

Not only is the Christian vocabulary scarce, but the acts, gestures, and ideas which are unavoidable in any Christian social world are also absent. Prayer is never mentioned. The Russian warriors do not pray when they are starting on their risky expedition; they do not pray before or during the fatal battle. Death is not accompanied by reflections on the destiny of the departed souls. Among so many omens of natural order there are no visions or revelations of the Christian celestial world: no angels or saints protect the Christian army going on this strange crusade.

The French medieval epic *Chanson de Roland* also contains very few Christian elements. Yet external signs and symbols abound; the author rejoices in opposing "the law of Christ" to "the law of Mohammed" as being at stake in the sacred war. Every one remembers the scene of the hero's death when the Archangel Michael descends in person from heaven to receive the soul of Roland. The dying warriors of Igor are laid in the bosom of mourning nature, facing their merciless fate alone.

The distance between Christian providence and pagan fate is not always clearcut. Many Christians in our day believe in blind destiny. A newly converted heathen could easily cover his inveterate belief in fate with the name of God. The above quotation from Boyan is too fragmentary to discern with what connotations the poet used the phrase "the judgment of God." But it must be noticed that the Russian word for judgment—*sud* has precisely this double meaning: judgment and destiny. The modern Russian word for destiny is *sud'ba, suzhdeno* it is destined, *suzheny* is predestined husband. Yet, on the other hand, *sudy Bozhy*, God's judgments, is the translation of the Biblical "God's counsels."

Not much can be elicited from the author's applying the same word *sud* to the battle or to death on battlefield. "Glory brought Boris Viacheslavich to judgment," (or to his destiny). We have seen that in the Russian *Chronicles* princes often go into battle to determine the judgment of God. In some Christian Slavonic documents, such as *The Life of Saint Constantine-Cyril*, *sud* is a simple synonym for death. But when the name of God is sometimes omitted the word *sud* sounds ambiguous, especially in *Igor's Tale*. It can be a simple linguistic rudiment or it can imply some religious idea—Christian or pagan.

Later we shall come back to the Christian ingredients of *Igor's Tale* in order to investigate Christian traces in the ethical ideas and sensibility of its author. Now it can be stated fairly that its apparent Christian content is very poor.

Incomparably richer is its heathen counterpart, the interpretation of which, however, presents many difficulties. The general skepticism of modern scholars towards the problems of Slavic mythology was reflected in their appraisal of the heathen world of *Igor's Tale* as a simple poetic convention. A distinguished student compared the paganism of the *Tale* to the mythological names in the classic poetry of the eighteenth century. The exaggeration in this view is obvious. The medieval poet lived in a time when Christianity in Russia had to wage a serious struggle with the survivals of paganism; when, after the acknowledgment of ecclesiastical preachers, the folk were still devoted to the "double faith." This historical situation, on the border-line between the two religious worlds, requires the most accurate investigation of the poet's religious background.

The pagan elements of the *Tale* can be found in the names of the great gods of the Russian Olympus, in a number of minor divine entities or personifications and in the poet's general attitude to nature and life.

Among the great pagan gods known from other sources, the poet names four, three of them in an indirect way, as the ancestors or masters of men and elements. The formula is always the same: the grandsons of Stribog, the grandsons of Dazhbog, the grandson of Veles. The poet likes to desig-nate the relation of descent by employing the expres-sion "grandson" rather than son. Striborg's grandsons are the winds; Veles' grandson is Boyan, the poet,—on what particular ground, we do not know. Veles (or Volos), to-gether with Perun, is one of the greatest of the Russian gods; very often he appears as god of cattle and of riches; here he is a patron of the poet, a "magic" poet. Perhaps for a wizard the protection of a pagan god, or the descent from him, is not unfitting. We do not know who are the grand-sons of Dazhbog, the sun god; the context permits con-ceiving of them as Russian princes, or Russian folk in gen-eral, or even the whole of mankind. The poet says that during princely feuds "the life (or wealth) of Dazhbog's grandson was being ruined." The fourth god Khors, who is also a solar god, probably of Iranian origin, is named di-rectly but obviously as the synonym of the sun itself. The prince Vseslav "raced, as a wolf, across the way of great Khors." The word "great" reminds us again that the divine meaning of Khors is not forgotten: he is more than the luminary itself. In what spirit, with which emotional strain are these names used by the Christian author?

As poet, the disciple of Boyan, he was the inheritor of a poetic tradition going back to pagan times. This tradition probably transmitted the names of gods who once were full of life and glamour and who, certainly, were dimmed by the victory of the new faith. But even for the official spokesmen of Christianity the ancient gods did not turn into nonentities. Unlike modern theologians, the ancient Church did not deny the existence of gods. The medieval theology considered them either as demons or as deified men. The second theory, that of Euhemerism, was very popular in Russia. Thus, one finds in the Ipatian *Chronicle* (1114) which transcribes the Greek chronicle of Malalas, the history of Egyptian kings who became gods. The king Feost "was called the god Svarog. . . After him reigned his son, by the name of Sun, who is called Dazhbog. . ." It is noteworthy that the chronicler gives to Egyptian king-gods Slavic names. Like the author of these lines, the poet of Igor could believe in the historical existence of the gods. But, whereas for the Christian preachers their names were an abomination, he treated them with the veneration of a son or grandson. Perhaps he had no theological theory at all about the gods: whether they were demons of nature, such as the Sun or Wind, or human ancestors. Christian theological ideas among the Russian folk were very confused, even in the nineteenth century. Essential is the fact that these names conveyed to him great and magical associations. He used them as symbols; but as realistic symbols, necessary for his mythical world-outlook.

His *Weltanschauung* is indeed mythical. It is very interesting for a scholar of religion to observe in him a living process of mythical creation. Most of the great poets have

mythical elements in their world-outlook; but in primitive
poetry it is quite impossible to draw the line between religious mythology and the creation of poetic fictions. The
poet of *Igor* is no primitive, but he stands near the primitive
world of paganism. He blends popular mythological tradition with his own more or less pantheistic symbolism.
There is hardly one abstract idea which could not be turned
by him into a living being or living symbol. Such is, for
instance, *Obida*, Outrage, one of his favorite symbols, and
a symbol necessary for a mourner, for a poet of woe. According to the recent discovery by Professor Jacobson the
image of Outrage was borrowed by the Russian poet from
a translation of a Greek work by Methodius of Patara (Outrage, *Obida*, ἀδικία). Outrage to him is a maiden. "Outrage arose among the hosts of the Dazhbog's grandson,
stepped as a maiden on the Troyan land near Don, and
splashing with her swan wings in the blue sea, she chased
away the happy times." But Russian folklore always
knew Woe (*Gore*) as a being who pursued an accursed man,
sitting on his neck, accompanying him to the grave. Fever,
or rather Fevers, were, to a Russian, demonic females of
whom he tried to rid himself by the aid of magic spells and
incantations.

The maiden Outrage does not stand alone in the poem.
Together with her, one finds personified Woe, Lie (*Lozh*),
and two female beings *Karna* and *Zhlia* who, according to
the probable meaning of their names, must be interpreted
as incarnate Lamentation and Mourning: "Karna shouted
and Zhlia rushed over the Russian land shooting forth fire
from a flaming horn."

Among these demonic entities who originated as personifications of fate and destiny there is one being of quite
a different origin and unclear significance. It is *Div*, whose
nature has not yet been fully explained. "Div is crying at

the top of a tree," foreboding the misfortune. The same Div rushes to the land when the catastrophe is fulfilled. Most of the commentators take him for a demonic bird-like being, of Slavic or Iranian mythology, who is ominous, evil-bearing, and, consequently, close to the symbolic Woe and Outrage.

All these divine or demonic beings are represented as dwelling and acting within a nature setting which is more than scenery for their action. In fact, nature is living and animated through and through. It can be said without exaggeration that nature and its phenomena occupy in *Igor's Tale* at least as important a place as human society. Nature, of course, is not quite independent from the latter: it embraces human life with love but also challenges it with threats; it sends its warnings; it shares human woe and joy. That the narrative of the Igor's expedition is opened by the eclipse of the sun—an evil omen—has nothing peculiar about it. The Russian *Chronicles*, not unlike those of the western Middle Ages, are full of astronomical events to be interpreted in the same providential sense. But in *Igor's Tale* nature is not the organ of God's revelation. It is a living essence by itself. When Igor leads his warriors to the fatal campaign, "the sun with darkness barred his way, the night groaned with the thunderstorm . . . the whining of the wild beasts arose. Div cries at the top of the tree: he bids the unknown land hearken." Foreboding the bloody battle, "the wolves conjure the storm from the ravines; the eagles, with their shrieking, call the beasts to a feast of bones; the foxes yelp at the red shields." After the Russian defeat—"the grass drooped in pity, and in grief the tree bowed low to earth."

In conformity with the general tragic character of the *Tale*, nature reveals itself chiefly in the quality of mourner. Yet it can rejoice as well, in sympathy with human happiness. At Igor's escape from captivity "the woodpeckers show him the way to the river with their tapping, the nightingales herald the dawn with their merry songs." Nature is not only the witness of human destinies. It can be either a mighty helpmate or the enemy of man. During Igor's flight, the Donets river "caressed the prince on its waves, spread out green grass for him by its silvery banks, clothed him with warm mists beneath the shade of the green trees." Igor himself gives thanks to the Donets, his savior, in a poetic dialogue with the river. But the river can be malicious and evil, like the Stugna whose bad temper is mentioned in contrast with the mild Donets. "Quite another was the Stugna river; it has an evil current, it had swallowed strange brooks and scattered the barges among the bushes. It had closed the Dnieper to the youth, Prince Rostislav [who was drowned in Stugna in 1093]."

Igor enters into conversation with a river. His wife, Iaroslav's daughter, on the walls of the town Putivl', in lament over her captured husband addresses the Wind, the Dnieper River, and the Sun with complaints and incantations which read like heathen prayers. It is worth noticing that the elements are addressed with the title "lord," which suggests not so much sympathetic intimacy with nature as awe and reverence towards it.

O Wind, mighty Wind! Why dost thou blow so violently, O lord? Why dost thou hurl the Huns' arrows with thy light wings against my beloved's warriors? Why hast thou, O Lord, scattered my joy over the feathery grass? . . . O Dnieper Slovutich [son of the Glorious]! . . . bear fondly my beloved one to me, O lord, that I should not send him my tears toward the sea at the dawn. O bright and thrice-bright Sun! Thou art warm and beauteous towards all. Why didst thou, O lord, spread thy burning rays upon my beloved's warriors?

Thus far we have seen in *Igor's Tale* nature personified

or acting. But the instances are countless where nature gives substance to similes and poetical figures. Prince Vsevolod's constant surname is "aurochs." Warriors are compared with wolves, princes with hawks, musician's fingers on the strings with ten hawks loosed upon a flock of swans. In the human and even in the political world the poet does not abandon the world of nature. He lives by its recollections, images, by its inspiring spirit. There is probably no other poem or work of art belonging to the European sphere of culture in which the unity with nature is so complete and so religiously significant.

Most of the Russian literary historians envisaged the world of *Igor's Tale* as a purely poetic fiction. A strong pantheistic feeling permeates modern Russian poetry both literary and oral, cultivated and popular. Reared in this poetic tradition, Russians pay no attention to it nor question its roots. In the oral poetry of Russian peasants, artistic pantheism lives hand in hand with the remnants of ancient paganism. The literary Russian poetry of the nineteenth century was strongly influenced by the art of the people, though often ignoring its pagan sources. In the twelfth century, when sacrifices to the gods were still offered in the countryside, the impact of the imaginative and emotional pagan world upon popular art must have been immensely stronger than nowadays.

We certainly do not think that the poet of *Igor's Tale*, still less Igor himself and his wife, worshipped ancient gods. They were good Christians in their conscious minds. But, the poet, at least, in the subconscious depths of his soul where he communicated with the soul of the people, lived in another, hardly Christian world. It is true that most of his images of nature are purely poetical. But in speaking of nature he can not help feeling it as a living being, and his imagination immediately enters upon mythological creation. In this natural-supernatural world the names of ancient gods, preserved probably by the poetic tradition, find the place which is refused at that early stage of Russian poetry to the saints and spirits of the Christian heaven. The poet feels that the name of the Archangel Michael or Saint George would spoil the poetic form which requires the names of Veles and Dazhbog. This is the function of the paganism prevailing in *Igor's Tale*.

If we do not know how far Igor's poet shared the pagan beliefs and superstitions of the Russian folk we can be certain, at least, of his belief in magic. Moreover, magic is treated by him without any repulsion and even with a certain reverence. Several times he calls Boyan, his master poet, *veshchy*. This word which in later Russian has acquired the meaning "wise" with the nuance of "clairvoyant" and "prophetic," has, in ancient documents, only the sense of "wizard." *Veshchy* is applied by the poet to the ancient Prince Vseslav of Polotsk, of whom it is told: "Vseslav judged the people, distributed towns to princes, but, by night he raced as a wolf: from Kiev he reached Tmutorakan before the rooster [the dawn], racing, as a wolf, across the way of great Khors [the sun]." In this Vseslav the werewolf, rationalist critics wished again to see a simple metaphor. But of this ancient prince who had died about a hundred years before the *Tale* was written, a monastic chronicler, his contemporary, related that his mother conceived him by enchantment. (1044) The same belief existed in Bulgaria concerning one of the princes of the tenth century. Hardly any one in the Middle Ages could doubt the existence of werewolves. Remarkable in our poet is the great esteem with which he treats one of them, Prince Vseslav.

If nature in *Igor's Tale* is saturated with pagan elements which can hardly find their parallels in the Russian *Chronicles*, in the attitude to society, in social or political ethics, the

Tale and the *Chronicles* come nearer to each other without reaching, however, a full identity. The main difference consists in a complete secularization of the poet's social ethics. It is purely laic, or neutral, neither Christian nor pagan, at first glance, whatever may be the secret sources nourishing it from the two religious worlds. Let us consider first of all its face value, without heeding its religious significance.

Studying the moral world of the chronicler we observed the continual struggle between the two outlooks: that of the clerical author and interpreter and that of the feudal society he portrays. We saw how the second scale of values made its intrusion through the pious surface of the narrative, the more frankly, the further one goes down through the twelfth century. The same feudal world speaks in *Igor's Tale* but here it speaks by itself without any censorious interpreter. It is purified, so to speak, or devoid of any obvious Christian impacts in language and symbols which are to be supposed as obligatory and inevitable to every member of Christian society, however worldly or impious he might be. This absence of Christian elements may have partly the same stylistic motivation as the presence of pagan mythology in the landscape.

Three main social ethical streams flow through *Igor's Tale*—the same which can be distinguished in the lay sections of the *Chronicles* as well: the ethics of clan or charity of blood; the ethics of class, or feudal and military virtues; and the ethics of mother country or patriotism of the Russian land. Clan or family consciousness in *Igor's Tale* is perhaps not stronger than in the *Chronicles,* but it is strong enough and finds eloquent emotional forms for its expression. Prince Vsevolod addresses his brother as they start on the campaign: "My only brother, my only bright light, Igor! We are both Sviatoslavichi (Sviatoslav's sons)." The patronymic names are used by the poet very often instead of first names: Iaroslavna, Glebovna—speaking of women, or "the brave sons of Gleb."

Prince Igor and his brother, the unfortunate heroes of the *Tale*, belonged to the great Chernigov line of the Russian princely dynasty, descending from the famous Oleg Sviatoslavich who died in 1116. The poet is conscious of the common destiny and the common honor of this clan: "In the field the Oleg's valiant brood is slumbering: afar has it flown. It was not born to stand an insult," says he of the Russian camp in the steppe. He dedicates some touching lines to the memory of Oleg, the unfortunate but glorious ancestor. We have seen also how the clan feeling of the poet induced him to use patronymic names even for the elements of nature: winds as grandsons of Stribog, Dnieper-Slovutich; Russian princes are grandsons of Dazhbog or, otherwise, Rusichi, the favorite patronymic commonly used by the poet and coined, perhaps, by himself.

This clan ethics is linked with and overshadowed by the feudal or military ethics—the elements of which we also had noted in the *Chronicles*. Here all the facets of the warlike virtues are glorified without any restraint: courage, bravery, boldness. In the style of the historic tales (and the *Chronicles*) the poet begins his praise of Igor: "He strengthened his mind and sharpened his heart with manliness; and, filling himself with warlike spirit led his brave hosts to the land of the Polovtsi." This is still a reasonable courage, the dutiful way of a Christian prince. "Igor said to his druzhina: Brothers and druzhina! It is better to be slain than to be captured." This can also be parallelled in the *Chronicles*, but, significantly, in the tenth century records of the great pagan warrior Sviatoslav. Even an imprudent, impassioned boldness, beyond the reason of war, is glorified. Such was, indeed, the whole campaign of Igor, which is justified in these words by the prince: "I wish to shatter a spear on the farthest borders of the Polovetsian land. With you, O Rusichi, I wish to lay down my head, or to drink of the Don in my helmet."

The heroic fight of Vsevolod in the last desperate battle is described with the features reminiscent of the popular Russian epics, *byliny*, known only through the records of modern times:

O fierce aurochs Vsevolod, thou standest in the battle, dartest thy arrows on the hosts, crashest with steel swords on their helmets. Wherever thou, aurochs, didst leap, gleaming forward with thy golden helmet, there lie the heads of the heathen Polovtsi, and their Avar helmets are split by tempered sabre, by thee, fierce aurochs Vsevolod.

Nowhere in Russian literature, written or oral, can be found such a pitch of warlike intensity, such superhuman or subhuman fierceness as in this portrayal of Vsevolod's warriors, the men of Kursk:

My men of Kursk are skillful fighters, nursed amid trumpets, rocked in helmets, fed at the spear-blades; well-known to them are the paths; familiar the ravines; their bows are strung; their quivers open; and their sabres whetted. Like grey wolves in the field, they gallop seeking honor for themselves and glory for their prince.

This last motive of "honor" and "glory" reveals the other side of the same feudal ideal. Glory for real greatness, particularly after death, and honor on a lesser scale, constitute a moral good, the fruit and privilege of the military virtue, valor. Glory is given not by success or political might, but by intrepid conduct. That is why the poem ends with a "glory song" to Igor and his kinsmen, although from the political point of view their campaign was a failure and defeat. In the same spirit the poet glorifies the ancestor of the Olgovichi house to whom he himself gives the surname Gorislavich, a compound of *Gore*, woe, and *slava*, glory. He glorifies also the ancient Vseslav—the "wizard," from "whose glory fell away" his weak descendants. Both Oleg and Vseslav left a sad memory after them in the annals of Russia which were well known to our poet. They were the chief "forgers of feuds," the heroes of civil wars. If they remained for the poet or Igor the pattern of glory, as Oleg was for Boyan, it was only because of their personal valor, of the adventurous spirit which is common to Igor together with the whole of Oleg's house.

What is glory to princes honor is to the druzhina, their retainer-warriors. The refrain, already quoted, "seeking honor for themselves and glory for the prince," is repeated twice in the battle scenes. The idea of "honor," in the sense of personal value based on warlike virtues, is very important for the historical appreciation of ancient Russian culture. It was extremely strong in the medieval feudal West. It undoubtedly lies at the base of aristocratic freedom—and, consequently, of modern democracy. On the other hand, the opinion was often maintained that it was alien to the Russian national character and to Orthodox Christianity as a whole. Indeed, one looks in vain for its premises in Byzantine social ethics nor does one find it in the later Muscovite society where "honor" was understood as social dignity determined by state rank. In the un-Christian East, however, in the world of Islam and Japan, the consciousness of personal honor is also strong, though lacking the same religious support against the State which the medieval Catholic Church gave to the individual.

The truth is that the concept of personal military honor has little, if anything, to do with the specific character of Teutonic nations and can be found in every society in which military service is based on feudal or feudal-like organization. Ancient or Kievan Russia was such a feudal society and developed the corresponding idea of military honor— perhaps, not without Varangian influence. On the pages of the *Chronicles* we had found this idea still veiled and only sporadically breaking through the Byzantine ideal of a humble Orthodox warrior. In *Igor's Tale* it reaches its free and eloquent expression.

The third source of social ethics for the poet of *Igor* is his strong patriotism which embraces not any one of the Russian principalities, but the whole of the Russian land. This pan-Russian consciousness, as we had seen, was in its decline at the end of the twelfth century and few traces of it can be found in the contemporary *Chronicles*. In *Igor's Tale* it is as vital as in the eleventh century; its poet is, in fact, a true inheritor of Boyan's age. There is no phrase repeated as frequently in the *Tale* as "the Russian land." This expression is taken not in the narrow sense of Kiev and its surrounding lands as it usually was at that time, but in the large sense of all the principalities and countries inhabited by the Russian people. Igor's foray, in itself a very insignificant episode of frontier fighting, is treated as a national tragedy. Igor marches on for the "Russian land," he fights for the "Russian land." His defeat produced a national mourning. The poet goes so far as to complete the sentence of Boyan: "It is heavy upon thee, O Head, without the shoulders; evil is it to thee, Body, without the Head," by the daring conclusion: "the Russian land without Igor." It looks as if, for him, Igor were the real head or leader of all Russia.

That the "Russian land" is not only a hyperbole serving to enhance Igor's glory appears from the general political outlook of the poet. Spokesman of the poet's political ideals is Prince Sviatoslav of Kiev, the head of the Olgovichi house. In a grand and poignant call to all princes of Russia, Sviatoslav urges them to intervene for the Russian land, "for the wounds of Igor, fierce Sviatoslavich." Smolensk and Polotsk, Galich and Suzdal, the remotest

border lands of Russia, are included in this impassioned
call. In the panegyrical enumeration of Russian princes the
poet makes no discrimination between the branches of the
Rurik house. The Monomachovichi, the traditional enemies
of the Olgovichi, even take predominant place because of
the political importance of their seats. On the contrary, one
of the strongest representatives of the Olgovichi clan, Iaroslav of Chernigov, is rebuked for his dishonorable conduct:
he abstained from all common expeditions against the
Polovtsi.

Here the national consciousness of the poet crosses
that of his clan. But it crosses also his feudal ethics of un-
bounded honor. The poet, as patriot, could not help seeing
the fatal effects of princely feuds and he condemns them
in a most unambiguous way:

> Brother spoke to brother: "This is mine and that also is mine."
> And the princes began to say of a paltry thing "this is great"; and
> amongst themselves to forge feuds; and the heathen from all sides
> advanced with victories against the Russian land.

Here is avarice rather than pride, the political original
sin, a view which is not incompatible with feudal ethics. But
"this is great" points to the exaggerated sensitivity of personal honor. The poet fully acknowledges the national
reverse resulting from the search for glory while speaking of
his great hero, the ancient Oleg:

> That Oleg forged feuds with his sword and sowed arrows over
> the earth. . . . Then, in the time of Oleg Gorislavich, feuds were
> sown and grew apace; the fortune of Dazhbog's grandson was wast-
> ed in the factions of the princes, and the life of men was shortened.

This political condemnation of Oleg does not diminish
the poet's admiration for his "glory" and bravery. The
same dualism of appreciation is found even for the person
of Igor. Speaking for himself, the poet dare not utter any

word of blame for the adventurous and inconsiderate foray which ended with calamity for the "Russian land." But the political lesson is put into the mouth of Sviatoslav of Kiev who, amidst tears and lamentations, sends the words of rebuke to his captured cousins:

O my nephews, Igor and Vsevolod! too early have ye begun to harass the land of the Polovtsi with your swords! But ingloriously were you defeated, ingloriously have you shed the blood of the heathen. Your brave hearts are forged of cruel steel and tempered in fierceness. What have you wrought to my silvered hair!

One is here in the presence of an ethical conflict which the poet does not resolve. His heart is equally responsive to the call of "glory" and to the call of suffering Russia. He is obviously not in sympathy with domestic feuds. He prefers to see his admired military valor exercised in the war against the common foes of Russia, the heathen. In this he stands on common ground with the best traditions of the *Chronicles*.

At this point it would be interesting to compare with the poet's praise of Igor, the appreciations of this prince and his foray by the contemporary chroniclers. There are narratives preserved in the Lavrentian and Ipatian *Chronicles*. They give very divergent opinions about Prince Igor. The Lavrentian *Chronicle* (1186), which is that of the city of Vladimir, reflects the political tendencies of the northern branch of the Monomach's house, the view of Igor's adversaries. This view is very severe. The chronicler stigmatizes the adventurous spirit and the inconsiderate boldness which cost Igor and his army the unglorious defeat. The tone is sometimes ironical:

At the same year Oleg's grandsons decided to go against the Polovtsi, because they did not go in the past year with all the princes, but they went by themselves, saying: Are we not also princes? Let us win praise for ourselves.

After the first easy victory their elation grew immensely. Three days were spent in amusements and boastings:

> Our brothers went with the great Prince Sviatoslav and fought
> the Polovtsi under the cover of Pereiaslavl (a fortress). . . . .
> They did not dare to go into their land; and we are in their land,
> we have beaten them and hold captive their wives and children;
> and now let us go against them beyond the Don and beat them up
> to the end; if we have victory there, we shall go to the shore of the
> sea where not even our grandfathers had gone and we shall take our
> final glory and honor—

"not knowing God's providence," adds the author. The
conduct of the Russian warriors in the second battle is far
from brave:

> Our men, having seen them (the Polovtsi), were frightened
> and fell down from their pride, not knowing what was said by the
> prophet: there is no wisdom for man, no courage, no thought against
> the Lord. . . . And our men were defeated through the wrath of God.

The lamentations of the author over the misfortune
of the Russian army are mixed with pious reflections on
God's chastising providence. Igor's escape is naturally
scored with satisfaction and interpreted as the sign of divine pardon. "And after a few days prince Igor fled from
the Polovtsi: for God does not leave the just one in the
hands of the sinners." The qualification of Igor as a "just
one" is rather unexpected, but it can be understood with
regard to his Christian faith as opposed to the heathen; besides, it is a Biblical quotation.

The Ipatian *Chronicle,* that of Kiev, is more than
friendly to Igor and gives the story of his misfortune with
much detail and in an elaborate religious frame. It is very
likely that this part of the Ipatian *Chronicle* includes the
annals written in the house of Prince Igor himself. Igor
is represented as a wise, pious prince who is purified by his
distress and achieves a high level of Christian humility.

His reflection on the ominous significance of the eclipse of the sun is quite different in tone from his proud challenge to the omen which occurs in the *Tale*. He says in the *Chronicle*: "Brothers and druzhina! nobody knows the mysteries of God. God is the creator of this portent as well as of His whole world; what good or evil God will do for us we shall see." When the scouts warn him of the dangerous readiness of the enemy he answers: "If we return without fighting then our disgrace will be worse than death; be it as God will." The thought of honor is present, but mitigated by resignation and confidence in God. These are his reflections after the first victory: "Thus hath God by His might given us victory over our foes, and honor and glory to us."

The second, unhappy battle is described in much more detail than in the *Tale*; we learn that Igor himself was wounded. One feature reminds us vividly of the epic: the love linking Igor with his brother Vsevolod in the moment of deadly danger: "Igor, captured, saw his brother Vsevolod fighting stoutly; and prayed for the death of his soul that he might not see the fall of his brother." The capture of Igor is accompanied by a page-long monologue of the prince in which he assigns his misfortune to a just punishment of God and offers repentance for his sins. One of his sins particularly weighs on his conscience: the cruel sack of a Russian town:

I recollect my sins before the Lord, my God, that I have wrought much killing and bloodshedding in the Christian land; I showed no mercy to the Christian folk and took by storm the town Glebov near Pereiaslavl. No little evil then befell the innocent Christians; fathers were parted from their offspring, brother from brother, friend from friend, wives from their husbands—old men were swept aside and youths received wounds cruel and ruthless; grown men were hewn down and mutilated and the women raped—and all this have I done; I am unworthy to live, and now I see the vengeance of the Lord my God. . . .

The particular episode of the sack of Glebov points to Igor himself as the source of this recollection, although the general pious development must be ascribed to the chronicler.

The same repentant spirit does not leave Igor in his captivity. He repeats: "I have justly, according to my deserts, received defeat at Thy command, O Lord, and it was not the bravery of the heathen that broke the strength of Thy servants." At the same time, Igor is far from depressed. The sense of honor, even in exaggerated sensitiveness, did not abandon him. It found its drastic proof in the circumstances of his escape. At first, Igor was opposed to the scheme of the flight offered to him by the Polovets Lavor (Ovlur in the *Tale*). He "was keeping the high spirit of his youth" in these generous considerations: "For the sake of glory I did not run away from my druzhina [in the battle] and now I myself will not depart ingloriously." His boyars, who shared his captivity, did not approve of his pride: "You cherish a haughty spirit within you, and one displeasing to God." The insistence of his counsellors and the imminent danger of death finally overcame his scruples of honor or pride.

Both the chronicles note the motive of honor in Igor's conduct, but they deal with it in quite different ways. The Lavrentian has no sympathy with this motive, ridicules it, and sees in it the reason of the catastrophe. The Ipatian tries to mitigate and merge it into the general strain of a deep piety which transfigures the character of Igor into that of a saintly Christian hero.

The poet of *Igor's Tale* has no words of blame for his prince; he himself is highly enthusiastic about honor and glory. He needs no religious mitigation for, nor limitation of it. He only dares, through the lips of Sviatoslav, to point at the fatal consequences of Igor's bold imprudence for the Russian land.

Coming back to the poet's warlike ardor one finds another restraint for its display—and this not of a social, but rather of an emotional, nature. The poet manifests such a degree of kindness, sensitivity, and delicacy that it is positively incompatible with joy in killing. He likes the audacity, the impetus, even the intoxication of a fight. But he obviously dislikes the act of killing, of bloodshedding. This can easily be seen in his treatment of combat. The fatal battle at the Kaiala river is the main subject of his epic. It forms the first, the longest part of it. But the battle itself is depicted rather indirectly. At first a series of omens, presentiments, forebodings. After follows the mourning, the picture of the fatal consequences of the defeat. Concerning the fighting iself, a few lines suffice. The first act, successful for the Russians, is told in one simple sentence: "From dawn on Friday they trampled the heathen hosts of the Polovtsi." The second, with tragic issue, is embodied in the exploits of Vsevolod—already quoted: "there the heathen heads of the Polovtsi lie, their Avar helmets are split by tempered sabres." To this may be added the third passage depicting the general horror of the combat: "Tempered arrows fly, sabres thunder upon the helmets, lances crack in the foreign field. . . The black earth beneath the hooves was sown with bones, and was watered with blood; and it came up a harvest of sorrow upon the Russian land."

Indeed, there is very little about the fury of the battle which is the climax, or the first climax, of the poem. The joy of killing, the sensual delight in running blood is common to primitive epics in most national literatures. But nothing can be found in *Igor's Tale* recalling this familiar image of the *Iliad* (xx, v. 482-83):

$$.\,.\,.\,.μυελὸς αὖτε$$
$$σφονδυλίων ἔκπαλθ' ὃ δ' ἐπὶ χθονὶ κεῖτο τανυσθείς$$

or these verses of the *Chanson de Roland*:

La battaille est merveilluse et hastive,
Franceis i ferent par vigur e par ire,
Trenchent cez points, cez costez, cez eschines,
Cez vestementz entresque as chars vives,
Sur l'herbe verte li cler sancs s'en afilet. . . .

(v. 1610-1614)

The mildness and gentleness of the Russian poet can be tested by still other criteria. The whole composition with its tragic tension and joyful solution seems to require, after the hell of the dark defeat, the compensation of revenge or, at least, the final victory. But the poet—and the reader as well—is satisfied with the escape, the flight. From the point of view of strict feudal honor, that is not compensation. Without revenge the hero would feel dishonored. But for some reason the idea of revenge does not come into the reader's mind. It was Igor, and not the Polovtsi, who began the fighting, in the frame of the epic, and Igor himself caused his misfortune. The Polovtsi committed no cruel deeds and one of the heathen helps the prince in his escape. From the lips of the pursuing khans we are informed of the plan to marry young Vladimir, Igor's son, to a Polovtsian princess. So, the Polovtsi may not be so bad, after all. The poet seems to have pardoned them from the joy of seeing his prince free again.

It is remarkable that in the *Tale* even the word "revenge" is used only once, and that in speaking on behalf of the enemies: "The fair maidens of the Goths . . . cherish vengeance for Sharokan" (one of the Polovtsian khans). In analysing the chronicles we have seen that, through the best times of Russian historiography, the word "revenge" was used in speaking of pagan times and heroes. Only since the middle of the twelfth century does it become fitting for a Christian prince. The poet of Igor had a milder temper than many an ecclesiastical writer among his contemporaries.

With this tenderness of heart is linked the particular attention paid by the poet to woman. He is certainly not a poet of love, least of all of romantic or chivalrous love, though he likes the epithet "fair" applied to the maidens, even to those of enemy nations: "fair maidens of the Polovtsi," "fair maidens of the Goths." He likes the words designating different nuances of love and friendship: *lado*, *khot'*, (lover, beloved, espoused, friend, and so on) but he uses them mostly in metaphors. "The beloved maiden" of Vseslav is his ambitious dream: the princedom of Kiev. But where the poet really appreciates woman is in the beauty of her suffering. If the whole *Tale of Igor* is a poignant lament its best organ is the voice of woman. All the Russian women share in the lament over Igor and his warriors: "Now can we no longer imagine our dearests in our thoughts, nor see them with our eyes, nor play with gold or silver. . ."

The climax of the *Tale*—the second one—is the lament of Iaroslavna, Igor's wife. Poetically it has always been considered the best part of the epic. We are acquainted already with her impressive incantations addressed to the elements of nature: Wind, Dnieper River, and Sun. Is it mere chance that, immediately upon the half-magical incantations of Iaroslavna, the poet shows prince Igor in the midst of flight? It is as if the incantations of the woman wrought their effect upon the elements, which return to the princess her deplored husband. Indeed, the next part—the flight— begins with the stir of elements: "The sea spurted at midnight; waterspouts move in mists. God shows the road to prince Igor from the land of the Polovtsi. . ." By this artistic effect the poet gave the woman—side by side with old Sviatoslav—a predominant place in his *Tale*. She is, or can be, the savior. Sviatoslav tried to save Igor with political speeches. His call sounded in vain. Iaroslavna—

with cries from her heart and with the power which a passionate desire gives over the elements—succeeded.

Mildness and tenderness of heart, limiting warlike ardor, do not yet exhaust the sensibility of Igor's poet. There is in him a trait which perhaps gives a key to the deepest strata of the Russian soul. It is linked with the general tragic tone of the poem; yet it needs a closer examination.

Tragic is almost every great epic of any historical nation: the *Iliad*, the *Chanson de Roland*, the *Niebelungenlied*. It is not irrelevant that great epic poets, representing the deepest poetic tradition of a primitive nation, choose for their song of glory some tragic event: a defeat, the ruin of a realm, the death of a young hero. A general law of moral life as well as of artistic creation reveals that the greatest in man is awakened not by happy life but by heroic death. *Igor's Tale* is not an exception. Yet in it there are some particular traits which are uniquely Russian. First, one can easily notice that the accumulation of tragic impressions is not sufficiently motivated by the subject. *Igor's Tale* is a drama with a happy ending. Thus, the richness of ominous spells is somewhat gratuitous. Secondly, the tragic effect is achieved not by the death of a struggling and doomed hero (the idea of Achilles, Roland, Siegfried) but by suffering and humiliation: in *Igor*, the suffering and humiliated being is the Russian land itself, oppressed by the Polovtsi.

Especially striking and unexpected is the return of the tragic theme before the happy end. Prince Igor is riding to his homeland; escaping from captivity, he praises the Donets River for his salvation; and just at this moment, by a strange association the poet remembers another evil river, the Stugna, which drowned in its waves the young Prince Rostislav. This event has nothing to do with Igor. It took place about a hundred years before. But the poet dedicates the whole stanza to this irrelevant association.

He introduces—a favorite device of his—a lamenting woman, the prince's mother, and lets all nature participate in the mourning: "The flowers drooped for pity and the trees bowed low to earth in grief." The poet repeats one of his best refrains, used previously for Igor's defeat, in this passage where it is out of place from the point of view of composition. The poet simply could not help pouring some drops of sorrow into the final cup of triumph. Both the absence of final revenge or its promise, and the insertion of the superfluous theme of mourning are highly revealing. The evaluation of suffering as a superior moral good, as almost an end in itself, is one of the most precious features of the Russian religious mind. Here, it is found, in an esthetic transposition, with a bard of military valor and honor in whom one would least of all expect to find it: the poet who abhors Christian symbols and Christian vocabulary.

This discovery forces us to return to the question of religious elements in *Igor's Tale*, which so far we have gauged, at least for the Christian elements, by merely external expressions. If it was legitimate to trace the influence of paganism in the poet's sense of nature it is only fair to ask for the Christian influence in his general ethical attitude. The question is easier to pose than solve. In this domain one is guided by intuition rather than factual data.

As a rule, all deeper ethical or social norms and attitudes, even merely secular in appearance, have some religious origin and are supported by religious beliefs or their survivals. It is possible, then, to suppose behind Russian clan ethics, with its strong and tender feeling of blood-kinship, the pagan roots, or pagan sanctification of primitive tribal institutions. In Christian times they were reinterpreted in terms of evangelical charity and remained for ever one of the main bases of Russian social ethics. It is also legitimate to suppose some pagan connections for warlike ethics of bravery, though they were socially necessitated by the feudal institutions of Christian times. Here, however, the student of *Igor's Tale* is confused by the absence of any pagan Slavic god of war, like Perun, who would correspond to Dazhbog and other deities of nature. This recalls the theories of some modern scholars who see in the military cult of Perun, but not in Perun himself, the reflection of the Scandinavian Thor. If Perun, as god of war, was an artificial creation of Vladimir or the Varangians of Kiev, he was likely to be dropped out of poetic memory after the Christian conversion. In this case one must admit that the Russians had no specific god of war and, consequently, no pagan Slavic sanctification of war ethics. Some religious support for it must have been brought from the Scandinavian sources.

Conceding a place to the pagan sway in war ethics, one is the more obliged to look for Christian influences in accounting for the mildness and tenderness of Igor's poet. Two centuries of evangelization could not pass in vain; it had gradually transformed the general moral attitude of people, and even their sensibility. The poet of Igor feels no longing for revenge; but for a pagan Russian princess (Saint Olga), before her conversion, revenge, of a most cruel pattern, constituted an important part of her glorious tradition. It was related calmly and objectively by the monk-annalist and probably belonged to the epic store of ancient times.

Yet, while Christianity accounts for the mildness of the Russian epic, it may also have had its pagan antecedents. From all the scanty records of Russian paganism, it appears to have been much milder than that of many other tribes, for example, the Teutons. The charity of the Gospel found a particularly fertile soil in Russia. Indeed, the Byzantine interpretation of Christian ethics was not marked by any particular mildness. Nor was the Western doctrine or life of the early Middle Ages. In Russia itself this charitable spirit is felt strongly in the literary documents which are less colored by the Byzantine culture; often in the laic, and rarer in official ecclesiastical works.

Yet, after all is said, one must keep in mind that the mildness of Russian paganism can only have been relative. Not only Princess Olga, but also Vladimir (both canonized saints) are depicted as cruel before their conversion. Acts of cruelty are reported of the pagan magicians in the eleventh century as well. And the pagan Viatichi killed a Christian missionary, Saint Kuksha, about 1100. So the Gospel really did transform, or was transforming, the coarse hearts of the heathen; and to it, in great part, are due the most touching and morally the finest features in the only preserved work of the ancient epic tradition of Russia.

XII

PAGANISM AND CHRISTIANITY

*T*HOUGH undoubtedly written by a Christian author, *Igor's Tale* revealed to us a mighty understream of heathen world-outlook. Most of the Russian literary historians tried to depreciate the strength of this heathen influence by citing the fact that Russia had been a Christian nation for two hundred years. Yet the historical documents give abundant evidence of the vitality of the vanquished religion, both in its pure, un-Christian manifestations and particularly in its fusion with the victorious Christianity.

Throughout the eleventh century, the first Christian century of Russia, the *Chronicles* mark many violent revolts of the heathen masses instigated by the *volkhvi*. This old Russian word designates heathen magicians, men learned in the tradition of incantations, healings, and divinations. In some features they are closely akin to the Finnish *shamans* indicating, perhaps, the Finnish influence upon Russian-Slavic popular magic. In the year 1024 according to the chronicle, *volkhvi* arose in Suzdal; they murdered aged people saying, "these hold up the harvest." Natural calamities, particularly bad harvests, were generally the pretext for these pagan reactions. Some time before 1071, on the occasion of the famine in Rostov, two volkhvi murdered a priest and many noble women, as being responsible for the bad harvest, and tried to kill the prince's envoy. Still more impressive are the events in Novgorod at about the same time:

344

A volkhv appeared in Novgorod in the time of Prince Gleb. He harangued the people, representing himself as a god and deceived many of them, almost the entire city. For he claimed to know all things, and he blasphemed against the Christian faith, announcing that he would walk across the Volkhov River in the presence of all. There was an uprising in the city; all believed in him and wished to murder the bishop. But the bishop took his cross, put on his vestments, and stood forth saying, "Whosoever has faith in the volkhv let him follow him; but who ever is a faithful Christian, let him come to the cross." So the people were divided: Gleb and his retainers took their stand beside the bishop; all the people followed the volkhv.

Thus eighty years after the official baptism of Novgorod, at a critical moment, Christianity finds support only in the military retainers of the prince. Even in Kiev, the center of Russian Christianity, a volkhv in 1071 prophesied wonderful events: "that after five years the Dnieper would flow backward and the various countries would change their localities so that Greece would be where Russia was, and Russia where Greece was." It was on this occasion that the Kievan chronicler recalls other more dangerous examples of the activity of the volkhvi in the north and northeast of Russia. His stories were taken from fairly recent times. It means that we possess only fragmentary and sporadic knowledge of the pagan revolts in ancient Russia. It is hardly accidental that in all the cited cases the pagan revolts were repressed by the secular power: the prince or his men kill the volkhvi and the popular commotion is calmed. The clergy seems to have little influence upon the masses: either they themselves become victims of the rioters, or their appeal, as in Novgorod, has no effect at all. In the twelfth century we have no notices of pagan riots. Yet, at the beginning of this century, Saint Kuksha, a monk of the Kievan Pechersk monastery, was killed by the heathen Viatichi (not so far from Kiev) during his missionary journey in their land. The *Lives* of some Russian saints preserved the memory of the pagan resistance to the Christian missionaries in Rostov and Murom, although the legendary character of these later works invalidates their historical evidence.

There can be no doubt that in the country places remote from the big centers and the highroads, heathendom held on partly at least through the whole pre-Mongolian period. The Russian Church historians dated the end of Russia's conversion at approximately the fifteenth century. The conventional character of this date appears from the fact that heathen survivals were abundant even in the nineteenth century. What is essential is that Christianity, the religion of the upper classes in Kievan Russia, became the universal or national religion in the next period.

A literature of sermons and canonical rules which is preserved from the eleventh to the seventeenth centuries aimed at one purpose: the uprooting of pagan survivals in Christian society. This literature, mostly anonymous or pseudepigraphic, eludes exact dating. Many manuscripts transcribe the ancient originals with new additions. Some Russian compilations have a translated Greek text as their basis, where the names of the Greek or even Egyptian Pantheon are supplanted by Slavic gods. In their skepticism about mythology the last generations of scholars have found an easy task in discrediting this whole branch of sources. Since we are not pursuing the study of mythology, however, but only trying to elucidate the character of the Russian religious mind and worship, we can consider our material reliable. The pre-Mongolian origin of most of it seems to be certain; a more precise dating is perhaps impossible.

What these sermons and canons fight against is, in their own words, the "double faith"; they accuse the Christians of being addicted to pagan practices and superstitions. The zealots immoderately exaggerate the limits of the supposed paganism. For instance, the whole domain of secular music and dance is pagan or devilish in their estimation. We shall not follow them in enumerating the several kinds of superstition undoubtedly of pagan origin, but common to all races and times. We shall limit ourselves to those survivals of Russian paganism that throw some light on the character of the Russian religious mind.

In the middle of the twelfth century, a bishop of Novgorod emphasizes to the women the prohibition against consulting the volkhvi because of the "homicides and many evils" which result from this practice. A contemporary priest of the same city tells that the women used to visit volkhvi especially for the cure of children's diseases. A healer-magician in country districts remained a constant figure even in nineteenth century Russia. But in the twelfth century the magician was more than a healer; he must have been an adept of the pagan cult. Many sermons of undated origin insist that sacrifices to ancient gods were still being offered by so-called Christian people. On this occasion they give some questionable catalogues of pagan deities. Some enumerations are rather the product of "scholarly" erudition than of personal observation. Yet one cannot put aside such concrete evidence as this: "Even now, in remote places they pray to him, the cursed god, Perun; but they do it in secret and cannot dispense with it."

As to the sacrifices to the gods, they are of two kinds: unbloody, as bread, millet, honey; and bloody ones, among which the slaying or drowning of chickens is particularly mentioned. The last form of sacrifice is that performed to the water deities who occupy an important place in the pagan cult. Indeed, if the personal names of the great gods which are cited are subject to criticism, there is not the least doubt that the main object of pagan worship was the cult of natural elements: water, fire, plants, and stones. Personified or not, these elements are mentioned most often; the Russian pagans or semi-Christians "sacrificing to the plants and to the fountains" are the continual theme of all descriptions. Collective deities or "semigods," to use the classical term, are most probably the embodiment of these elements. "Bankspirits," (*beregini*), "vampires," and *vily* are mentioned. Modern Russians have long forgotten these names; they were changed for new ones, but probably new ones of the same meaning.

The cult of fire is more personal with even a proper name for it: "They pray to fire calling it Svarozhich (Svarog's son)." The patronymic form reminds us of the poet of *Igor* who calls the elements—for instance the winds the grandsons of Stribog. Svarozhich is a very popular Russian or Slavic deity; but only once is the form Svarog found. The Ipatian *Chronicle* (1114) translates by Svarog the Greek Hephaestus, and puts him in relation to the Sun, Helios. For him Svarog, the fire, is the father of the Sun, Dazhbog. The tie between Sun and Fire as Russian deities is obvious, as well as the agricultural meaning of their cults. "The fire makes the harvest, it dries the crop when it is ripening; that is why the damned people venerate the South and bow toward the South," relates a Russian sermon circulating under the name of Saint Gregory; and most of the polemists mention: "They pray to the fire under the grain kiln (where the corn was dried by fire)." At these places sacrifices to Fire or Svarozhich were also offered.

Of an entirely different meaning are the deities known by the names of *Rod* and *Rozhanitsy*. Their cult is the main object of clerical denunciations, indicating its religious importance to the people. Strangely enough the modern population has entirely lost the memory of those divine powers although preserving fully the religious bearing of their cult.

Their meaning is clear from the etymology. *Rod,* as we know, means clan, tribe, or family—corresponding completely to the classical gens (γένος). But it can also have a more general meaning embracing birth itself (*rozhdenie* in Russian). Rozhanitsy are the female powers presiding over birth. They are mentioned only in the plural, for they are collective deities. Their male correspondent, however, is used only in the singular. This incongruity is explained by modern historians as the difference in the functional extension: *Rod* is the general power of birth or reproduction, and Rozhanitsy the special mistresses of individual birth and individual destiny. It was supposed that every man had his own Rozhanitsa presiding over his birth and life. The Russian deities bring to mind the parallel of the celtic fairies, but this connection is by no means assured, even the meaning of Rozhanitsy as goddesses of destiny is not certain, so scarce is our evidence. The last interpretation of Rozhanitsy as deities of fate is corroborated, however, by the Slavonic translation of a Biblical passage. In Isaiah 65:11 τύχη (*fortuna*) is rendered by *rozhanitsa.* Yet this meaning cannot be original, as the etymology of rozhanitsa clearly indicates. The central idea was undoubtedly the mystery of birth, in which the tie with the ancestral clan determined the destiny of the individual. The past was perhaps more important than the future in the chain of generations. The person felt linked with an unbroken chain, with few chances of escape by the decision of his own free will. "It is written for him from birth," is a popular Russian saying. Russian folk tales and epic songs are full of instances of the overwhelming power of destiny. No force can cross or check what is "written" for man. "You cannot ride past your predestined bridegroom" is another common proverb. In their belief in predestination, the Russian people are probably no exception among the nations. What is peculiar to the Russian is that there

is close connection between destiny and birth, that their
divinities of fate, corresponding to *Moirai, Parcae,* or *Fatae,*
have names identical with birth and are represented as the
mystery of birth itself in its blood union between generations.

The sources themselves give nothing more than the
names and one constant characteristic of their cult: the sacrificial meal. Most of the sermons repeat: "They lay out the
table (or "the second table") to Rod and Rozhanitsy." It
means that at certain feasts some food was served to these
deities. We even know of what this "second table" consisted.
It held only meatless dishes: bread, gruel, cheesecurd, and
mead.

Besides the meals for the Rozhanitsy the sermons mention specific meals for the dead (*nav'e*) offered in bathhouses. Our sources give us a clear idea of the rites and
their meaning. A sermon under the name of Saint John
Chrysostom gives the following details: "They arrange baths
for the dead; spread out ashes amidst bathhouses; put meat,
milk, butter, and eggs and all things needed by the demons,
and pour water on the stove bidding them wash; they also
hang linen and towels in the bathroom." The banquet is
connected with the bath as it is in all Russian folk tales. The
ashes spread on the floor serve for footprints, making the
visit of the dead seem more real. The preacher himself believes that the demons, exploiting the superstitions of the
people, enjoy the banquet and leave their actual traces
in the ashes "for their seduction." The same practice,
particularly observed on Maundy Thursday, still persisted
in White Russia in the nineteenth century. Since the dead
were believed to come at any time to bathe in the empty bathhouses after the living, these buildings were considered dangerous by night, but therefore the more suitable for divinations. The nearest modern parallel to the ancient "second

meals for the Rozhanitsy" was the feast of *Dziady* in White Russia. Here separate courses were left for the dead, who were called *Dziady* (grandfathers) and special prayers or incantations were said. It is possible that here the ancestors have replaced the ancient goddesses of birth as less exposed to the incrimination of paganism and more innocent in the eyes of the Church. If it be so, the interpretation of Rozhanitsy as goddesses of Rod rather than of Fate receives confirmation.

Scarce as they are, these evidences of pagan survivals in ancient Russia corroborate the general impression outlined in Chapter I. The core of Russian paganism was not the belief in great gods but the religious veneration of nature herself in her elements and phenomena, only in part personified, and the cult of Rod, or blood kinship, under the double aspect: the veneration of ancestors, and the faith in destiny. Nature religion was found in *Igor's Tale* and has left its traces in all modern Russian poetry. The Rod religion, at least in its moral implications, is observed not only in the ancient chronicles, but also in *Igor's Tale,* as well as in all Russian folklore and all pre-revolutionary life.

There is still another element among these pagan survivals which is very important for knowledge of the Russian mind but which requires great caution in its treatment. As a matter of fact it is not strongly emphasized in the sources, and it acquires its full meaning only in the light of later and even modern Russian life. This element I should like to call Dionysiac or orgiastic. Strong Christian and social discipline, particularly in the Muscovite period, repressed or relegated this ancient trend into the background. Yet it came to the surface every time a political or cultural outburst freed the chained chaos of the Russian soul.

In ancient sermons are mentioned a phallic rite observed at wedding-banquets, sexual promiscuity during the feast

gatherings of young people, especially on the day or night
of Saint John and the dissolute character of banquets in general. All these were features of modern Russian life as well.
There is another allusion which would give us a precious
revelation of the Russian Dionysiac spirit were it not so short
and possibly corrupted that it resists every explanation.
Among the other real or fictitious Russian pagan deities an
unknown name is mentioned: "They believe . . . also in Pere-
plut and, whirling, they drink to him from horns." If this
translation is correct one can see here the combination of violent dance and intoxication in honor of a god, that is, the
Dionysiac element in its primitive and purest form.

Numerous are the sermons devoted to invectives against
drunkenness and the pagan character of banquets. They
even induced one of the modern scholars in Russian paganism, E. V. Anichkov, to see in these invectives the only sub-
stantial content of antipagan literature. This is an exaggeration, yet obviously the Christian moralist stood in despair
before the rage of these bacchanals. No pagan gods are mentioned in connection with the banquets. But their pagan
character was proved to the preachers by the use of musical
instruments and secular songs. Ancient Russian preachers in
their puritan zeal condemned all kinds of secular music, including dancing. Yet the very radicalism of clerical denunciation was partly provoked by the orgiastic features of popular amusements. Let us read one item of condemnation
by the Metropolitan Cyril:

> On Saturday evening men and women come together, play and
> dance shamelessly and indulge in obscenities on the night of the
> Holy Resurrection, just as ungodly pagans celebrating the feast of
> Dionysos; men and women together, like horses, frolic and neigh
> and make obscenities . . . And now let them cease.

Or this indictment by the Synod of Vladimir of 1274:

We have also learned that they still hold the custom of the thrice-accursed heathens: on the divine feast-days they celebrate demonical plays with whistling, shouting, and howling; they call together base drunkards and beat one another with poles to the death, even stripping the killed of their clothes.

This wild debauch of popular feasts was preserved until the twentieth century, with the same scenes of drunken fighting and killing as are depicted in this document of the thirteenth century. Orgiasm, though not necessarily in the specific sexual meaning, unrestrained emotional outbursts, stimulated by alcohol, dancing, fighting, or sex, always has been an outstanding feature of the Russian temperament. As to drunkenness, the abundance of the sermons especially denouncing it has little weight as proof. There was hardly a nation in the Middle Ages which, in some period, or in the eyes of some neighbors, did not have the reputation of being particularly bad drunkards. But the uniqueness of Russia's case is emphasized by the legend according to which its devotion to drinking was one of the motives for Russia's conversion to Christianity. The chronicler relates very calmly, or perhaps, with a slight smile of satisfaction, the answer of Prince Vladimir, then heathen, to the Moslem missionaries: "Drinking is the joy of Russians; we cannot do without it." Thus the national vice was represented in official tradition as the means by which Providence saved Russia from the evil lot of becoming Moslem.

At this point of our investigation it is pertinent to raise the problem of the presence or absence of Bogomil trends in popular Russian piety. Although Bogomilism is by no means a heathen religion but rather a Christian sect, one would expect its refutation or at least its denunciation in the same sermons or penitential canons which deal with pagan survivals, magic, and all kinds of superstitions. Bogomilism was a dualistic sect, a remote offspring of ancient Manicheism, which appeared in Bulgaria in the ninth century and became a mighty rival of the Church in all the Slavic Balkan countries. From there it penetrated western Europe in the eleventh century and began a very spectacular career under the name of Cathars, Albigenses, and others. Considering the close cultural relations between medieval Bulgaria and Russia and the identity of their literary language, the infiltration into Russia of the Bogomils or their teaching would have been very natural. An eminent literary historian, A. N. Veselovsky, affirmed that at the base of Russian folklore (so-called "spiritual songs") are apocrypha or legends of Bogomil origin. The theological analysis of both the existing apocrypha and the Russian songs, however, does not justify this theory. First of all, the dualistic elements in the apocrypha as well as in the songs are very slight. They are reduced to the not quite orthodox legends on the role which Satan took in the creation of the world. Some stories of this kind, well-known also in popular tales, Ukrainian and others, are not sufficient to prove the popular world-outlook dualistic. Most of the apocrypha, whose Greek originals were ascertained, go back to the earliest times of Christianity. If any heretical views are reflected in them, these are of the ancient gnosticism. But expunged, and received by the Church for popular use, the apocrypha represent simply the lower popular stratum of Greek and Byzantine Christianity. It is proved that the Bogomils enriched this literature by some additions, but traces of specifically Bogomil apocrypha in Russia have not been found.

One of Veselovsky's disciples, E. V. Anichkov, claimed to have discovered a mention of the Bogomils in the polemical sermons against paganism. But it is a pure misunderstanding. The Bulgars mentioned there are not heretical Slavs but Turkish Moslems. Since the seventh century the Turkish Bulgar state had existed on the middle Volga, and from these Bulgars came the Moslem missionaries to Prince Vladimir. In relation to the same Bulgars the chronicler mentions some obscene rites which are repeated by later preachers denouncing paganism.

There is in the *Chronicle* itself a passage which, if taken at face value, implies the dualistic theology of the pagan volkhvi. In the middle of the narration of the pagan riots mentioned above, the *Chronicle* cites some examples of the theological disputes between Ian, the prince's envoy, and the volkhvi. The two volkhvi of Belo-ozero give the following myth of the Creation, familiar from Ukranian folk tales:

> God washed himself in the bath and after sweating, dried himself with a piece of cloth and threw it from heaven upon the earth. Then, Satan quarrelled with God as to which of them should create man. The devil made man, but God set a soul in him. Therefore, whenever a man dies, his body goes to earth and his soul to God.

To the following question of Ian: "In what god do you believe?" they answered, "In the Antichrist."—Where is he?—"Sitting in the abyss." Another magician of the Chud tribe explains his faith to a Christian citizen of Novgorod upon his asking, "Who are your gods and where do they dwell?"—"In the abysses; they are black of visage, winged and tailed, and they mount under heaven listening to your gods. For your gods dwell in heaven. If any of your people die, they are carried up to heaven. But if any of ours die, they are carried down into the abyss to our gods."

At first sight it is clear that we are dealing here, not with an objective description of the heathen faith, but with a satire. The point of this satire consists in the identification of the heathen gods with devils. It is very likely that the author or his source of information used some features of Bogomil legends for his distorted picture, as he used the customary iconographic pattern for demons for the external appearance

of the gods. And yet in order that this satire should have
made any sense at all, it must have borne some resemblance
to reality; in other words, the religion of the volkhvi was
really tinctured by dualism. In comparison to the dualism
of the Bogomils, it was a dualism turned upside down.
Wheras the Balkan heretics rejected, in a most energetic way,
the earthly or evil god in all forms of his activities—creation,
sexual and social life, and even the Church,—the Russian
volkhvi seemed to worship inferior or subterranean powers
as their gods. Here also much must be attibuted to polemical distortion. The dualistic religious systems which admit
the worship of evil gods always combine their cult with that
of good, beneficent deities, so that "gods" and "devils" have
their equal share. And, indeed, traces of such dualism are
really observed in the folklore of the semipagan Finnish
tribes of northeastern Russia.

It must be noted that the volkhv of the last story dwells
in the country of the Chud, a Finnish tribe. So his theology,
whatever it may be, is probably not that of the Russian Slavs.
But the same can be said of the volkhvi in the *Chronicle* in
general. It can hardly be accidental that, with one exception, all cases of pagan riots, where the volkhvi appear, belong to the North (Novgorod, Belo-ozero) where Slavic
tribes dwelled in close contact with the Finns. Chud, Meria,
together with the Slavs of Novgorod, are represented by the
chronicler as active tribes, building the primitive Russo-
Varangian state in the North. In all Finnish tribes the
shamans (professional magicians) have been deeply influ-
encing the popular religion up to the present. It is natural
to admit the Finnish influence on the primitive and undevel-
oped paganism of the Russian Slavs in the regions of their
cohabitation. From this point of view all or most of the
volkhvi appearing on the pages of the *Chronicles* can be considered as Finnish magicians or their Slavic disciples. In this

case their religious features are not characteristic of Slavic
paganism, but of the Finnish influence upon it.

That is the import of the real or fictitious dualism of the
Volkhvi. The main orientation both of Russian religious
folklore, and Russian culture in general indicates that the
bias of the Russian religious mind is quite opposed to any
kind of dualism. It is naturalistic monism that was a perpetual temptation to Russian Christianity. The Russian people as well as the Russian poets hold nature pure and holy,
exempt from every sin inherent to human history and culture. In the communion with nature, man finds his redemption. This is the Russian heresy that becomes intelligible
only upon the premise of a strong original monism underlying all strata of historical Russian Christianity. Yet, Christianity neither of the Byzantine nor Roman type, is liable
to this monistic naturalism. It must then be sought in the
deeper, pagan layers of the Russian soul.

It remains for us to mark the initial stages of the gradual
fusion of dying paganism with victorious Christianity, so far
as they are reflected in our sources. These beginnings are
very meager. The Church, essentially a Greek Church on
Russian soil, mercilessly assailed any kind of heathen survival, showing none of the pedagogical condescension or
accommodations of which the mission of the Western Church
knows so many striking examples. Christianity in Kievan
Russia is mainly the civilized, urban religion, the faith of
the aristocratic society. It was in later more democratic and
nationalistic centuries, that the fusion of old and new per-
meated more easily and deeply the life of the folk. However, even in Kiev some interesting developments of religious
syncretism or fusion can be traced. Such are the cults of some
Christian saints who inherited the mythological tradition of
pagan deities, as the prophet Elias replacing Perun in his
character of thunder-lord, Saint Blasius, the protector of

THE RUSSIAN RELIGIOUS MIND

cattle, in name and function akin to Veles or Volos, the "god of cattle," and Saint George, whose legend on the Russian soil assumed some definite mythological features.

From several sermons, treating the subject *ex professo*, one learns about idolatrous rites connected with the cult of Sunday (*Nedelia*). The Sunday or Nedelia was represented in visual form, painted or carved; the sermons speak both of statues *bolvani* and painted images. The emphasis of the preacher is indicated in the title itself: "It is not becoming to Christians to venerate the Nedelia nor kiss it because it is a creature."

The argument of the ancient preacher is not entirely clear. Certainly he did not wish to protest against the cult of the saints who are also "creatures." In the Greek Church, Sunday under the name of Anastasia (resurrection) was venerated as the name of one of the virgin martyrs. Most likely the symbol of the Resurrection of Our Lord was venerated under this human guise. On ancient Russian icons Saint Anastasia can be seen, in most cases together with Saint Paraskeva (Friday). Whether the preacher had in mind the confusion between a saint and weekday, or some particular forms of veneration, such as sculptured images, we do not know. Yet the meaning of the cult of Sunday as a particular spiritual entity is very important for Russian piety. However, it can be studied only on the evidence furnished by later centuries, together with the cult of Saint Friday which practically evicted Nedelia in the popular worship.

There is one fact of Christian-pagan syncretism mentioned with particular emphasis in the sources of this period. It is a revealing feature of the main stream of the popular Russian religious mind, the full development of which belongs, however, to a later epoch. It is the fusion of the cult of the Rozhanitsy with that of Theotokos, the Mother of God. In the sermon of the so-called "Christ-lover" one reads:

"We do not do a simple evil, but we intermingle some pure prayers with the accursed idol-worship—the most Holy Mother of God with the Rozhanitsy." More explicit is the sermon of Pseudo-Gregory: "The priests who serve their belly have established the custom of adding the troparion to the Nativity of the Mother of God to the repast for the Rozhanitsy, setting aside dishes for them." The troparia are the ecclesiastical hymns for Christian feast days. It is not quite certain which Nativity is meant here: that of Christ, to judge from certain Greek precedents, or that of Our Lady, as the literal sense appears to indicate. But the meaning of the ritual is clear. As of old, in connection with childbirth, festive meals were laid and separate courses were put aside for the goddesses of birth. It was on the instigation of the "popes," Christian priests present at the table, that the prayers to Our Lady were sung. The practical intention of the popes is clear: they tried, by invoking the name of Mary, to substitute Our Lady for the pagan Rozhanitsy. If they had succeeded in this innovation the old rite would have remained, with the pagan names forgotten and the whole festivity invested with a thoroughly Christian character.

That this did not happen and that the whole rite disappeared from Russian folklore are due to the zeal of the first Russian missionaries. They wanted no compromise with Satan. The same preacher quoted from the so-called Apocalypse of Saint Paul, which he naturally took for a genuine work of the Apostle. "Paul said: I saw a cloud of blood spread all over the world. And I asked, saying: O Lord, what is it? And He said unto me: 'This is the prayers of men, mixed up with iniquity.'" Iniquity is idolatry. The confusion of Christian prayers with idolatrous acts is worse than the "simple evil" of paganism.

The zealous preacher not only accuses Christian priests of initiating this contamination, but he gives also the least honorable motives for their action; very remote, indeed, from the pedagogical tolerance of Gregory the Great towards heathen rites. He calls them "popes serving their belly," adding a still stronger epithet, *kormoguztsy.* He supposes that they took part in heathen festivals for the sake of gluttony, and in order to justify their conduct, they spread a Christian veil over the pagan practice. One could doubt the fairness of this indictment but for the general observation that most Russian sermons directed against paganism are also directed against bad priests who appear guilty not only of negligence in fighting pagan practices but even of participating in them. The same "Christ-lover," after inveighing against the survival of heathen sacrifices and obscene rites, continues his incrimination:

> This is done not only by the ignorant but also by the knowing, by priests and book-scholars; if the knowing ones do not do it (offer sacrifices), they drink and eat those meals which have been prayed upon; if they do not drink nor eat they see evil doings; if they do not see, they hear; and do not wish to teach the people.

Most of this sermon consists in indictments of bad priests. The author appears not to have belonged to their category, either as a bishop, monk, or a learned layman.

We are not interested now in the priests' role in the Christian-pagan syncretism, but in the religious meaning of the troparia at the repasts of the Rozhanitsy. The Mother of God was not casually chosen to replace the goddesses of birth. She was obviously the embodiment of motherhood, divine Motherhood itself. It is noteworthy that the most common name of Mary among Russian people is *Bogoroditsa,* the literal translation of the Greek *Theotokos*: not Blessed Virgin (or "La Sainte Vierge"), not our Lady (though the "Queen of Heaven" also is common), not "Liebe Frau," but "Mother of God." The Theotokos, in which name the Greek theology of the fifth century celebrated its great tri-

umph over Nestorianism, was adopted by the West, in a
Latin translation of *Deipara*. But it never really became
popular in the Catholic West. In Russia it has no abstract,
theological flavor, but it is full of emotional power. It
speaks directly to the heart because it touches the very core
of the Russian religion: divine Motherhood. Differing
from Greece where Theotokos was once the object of discussion, Russia laid the stress not upon the first but upon the
last part of the compound name: not "theo" but "tokos," the
Parent, the Birthgiver, the Mother. The Russian Mary is
not only the Mother of God or Christ but the universal
Mother, the Mother of all mankind. In the first place she
is of course Mother in the moral sense, a merciful protector,
an intercessor for men before the heavenly Justice, the Russian version of redemption. But in another ontological sense
she was really believed by the folk to be the Giver of life to
all creatures, and in that dignity she rightly succeeded to the
modest and nameless, somewhat shadowy Rozhanitsy.

We must confess that practically all features of this image
of the Russian *Bogoroditsa* are taken from the sources of
later periods, mostly from modern Russian folklore. For
the Kievan age the sources of Russian Mariology are very
scanty. The extension and significance of her cult is
evidenced by the number of churches consecrated to her
name, her feasts celebrated, her icons venerated. But in
written sources the religious meaning of her cult is little
stressed, her name is seldom used in comparison with later
times. The first stage of her cult seems to have been veiled
in silence. Greek theology had little to do with its development; Greek liturgy and iconography did the most. But,
as we have seen, the national source of Mariological religion
was in Russian paganism.

Was the cult of Rozhanitsy the only heathen precedent
of the Mary worship in Russia? We do not know. Our

sources for the mythological aspect of Russian paganism are too scanty. Yet, if the Russian Slavs had no name for the Great Goddess it does not mean that they did not know her. The great anonymous goddess of the Scytho-Iranian world appears to have been living until the present day in the pattern of Russian peasant art. Unmistakably pagan reminiscences were attached to the Russian cult of the Saint Paraskeva-Piatnitsa (Holy Friday), which played a great role in medieval and modern Russia. At every step in studying Russian popular religion one meets the constant longing for a great divine female power, be it embodied in the image of Mary or someone else. Is it too daring to hypothesize, on the basis of this religious propensity, the scattered elements of the cult of the Great Goddess who once had reigned upon the immense Russian plains?

Suppose this hypothesis is vain and such a goddess never existed on the Russian soil. The Christian conversion, indeed, overtook the eastern Slavic tribes at a very early stage in their mythological development. Perhaps they never had the time to evolve fully their primary religious intuition of the Divine Motherhood into the completed forms of myth and cult. This mythological and cultual process might have taken place under the Christian guise, fertilized and sublimated by the Christian images of Holy Womanhood. One thing is almost certain: Greek Orthodox Christianity alone is not sufficient to account for the deep and rich forms of the Divine Womanhood cults which took place on the Russian soil.

Conclusion

XIII

THE RUSSIAN RELIGIOUS MIND

*T*HE foregoing chapters have dealt analytically with the different currents of the Russian religious mind in various strata of society, giving little opportunity to stress the general characteristics of the ancient Russian religion. Our task now is to look for unity behind diversity. It must be pointed out that some essential elements of piety have not been treated as fully as they deserved simply because they were not expressed with enough emphasis in the sources analyzed. They are diffused instead throughout the entire field of ancient Russian literature. Before approaching any particular aspects of the Russian religion, however, it is necessary to dwell on a special problem which is of interest to all students of ancient Russian culture.

THE PROBLEM OF CHRONOLOGICAL DEVELOPMENT

Almost all literary historians admit their failure of putting into evolutionary order the existing works of the Kievan period. There is therefore no history of this period organized chronologically. Only analyses of separate works exist. The chronological arrangement of these works so far has little intrinsic significance. Modern critics' continual shifting of the dates, even in the case of such outstanding works as the Epistles of James and Daniel, is proof of the lack of a solid chronological frame.

This lack could be explained, and was explained by the

scarcity of the material that had been preserved and by the imitative, compilatory character of ancient Russian literature. Yet in the subsequent medieval period, the material is still less abundant, the Byzantine influence is no less strong, but the chronological skeleton is far more definite, because the evolutionary process is evident. The puzzling element in the Kievan period is the richness of content, the variety of literary styles and spiritual trends requiring not one but several evolutionary series. This complexity in the cultural life, together with the scarcity of existing materials, defies all attempts to arrange the material in an evolutionary sequence. The first impression, therefore, is a complete lack of unity. However, in a rare instance, when a chronological series is complete, as in the historical chronicles, it is easy to recognize inner development. The strong and severe claims of Christian ethics in the sphere of political life characterize the end of the eleventh and the beginning of the twelfth century until the death of Monomach in 1125, or possibly that of his son Mstislav in 1132. The twelfth century is marked by the prevalence of feudal ethics of loyalty and honor. By the end of the century local patriotisms disrupt the unity of Russian lands and a corresponding increase of political immorality follows. Such a clear evolutionary arrangement is unfortunately not possible in other fields as it is in political ethics. This field, however, gives us the key to drawing some other general conclusions.

The regressive character of this ethical line is striking, both from the Christian and the national points of view. The movement is from universal to particular, from evangelical to secular or to narrowly pious; in short, it is a movement of disintegration. The political development offers a key to this cultural paradox. The Kievan state reached the climax of its expansion and power in heathen times during the tenth century, under Sviatoslav and Vladimir. Iaroslav, the son and successor of Saint Vladimir, maintained this level for some forty years. His death in 1054, however, marks the end of political unity in Russia and the beginning of feudal disintegration. His grandson, Vladimir Monomach, was the last prince of Kiev with universal authority, based more on his personal qualities than on constitutional grounds. The end of the twelfth century is the third milestone in the downward movement, when the nomad tribes, now grown in strength, devastated south Russia and cut the commercial roads towards the Black Sea and Byzantium.

The first ascendant period of the Kievan State left no traces in literature except its commercial pacts with the Greeks. The whole Christian and literary stage of pre-Mongolian Russia coincides with the gradual decadence of political and economic life. One must keep in mind that the lines of political and cultural developments, while connected, are not parallel. The last great prince of Kiev, Iaroslav, laid the foundations for cultural progress by gathering around the Cathedral Church of Saint Sophia a circle of learned clergy and translaters. The quantitive growth of the intellectual elite continued for generations, in spite of political setbacks and catastrophes. The process finds its eloquent parallel in the West during the Carolingian Renaissance when the impulse given by Charlemagne to the cultural revival came to full fruition under his grandson Charles the Bald at a time when the Empire was already in ruins.

The corresponding cultural climax in Russia can be hypothetically dated around the middle of the twelfth century. Indeed the two outstanding figures of Russian Byzantinism, Clement and Cyril, belong to this age. Since no literary figure of such importance is known in the thirteenth century one may infer that by that time political disintegration had already paralyzed cultural life. However, the greatest literary figure of ancient Russia and the most scholarly among its prelates, Hilarion of Kiev, belongs to the reign of Iaroslav, that is, to the very first years of Russian literature. The circle of the adepts of new Christian learning must have been very limited by his time. Yet, this narrow circle was inspired with the high vision of the new calling of Russia, as a newly-accepted member among the Christian and cultured nations of the world. The Christian idealism of this generation partly explains the appearance of this greatest literary figure at the threshold of Russian literature.

The climax of religious life, as embodied in the figures of great national saints, also falls into the first Christian generation. The princes Boris and Gleb and the Abbot Theodosius belong to it. With them Russian kenoticism, the most original creation of the Russian religious spirit, comes into being. Its first achievements remain unsurpassed for centuries until the days of Saint Sergius in the fourteenth century. Thus the first response of the newly-converted nation to the Christian call was most spontaneous and powerful. Afterwards, in the strict school of the Greek Church, Russian piety became more conventional. Since these last types of devotion and doctrine are less original and more imitative they cannot be placed in any evolutionary scheme either progressive or retrogressive. But a further and more detailed study of the literary documents in the light of contemporary developments in Byzantium will some day offer new landmarks for their chronological arrangement and, consequently, for the history of the Russian religious mind.

NATURE AND RELIGION

It is a commonplace among historians of religion that Eastern Christianity stresses the cosmological aspects more strongly than the Christian West which puts unquestionable emphasis upon anthropology. This is, beyond doubt, the Hellenistic legacy to Eastern theology, clearly discernible

from Origen to the Damascene. A symbolic expression of
this tendency can be found in the representation of the Cosmos on the Greek icons of the Pentecost. Around the Blessed Virgin the twelve Apostles are depicted receiving the
fiery tongues of the Holy Ghost; but beneath their seats the
half-figure of a bearded man with a crown on his head is
seen as if coming from under the earth. This is the "King
Cosmos" also participating in the outpouring gifts of the
Holy Ghost. The same cosmological motive is strong in
Greek hymnology as well, especially in the hymns dedicated
to Our Lady. She is always thought of and venerated in
connection with the Cosmos which stands under her protection.

It is true that, compared with the Hellenistic age, the
Byzantine attitude to nature seems cold, abstract, and rational. Cosmos became an idea rather than a feeling of man's
ties with nature. On the other hand, the medieval West,
particularly Celtic and Teutonic, also possessed a very strong
religious feeling for nature and tried to graft it upon the old
Roman stem. But Russia, taking over Byzantine cosmology,
imparted to it a warmth, spontaneity, and even poignancy
which went far beyond the western medieval sense of nature.

The most beautiful expression of the Russian sense of
nature is in *Igor's Tale;* here it is religious, though not Christian. Together with numerous remainders of naturalistic
heathen cults *Igor's Tale* points to a pre-Christian source of
Russian cosmology. But we do not lack instances of its Christian transformations.

Cyril of Turov had the reputation of being the most
eloquent poet of nature in Russian theological literature.
As we have seen, this reputation was hardly a deserved one.
The learned bishop simply adapted for his own use one of
the paschal homilies of Gregory of Nazianzus. The Byzantinist school in Russia, with its pursuit of abstract symbol-

ism, was the least favorable setting for a strong and sincere
sense of nature. It is true that Gregory's description of a
Hellenistic spring, completely lacking local Russian features,
had a long and notable career in Russia. It was transcribed
and imitated until the seventeenth century, as has been shown
in a recent study of the landscape in ancient Russian literature
by A. Nikol'skaia. The slavish dependence upon the Greek
original and the lack of any ingenious approach to nature
shows how extremely difficult nature-painting is for any
primitive literature. Against this barren background *Igor's
Tale* stands out as a work of genius, nourished, besides, by
quite a different tradition of folk poetry.

Vladimir Monomach strikes a more intimate and deeply
Christian note when he speaks of nature as the manifestation
of God's loving kindness. He knows hardly more than to
name all the wonders of God's creation, the sun, the moon,
the stars, and the different animals and birds, but his un-
feigned admiration throbs with joy and tenderness. It is one
of the foundations of Vladimir's religious optimism, of his
confidence in God's wisdom and love.

In the eschatological *Sermon on the Celestial Powers* the
anonymous Russian author concludes his picture of the Last
Judgment by the vision of a new earth in all its beauty and
magnificence. The redemption of nature is, for the author,
the major feature of the eschatological hope and even makes
him forget about the bliss of the saints.

In the most popular and artistic hagiographic monument
of Kievan Russia, the *Legend of Saint Boris and Saint Gleb*
(the *Skazanie*), warm and touching images of the life of
nature unexpectedly enhance the tragedy of slaughtered
innocence. One reads among the supplications of Gleb addressed to his murderers: "Do not reap the unripe ear.... Do
not cut down the vine-shoot which is not yet grown."

The Russian *Chronicles,* even those composed by the

monks of the Caves Cloister, sometimes reflect a sympathetic feeling for nature, perhaps under the influence of folk traditions and legends. Such is the description of the battle between Saint Vladimir's sons Iaroslav and Mstislav in 1024. "When night fell, there was darkness with lightning, thunder, and rain. The combat was a violent one. As the lightning flashed, the weapons gleamed and the thunder roared, and the fight was violent and fearsome." Here it is obvious that the thunder, accompanying the fight, is mentioned not simply as a detail of setting, as a mere weather phenomenon, but serves to enhance the impression of the fierceness and rage of the battle. Its function is the same as that of the thunderstorm in *Igor's Tale*.

THE ROLE OF BEAUTY

The Russian sense of nature has two aspects, both of which can acquire a religious significance. The first is the consciousness of belonging to nature, of being deeply rooted in it. This consciousness brings with it the religious acceptance or rejection of the human body and the physiological processes. Traces of such religious physiology can be found in the canonical ritualism of Kirik and his fellow priests among the Russian clergy.

The other aspect of nature is beauty. The above-mentioned instances of the religious appreciation of nature involve a sense of beauty. But the sense of beauty finds its way not only into nature but also into art. There is no doubt that the Russians are and always were gifted for the arts, although in different epochs different arts rose to the top in the national esteem. Thus in ancient Russia poetry and music, at least secular poetry and music, were thwarted by ecclesiastical condemnation. The pictorial art, however, was not only protected, but created by the Church, at least in its higher forms.

The influence of the religious art upon the Russian religious soul was extremely great. The Kievan *Chronicle*, in its legendary account of the conversion of Saint Vladimir, ascribes the choice of the new religion to the overwhelming impression produced by the beauties of the Greek liturgy upon Vladimir's envoys. According to this account the Kievan prince, having made up his mind to change his religion, sent his envoys to the centers of different confessions, Moslem, Jewish, Roman Catholic, and Greek Orthodox to investigate whose faith was the best. The envoys performed their task in the only manner available to them—by observing the liturgical rites of the respective nations. They were deeply disgusted by the Jewish and Moslem worship and not affected by that of the Roman Catholics.

But their enthusiasm for the Greek service was immense. In Constantinople the Emperor sent them to a solemn celebration in Saint Sophia, organized especially for their benefit. They hardly could understand the words of the Greek liturgy or its religious meaning, but its beauty was the decisive factor in their final choice. They reported to Vladimir in the following words:

> We went on to Greece, and the Greeks led us to the edifice where they worship their God, and we knew not whether we were in heaven or on earth. For on earth there is no such splendor or such beauty and we are at a loss to describe it. We only know that God dwells there among men, and their service is fairer than the ceremonies of other nations. For we cannot forget that beauty. Every man, after tasting something sweet is afterwards unwilling to accept that which is bitter.

Certainly this is no more than a legend. Prince Vladimir had other reasons to embrace the Greek form of Christianity besides its esthetic values. But the legend is characteristic of the mood of the religious elite in Kiev at the end of the eleventh century. Apparently, the chronicler, a learned monk of the Caves Cloister, considered the beauty of the cult a normal and not unworthy motive for the choice of a religion. His is not an isolated reaction. At all times the liturgical beauty of the Orthodox Church was considered by the Russians as the best missionary argument in the conversion of the heterodox. In the panegyrical entry on Prince Andrew Bogoliubsky, the chronicler recalls his pious custom:

In former days when a merchant came to him from Constantinople or from other countries, from the Russian land or from the Latin, from the whole of Christendom and even from all heathen lands, he led them into the galleries of the church, that they might see the true Christianity and be converted (1175).

The same missionary device was employed in the fourteenth century by Saint Stephen for the conversion of the heathen Zyrians, and in the Muscovite period the appreciation of the esthetic side of worship went still further. It remains one of the most constant features of Russian religion. Very seldom is kenotic poverty extended into this sphere of the cult. In the Kievan period not a single instance is known of ascetic denial or neglect of temple beauty. The chroniclers do not omit to mention and even to describe in detail the magnificence of new churches or richly-ornamented icons. Because of the poverty of their means of expression their descriptions stress not so much the beauty of forms as the luxury of ornamentation. Gold and silver, pearls and precious stones, silks and embroideries take the major place in these descriptions. They fill, in a rather monotonous enumeration of sacred objects, no less than two columns in quarto in the Ipatiev *Chronicle,* in depicting the glory of the ecclesiastical buildings of Prince Andrew Bogoliubsky. Certainly this prince had every reason to display proudly his gorgeous churches to foreign guests, even if one might doubt the effect of this show upon their religious sentiments.

To give up all one's substance for the adornment of a

church was considered a God-pleasing deed, even in the
Kievan period. Among others, this was done by Erasmus,
one of the Kievan monks, but the Patericon tells us that this
did not save the future saint from temptation and temporary
moral laxity. The story shows a fine understanding of religious psychology among the Kievan hagiographs: of all Christian virtues the devotion to beauty of ritual is the least secure
way to salvation. How different is the creative work of an
artist if inspired by high religious spirit! One of the most
attractive figures of the same *Patericon* is Alypius, the icon
painter, the first in a series of canonized religious artists in
Russia. All his works are lost, but if his style can be recon-
structed in accordance with the legend of his life, it must
have been a light, spiritual art, almost dematerialized and
transparent with the vision of celestial beauty.

THE TESTIMONY OF THE ICONS

In the present book only literary material has been used
for the reconstruction of the Russian religious mind. Yet
it often has been affirmed that the deepest religious experiences and ideas of ancient Russia were expressed not in words
but in colors: in her religious painting. What have icons to
teach us about the Russian religious mind of the first Christian centuries?

Unfortunately this source of information for the Kievan
period is very scanty. Besides mosaics and the frescoes of
some churches (Saint Michael monastery in Kiev, Saint
Savior in Nereditsa near Novgorod), hardly more than a
score of Kievan icons, that is, separate paintings on wood,
are extant. The second, and the major reason for their in-
adequacy is their imitative character. In the first centuries
of its development, Russian religious art followed Byzantine
patterns strictly. Russian icons of that period are, in most

cases, copies of Greek originals. There are some good copies among them promising a great future, but still lacking in original spirit. Sometimes, it is impossible to tell the Russian copy from the Greek original.

It is likely that these difficulties will be partly overcome with the progress of studies in this field, only recently opened to research. Perhaps it will at length be possible to speak of the particular features of Russian style in the Russian iconography of this period. So far we can make some general observations not limited to the early times alone.

The fundamental religious dualism in the worship of Christ does not find its iconographic expression in different treatments of Christ. The Lord on the icon is always the Pantocrator, never a humiliated Christ. Yet, His countenance is liable to slight changes, from severe and wrathful to mild and sorrowful. Sometimes these nuances were almost imperceptible; sometimes, in later time, they were grasped even by contemporaries who gave particular names to the types of the most venerated icons. In Kievan art it is sufficient to state that both types derived from Byzantium are represented, but not yet strongly differentiated.

The corresponding dualism is also observed in the Madonna types. Apart from the Orante, with the Infant represented in a medallion on her waist (the patron of Novgorod), all Russian icons of Our Lady can be traced to the two Greek patterns: in one Mary is represented as the heavenly Queen, in the other as God's Mother. The idea is indicated by the mutual situation of the two heads, Mother's and Son's. The head of the Queen is erect, facing forward, as well as that of the Infant; both look ahead without any relationship to one another. On the icons of the Mother her head is bent toward the Son in a token of tenderness. Very often the feeling of motherly love is indicated, slightly and reservedly, in the expression of the eyes—always

marked with sorrow as if foreseeing the Golgotha. The
Queen type is called in Greek *Hodegetria,* after the famous
miraculous icon of Constantinople. In Russia Our Lady
of Smolensk, a Greek icon, is the main representative of this
type. The best presentation of motherly tenderness is found
in Our Lady of Vladimir, also brought from Greece—perhaps the most beautiful example of all Greek icons extant.
In Russia this type is called by the familiar name of *Umilenie.* There was a time when the art historians believed that
the *Umilenie* type was a Russian creation. We know better
now, but the very possibility of this error is the proof of the
rareness of this Madonna type in Greece. The Russians
took over both iconographical patterns from Greece; but
they gave their preference to the less common one, revealing by this choice the prevailing leaning of their mind.

We know that in the cult of Our Lady on the Russian
soil divine Motherhood and not Virginity is emphasized.
A corollary of this devotional trend was that, in contrast with
the West, beauty was not the main feature of her image.
That means that the strong Russian need for the worship
of beauty had to find its gratification elsewhere. Since icons
of holy women and virgins were rare or even absent, the
Russian religious artist found the embodiment of the idea
of the beautiful in the icons of angels. Their icons are preserved from all periods of Russian art—angels in general,
or Saint Michael and Gabriel in particular, always extremely
refined and enchanting. The antique model of a young
god or genius is still conspicuous. But the beauty of the
human face is here purified of all sexual fascination and
sublimated into celestial spirituality.

In spite of the infancy of Russian art, its refinement is
characteristic not only of the angels' icons. The whole school
of Suzdal-Vladimir is marked by aristocratic elegance in
lines and colors; a certain rudeness of Novgorodian primi-

tives, more popular and plebeian, is the opposite of Vladimir aristocracy.

LEARNING AND SCIENCE

The religious meaning of beauty to the Kievan Christian élite is beyond doubt. More questionable is their attitude towards learning and science. Tested by her production in this field ancient Russia would fare badly. The "backwardness" of Russia, if compared to the West, is strongly marked even in the middle of the eleventh century, when the first flight of philosophical thought started in France. And yet ancient Russia never knew any ascetic denial of culture, such as was familiar to the monks of Cluny in an acute form, as well as to some currents of Byzantine monasticism. In Kiev one constantly meets with eulogies of wisdom, and explicitly of book wisdom. The most famous of these is included by the chronicler in the description of the cultural activities of Prince Iaroslav around 1037:

> Great is the fruit of book learning; by books we are shown and taught the ways of repentance, we acquire wisdom and conscience from the words of books; they are rivers watering the universe, they are the fountainhead of wisdom, by them we are comforted in sorrow, they are the bridle of temperance.

A long quotation from the Wisdom of Solomon helps to enhance the authority of book wisdom.

The first Russian *Collection* of 1076 is opened by an article on book reading attributed to Saint John Chrysostom. In the later collections of this kind, many such articles are included, stressing the high value of books and suggesting the best methods of using them. Nowhere is there to be found a warning against possible misuse or the danger of free and critical thought connected with reading.

Very illuminating in this respect is the comparison of the Greek and Russian *Lives* of saints. Generally speak-

ing, the first part of every hagiographical document, that
dealing with the childhood history of a saint, is the least
reliable part.   One has to deal with legends or, in most
cases, simply with literary clichés.   In the Greek hagiography
two different clichés were used.   One of these describes the
great gifts of the child and his precocious progress in learning, the other his ascetic aversion to learning and school.
Both were represented by highly authoritative sources.   The
first by the lives of Saint John Chrysostom, Saint Euthymius,
Saint Sabbas of Palestine; the second by that of Saint Anthony the Great.

It is a remarkable fact that in Russia only the first tradition took root.   All Russian saints in their childhood are
zealous and talented scholars.   Of Saint Theodosius we are
informed that as a child he "learned all grammatikia."
Whatever the author had in mind in using this Hellenism,
he certainly meant more than a mere knowledge of reading
(in Russian *gramota*).   Probably "grammatikia" embraced
the content of the "Grammar Schools" as they existed in
Byzantium and the Roman Empire.   In this case it was a
great exaggeration, considering the place and the time, a
small provincial town (Kursk) during the first decades after
Russia's conversion.   We still possess some examples of
Theodosius' writings from the years of his maturity.   Although of a rare religious power, they bear no witness to
the author's literary learning.   The exaggeration of his
biographer is obvious, but the tendency itself is precious.

Saint Theodosius is no exception.   In a Smolensk monastery Saint Abraham copied with his own hand and by the
hands of other scribes the whole library of the fathers.
Saint Euphrosynia of Polotsk who died in 1173, a nun
living at the cathedral church of Saint Sophia, occupied her
days with copying books, and by selling them she received
money to distribute to the poor.   The young princes Boris

and Gleb are depicted by Nestor as addicted to reading pious books, the *Lives* of saints in this case. In the Kievan *Patericon* books are mentioned on every page. During the life of Theodosius, the monk Hilarion spent "days and nights" in writing (copying) books while the holy abbot himself made threads for the great Nicon, the master book-binder. His disciple Gregory possessed books in his cell that tempted thieves. Nicholas Sviatosha, the prince-monk, offered to the monastery many of his books and had a Greek monk, another Theodosius, translate for his theological instruction the famous letter of Pope Leo I on the two natures in Christ.

In an anonymous article inserted into many later collections but used by the above-quoted *Preface to Repentance*, ignorance is considered "worse than sin":

those who have sinned and repent truly are saved; but the sense-less who have erred in the sense of Writ, having no sober and sane mind, fall into heresy and perish. Learn books one from another, and God will give reason to whomever he wishes—to him who will keep His commandments.

It is clear that all the books spoken of in these sources are books of religious content, "divine" in the old Russian sense. On the other hand, the whole-hearted acceptance of culture, the freedom from obscurantism, is very often a sign of the barbarian youthfulness of a nation attracted mightily by a higher and "sacred" culture and unable to perceive the spiritual dangers inherent in every product of the human mind. Saint Augustine is obscurantist in his relation to Plato or the ancient culture in general, but Bede and Columban are not. The first Christian generations in Russia worship the sacred Greek culture in the same way in which the Celtic or Saxon monks worshipped the Latin one. But the culture available for the Russians (in translations) was more limited and homogeneous; secular elements were practically excluded.

That this exclusion had no doctrinal foundation is proved by the fact that many of the translations made in Russia or by Russians were of secular content; books on history, geography, even fiction, as the Byzantine poem *Digenes Acritas.* Obviously, the Russians tried to fill up the gap left by their Bulgarian predecessors from whom they had inherited all their library. Unfortunately, the Greek monasteries where they looked for their books were extremely poor in secular literature. The Russians did not venture to turn to the richer libraries of Constantinople, the general content of which was much higher than their level of capacity. How could they make a choice in this maze of wisdom? And how could they imagine that the fathers in Studion or in Mount Athos lacked something essential in their book treasures? Thus Russian cultural aspirations, however open and sincere, found a drawback in their Slavonic language, narrowly limiting the circle of available translated literature. This fact, be it by contingency or destiny, explains a tragic lack in ancient Russian culture, a complete absence of rational scientific thought, even in the theological field. Apart from practical and concrete matters, Russian thought was not awakened before the eventual Europeanization of the country. A real and full-fledged scientific investigation in Russia started only in the nineteenth century.

HISTORICAL THEOLOGY

There was, however, one branch of learning, or, at least, literary activity, in which ancient Russia did not yield to the medieval West: it was historiography. The first European scholar who studied Russian *Chronicles* in the eighteenth century, the German historian Schloetzer, thought

that the Russian Nestor, the supposed author of the ancient
Chronicles had no rivals in the West. The Russian *Chronicles* are marked by a realistic historical sense, a richness of
detail and an artistic representation of events. The part of
rhetoric is very limited. The *Lives* of the Russian saints, at
least in the Kievan period, shared the same literary merits
with the *Chronicles,* and in particular, their obvious preference for historical narrative rather than legendary adornment. In all these qualities the Russians owed little to their
Greek teachers. In fact, the prevailing type of Byzantine
historiography, the contemporary memoirs with an elabo-
rated style and an attempt at historical pragmatism, of
which Thucydides gave the pattern, found no imitators in
Russia. Gregory of Tours and the Italian chroniclers of
the twelfth and thirteenth centuries bear a greater similarity
to the Russian annalists than Cedrenus or Psellus.

One branch of Byzantine historiography, however, was
appreciated in Russia and found its entrance by way of
translations: it was the world chronicle, a theological frame
for the history of mankind with its center in the God-chosen
Jewish nation, but including some information about the
peoples of the ancient Orient, Greece, Rome, and Byzantium.
One of these chronicles, that of Georgius, surnamed Ham-
artolus, was most probably translated by the Russians in the
eleventh century. John Malalas and Georgius lay at the
base of numerous Russian adaptations and summaries, under
different titles but under the general name of "Chrono-
graphs." Unfortunately all the preserved manuscripts belong to a later period, but the work of the Russian compilers
must have begun very early. The author who edited the
book of Russian *Chronicles* about 1100 (he may have been
Nestor) prefaced his annalistic exposition by a vast introduction of world history. Not satisfied with Byzantine
sources, he gives a geographico-political survey of the Slavic

and Germanic peoples of the West. To the thirteenth century belongs the Russian historical composition known as *Palaea Interpreted*. *Palaea* was a short history of the Old Testament translated from Greek, which practically took the place of the Bible in ancient Russia. One Russian scholar used this textbook as a frame for a vast polemical treaty directed against the Jews, along lines well known to us from the works of all the Russian theologians of the Kievan period.

All this bears witness that the Russian chroniclers possessed not only the sense of the concrete, the love for artistic shaping of historical events, but also the sense of larger connotations, the desire to find the meaning of history as a whole. Without unfair exaggeration one might say that they possessed a feeling for the religious philosophy of history. They used this universalistic outlook even in short writings like Nestor's *Lives* of the first Russian saints. The central idea is the Messianic fulfillment of the Old Testament and, after the repudiation of the Jews, the spreading of the Gospel among the Gentiles. We found this idea to be the core of Russian theological thinking in general. In fact, because of the lack of rational or logical elements, ancient Russian theology was entirely historical.

In the legendary story of the conversion of Saint Vladimir the chronicler introduces the person of a certain Greek Byzantine "philosopher" whose long oration produced a deep impression on the heathen prince. Now this would-be apology of Christianity has no arguments at all, except for some messianic prophecies which would be convincing to a Jew but not to a Slavic heathen. Instead of the religious or ethical presentation of Christianity the "philosopher" gives a long and detailed exposition of Old Testament history, mixed with some apocrypha. The place of Christ at the summit of the history of the Jewish people is, by itself, a proof of His divinity.

This inserted piece of historical apologetics seems to have originally belonged not to a Russian, but to a Bulgarian pen and to have been transferred to the Vladimir legend from the Bulgarian Tsar Boris. But, if a Russian compiler found it fitting for his work, he had his reasons. The story, unconvincing to a modern reader and hardly convincing to any pagan prince, had its full meaning for a learned Russian Christian. God spoke to him through history as He spoke to Vladimir Monomach through nature.

Another still more paradoxical example of historical theology can be found in the Life of Saint Alexander Nevsky written in the thirteenth century, soon after the Mongolian conquest. The author tells of the envoys of the Pope trying to convert Alexander to Roman Catholicism. The proud answer of Alexander is given as follows:

> From Adam up to the flood, and to the division of languages, and to the beginning of Abraham, from Abraham to the passage of Israel through the Red Sea . . . to Augustus and the Nativity of Christ, the Passion and Resurrection, from Resurrection to the Ascension into heaven, and to the reign of Constantine, to the First Council and to the Seventh, I know well all this. Our doctrines are those preached by the apostles . . . The tradition of the holy fathers of the seven councils we scrupulously keep. As to your words, we do not listen to them and we do not want your doctrine.

At first glance, this enumeration of Biblical data has no relation whatsoever to the papal claims. But in the mind of the author the knowledge of them is equivalent to theological initiation. A remarkable feature: the mystical truths upon which the Christian dogma is founded, the Incarnation and the Resurrection of Christ are simply included in the chain of historical facts. Augustus and Constantine are cited on the same level with Adam and Abraham. That means that the whole history, without distinction between a sacred and profane has a religious meaning. Morover, the

knowledge of the historical tradition, based of course, on
Revelation, is the only way to dogmatic truth. That is the
Russian answer to the speculative theological approach of
the Catholic West.

The Russian religious feeling of history has nothing
mystical about it. It is lacking in the sense of the dualism
of the two worlds which is a necessary premise for every
symbolic interpretation. God is immanent in history, as
He would be in nature too. Therefore every historical
fact receives its own value. The historical world is as grand
and meaningful as the physical world. This explains why
the religious interpretation of history did no harm to the
concreteness and matter-of-factness of Russian historiography. The Russian chronicler keeps himself free from
theological speculations; he keeps his eyes and ears open to
the impressions of social realities.

We have seen another tendency in a group of Russian
writers. Hilarion, Clement, and Cyril, the theologians, are
allegorists in their interpretation of history. Under their
skilful pens the Bible loses all its historical content. Cyril
of Turov has lost the understanding of the Gospel apart
from Christological speculations. All these writers are representatives of Byzantinism on the Russian soil, exaggerating
like freshmen the intellectual vices of their teachers. We
see the national reaction to this "Alexandrinism" in the
priest Thomas of Smolensk who, in the name of a circle of
students, opposed the immoderate allegorism of Clement.
Perhaps the Antiochean school of historical theology, had
it been known in Russia in addition to its ethical exponent,
Saint John Chrysostom, would have better fitted the Russian historical mind. The best national products in the historical field, the *Chronicles* as well as the biographies, would
support this view.

It is extremely pertinent for a properly balanced evaluation of the Russian religious mind, to stress the religious bearing of both history and nature. This trait helps to define Russia in its true historico-geographical place between the East and the West. For the East, nature is divine, history has no religious sense; it is a perfect truth for India. But in Greece too Platonism had no historical feeling, and even Aristotle could say his famous: Φιλοσοφώτερός ἐστι ἡ ποίησις τῆς ἱστορίας. The Greeks had some excellent historians, but their philosophers, poets, and mathematicians were still greater, whereas in Rome, history, together with morals, constitutes the very essence of national genius. In Christian times, the distance was not so wide between the Byzantine and Roman worlds, after so many centuries of the Hellenistic sway in the West. Yet the difference persists, and Russia is nearer to medieval Europe in its sense of history than to Byzantium. Her emphasis on religious cosmology, however, as against the Western anthropology, relegates her again into the domain of the Sacred East.

ESCHATOLOGY

For a complete appraisal of the Russian historical sense one has to keep in mind its eschatological trend. For a Christian, history is not an endless circle of repeated developments, as it was for Aristotle or Polybius, nor is it an endless straight line of progress, as it is for the moderns, but a finite and closed process having both a beginning and an end. In this historical outlook the Russian annalist is not different from the chronicler of the Christian West. One is entitled, however, to speak of a particular eschatological interest in Russia judging by the great number of translated apocryphal apocalypses and the works, also half apocryphal, of the Greek fathers—Hippolytus, Methodius, Cyril of Jerusalem, Ephrem and "Palladius." There are no signs,

however, that in Russia this interest took the morbid character of an immediate expectation and fear of the End. It
could, in a particular case, deeply impress the sensitive religious mind of a monk like Abraham of Smolensk, and
direct his way of devotion and preaching along the line
of repentance. It could produce a work, like *The Sermon
on the Heavenly Powers*, of severe and gloomy prospects.
Yet, this gloomy vision never was a prevailing feature of
Kievan Christianity. The last fulfilling event of history,
the coming of Christ, could be envisaged not only as retribution, as "Terrible Judgment," but also as salvation, the
end of the suffering of the innocent, the "apocatastasis" of
creation. We have seen that even the gloomy *Sermon on
Heavenly Powers* ends upon a jubilant note of the transfiguration of the Earth.

Still more interesting is the eschatology of Hilarion of
Kiev. He gives only short allusions, but they are precious.
For him the end and fulfillment appears not in the aspect
of Judgment but of the "world to come" and of the "incor-
ruptible life." It is a new, third world eon following the
Church of the New Testament.

Law was precursor and servant to Grace and Truth, but Grace
and Truth are servants to the World to come, to the incorruptible
life . . . Moses and the prophets had preached the Christ's coming.
Christ and His apostles, the Resurrection and the World to come.

At least one can say that Russian eschatological consciousness was divided between the negative and positive sides of
the expectation, or putting it in other terms between the
medieval image of Judgment and the ancient Church expectation of eternal life. The last trend is perhaps responsible for the strange popularity in Russia of some pre-Nicene
fathers, commonly neglected as "superseded" by the classical and post-classical patristic thought.

ASCETICISM

Asceticism has multifarious roots in human nature and its religious needs; so it is common to both religious trends orientated on love and on fear. One expects—and this expectation is confirmed by historic evidence—that the Phobos religion produces more severe and more acute forms of asceticism. At an average level, Russian asceticism does not achieve the stupendous record of the Christian East, nor, in certain regards, that of the Catholic West. Generally speaking, the Russian type is marked by relative moderation, though this moderation may appear extreme to the modern eye. The most cruel life, in underground caves and seclusion, was led by the disciples of Anthony of Kiev who was trained in the school of Mount Athos. Through Mount Athos one can trace the influence of monastic Syria upon this school of devotion. One of the ascetic inventions of Syria, breast chains, found their way into Russia and were in use until recently. Stylitism, column-standing, on the other hand, left no traces in pre-Mongolian Russia. It appears, in a mitigated form, in later centuries.

The kenotic school of Saint Theodosius contented itself with moderate ascetic exercises borrowed from the experience of Palestine: fasting, manual work, deprivation of sleep. The war against the devil and the flesh was waged courageously and indefatigably. Yet, instead of frontal attacks in the form of self-inflicted pain, they recurred to the tactics of besieging, harassing, and exhausting the foe. The fierceness of battle was here replaced by constancy of effort. For this reason the Russian ascetics preferred to the classical, Graeco-Latin terminology of war the terminology of labor. This conception of asceticism was not confined to kenotic circles in Russia. The ascetic aggressiveness of Anthony's school remains an isolated fact in the history of Russian holiness, much admired but little imitated.

MYSTICISM

Out of all monastic schools of the Christian Orient, ancient Egypt seems to have least influenced Kievan Russia, although Egyptian *Paterica* and *Lives* of saints were well known there. In Egypt, under the impact of Alexandria's Platonic theology, asceticism was the way to contemplation. No contemplative trends can be traced in Russia before the Mongolian conquest. Least of all is one entitled to speak of any kind of mysticism. The revival of mystic life in Constantinople of the tenth and eleventh centuries, thanks to Simeon the "New Theologian," seems to have remained unnoticed in Kiev. It is true that the Studion, the great spiritual beacon for Russia, rejected the new mystical doctrine and its practices. Russia had to wait for some three centuries before she could adopt and bring to a high perfection the mystical way of life.

Saint Theodosius taught the practice of the Jesus-prayer which was used by mystics. This prayer was in use among certain of his disciples and permanently remained on the lips of pious Russian people. But for Theodosius, as for Monomach and pious laymen, it is but a form of ejaculatory prayer, the shortest and easiest formula for "perpetual" praying.

ETHICAL DUALISM

Ethical emphasis goes through all the religious literature of Russia. However strong may have been the cultural, esthetic, or historical interests of ancient Russia, especially as compared with the later and modern Russian Church, the dominating trend was ethical. The main problem was: how to live and what to do for one's salvation? That the answer was sought in the way of moral life more than in sacramental sanctification, constitutes a notable difference between the Russian and Byzantine religious minds.

If one has to look for the dominant ancient Russian ethical attitude it is to be found in charity. It seems to be a commonplace for every brand of Christian ethics, but it is not. Very often Christian moralists or whole nations pay lip service to the evangelical commandment while looking elsewhere for a real moral ground in life. We have seen the average Byzantine ethics based upon fear of God or men. The same might be justly asserted of the Muscovite society of the sixteenth and seventeenth centuries. Without doing too much violence to the facts, one might venture to say that Anglo-Saxon ethics is centered round purity and law in various combinations. The last example may serve as a device for approaching Russia. Never in Russian history was either purity or law dominant morally. Their importance was raised in modern times, when Russia went to the Western school.

One fact is curious and even amazing in ancient Russia— the coolness in the veneration of holy virgins. The Russian church canonized only twelve female saints, and only one of them was a virgin, Princess Euphrosynia, who took the veil in a Polotsk convent. Numerous virgin saints of the Greek church found their place in the Russian calendars and martyrologues (*Chet'i Minei*). But one looks in vain for their images in ancient icons. Among all rich collections of Russian icons Saint Paraskeva alone (with Saint Anastasia) represents saintly womanhood. But Paraskeva, Friday—like Anastasia, Sunday—are images of Christian mythology rather than human saints, and virginal at that. Indeed Saint Paraskeva became the giver of fertility to praying wives. The exclusive cult of sacred or divine Motherhood—from Mother-Earth to the Mother of God—overshadowed the

Christian value of virgin purity. Purity spoke more strongly to the Russian heart as a physiological virtue, a relic of naturalistic religion blended with ritualistic canons of the Church. Yet ritualism was not predominant in the Kievan age of Russia.

As to law, or justice, the same age was more favorable to them than any period of Russian life. Yet we have observed the tendency, even in Kiev, to interpret justice as a particular application of charity. Justice has moral value only if exercised for the benefit of the poor and the oppressed, and this returns us to the same caritative element.

A particularly Russian aspect of Christian charity is its connection with the ethics of the clan or *rod*. Russian charity not only finds its strongest expression in the love between brothers or blood relatives, but it attempts to embrace, in a fictional kinship, all fellowmen. All men are brothers not in a spiritual Christian sense, as having the common Father in heaven, but in an earthly sense, of a common origin, or common blood. It imparts a certain warmth, a residuum of family tenderness in human relationship, but this warmth has something sensual and naturalistic in it and therefore has to be limited to the bounds of national or racial community.

Charity is a common denominator of Russian ethics. But this ethics is not uniform. In all epochs of Russian history one finds a constant ethical dualism. In a superficial way it can be characterized as the opposition of severe and mild tendencies. We have seen, however, that this thoroughgoing opposition is not in the degree, but in the quality of the underlying religious vision. The severe or Byzantine type is rooted in the religion of Christ-Pantocrator, the heavenly King and Judge. The mild, or more purely Russian ethics has, as its premise, the religion of the humiliated or "kenotic" Christ.

In the religion of the Pantocrator type, charity has the tendency of being limited to almsgiving as one of the divine precepts, and the propitiation of God becomes the main purpose of religious life. In the kenotic Christianity, charity, while remaining the focal point, is enriched and qualified by self-humiliation as the second element. Both types of religious ethics stand under the strong influence of monasticism. Both accept and even emphasize monastic virtues of humility, obedience, and repentance. Yet the same words have different connotations. The humility of the Byzantine type is based upon a strict sense of hierarchy. Man, knowing his place in the world, has to humiliate himself before the higher: God, emperor, the superior, the rich, and so on. Toward his inferiors he owes condescending, patronizing charity. In the kenotic religion, which takes its pattern in the humility of Christ, man humiliates himself not only before God but before the lowest members of society. This kind of humility takes, of necessity, an external and social aspect: it finds its most drastic expression in the "uncouth garb" of the saintly Russian monks. Saint Theodosius tried, even as a layman, to degrade himself socially by sharing the manual labors of his serfs or taking ignoble professional work upon himself. Toward the higher persons of society, however, the kenotic saint can be exacting and severe. He approaches them not with humble gestures but with authoritative prophetic power, insisting on justice and threatening them with the wrath of God. Thus, the effect of the kenotic attitude is the reversion of social hierarchies, whereas the Pantocrator or Phobos religion supports mightily the existing hierarchical structure.

The difference in the types of obedience follows immediately from the foregoing. The Phobos obedience is always to one's superiors in both secular and ecclesiastical hierarchies. Fear is considered not only as an accompanying token but

as an inspiring motive. Kenotic obedience is grounded upon
charity or at least meakness. It is mutual obligation practiced among equals as well as between the low and the high.
"Obey one another," is the precept of Theodosius to his
monks. Obedience in this case means hardly anything else
than mutual serving, yielding, submitting. The hierarchical obedience is little emphasized, although it is presupposed.
Theodosius considers disobedience or breaking of the monastic rule a great sin, but does not maintain discipline with
punishments. With Russian kenotic abbots of this type the
result is often the loosening of discipline in their monasteries.
Theodosius was deeply distressed by the low religious level
of his flock, and, finding purely spiritual motives ineffectual,
descended to the external devices of regular conduct.

The third monastic virtue, that of repentance, is perhaps
the most common link between the two religious types. For
the Byzantine Phobos religion, it is the most sincere and
profound ingredient. For the kenotic Russian saint, repentance is also the most serious thing: there is nothing of
optimistic joyfulness or cloudless serenity about him. Both
have their teacher and model in Ephrem the Syrian. If one
has to point out the difference, it must be found in the predominance of the fear motive in one type and the vision of
Christ's perfection in the other. The first is enhanced by
the terrifying meditation on future Judgment and eternal
fire; the second, by the image of Christ's love and suffering
for mankind and man's unworthiness and betrayal of this
love. The first may be more acute and bitter; the second is
softened by the vision of Christ's pardoning love.

Since so early a date as the end of the fourth century
Eastern monasticism, both in Egypt and especially in Syria,
highly appreciated the penitential value of tears. Tears were
the external token of a true repentance and at the same time,
a physiological means of eliciting it. They were considered

as a special charisma, a "gift of tears." Russia inherited
this ideal together with a practical training in this virtue.
She seems to have been particularly favored with this grace.
She always was inclined to look for comfort and spiritual
exaltation to grace-given tears. Now, the tears of Phobos
are bitter; the tears of Kenosis are sweet. The tears of repentance are fused with tears of other feelings both comforting
and sublime. There are the tears of compassion, the tears
of joy, the tears at the contemplation of celestial beauty.
Even laymen, like Prince Vladimir Monomach, were blessed
with this gift of tears, and Monomach was far removed from
the fear complex; his tears must have been of a sweeter
brand.

There is a Russian word *umilenie*, untranslatable because
of the richness of sense inherent in it. It renders the Greek
κατάνυξις and is rendered usually by "tenderness," "attri-
tion," "emotionalism." All kinds of valuable, fruitful emotions which at their highest pitch evoke tears, at a moderate
level produce what the Russians call *umilenie*. The beauty
of the Church service and even the beauty of nature, the
contemplation of the innocence of childhood or the perfection of holiness engender this state of mind. *Umilenie* is a
particular grace of the kenotic religion.

THE LAYMEN'S ETHICS

Monastic religion in all its currents attracted the laymen
also, drawing them into the circle of its influence. Byzantium
never knew the dualism of monastic and lay ethics, but considered the Christian ideal embodied only in a perfect monk.
For them monasticism was merely a correct and uncompromising interpretation of the Gospel. No doubt this doctrine
did not lack its spokesmen in Russia, Cyril among them.
But other teaching was also found which showed their own
particular vocation to laymen. We have seen the abbot

Polycarp restraining Prince Rostislav from taking monastic
vows. In canonizing so many laymen princes, the Russian
Church officially acknowledged a laic way to salvation.

In the literature of Admonitions destined for laymen
two currents can be distinguished corresponding, though not
exactly, to the two monastic tendencies. Yet charity in lay
interpretation is not a heroic or evangelic way; it hardly can
be understood as kenotic, in spite of its partaking of Christian
humility. Laymen, even those as religiously advanced as
Vladimir Monomach, shunned a direct approach to the
Gospel as if yielding it to the monks. They turned for inspiration to the less sublime but more practical store of the
Old Testament. They found it in the Wisdom literature and
Psalms. In Wisdom books the ideal of charity and law-
abiding duty was moderated and diluted by practical considerations and concessions to life. The Psalms gave a deeper
religious inspiration with their idea of God's creation, providence, and retribution for human acts. The two currents of
lay ethics may be characterized, in the terms of patristics,
as the ethics of fear and that of hope, instead of love. A pious
layman approached God either as a slave, in trembling prostration, or as an honest worker in a confident but humble hope
for remuneration. Filial love was too high for him, or too
daring for his humility.

The influence of the New Testament is not entirely absent, however. Its presence is felt as warming and lighting
the more terrestrial doctrines of the Old. In critical moments of life, as when Vladimir's son was killed, man expresses his emotions in pure and sublime evangelical tones.
The Gospel is working continuously upon the stuff of human
souls, though its influence is not so conspicuous as that of the
Old Testament.

In sensitive and religiously gifted natures the Gospel
could explode the heroic Christian virtues. The way of high

kenoticism remained open to laymen as well as to monks. For laymen it meant self-sacrifice of love, in following Christ up to the death on the Cross. The nonresistance of Boris and Gleb remains forever the summit of Russian kenotic Christianity.

SOCIAL ETHICS

One cannot overstress the social aspect of Russian religious ethics. Against the widespread opinion of the exclusively personal character of Eastern Christianity, one must keep in mind that through all the centuries of medieval and Muscovite Russia her religion was predominantly social, though in varying forms. An enforced individualism enters the Russian Church life only since the reform or revolution of Peter I.

In Kiev the social energies of Christianity were freed by the extensive concept of charity, as well as by the great part played by the Church in civilizing and organizing a newly created society. The Church was looked upon by everybody, the princes included, as guide and adviser in all important matters, secular as well as religious. The state had little, if any, deep-rooted traditions, was plastic and malleable and eager to know the true Christian way. The new Russian Church, on the other hand, was not a simple offspring of the Byzantine, inheriting the age-old shackles of her mother Church. Russian Christianity was fresh, creative, responsive to the call of Christ. Its social message springs immediately out of its evangelical spirit.

Charity as its central virtue was preached particularly with regard to the destitute and poor. In the Kievan period it was inseparable from justice, in the Russian caritative sense. Here Russia had a great teacher in Chrysostom, whose selected works made available in anthologies (*Zlatostrui*) were her favorite reading. His interpretation of the parable of the Dives and Lazarus impressed the Russian conscience deeply. Another mighty prod in the same direction was given by the half-mythical figure of Saint Nicholas, the greatest saint of the Eastern Church, whose legend is a poem of stormy, elemental power of charity and justice. The third great teacher of charity was Saint John Eleemosynarius, the patriarch of Alexandria of the seventh century.

There is nothing pale, rosy, and conventional in the Russian concept of charity grown in such a school. The tremendous menace of the Last Judgment impending for the unmerciful and, at the other pole, the image of a meek and loving Saviour, destitute and suffering Himself, worked in the same direction. Both the Phobos and the Agape religions concurred to produce a common effect upon the receptive Russian soul.

Among the common charitable duties insisted upon in Russian sermons and admonitions, charity towards slaves and servants is alway stressed. The greatest sin, in the opinion of many Russian spiritual guides, is the profit extorted at the manumission of slaves (*izgoistvo*). Together with usury *izgoistvo* is the chosen form of social injustice against which the Church is never weary in raising its denunciations.

The predominantly social trend of Kievan monasticism is proved by the fact that all the known monasteries of this period were situated in towns or on their outskirts. It gave the monks the chance of fulfilling their duties as spiritual fathers to the laity, which was a general custom in Russia. Of course, ascetic exercises of the recluses in the Cave Cloister of Kiev or the monastic ideal of a Cyril of Turov had nothing to do with social or caritative works. But, as we know, the great leader was Theodosius and according to his idea, a monastery was not only a spiritual center for the laity but a source of food for the poor from the work of its monks.

Moreover, he took upon himself the right and duty to show princes and their officers the way of justice. Political crimes such as the usurpation of the Kievan throne was for him as obvious a break of Christian obligations as injustice in courts and personal sins. In this he did not stand alone. With less audacity perhaps, the Russian clergy in general followed his example.

THE IDEAL OF STATE POWER

Of all phases of Byzantine culture, political Byzantinism had the least chance to be transplanted to Russia. Russia was not a centralized but a semifeudal state—more exactly, a loose union of small independent states without any central power corresponding to the West European kingship, not to speak of the Empire. Thus Russia was not a subject of sovereignty capable of bearing Byzantine imperial claims. Moreover, the emperors of Constantinople considered Russian princes as their vassals on the ground of their conversion to the Orthodox faith: the Emperor was the head of all Orthodox Christians throughout the universe. Nothing proves that this Greek theory was accepted in Russia, but in the Byzantine palace Russian princes were "honored" by the title of "chamberlain" (ὁ ἐπὶ τῆς τραπέζης). The head of the Russian Church, the Metropolitan of Kiev, himself a Greek subject appointed by Constantinople, must have looked upon Russian princes with the eyes of his emperor.

That means that the Byzantine political doctrine of sacred autocracy was not preached in Russia by the Greek clergy and could only trickle in through general channels of religious literature. On the other hand, no work of Greek political literature was found among the store of the translations available in Kiev.

There could therefore be no question of the unlimited,

or autocratic power of Russian princes, either in practice or in theory. The Russian *kniaz'* or prince was translated by the Greeks as ἄρχων, which corresponded to the Byzantine governors or high officers of the imperial administration. What could be applied to Russia was the general Christian appraisal of political power: its origin, mission, rights, and duties.

The divine origin of the princely power stood firm, based upon Biblical and patristic traditions. It endowed the prince with a high dignity and implied obedience to him as the "minister of God" (Romans 13; 4). Yet, it was a quite exceptional case when the author of the panegyric of Prince Andrew of Vladimir dared to apply to him the famous definition of Chrysostom-Agapit, so popular in later Moscow: "Caesar by his earthly nature is similar to any man, but by the power of his dignity he is similar to God alone." In Kievan Russia, far from any "deification" of power, the divine investiture required from the holder of power obedience to religious and moral law. The necessity of the obedience to law by the princes is a more frequent topic in Kievan literature than the obedience of the subjects to their princes.

In his Lenten missive to Vladimir Monomach Metropolitan Nicephorus, a Greek himself and full of praises for the prince's piety and virtues, finds, however, one weak point in his administration and suggests a correction: the prince ought to be more cautious in listening to his counsellors and to return all those deported without sufficient reason.

Kievan chroniclers are very outspoken about the vices and flaws of their princes; they obviously felt no restraint imposed by princely dignity upon the freedom of their judgment. All they can afford to do, in order to alleviate the guilt of a prince, is to attribute his deficiency to the influence

of bad counsellors. Bad counsellors, mostly "young ones"
(compare Isaiah 3: 1-4), are the root of all political evils.
The youth of the prince himself is often considered as a
great misfortune and a sign of God's wrath against the
country.

Good and bad princes alike are sent by God as a reward
or punishment to the people. "If a country is right before
God, He ordains in it a just Caesar or prince, loving law and
justice, and he installs governors and judges administering
justice." But "woe to the city where the prince is young,
and likes to drink wine at the sound of the *gusli* with young
counsellors. . . Such are given by God for our sins." (*Lavr.*
1015).

If a bad prince is sent by God and his tyranny has a penitential significance this seems to exclude revolt against the
tyrant as a legitimate political action. This conclusion would
be quite correct in the spirit of the Byzantine and even early
Christian ethics; it was indeed the doctrine of Anastasius
Sinaitas in the seventh century and it was repeated by some
Russian moralists as well. And yet the import of this doctrine of obedience was greatly exaggerated by the modern
historians who often viewed the early Russian ways of life
from the viewpoint of Muscovy. The Kievan chronicler
may consider a revolt of the citizens against their prince as
the act of God's will, punishing the prince in his turn (*Lavr.*
1068). This inversion of the doctrine of obedience was the
more natural because of the constitutional place of the *veche,*
the people's assembly, in Kievan Russia. The Byzantine
theory gave no justification for democracy, but it was capable
of shrinking and waning in the new social and political surroundings. The chastising providence of God, in the political sphere, is double-faced; occasionally, it can use to its
own ends even a popular revolution.

There was, however, one thing before which ancient

Russia, unlike Byzantium, stopped with horror: the murder of a prince. Regicide in Byzantium was so common that it seems a part of the political system, a necessary corrective to autocracy. In Russia, where the killing of a prince in an honest battle was considered an abnormal disaster, a revolt, although it was sometimes justified if it ended in the overthrow of a prince, was never pardoned if it resulted in his murder. The assassination of an unpopular, even tyrannical prince could lead to his canonization as a "sufferer," no doubt a means of expiation for the crime.

Thus, although the doctrine was not particularly favorable to political freedom or popular government, it did not restrain their development in ancient Russia. The Church made no effort directly to transplant Byzantine political institutions into Russia or to preach absolute monarchy. Religious ideas favorable to autocracy or even to despotism certainly trickled in, together with Phobos ethics. But the general social atmosphere was not propitious for their growth. Never in her historical life has Russia been nearer the realization of political freedom than in the glorious days of her youth.

CHURCH AND STATE

Freedom was especially enjoyed by the Church. The relations between Church and State took forms which were more advantageous for the former. One cannot say, however, that the Church abused its privileged and influential position. In the dramatic and even tragic history of the relationship between the Christian Church and the Christian State the Kievan experience, short and unstable as it was, can be considered as one of the best Christian achievements.

There was certainly no attempt at the separation or at the strict division of the functions between Church and State. The Byzantine system was termed a "harmony" or

"symphony" of the two spheres of life. But, whereas in
Byzantium the overweight of political power most often led
to the domination of the State over the Church, in Russia
their collaboration was sincere.

Saint Vladimir gave the Church the chart of immunity
("Ecclesiastical Ordinance") which made the extent of
ecclesiastical jurisdiction much wider than it was in Byzanti-
um. It embraced all kinds of persons dependent on the
Church or else deprived of class or clan protection (*izgoi*).
Among the juridical objects or cases the Church possessed
in large measure the jurisdiction over family and inheritance
disputes, besides religious and many moral transgressions.
This extension of ecclesiastical jurisdiction, confirmed by
Vladimir's successors, does not find its precedent in Greek
Canon Law, in spite of constant official references to it. It
corresponds more to Western legal conditions, as does the
obligatory payment of the tithe for the benefit of the Church
which was established by Vladimir.

Besides a great extent of jurisdiction over lay persons
and in lay matters, bishops were often invited by princes to
give their advice in the most important political issues such
as war and peace, pacts with other princes, new legislation,
and the like. On the other hand, the Church expected from
the pious prince defense against heathens and heretics, the
material support of the clergy, and the building of churches
and monasteries. This protection was paid for by recognizing the influence of the prince in the nomination of bishops
and other church dignitaries whose appointment depended
formally on the Metropolitan or bishops.

Collaboration and encroachment of this kind was com-
mon to the Christian world—western and eastern. The
Russian type is characterized by the predominence of the
Church and the rarity of conflicts.

The predominance of the Church was based upon one

essential fact: the dependence of the Russian Church on
Constantinople. The head of the Russian Church, the Metropolitan of Kiev, was appointed by the oecumenical Patriarch who held in his hands the general control over the
church administration in Russia. Greek interference with
Russian affairs was rare and moderate. Yet it was sufficient
to keep a rein on the possible encroachment by Russian
princes. Two attempts of the Kievan princes to get rid of
the Greek supremacy in the Church by electing a Russian
Metropolitan through the council of Russian bishops had
failed. The prince of Kiev had to conform with the Greek
prelate sent from the capital of the mighty Empire. That
dependence, complained of by all Russian nationalists of
ancient and modern times, was the main reason for a happy
Church and State relationship in early Russia.

The Metropolitan, representing the Church Universal
and the great Empire, faced a weak local prince in Kiev, one
among many, who could not confront the Greek prelate with
an all-Russian political might. Indeed, the prince of Kiev
was not a king nor even a grand duke, and he had no power
at all over his princely kinsmen. The unity of Russia was
kept and warranted much more by the person of the Metropolitan of the whole Russia than by the prince of the city
and territory of Kiev.

The Metropolitan was greater than the prince or any
princes in Russia. But he did not try to transform his influence into political power. For this his Greek training and
previous career was a good antidote; in Greece he learned
how to honor secular authority. Without attempt to rule
Russia he used his right and duty of teaching more largely
and freely than he could in Byzantium: "The order and the
law of the Church requires me to say something useful to the
princes at this time [Lent]," writes Metropolitan Nicephorus
(d. 1121) to Monomach. Another Nicephorus (1195),

speaking to a prince about a concrete political matter, states
a general rule: "We are installed by God to restrain you
from blood-shedding."

In this duty of preaching the Metropolitan found limitations in his foreign origin, in a certain estrangement from
the native population, and sometimes in the insufficient knowledge of the national idiom. The Russians seem to have had
little veneration for their Greek prelates; they never canonized them in this period as they did canonize numerous Russian bishops; the chroniclers seldom mention the activity of
the Kievan hierarchs. But the same idea of the moral responsibility of the clergy for the sins of the laymen, especially of princes, was taken over by the Russian Church. A
prince had to receive with humility the words of admonition
dispensed to him by bishops, abbots, saintly monks, and his
personal spiritual father.

Some princes were recalcitrant. Several conflicts between
them and their bishops left their traces in the *Chronicles*.
The most troublesome prince for the Church was the most
ambitious one—Andrew of Vladimir who strived, without
success, for the creation of the second Metropolitan see in
his city. In Novgorod the bishop, elected by the people
assembly or *veche*, sometimes became the victim of conflicting
parties. Yet, one never hears about the conflicts of jurisdiction concerning the limits of power between the secular and
ecclesiastical authorities.

It is puzzling for a modern student to learn that most
of the clashes between princes and bishops concerned liturgical issues or, more exactly, one issue: that of the week fast-
days coinciding with great calendar feasts. We have already
touched upon these conflicts in speaking of Russian ritualism.
It is noteworthy that with regard to this particular item not
only Andrew but also other more modest princes dared to accuse their bishops of the breach of canons and began formal

canonical suits in Constantinople before both the Patriarch
and the Emperor.

This occasional interference of Russian princes with the
liturgical rules of the Church was an obvious transgression
of their sphere of responsibility. Here, as in other cases, the
existence of a higher, more embracing, and oecumenical authority over the local church proved to be beneficial. Byzantium, through the "oecumenical" Patriarch, checked the un-
wise zeal of Russian princes and taught them submission to
spiritual authority in spiritual matters. The only document
extant of the correspondence between the Patriarch of Constantinople and Russia of the Kievan period belongs to this
category: it is the letter of Patriarch Lucas Chrysobergas to
Prince Andrew on the occasion of his liturgical conflict with
the bishop of Rostov. The Patriarch had taken the side of
the bishop and sends to the prince of Vladimir a severe re-
monstration:

> If you disobey his teachings and admonitions and, moreover,
> begin to persecute your bishop and teacher, embracing other doctrines
> against the law, you must know, my blessed son, that, even if you fill
> the whole world with churches and build innumerable towns but
> persecute your bishop, the head of the Church and the people, those
> will be no churches but sties, and you will have no reward nor
> salvation.

All the venom of this arrow could be fully appreciated
by the prince, a great builder of churches and towns.

In a calmer and positive form the idea of the independence of spiritual power is developed at the close of the
missive:

> Ask your head [that is, your bishop] and do what he tells you.
> For nobody among all men, neither bishop nor priest nor monk
> nor angel, nor even an angel from heaven, has such power to bind
> and to loose, only your God-beloved bishop whom God our Lord
> made the head of your land and yourself. If you honor the bishop

you honor Christ, for he has the image of Christ and sits on the seat of Christ.

In this way the Patriarch could speak to the Russian princes in language which he dared not use before the Emperor. The historical situation was such that even Byzantinism became the guardian of freedom for the Russian Church.

RELIGIOUS NATIONALISM

Life within the oecumenical organism of the Church favorably shaped young Russia's national consciousness. Russia as a nation was born out of the mixture of Slavic and non-Slavic tribes simultaneous with her conversion. In meditating about the destiny of their people, baptised "after all others," the authors of the eleventh cenury inspired by the Slavic tradition of Saint Cyril and Saint Methodius created a doctrine of national calling of Russia which is much more orthodox, because it is more Christian than later Muscovite messianism.

In Kiev one cannot speak of Russian messianism in the sense of uniqueness or exclusiveness of national religious calling. All peoples are called by God, and Russia among them. It is a view taken from a universal, oecumenical standpoint, and not from a national one. On the other hand, the nation is not an indifferent category in the kingdom of God. As man stands before God, responsible for his own life, so stand all nations, as spiritual entities, with their sins and their holiness, in the earthly Church and in eternity. This religious idea of the nation could not be born in the medieval West, with its unity of Latin culture. It has its natural origin within the Eastern Church, with its plurality of languages and cultures: oriental, Greek, Slavic. Let us not forget that the Latin world, in the mind of eleventh century Russia, also entered into this Christian Universsum, though not as its center.

The later Jewish belief that every nation has its celestial patron in the person of an angel (Daniel 10) was familiar to Russians, especially through the intermediary of Epiphanius of Cyprus. But much more widespread was the idea that each Christian nation is headed in the kingdom of God by her holy founder in Christ.

The Roman country praises with laudatory words Peter and Paul by whom she was led to believe in Jesus Christ, son of God; Asia—Ephesus and Patmos, John the Theologian (Evangelist); India, Thomas; Egypt, Mark. All countries, cities, and nations venerate and glorify each their own teacher who had taught them the orthodox faith.

These are the famous words of Hilarion of Kiev repeated by Russian hagiographers through the centuries. The Russian Church cannot claim an apostolic origin; at least, this was clear to the first Christian generations in Russia. The Russian heathens "heard from no one the word on Jesus Christ, our Lord, for the apostles did not come to them," admits Nestor in his *Lection of Saint Boris and Saint Gleb.* In place of the great apostolic names of other church-founders Hilarion suggests that they exalt the name of Prince Vladimir, the "Baptiser," a not-yet-canonized father of Russian Christianity. Nevertheless, this comparison with other nations is far from inspiring Russian society with pride; certainly they have no claim to the first place in the hierarchy of the earthly Church. The only ground for their national self-respect is the Christian reversal of all human values; and Nestor actually proceeds on this way.

In his prologue to the *Lection of Saint Boris and Saint Gleb* he tells at length the Gospel's parable of the workers in the vineyard. The Lord of the vineyard equalizes the reward of the workers in spite of the difference of their working hours. The Russians are not the first, but the last ones, the workers of the eleventh hour. "Indeed, they had been idle, serving idols and not God . . . but in the last days God had mercy of them and did not let them perish to the end in the error of idolatry."

This salvation is the act of God's mercy and implies no merit on the side of the heathen people. "God had mercy toward all countries, and we also were not neglected by Him," says Hilarion. But the last called can yield greater fruits in the Church. "Many last ones will be the first, if these last are better than the first fathers." This is the reflection of Nestor on the virtues of the great Theodosius. This recent Russian saint has refuted the prediction of an ancient *Patericon*: "Weak will be the last generation."

The same national idea underlies the cult of the "sufferers." Boris and Gleb "took off the shame from the sons of Russia," the shame of inveterate heathendom. The authors of their *Lives* insist, with obvious exaggeration, that the veneration of those first saints of Russia is not limited to their mother country but already has become universal.

According to Hilarion, James, and others, it was Prince Vladimir himself who saved the Christian honor of Russia. But no one yet seriously claims the first place for her: "Not the worst, though the last," is the dominant tone: "Lo, we also with all Christians already praise the Holy Trinity," said Hilarion.

In comparison with the Christian present the recent heathen past appears in the darkest colors. "Formerly we lived like beasts or animals," asserts Hilarion, "not knowing the right from the left, heeding the earthly things and having no thought of the heavenly." That the Slavic ancestors lived "in a beastly manner" is a common idea of Russian chroniclers who apply it either to all Russian tribes or to particularly backward ones like the Drevliane and Viatichi. But in Hilarion one already meets the first attempt at the rehabilitation of pre-Christian Russia. Hilarion here con-

tradicts himself. Embarking on the panegyric of Prince
Vladimir, he cannot stop before the honor of his dynasty
and his country:

> Let us praise the great kahan (prince) of our land Vladimir,
> the grandson of old Igor, the son of glorious Sviatoslav who, reigning
> in their times, were famous in many countries for their valor and
> gallantry . . . For they had reigned not in a small or unknown
> country but in Russia which is known and heard of in all ends of
> the earth.

Historical appreciation in two directions is also found
in the *Chronicles*. The annalist depicts with obvious satisfaction the warlike exploits of pagan princes, even when
directed against the Christian Greek Empire, forgetting in
this case his own disparaging characterization of Russian
paganism. Obviously the natural national feeling and the
new Christian idea of national dignity based upon Christian
calling and self-denial are not yet fully reconciled. But the
pagan nationalism is relatively harmless and the Christian
one still modest.

One small step forward (or backward) was made at the
end of the eleventh century when the legend of the travel
of Saint Andrew, the apostle, to Russia was created. It was
an attempt at the ennoblement of the Russian Church by
the way of obliterating its late origins. In spite of the contradiction of this legend against the ancient tradition, it took
roots. In the Nóvgorod province the wanderer's staff of
Saint Andrew was shown; later on in Rostov appeared the
staff of the John the Evangelist. Rostov did not want to
stand behind Novgorod. All these are harmless features
of religious patriotism with parallels in nearly all Christian
countries.

No one in Russia in those centuries conceived of their
country as the center of the Christian world, or the land of
the truest faith, or of the greatest saints. A filial reverence

tied Russia to the Greek mother Church. They did not
compose eulogies in the honor of "Holy Greece," but in all
practical issues they conformed to her. Greece gave the
norms for all the canonical, liturgical, and ritual orders.
Although Russia began to develop some national peculiarities
in all these spheres of religious life, the supreme authority
of the Greek Church arbitrated in every disagreement, such
as the one concerning fast days.

Nobody was shocked in Russia when the Church calendar
marked a feast celebrating the victory of the Empire over the
pagan Slavs, ancestors or kinsmen of the Russians. Saint
Demetrius of Salonika, the great protector of his city against
the Slavic invaders, became one of the most venerated
saints of the Russians. They went still farther on the path
of Christian humility. Kievan Russia created a new feast,
unknown in the Greek Church; that of the "Veil" or "Protection" of Our Lady (*Pokrov*) which commemorated the
rescue of Constantinople by the prayer of the Holy Virgin
from the besieging Slavs. The origin of this Russian feast
is not clear. Strangely enough, it became one of the most
venerated and favorite with the people. Nobody was ever
offended by the fact that its historical nucleus was the
triumph of the Greeks over the Slavs. One may safely conclude then that under the rule of Greek Patriarchs and
Metropolitans, the young Russian Church was able to develop a deep and sincere national consciousness which remained quite free from venomous nationalism.

Some of the modern Russian historians, such as M. D.
Priselkov, tried to discover, by a violent interpretation of
sources, the traces of the mighty anti-Greek current within
the Kievan church. These artificial constructions, reflecting
modern trends of mind, have little ground in historical
facts.

Looking back upon their recent heathen past and comparing it with the happy present state of grace the Russian Church leaders, during the reign of Iaroslav (1020-1054), were filled with pious joy and exaltation. This triumphant feeling pervades the most ancient documents of Russian literature, gradually waning towards the end of the century. The most eloquent spokesman of this national exultation was Hilarion.

The darkness of the demonic cult perished and the sun of Gospel shone over our land. The temples of idols were destroyed, and the churches were built, the idols were broken and the icons of the saints appeared. Demons fled away, the cross sanctified the towns; as shepherds of spiritual lambs, came bishops, priests and deacons, offering the immaculate sacrifice. They adorned all the sanctuary and vested holy churches with beauty. Angel's trumpet and Gospel's thunder sounded through all the towns. The incense rising towards God sanctified the air. Monasteries stood on mountains. Men and women, small and great, all people filled holy churches.

It is easy to discover in this piece of oratory some specific Russian features: the religious emphasis on beauty and the sanctification of nature symbolized by incense rising through the air. Yet, it would be misleading to interpret this and similar oratorical expressions of grateful joy for national salvation as signs of general religious optimism. Some recent historians, such as N. K. Nikol'sky and M. D. Priselkov, misled by the contrast of these joyful panegyrics of the eleventh century with the subsequent literature, went so far as to construe a dualism in Russian Christianity; a joyful, this-wordly, easy-going religion of the first generations and the ascetic, gloomy, other-wordly religion of the later time.

As a matter of fact, the cave life of Anthony and his disciples falls precisely into the time of Iaroslav and precedes the more humane and social life under the rule of Theodosius. On the other hand the kenotic trend of the very first Russian saints, Boris and Gleb, as well as Theodosius, is by no means an easy or joyful way of salvation. The imitation of Christ, though different from classical monastic asceticism, leads through self-humiliation to sacrificial death. The same Nestor who described the heroic life of the first Russian saints exults in his prologues with the joy of national triumph. Likewise, the "joyful" Hilarion also began his ecclesiastical career with a solitary cave life. In fact, the triumphant feeling of national salvation gives no key to the way of personal salvation. It is found in men of opposite spiritual tendencies: in Hilarion, Nestor, and Cyril of Turov alike.

It is a still greater error to see, as Nikol'sky does, the origin of the ascetic tendency in the dualistic heresy of the Bogomils. Byzantium and Christian antiquity supplied the ascetics with enough pattern and inspiration. What demands an explanation is the kenotic, specifically Russian, way. It is most strikingly represented in the first Christian generations of Russia. Its origins are evangelical. The early time of its appearance in Russia can be explained by the freshness and receptivity of the newly awakened religious mind which, like the first gropings of a child's art, reveals its most intimate and deepest aspirations.

However rich and multiform was the blossoming of Russian Christianity in the Kievan period, one has to be cautious and not believe that it exhausted all the possibilities of the Russian religious mind. There were strata in it which awaited a more elaborate cultivation; others which had to be first opened into the light of conscious life. One does not see in Kiev the "holy fools," a specific form of Russian kenoticism found in the Greek tradition but typical of later, Muscovite Russia. Contemplative mysticism was awakened only in the fourteenth century and made the Russian middle ages (the fourteenth and fifteenth centuries) the "golden

age" of holiness. The same age saw the highest development of religious art in which the Russian mind expressed
its most sublime theological intuitions. Muscovy in the sixteenth and seventeenth centuries emphasized social ritualism and the strength of duty in order to build upon it a
mighty Empire. In the Petersburg period, the eighteenth
and nineteenth centuries, the ancient religious tendencies revived under the touch of western culture, partly refined and
enriched, partly secularized and deformed in radical and
revolutionary disguise. At the same time ancient Christian
and semipagan religious trends in the life of the people came
to light and were traced for the first time by ethnographical
and folkloristic research.

Yet, Kievan Russia, like the golden days of childhood, was never dimmed in the memory of the Russian
nation. In the pure fountain of her literary works anyone
who wills can quench his religious thirst; in her venerable
authors he can find his guide through the complexities of
the modern world. Kievan Christianity has the same value
for the Russian religious mind as Pushkin for the Russian
artistic sense: that of a standard, a golden measure, a royal
way.

Selected Literature

GENERAL AND INTRODUCTION

Brémond, Henri, *Histoire littéraire du sentiment religieux en France*, 11 v., Paris, 1916-33. (3 v. in English translation)

Fedotov, G. P., *Treasury of Russian Spirituality*, Sheed and Ward: in press.

Frere, W. H., *Some Links in the Chain of Russian Church History*, London, 1918.

Graham, Stephen, *The Way of Martha and the Way of Mary*, New York, 1915.

Kliuchevsky, V. O., *A History of Russia*, 5 v., London, 1911-31.

Lapchine, I. I., "La Phénomenologie de la conscience religieuse russe dans la littérature russe," *Zapiski nauchno-izsledovatel'skago ob"edineniia*, v. V-VI, nos. 28 and 35, Prague, 1937.

Leger, L., *La Littérature russe: notice et extrais*, Paris, 1892.

Leroy-Beaulieu, Anatole, *The Empire of the Tsars and the Russians*, 3 v., New York, 1893-96.

Lo Gatto, Ettore, *Storia della letteratura russa*, Roma, 1928-39.

Luther, Arthur, *Geschichte der russischen Litteratur*, Leipzig, 1924.

Masaryk, T. G., *The Spirit of Russia*, 2 v., London and New York, 1919.

Miliukov, P. N., *Outlines of Russian Culture*, edited by M. Karpovich, 3 v., Philadelphia, 1942.

Miliukov, P. N., Ch. Seignobos, and L. Eisenmann, *Histoire de la Russie*, 3 v., Paris, 1932-33.

Mirski, D. S., *A History of Russian Literature from the Earliest Times*, London, 1927.

Orthodox Spirituality, by a monk of the Eastern Church, S.P.C.K., London, 1945.

Palmieri, Aurelio, *La Chiesa russa*, Firenze, 1908.

Pares, Sir Bernard, *A History of Russia*, London, 1937.

The Russian Church; Lectures on Its History, Constitution, Doctrine and Ceremonial, London, 1911.

Staehlin, Karl, *Geschichte Russlands*, 5 v., Stuttgart, 1923-39.

Sumner, B. H., *Survey of Russian History*, London, 1944.

Vernadsky, G., *A History of Russia*, revised, New Haven, 1930.

Vernadsky, G., *A History of Russia: Ancient Russia*, New Haven, 1943.

Zernov, Nicolas, *The Church of the Eastern Christians*, London, 1942.

Akademiia Nauk SSSR, *Istoriia russkoi literatury*, v. 1, Moscow-Leningrad, 1941.

Anichkov, E. V., A. K. Borozdin, and D. N. Ovsianiko-Kulikovsky, *Istoriia russkoi literatury*, v. I and II, Moscow, 1908.

414   THE RUSSIAN RELIGIOUS MIND

Fedotov, G. P., *Sviatye drevnei Rusi (X-XVII st.)*, Paris, 1931.
Florovsky, G. V., *Puti russkago bogosloviia*, Paris, 1937.
Golubinsky, E. E., *Istoriia russkoi tserkvi*, 4 v., second edition, Moscow, 1901-17.
Grekov, B. D., *Kievskaia Rus'*, fourth edition, Moscow-Leningrad, 1944.
Gudzy, N. K., *Istoriia drevnei russkoi literatury*, second edition, Moscow, 1941.
Ikonnikov, V. S., *Opyt russkoi istoriografii*, 2 v., Kiev, 1891-1908.
Istrin, V. M., *Ocherk istorii drevne-russkoi literatury*, Petrograd, 1922.
Kadlubovsky, A. P., "Ocherki po istorii drevne-russkoi literatury zhitii sviatykh," *Russkii Filologicheskii Viestnik*, Warsaw, 1902.
Makary (Bulgakov), *Istoriia russkoi tserkvi*, 12 v., second and third editions, Moscow, 1886-1910.
Nikol'sky, N. K., *Materialy dlia povremennago spiska russkikh pisatelei i ikh sochinenii X-XI v.v.*, St. Petersburg, 1906.
Nikol'sky, N. K., "O drevne-russkom khristianstvie," *Russkaia Mysl'*, no. 6, 1913.
Orlov, A. S., *Drevniaia russkaia literatura, XI-XVI v.*, Moscow, 1937.
Pietukhov, E. V., *Russkaia literatura*, v. I, Iuriev, 1911. (Drevnii period)
Priselkov, M. D., *Ocherki po tserkovno-politicheskoi istorii Kievskoi Rusi, X-XII v.*, St. Petersburg, 1913.
Presniakov, A. E., *Lektsii po russkoi istorii*, 2 v., Moscow, 1938-39.
Shevyrev, S. P., *Istoriia russkoi slovesnosti*, 2 v., third edition, St. Petersburg, 1887.
Speransky, M. N., *Istoriia drevnei russkoi literatury*, third edition, Moscow, 1921.
Vernadsky, G. V., *Zvenia russkoi kul'tury*, part 1, no. 1., Drevniaia Rus', Bruxelles, 1938.
Vladimirov, P. V., *Drevniaia russkaia literatura kievskago perioda X-XIII viekov*, Kiev, 1901.

CHAPTER I. PRE-CHRISTIAN PAGANISM

Brückner, A., *Mitologia slava*, Bologna, 1923.
Cross, S. H., "Primitive Civilization of the Eastern Slavs," *Slavic and East European Review*, v. V, parts 1-2, 1946.
Iagich, V., "Mythologische Skizzen," *Archiv für slavische Philologie*, v. IV.
Krek, G., *Einleitung in die slavische Literaturgeschichte*, second edition, Graz, 1887.
Leger, L., *La Mythologie slave*, Paris, 1901.
Machal, J., "Slavic Mythology," *Mythology of all races*, v. 3, Boston, 1918.
Mansikka, V. J., *Die Religion der Ostslaven.*, v. I, *Quellen*, FF Communications edited for the Folklore Fellows, v. X, no. 43, Helsinki, 1922.
Niederle, L., *Manuel de l'antiquité slave*, v. II., Paris, 1926.
Niederle, L., *Zivot starych slovanu*, II, 1, Prague, 1924.
Rostovtseff, M. I., "Le Culte de la Grande Déesse dans la Russie méridionale," *Revue des Études Grècques*, 32, 1919.
Sakhanev, Vsev., "Études sur l'origine de l'art populaire russe," *Eurasia Septentrionalis Antiqua*, v. IV, Helsinki, 1929.
Zelenin, D., *Russische (ostslavische) Volkskunde*, Berlin, 1927.

SELECTED LITERATURE   415

Afanas'ev, A. N., *Poeticheskiia vozzrieniia slavian na prirodu*, 3 v., St. Petersburg, 1865-69.

Dintses, L. A., *Russkaia glinianaia igrushka*, Akademiia Nauk SSSR, Trudy Instituta Antropologii, Etnografii i Arkheologii, Arkheologicheskaia seriia 3, Moscow-Leningrad, 1936.

Gorodtsov, V. A., *Dako-Sarmatskie religioznye elementy v russkom narodnom iskusstve*, Trudy Gosudarstvennogo Istoricheskogo Muzeia, 1, Moscow, 1926.

Kagarov, E. G., *Religiia drevnik slavioan*, Moscow, 1918.

Potebnia, A. A., "O mificheskom znachenii niekotorykh obriadov i povierii," *Chtenia v Obshchestvie istorii i drevnostei rossiiskikh*, nos. 2, 3, 4, Moscow, 1865.

Potebnia, A. A., *O niekotorykh simvolakh v slavianskoi narodnoi poezii*, Khar'kov, 1914.

Sokolov, I. M., *Russkij fol'klor*, Moscow, 1938.

Trever, K. V., "Sobaka-ptitsa: Senmurv i Paskudj," *Izvestiia Gosudarstvennoi Akademii Istorii material'noi Kul'tury*, v. 100, Leningrad, 1933.

CHAPTER II. RELIGIOUS BYZANTINISM

HISTORICAL BACKGROUND

See Works of Makary, Golubinsky, and Priselkov under "General."

Fedotov, G. P., "St. Vladimir et la conversion de la Russie," *Irenicon*, 1938.

Laehr, G., *Die Anfänge des russischen Reiches*, Berlin, 1930.

Makary (Bulgakov), *Istoria khristianstva na Rusi do ravnoapostol'nago kniazia Vladimira*, second edition, St. Petersburg, 1868.

Parkhomenko, V. A., *Nachalo khristianstva na Rusi*, Poltava, 1913.

Polonskaia, N., "K voprosu o khristianstvie na Rusi do Vladimira," *Zhurnal Ministerstva Narodnago Prosveshcheniia*, September, 1917.

Vernadsky, G., "The Status of the Russian Church During the First Half-Century Following Vladimir's Conversion," *The Slavonic Year-Book*, Menasha, Wisconsin, 1941.

THE FORMULA OF BYZANTINISM

Baines, N. H., *Byzantine Empire*, New York, 1926.

Buckler, G. G., *Anna Comnena*, London, 1929.

Byron, Robert, *The Byzantine Achievement*, London, 1929.

Diehl, Charles, *Byzance; grandeur et décadence*, Paris, 1929.

Diehl, Charles, *Byzantine Portraits*, New York, 1905.

Diehl, Charles, *Études byzantines*, Paris, 1905.

Dieterich, Karl, *Geschichte der byzantinischen und neugriechischen Literatur*, Leipzig, 1902.

Fuchs, F., *Die höheren Schulen von Konstantinopel im Mittelalter*, Leipzig, 1926.

Hesseling, D. C., *Essai sur la civilisation byzantine*, Paris, 1907.

416   THE RUSSIAN RELIGIOUS MIND

Hussey, J. M., *Church and Learning in the Byzantine Empire, 867-1185*, London, 1937.
Krumbacher, Karl, *Geschichte der byzantinischen Literatur*, second edition, München, 1897.
Ostrogorsky, Georg, *Geschichte des byzantinischen Staates*, Munich, 1940.
Rambaud, A. N., *Études sur l'histoire byzantine*, Paris, 1912.
Runciman, S., *Byzantine Civilisation*, London, 1933.
Soyter, G. B., *Byzantinische Dichtung*, Athens, 1938.
Strzygowski, Joseph, *Orient oder Rome*, Leipzig, 1900.
Vasiliev, A. A., *History of the Byzantine Empire*, 2 v., Madison, 1928-29.
Uspensky, F. I., *Ocherki po istorii vizantiiskoi obrazovannosti*, St. Petersburg, 1891.
Vasil'evsky, V. G., *Trudy*, 4 v., St. Petersburg, 1908-30.

THE RELIGIOUS MIND OF BYZANTIUM

Bardenhewer, Otto, *Geschichte der altchristlichen Literatur*, Freiburg im Br., 5 v., 1902-32.
Dvornik, Fr., *Les Légendes de Constantin et de Méthode vues de Byzance*, Prague, 1933.
Fliche, Augustin, and V. Martin, *Histoire de l'Eglise depuis les origines jusqu'à nos jours*, Paris, [1934]—.
Fortescue, A., *The Orthodox Eastern Church*, London, 1907.
Gardner, Alice, *Theodore of Studium*, London, 1905.
Gass, W., *Symbolik der griechischen Kirche*, Berlin, 1872.
Harnack, Adolf, *History of Dogma*, 7 v., London, 1894-99.
Heiler, Fr., *Urkirche und Ostkirche*, München, 1937.
Hergenroether, J. A. G., *Photius, Patriarch von Constantinopel*, 3 v., Regensburg, 1867-69.
Holl, Karl, *Enthusiasmus und Bussgewelt beim griechischen Mönchtum*, Leipzig, 1898.
Holl, Karl, *Gesammelte Aufsätze zur Kirchengeschichte*, v. 2., Der Osten, Tübingen, 1928.
Kidd, B. J., *The Churches of Eastern Christendom from A. D. 451 to the Present Time*, London, 1927.
Mercier, E., *La Spiritualité byzantine*, Paris, 1933.
Neale, J. M., *Introduction to the History of the Holy Eastern Church*, 2 v., London, 1933.
Oeconomos, I., *La Vie religieuse dans l'empire Byzantin au temps des Comnènes et des Anges*, Paris, 1918.
Pargoire, J., *L'Eglise Byzantine de 527 à 847*, Paris, 1905.
Rehrmann, A., *Die Christologie des Heiligen Cyrillus von Alexandria*, Hildesheim, 1902.
Seeberg, Reinh., *Lehrbuch der Dogmengeschichte*, 5 v., third edition, Leipzig, 1913-23.
Dobroklonsky, A. P., *Prepodobnyi Feodor, ispoviednik i igumen Studiisky*, Odessa, 1914.
Florovsky, G. V., *Vizantiiskie ottsy V-VIII v.v.*, Paris, 1933.

Skabalanovich, M. N., *Vizantiiskaia tserkov' i gosudarstvo v XI v.*, St. Petersburg, 1884.

Vernadsky, G. V., "Vizantiiskiia ucheniia o vlasti tsaria i patriarkha," *Recueil N. P. Kondakov*, Prague, 1926.

SLAVIC BYZANTINISM

Dvornik, Fr., *Les Slaves, Byzance et Rome au IX s.*, Paris, 1926.

Leib, J., *Rome, Kiev et Byzance à la fin du X siecle*, Paris, 1924.

Murko, M., *Geschichte der ältern süd-slavischen Literatur*, Leipzig, 1908.

Palauzov, S. N., *Vek bolgarskago tsaria Simeona*, St. Petersburg, 1852.

Zlatarsky, V. N., *Istoriia na b'lgarskata drzava pr'ez srednite viekove*, I, 2, Sofia, 1927.

SLAVONIC TRANSLATIONS

Arkhangel'sky, A. S., *Tvoreniia ottsov tserkvi v drevne-russkoi pis'mennosti*, 4 v., Kazan', 1889-91.

Budilovich, A. S., *XIII slov Grigoriia Bogoslova v drevne-slavianskom perevodie*, St. Petersburg, 1875.

Evseev, I. F., "Ocherkl istorii slavianskago perevoda Biblii," *Khristianskoe Chtenie*, no. II, 1912.

Evseev, I. E., "Gennadievskaia Bibliia 1499," *Trudy XV Arkheologicheskago s"ezda v Novgorodie 1911*, v. II, Moscow, 1916.

Kalaidovich, K. F., *Ioann ekzarkh Bolgarsky*, Moscow, 1824.

Malinin, V. M., *Zlatostrui. Desiat' slov Zlatostruia XII v.*, St. Petersburg, 1910.

Rainov, T., *Nauka v Rossii XI-XVII vekov*, Akademiia Nauk SSSR, Moscow-Leningrad, 1940.

Shakhmatov, M. V., and D. Chizhevsky, "Platon v drevnei Rusi," *Zapiski russkago istoricheskago obshchestva v Pragie*, v. 2, Prague, 1930.

Sobolevsky, A. I., "Osobennosti russkikh perevodov domongol'skago perioda," *Trudy IX Arkheologicheskago S'ezda*, v. II., Moscow, 1895-97.

Speransky, M. N., "Perevodnye sborniki izrechenii v slaviano-russkoi pis'mennosti," *Chteniia v Obshchestvie Istorii i Drevnostei*, Moscow, 1900-05.

Tikhonravov, N. S., "Otrechennyia knigi drevnei Rusi," *Sochineniia*, v. I, Moscow, 1898.

Voskresensky, G. A., "Kharakteristicheskiia cherty chetyrekh redaktsii slavianskago perevoda Evangeliia ot Marka," *Chtenia v Obshchestvie Istorii*, Moscow, 1896.

THE GREEK LITURGY

Arsen'ev, N. S., *We Beheld His Glory*, New York, 1936.

Baumstark, A., *Die Messe im Morgenland*, Kempten-München, 1906.

Bjerring, Nicolas, *The Offices of the Oriental Church*, New York, 1884.

Bouvy, E., *Poètes et mélodes*, Nîmes, 1886.

Brightman, F. E., *Liturgies, Eastern and Western*, v. I, Oxford, 1896.

Cabrol, F., *Hymnographie de l'Eglise grècque*, Anger, 1893.

Christ, W., and Paranicas, *Anthologia graeca carminum christianorum*, Lipsiae, 1871.

Hapgood, Isabel, *Service Book of the Holy Orthodox Church*, Boston and New York, 1906.

Maltzew, A. P., *Andachtsbuch der orthodox-katholischen Kirche des Morgenlandes*, Berlin, 1895.

Maltzew, A. P., *Die Nachtwache oder Abend- und Morgengottesdienst der orthodox-katholischen Kirche des Morgenlandes*, Berlin, 1898.

Pitra, J. B., *Hymnologie de l'Eglise grècque*, Rome, 1887.

Salaville, S., *An Introduction to the Study of Eastern Liturgies*, London, 1938.

Tarchnisvili, M., *Die byzantinische Liturgie als Verwichlichung der Einheit und Gemeinschaft in Dogma*, Würzburg, 1939.

THE GREEK LANGUAGE IN RUSSIA

Wanczura, Alojzy, *Skolnictwo v starei Rusi*, Lwow, 1923.

Ikonnikov, V. S., *Opyt izsliedovaniia o kul'turnom znachenii Vizantii v Russkoi istorii*, Kiev, 1869.

Lavrovsky, N. A., *O drevne-russkikh uchilishchakh*, Khar'kov, 1854.

CHAPTER III. THE RUSSIAN BYZANTINISTS

CLEMENT SMOLIATICH

Loparev, Chr., *Poslanie mitr. Klimenta k smolenskomu presviteru Fomie*, St. Petersburg, 1892.

Nikol'sky, N. K., *O literaturnykh trudakh mitr. Klimenta Smoliaticha*, St. Petersburg, 1892.

CYRIL OF TUROV

Antony (Vadkovsky), *Iz istorii khristianskoi propovedi*, second edition, St. Petersburg, 1895.

Evgeny, *Tvoreniia sv. ottsa nashego Kirilla ep. Turovskago*, Kiev, 1880.

Kalaidovich, K., *Pamiatniki rossiiskoi slovesnosti XII vieka*, Moscow, 1821.

Sukhomlinov, M., *Rukopisi grafa A. S. Uvarova*, v. 2, St. Petersburg, 1858.

Vinogradov, V. P., "O kharakterie propovednicheskago tvorchestva Kirilla, episkopa Turovskago," *V pamiat' stolietiia Imper. Moskovskoi Dukhovnoi Akademii, Sbornik statei*, Chast' 2, Sergiev Posad, 1915. (This book was not available to me.)

HILARION OF KIEV

Gorsky, A. V., anon., "Pamiatniki dukhovnoi literatury vremen velikago kniazia Iaroslava I," *Pribavleniia k tvoreniiam sviatykh ottsov*, Chast' II, Moscow, 1844.

Zhdanov, I. N., "Slovo o zakonie i blagodati i Pokhvala kahana Vladimira," *Sochineniia*, v. I, St. Petersburg, 1904.

CHAPTER IV. RUSSIAN KENOTICISM

Vajs, Josef, ed., *Sbornik staroslovenskich literarnich pamatek o sv. Vaclavu a sv. Lidmile*, Prague, 1929.

Abramovich, D. I., editor, *Zhitiia sviatykh muchenikov Borisa i Gleba*, St. Petersburg, 1916.

Bel'chenko, "Prepodobnyi Feodosy Pechersky, ego zhizn' i sochineniia," *Zapiski Istoriko-fiologicheskago Obshchestva pri Novorossiiskom universitetie*, X, Odessa, 1902.

Bugoslavsky, A. S., "K voprosu o kharakterie i ob'emie literaturnoi dieiatelnosti prep. Nestora," *Izvestiia Otdieleniia russkago iazyka i slovesnosti Akademii Nauk*, nos. 1 and 3, St. Petersburg, 1914.

Chagovets, V. A., *Prepodobnyi Feodosy Pechersky, ego zhizn' i sochineniia*, Kiev, 1901.

Golubinsky, E. E., "Istoriia kanonizatsii sviatykh v russkoi tserkvi," *Chtenia v Obshchestvie Istorii i Drevnostei*, second edition, Moscow, 1903.

Nestor, "Zhitie prepodobnago Feodosiia," *Chteniia v Obshchestvie Istorii*, Moscow, no. 3, 1858; no. 1, 1879; no. 2, 1899.

CHAPTER V. ASCETIC IDEALS

Goetz, L. K., *Das Kieven Höhlenkloster als Kulturzentrum des vormongolischen Russlands*, Passau, 1904.

Smolitsch, Igor, *Das altrussische Mönchtum (11-16 Jahrh.)*, Würzburg, 1940.

Smolitsch, Igor, *Leben und Lehre der Stazzen*, Vienna, 1936.

Abramovich, D. I., *Izsl'edovanie o Kievo-Pecherskom Paterikie*, St. Petersburg, 1902.

Abramovich, D. I., editor, *Paterik Kievo-Pecherskago monastyria*, St. Petersburg, 1911. (A new edition in *Pamiatki movi ta pis'menstva davn'oi Ukrainy*, v. 4.)

Kazansky, P. I., *Istoriia pravoslavnago russkago monashestva*, Moscow, 1855.

Kubarev, "O Kievo-Pecherskom Paterikie," *Chtenia v Obshchestvie Istorii*, 1847.

Sychev, N., "Na zare bytiia Kievo-Pecherskoi obiteli," *Sbornik v chest' Sobolevskago*, Leningrad, 1928.

The works of St. Theodosius were published by Metropolitan Makary in *Uchenyia Zapiski vtorogo Otdieleniia Akademii Nauk*, v. II, and by A. I. Ponomarev, in *Pamiatniki drevne-russkoi uchitel'noi literatury*, v. I, St. Petersburg, 1894.

CHAPTER VI. RUSSIAN ESCHATOLOGY

SAINT ABRAHAM OF SMOLENSK

Fedotov, G. P., "Zhitie i terpienie prepodobnago Avraamiia Smolenskago," *Pravoslavnaia Mysl'*, v. 2, Paris, 1930.

Riedkov, N., "Prepodobnyi Avraamii Smolenskii i ego zhitie," *Smolenskaia Starina*, v. 1, 1909.

Rozanov, S. P., editor, *Zhitiia prepodobnago Avraamiia Smolenskago i sluzhby emu*, St. Petersburg, 1912.

THE SERMON OF THE CELESTIAL POWERS

Sakharov, V. A., *Eskhatologieeskiia sochineniia i skazaniia v drevne-russkoi pismennosti*, Tula, 1879.

Slovo o nebesnykh silakh, edited among the works of Cyril of Turov. (cf. Chapter III)

CHAPTER VII. THE RITUALISM OF THE CLERGY

Goetz, L. K., *Kirchengeschichtliche und kulturgeschichtliche Denkmäler Altrusslands*, Stuttgart, 1905.

Almazov, A. I., *Tainaia ispoved' v pravoslavnoi tserkvi*, Zapiski Novorossiiskago Universiteta, v. 63-65, Odessa, 1894-95.

Pavlov, A. S., editor, "Pamiatniki drevne-russkago kanonicheskago prava," *Russkaia Istoricheskaia Biblioteka*, v. VI, second edition, St. Petersburg, 1908.

Smirnov, S. I., *Drevne-russkii dukhovnik*, Sergiev Posad, 1899.

Smirnov, S. I., "Materialy dlia istorii drevne-russkoi pokaiannoi distsipliny," *Chteniia v Obshchestvie Istorii*, Moscow, v. 3, 1912.

CHAPTER VIII. THE RELIGION OF THE LAITY: THE TRANSLATED COLLECTIONS

Popov, N. P., "L' Isbornik de 1076, dit de Svjatoslav, comme monument littéraire," *Revue des Etudes Slaves*, v. XIV, Paris, 1934.

Iakovlev, V. A., *K literaturnoi istorii drevne-russkikh "Sbornikov," opyt izsliedovaniia "Izmaragda,"* Zapiski Novorossiiskago Universiteta, v. 60, Odessa, 1893.

Nikol'sky, N. K., "Materialy dlia istorii drevne-russkoi dukhovnoi pis'mennosti," *Sbornik Otdieleniia russkago azyka Akademii Nauk*, v. 82, St. Petersburg, 1907.

Pietukhov, D. V., "Drevniia poucheniia na voskresnyie dni velikago posta," *Sbornik Otdieleniia russkago iazyka Akademii Nauk*, v. 40, St. Petersburg, 1886.

Ponomarev, A. I., *Pamiatniki drevne-russkoi uchitel'noi literatury*, v. 1 and 3, St. Petersburg, 1894-7.

Shimanovskii, V., editor, *Isbornik Sviatoslava 1076*, Warsaw, 1894.

CHAPTER IX. THE RELIGION OF THE LAITY: THE RUSSIAN ADMONITIONS

THE SERMON OF LUCAS ZHIDIATA, BISHOP OF NOVGOROD

Ponomarev, A. I., editor, *Pamiatniki*, I, 3, St. Petersburg, 1894.

Bugoslavsky, A. S., editor, *Izviestia Otdielenia Russkago Iazyka Akademii Nauk*, v. 18, n. 2, St. Petersburg, 1913.

THE MISSIVE OF THE MONK JAMES TO HIS SPIRITUAL SON DEMETRIUS

Ponomarev, A. I., editor, *Pamiatniki*, I, 3, St. Petersburg, 1894.

THE ADMONITION OF MONK GEORGIUS OF THE ZARUB CAVE

Sreznevsky, I. I., *Svedeniia i zametki o maloizvestnykh i neizvestnykh pamiatnikakh*, St. Petersburg, 1881. (From *Sbornik Otd. russ. yazyka*).

THE RUSSIAN PENITENTIALS

Pavlov, A. S., editor, *Pamiatniki*, St. Petersburg, 1908.

THE ADMONITION OF PRINCE VLADIMIR MONOMACH

"Lavrent'evskaia Letopiss'," in *Polnoe Sabranie*, Leningrad, 1926-27.

Ivakin, I. M., *Kniaz' Vladimir Monomach i iego Pouchenie*, Moscow, 1901.

Protopopov, S., "Pouchenie Vladimira Monomacha kak pamiatnik religiozno-nravstvennykh vozzrienii i zhizni na Rusi v dotatarskuiu epokhu," *Zhurnal Ministerstva Narodnago Prosvieshcheniia*, v. 171, St. Petersburg, 1874.

Shliakov, N. N., "O pouchenii Vladimira Monomacha," *Zhurnal Ministerstva Narodnago Prosveshcheniia*, St. Petersburg, 1900.

THE SUPPLICATION OF DANIEL THE EXILE

Gudzy, N. K., "K kakoi sotsial'noi srede prinadlezhal Daniil Zatochnik?" *Sbornik A. S. Orlovu*, Leningrad, 1934.

Gussov, V. M., K voprosu o redaktsiiakh "Moleniia Daniila Zatochnika," Lietopis' zaniatii Ist.-Filol. Obshchestva pri Novorossiiskom Universitetie, v. I, Odessa, 1899.

Mindalev, P., *Molenie Daniila Zatochnika i sviazannye s nim pamiatniki*, Kazan', 1914.

Shliapkin, I. A., *Slovo Daniila Zatochnika*, St. Petersburg, 1889.

Zarubin, N. N., editor, *Slovo Daniila Zatochnika*, Leningrad, 1932.

CHAPTER X. THE ANCIENT CHRONICLERS

Cross, S. H., "The Russian Primary Chronicle," *Harvard Studies and Notes in Philology and Literature*, v. XII, Cambridge, 1930.

Aristov, N., *Pervye vremena khristianstva v Rossii po tserkovno-istoricheskomu soderzhaniiu russkikh lietopisei*, St. Petersburg, 1888.

Nikol'sky, N. K., "Provest' vremennykh let kak istochnik dlia istorii nachal'-nogo perioda russkoi pis'mennosti," *Akademiia Nauk SSSR, Sbornik po russkomu iazyku i slovesnosti*, v. II, no. 1, Leningrad, 1930.

Polnoe Sobranie Russkikh Lietopisei, edited by Arkheograficheskaia Komis-siia, v. I, Lavrent'evskaia lietopsis', Leningrad, 1926-27; v. II: Ipat'evskaia lietopis', second edition, St. Petersburg, 1908.

Priselkov, M. D., *Istoriia russkogo letopisaniia XI- XV v.*, Leningrad, 1940.

Shakhmatov, A. A., *Razyskaniia o drevnieishikh russkikh lietopisnykh svodakh*, St. Petersburg, 1908.

Sukhomlinov, M., "O drevnei russkoi lietopisi kak pamiatnikie literaturnom," *Uchenyia Zapiski* vtorogo *Otdieleniia Akademii Nauk*, no, III, St. Petersburg, 1856.

CHAPTER XI. THE TALE OF IGOR'S CAMPAIGN

"Geste de la Guerre d'Igor," symposium in *Annuaire de l'Institut de Philologie et d'Histoire Orientales et Slaves*, v. VIII, New York. (In press.)

Koulmann, N., "Le Dit de la campagne d'Igor," *Le Monde Slave*, vol. VII, Paris, 1937. (Translation)

Magnus, Leonard A., *The Armament of Igor* (edited and translated), London, 1915.

Barsov, E., *Slovo o polku Igorevie*, 3 v., Moscow, 1887-89.
Gudzy, N. K., and I. Novikov, *Slovo o polku Igoreve*, Moscow, 1938.
Orlov, A. I., *Slovo o polku Igoreve*, Moscow, 1938.
Perets, V., *Slovo a polku Igorevim*, Kiev, 1926. (Commentary in Ukrainian)
Potebnia, A., *Slovo o polku Igorevie, Tekst i primiechaniia*, Voronezh, 1878.
Rzhiga, V., "Slovo o polku Igoreve i russkoe iazychestvo," *Slavia*, vol. XII, 1933-34.
Shambinago, S., and V. Rzhiga, *Slovo o polku Igoreve*, Moscow- Leningrad, 1934.

CHAPTER XII. PAGANISM AND CHRISTIANITY

Krappe, A. N., "La chute du paganisme à Kiev," *Revue des Etudes Slaves*, v. XVIII, Paris, 1937.
Anichkov, E. V., *Iazychestvo i drevniaia Rus'*, St. Petersburg, 1914.
Azbukin, P., "Ocherk literaturnoi bor'by predstavitelei khristianstva s ostatkami iazychestva v russkom narode XI-XII," *Russkii Filologicheskii Vestnik*, nos. 28, 35, 37-39, Warsaw, 1882-98.
Gal'kovsky, N., *Bor'ba khristianstva s ostatkami iazychestva v drevnei Rusi*, Khar'kov, 1916; the documents in Zapiski Moskovskago Arkheologicheskago Obshchestva, Moscow, 1913.
Sreznevsky, I., "Rozhanitsy," *Arkhiv istoricheskikh i iuridicheskikh sviedienii* (*Kalachova*), v. II, St. Petersburg, 1855.
Tikhonravov, N. S., "Slova i poucheniia, napravlennyia protiv iazycheskikh vierovanii i obriadov," *Lietoposi russkoi literatury i drevnostei*, v. IV, St. Petersburg, 1862.

CHAPTER XIII. THE RUSSIAN RELIGIOUS MIND

Alpatov, M., and N. Brunov, *Geschichte der altrussischen Kunst*, Augsburg, 1932.
Anisimov, A. I., *Our Lady of Vladimir*, Prague, 1928.
Muratov, P. P., *Les Icones russes*, Paris, 1929.
Vasiliev, A. A., "Was Old Russia a Vassal State of Byzantium?" *Speculum*, VII, 1932.
Anisimov, A. I., "Domongol'skii period russkoi zhivopisi," *Voprosy Restavratsii*, v. II, Moscow, 1928.
D'iakonov, M. A., *Vlast' moskovskikh gosudarei*, St. Petersburg, 1889.
Istrin, V. M., *Knigi vremennyia i obraznyia Georgiia Mnikha*, 3 v., Petrograd, 1920-30.
Istrin, V. M., "O sostavie Tolkovoi Palei," *Izvestiia Otdieleniia russkago iazyka Akademii Nauk*, v. II-III, St. Petersburg, 1897-98.
Kondakov, N. P., *Ikonografiia Iisusa Khrista*, St. Petersburg, 1905.
Kondakov, N. P., *Ikonografiia Bogomateri*, 2 v., St. Petersburg, 1914-15.
Nikol'skaia, A. B., "K voprosu o peizazhe v drevne-russkoi literature," *Sbornik statei v chest' A. I. Sobolevskogo*, Leningrad, 1928.
Waldenberg, V. E., *Drevne-russkiia ucheniia o predielakh tsarskoi vlasti*, St. Petersburg, 1916.

INDEX

Abraham of Smolensk, Saint, 158-170, 272, 378, 386
Achilles, 340
acribia, 182
Adam, 65 f., 74 ff., 140, 213, 383
ἀδικία, 322
Admonition of the Father to his Son, 215
Admonition of a Spiritual Father to a Penitent, 239
admonitions, 44, 215, 217 f, Chapter IX *passim,* 268, 394, 396, 404
Afanas'ev, A. N., 8
agape, 46, 129, 206-210, 215-219, 221, 225 f., 228-231, 234, 240, 243, 249, 255, 257, 268 f., 271 f., 280-283, 370, 387, 390, 395 f.
Agapit, 145, 398
Albigenses, 354
Alexander the Great, 24, 188
Alexandrinism, 67, 384
Alexius, Metropolitan, 59
allegory, 384; in scriptural interpretation, 64-67, 70, 73, 90; in Cyril of Turov, 136, 140 f.
Almazov, 238
Alypius, 154, 374
Anastasia, Saint, 358, 389
Anastasius Sinaitas, 399; *Questions and Answers,* 48, 223
ancient Russia, *see* Russia, ancient Kievan
Andrew, Saint, the Apostle, 408
Andrew, son of Monomach, 280, 300, 303, 308 f.
Andrew Iurievich Bogoliubsky, Prince of Vladimir, 108 f., 200, 273, 278, 283, 295 f., 298, 301, 307, 373, 398, 403
Andrew of Crete 250
Andrich (Oldrich) of Bohemia, 288
Anichkov, E. V., 10, 352, 354
Annals, see *Chronicles*
Anthony, bishop of Chernigov, 200
Anthony, Saint, 110-113, 115, 118, 120, 128, 142 f., 147, 149 ff., 153-157, 378, 387, 410
Antichrist, 49, 170, 174, 355
antidor, 193
Antioch, monk, 48
Aphrodite, 13
Apocalypse of Saint John, 166, 174
Apocalypse of Saint Paul, 359
apocatastasis, 386
Apocrypha, 42 ff., 48 f., 76, 79, 88, 166 f., 174, 180, 271, 354, 382, 385

Apostle, the, *see Epistles*
Arethas, monk, 150
Arianism, 45
Aristotle, 24, 25, 63, 226, 385
Artemis, 14
ascesis, 152
asceticism, 44 f., 47, 53, 59, 68 f., 89, 95, 98, 100, 110-131, Chapter V *passim,* 161 f., 164, 166, 168, 183 f., 190, 208-212, 218, 220 f., 224 f., 231, 234, 238, 243, 246, 248, 252, 254, 263, 267 f., 273 ff., 377 f., 387 f., 396, 410 f.; salvation through, 31; and mysticism, 34; of Saints Boris and Gleb, 98; Egyptian and Syrian, 31, 39, 117, 155 f.; and "uncouth garb," 116 f., 121, 159 f., 391
Asclepius, 30
Athanasius, recluse, 149
Athanasius of Alexandria, Saint, 27 f., 76; *Contra Arianos,* 45
Athena, 20
Athonites, *see* Mount Athos
Augustine, Saint, 27, 207, 222 f., 379; *Speculum,* 226
Augustus, 383
Avvakum, 158

Baptism, 21, 33, 87 f., 98, 181, 199, 224; "second," 275
Barbara, Saint, 99, 103
Barlaam, Saint, 44, 119 f., 136
Barth, 34
Basil of the Caves Monastery, 150 f.
Basil the Great, Saint, 136, 160, 203, 246; *Hexameron,* 45, 246 f., 254 f.
Basil of Mangazeia, 109
Basil the Younger, Saint, 166
Bathos (the Depth), 167
beauty, of nature in religion, 371-374, 393, 410; of icons, 376
Bede, 379
Bee, the (Melissa), 48, 226, 260, 264, 311
Benedict of Nursia, 152
bereginyi, 348
Bible, 42 f., 64-68, 71, 73, 79, 86 f., 127, 141, 148, 155, 159, 161, 165, 169, 182, 184, 189, 225 f., 246, 252, 255, 271, 273, 278 f., 299, 311, 319, 334, 349, 382 ff., 398; Latin, 39; Slavic, 40, 57, 59
Blessed Virgin, *see* Mary
Blind and the Lame, The, 138
Bogomils, 43, 168, 353-356, 411

423